BRITISH RAILWAYS STANDARD STEAM LOCOMOTIVES

The Society has published a complete history of all locomotives designed and built by Riddles in 1951 in the BR Standard Classes and their work. Details of origins, dimensions, construction and withdrawal dates of each engine, detail variations, classifications, engine diagrams, allocation and work will be described, with illustrations.

Volume 1	Background to Standardisation and the Pacific Classes	Published 1994: second impression 2007
Volume 2	The 4-6-0 and 2-6-0 Classes	Published 2003: second impression 2012
Volume 3	The Tank Engine Classes	Published 1997: second impression 2007
Volume 4	The 9F 2-10-0 Class	Published 2008
Volume 5	The End of an Era	Published 2012

The Railway Correspondence and Travel Society is Britain's leading organisation for those iinterested in all aspects of railways past, present and future. It is highly regarded by professional railway people and enthusiasts alike, a position it has held since its formation over 80 years ago.

A monthly journal, *The Railway Observer,* is sent to each member and, in addition, there are indoor meetings at 30 branches throughout the country as well as organised visits to installations of railway interest. The RCTS has gained an enviable reputation for accurate and detailed railway literature.

Full details about the society, how to join as well as a list of current publications are available at our comprehensive website – rcts.org.uk

£27.95

Pictured in 1951, Hereford 'Saint' No.2920 *Saint David* was standing at the north end of Bay platform No.1 taking water. There were still 26 engines in traffic at the beginning of the year, a figure that had been halved by the end; throughout the year, two of the class were at Hereford and Cardiff.

D.K. JONES COLLECTION

LINES & BRANCHES CONNECTING WITH THE SHREWSBURY & HEREFORD RAILWAY

Line/Branch	At	Serving Station	Opened	Remarks
-	Shrewsbury			GWR Northern Main Line, L & NW Crewe line, see Vol 1
Severn Valley	Severn Valley Jct.	Shrewsbury	1st February 1862	See Vol. 1
Welshpool	Sutton Bridge Jct.	Shrewsbury	27th January 1862	Connected to Cambrian Rly at Butterley. Also served Minsterley branch. See Vol 1
Much Wenlock	Marsh Farm Jct	Craven Arms	16th December 1867	Connected at Presthope with existing route to Wellington.
Bishop's Castle Rly	Stretford Bridge Jct.	Craven Arms	1st February 1866	Running Powers over S & H to Craven Arms
Central Wales	Central Wales Jct.	Craven Arms	6th March 1861	to Knighton, extended to Swansea. L & NW/ LMS
Clee Hill	Clee Hill Jct.	Ludlow	1st August 1861	Mineral Line
Tenbury Wells	Woofferton Jct.	Woofferton Jct.	1st August 1861	Connected at Tebury to Bewdley Jct (August 1864)
New Radnor	Kington Jct.	Leominster	2nd August 1857	Connected at Kington with New Radnor (September 1875). Connected at Titley with Eardisley (August 1874) and Presteign (September 1875)
Bromyard	Leominster & Bromyard Jct.	Leominster	1st March 1884	Connected at Steens Bridge with Bromyard (September 1897), and thence to Worcester by existing route
Worcester	Shelwick Jct.	Hereford	15th September 1861	Connected at Malvern Wells with existing route from Worcester
Barton (NA & H)	Barrs Court North Jct.	Hereford Barton	16th January 1854	Thence by existing route to Newport
Gloucester	Barrs Court South Jct.	Hereford Barrs Court	1st June 1855	Broad Gauge route until 1869 (Vol. 3)

ACKNOWLEDGEMENTS

I must thank John Copsey for his hefty contribution to this book, especially the Traffic details. Thanks also to Brian Stephenson for permission to use the R.O. Tuck and C.R.L. Coles photographs, now part of his Archive; to Russell Mulford for the many negatives he loaned for me to print and photographs he supplied in the Shrewsbury area; to Michael Mensing for the superb prints he provided; and to David Cross for loaning his father's negatives for me to print. Thanks also to the perennial suppliers of hard-to-come-by material such as Roger Carpenter, Richard Casserley, Keith Jones and the Stephenson Locomotive Society Library. Tony Cooke's GWR layouts in the Hereford area book provided a world of useful data, and thanks to Chris Turner for digging out the OS and other maps for locations along the line.   *John Hodge, Haywards Heath, West Sussex.*

A detailed history of
BRITISH RAILWAYS STANDARD STEAM LOCOMOTIVES

Volume 5: The End of an Era

by John Walford

THE RAILWAY CORRESPONDENCE AND TRAVEL SOCIETY
2012

© RCTS 2012

www.rcts.org.uk

ISBN 978 0 901115 97 3

Published by The Railway Correspondence and Travel Society,
16 Welby Close, Maidenhead SL6 3PY, United Kingdom.

Printed by The Amadeus Press, Cleckheaton BD19 4TQ.
Typesetting and page layout by David Bird, RCTS.
Cover design by John Holroyd, RCTS.

COVER PICTURE

Watched by a number of very exuberant youthful enthusiasts, 70032, bereft of nameplates, departs from Carstairs on 28th March 1967 with the "Scottish Rambler No.8" rail tour bound for Carlisle where the train traversed the goods lines and travelled over the Alston and Langholm branches. The train returned to Glasgow via Dumfries and Kilmarnock behind 92009.

Ken Falconer

CONTENTS

LIST OF TABLES

LIST OF TABLES continued

A DEDICATION

The BR Standards series was conceived during the late 1970s under the editorship of Mr. D. L. Bradley. A group of authors was recruited and steady progress was made on researching the topic for the next few years. The untimely death of Don Bradley in 1986 meant that progress was disrupted until a new editor was appointed. Mr. R. K. (Dick) Taylor took over in the early 1990s and the first volume appeared in 1994, followed by others in 1997, 2003 and 2008.

Throughout these two decades, Dick Taylor's contribution to the realisation of the RCTS BR Standards project has been incalculable. Those who have had the pleasure of Dick's acquaintance over these years know that he is one of nature's gentlemen. He has been tireless in support of the authors, inspiring the highest standards, always ready to listen and advise and guiding them through the research, writing and production processes with which many were unfamiliar. The result is a series for which Dick can be justly proud.

As this publication is the last one in the RCTS BR Standards series, it is fitting that it is dedicated to Dick Taylor as an appreciation of all his efforts.

FOREWORD

In retrospect, the success of the BR Standard locomotive designs is debatable, because history overtook them and they were denied the long lives and fulfilment of many of their predecessors. Worse, several of the early diesel types which superseded them were far from satisfactory. Was a large amount of money wasted in pursuit of economy, wide route availability, progress and modern image?

It is, however, futile to dwell on what might have been, except perhaps for a few glimpses, such as the spectacular performances of the rebuilt and modified 71000 *Duke of Gloucester*. It is also fascinating, and mildly amusing, to look at the varying reputations of the Standard designs according to the depots to which they were allocated. Thus, the Britannias at Stratford and Stewarts Lane, replacing smaller types, enjoyed enviable reputations, whereas those at Polmadie, working alongside the LMS Pacifics, were less favourably judged. At many former Great Western Railway depots their reception at best was tepid.

Nevertheless, it is certain that without the Standard designs, the post-war nationalised railway would have been much poorer, and recovery to pre-war conditions distinctly slower. Short-lived or not, they made a worthy contribution to British railway history.

After publication of Volume 4 of this series – The 9F 2-10-0 Class – research continued. Volume 5 contains the fruits of these later investigations. Chapters reveal the history of British locomotive allocation and repair policy, on both the pre-1948 railways and on BR.

To demonstrate the varied duties performed by the Standards, this book features over 140 photographs, all in colour, of the locomotives at work.

The RCTS acknowledges with gratitude the contributions to this series made by the following authors: P. J. Chancellor, Andrew Dow, Dr. P. T. Gilbert, Paul Harrison, Andrew Lait and John Walford. Our thanks go to John Holroyd for designing the cover as well as the numerous contributors of information and photographs. A special mention and thanks must go also to the members of the Society's Publications Committee.

Hugh Gould
President
The Railway Correspondence and Travel Society

PREFACE

This is the final volume in the RCTS BR Standard Steam Locomotive series.

Section One discusses why BR continued to construct steam locomotives after Nationalisation in 1948 when other, more modern forms of traction were becoming available. It is clear that the main consideration was the urgent need to replace locomotives worn out by intensive use during World War II and its aftermath as quickly and as cheaply as possible. This did not mean that alternative motive power was dismissed out of hand; quite the contrary. Comprehensive reviews on the topic were commissioned and are summarised in this section. As soon as capital resources permitted, an almost headlong dash towards new traction forms was pursued. Included also is a discussion on whether, if the construction of already established designs had been continued, there would have been any need to embark on the BR Standards project at all.

As background to the RCTS BR Standards series, two sections appear next. Section Two on BR Shed Codes has been compiled by Mr. Andrew Lait, whose extensive research provided comprehensive locomotive allocation lists for previous volumes in the series. The lists here give details of the recoding and closing dates during the BR era of the sheds which had an allocation of steam power. A separate list refers to the BR Standard classes and includes the dates of first allocation to and final removal from individual sheds for the Standard classes as a group. For completeness, a list of the shed codes as designated by the four nationalised railway companies, the LMS, LNER, SR and GWR as at 1st January 1948 is given at the end of the section together with dates when they were recoded into the new BR system.

Section Three outlines the typical division of activities in a large locomotive Works in the early 1950s; the works in question is Crewe on the LMR. The material was derived from the collection held by the National Railway Museum at York of the papers of Mr. R. C. Bond, appointed Chief Officer for Locomotive Construction and Maintenance for the Railway Executive in 1948, and is a synopsis of several papers delivered by Mr. Bond to the Institute of Locomotive Engineers during 1953.

Locomotive naming is a perennial source of interest to railway enthusiasts. Section Four covers the fascinating history of the Britannia Pacifics' naming process, as first presented by Mr. Andrew Dow in his article in the magazine *Steam World* no. 251, May 2008, pp.8-14. The editor and author considered this 'insider' view of the subject to be of such interest as to merit inclusion in this final volume of the Standards series. Mr. Dow was approached and readily agreed to the reproduction of the article in full.

Performance data for the Standard classes was included in the respective volumes published earlier. Further performance logs have come to light, including ones for the 77xxx and 78xx classes which were not previously covered. The opportunity has been taken to compare performances not only with comparable steam classes but also with that of non-steam traction where possible. The annual average mileage and availability comparisons for the 9F 2-10-0 class displayed in Volume Four proved popular and data for the remaining Standard classes is included in Section Five.

Section Six provides a record of the repair history for those classes not covered in the earlier volumes whilst amendments and information additional to that given previously are detailed in Section Seven.

The material in Section Eight arose from a chance finding during research into the R. C. Bond papers for Section Three. The basis for the BR Steam Locomotive Power Classification provides a glimpse into how these things were decided, revealing that the methods were perhaps more of a mixture of 'art and science' than has been previously acknowledged.

Finally a snapshot of the status of preserved Standard steam locomotives at June 2011 is tabulated in Section Nine by Mr. Paul Harrison.

BR Standards Volume Five is the first RCTS publication to use colour photographs throughout. The selection, preparation and captioning of over 140 illustrations would not have been possible without the dedicated efforts of Mr. Rodney Lissenden and Mr. David Kelso, both of whom have assembled extensive photographic collections over the years. In addition, they have persuaded a number of contacts in the railway photography field to search through personal archives for suitable images for inclusion; many of these views have not been published before. Thanks must be also extended to Mr. David Bird who has spent a considerable amount of time in compiling the layout of the book and for proof reading the text and captions.

The editor and authors hope this 'Farewell Miscellany' on the BR Standard Classes will prove to be an interesting and enjoyable read.

1. THE BR STANDARD STEAM LOCOMOTIVE PROJECT: A WORTHY STOPGAP?

1. Introduction

Following the formation of the British Transport Commission (BTC) and the Railway Executive (RE) in January 1948, one of the early acts of the Executive was to commission a report on the recommendations for a series of standard steam locomotive designs to cover the major requirements of British Railways into the future.

E. S. Cox, Executive Officer (Design), produced a document dated 14th June 1948, entitled *Report on Proposed Standard Steam Locomotives*. This was used as the basis for the development of the twelve classes ultimately making up the Standard steam stock, the first of which, the Britannia Pacifics, appeared in 1951.

It is clear that alternatives to steam power were already actively being considered at this time. In April 1948 the BTC chairman, Sir Cyril Hurcomb, requested a meeting with the RE chairman, Sir Eustace Missenden, to review future motive power requirements for British Railways, with particular regard to the examination of alternatives to that of steam traction; a copy of the letter is reproduced at the end of this section.

The outcome of a series of meetings was the appointment by the RE of two committees. The first, constituted in conjunction with the London Transport Executive, was set up on 22nd September 1948 with the remit to review the methods of electric operations already employed on British railways and the system or systems to be adopted for future electrification schemes. The report was completed in April 1950 and issued by the BTC in 1951 with the title *Electrification of Railways*. It included also a synopsis of contemporary electrification projects in a number of other countries, including continental Europe, Scandinavia, South Africa, the USSR and the USA.

The main recommendation of the report was that for future electrification schemes the 1,500 volts direct current system should be adopted as standard, except where extensions of the third rail system of the former Southern Railway were proposed.

2. Report on the Types of Motive Power

The second committee appointed by the BTC in 1948 was constituted on 20th December and charged with reviewing the future balance of advantage between various types of motive power for future service on British Railways (BR). The report was concluded in October 1951 and issued in the same year with the title *Report of the Committee on Types of Motive Power*. The main types of motive power examined were steam, electric, diesel-electric, diesel mechanical and gas turbine; the question of atomic power, a subject of some debate at the time, was regarded as impractical for individual motive power units and not seriously considered.

The committee looked at the issue from a number of headings:

2.1 Characteristics of each type of motive power
2.2 Experience and economics of operation, both at home and abroad
2.3 Future commercial and operating requirements of British Railways
2.4 Environmental factors
2.5 Staff working conditions and recruitment
2.6 Fuel availability and national policy
2.7 Effect on the UK locomotive building and engineering industries
2.8 Strategic considerations
2.9 Assessment and Conclusions.

2.1 Characteristics of Each Type of Motive Power

Each type of motive power was assessed for its prospects of meeting, on an economic basis, the requirements and conditions envisaged for future BR operations.

Steam Traction

Contemporary research into the ability of the modern coal-burning steam locomotive to convert the energy in the fuel into useful work at the wheels put the thermal efficiency at no more than 8%; for older designs, the figure was 6% or less. The following table lists the sources of the 92% of losses:

	Per Cent
Exhaust steam	59
Residual heat in volatile products of combustion	14
Cinders	8
Radiation from boiler	3
Firebox	5
Cylinders	2
Mechanical friction	1
Total Losses	92
Useful Work	8
	100

Despite various attempts over many years to increase steam locomotive efficiency, for example compounding, turbine drive, steam condensing devices and auxiliary equipment such as feed-water heaters, these were more than offset by increased first and maintenance costs. The heat saved was not enough to justify utilising such systems and none universally had been adopted.

Although the increase in thermal efficiency of the steam locomotive was thought likely to be marginal, advances in its design and construction were expected to result in increased mileage between repairs, reduction in repair costs and greater availability in traffic. Such improvements would include, among other things, the provision of rocking grates, self-cleaning ashpans and smokeboxes, extended use of roller bearings, advances in boiler design and improvements in on-board water treatment systems.

The advantages of the steam locomotive were well documented; a basic design simplicity, low first cost, reliability in traffic and the ability to withstand rough treatment in service. These characteristics are offset by a number of disadvantages however:

the need for frequent replenishment with water of satisfactory quality, the supply of which requires significant infrastructure
coal transport from collieries to MPDs
standby costs
ash disposal at frequent intervals, requiring considerable

1

labour and also specialised equipment

lengthy boiler wash-out down-time periods

turning operations at terminals with many engine movements from sheds or yards requiring line occupation, often with fouling movements, resulting in much unproductive time for engine and crew

the fact that the loaded tender of modern main line express passenger engines may weigh as much as two coaches limited acceleration compared with diesel and electric motive power

the need for large coal to achieve highest efficiency

the lack of flexibility during peak traffic periods when continuous use of available equipment is necessary for full economy of operation.

Electric Traction

Experience with electric traction in the UK up to 1951 had been confined almost entirely to suburban and inter-urban passenger schemes, operated by multiple units. Various different electrification systems adopted throughout the world had been reviewed in the *Electrification of Railways* report completed in April 1950. Here the 1,500V d.c. system had been recommended for future schemes on BR, although developments in the use of a high voltage single phase alternating current were continuing and were not ruled out in the report. In the event, a subsequent review (1956) did opt for a 25kV a.c. system.

The advantages of electric traction compared with steam from the traffic point of view were listed as follows:

greater availability of the electric locomotive and motor coach

flexible working at terminals with much shorter turnaround time intervals

greater acceleration and much improved uphill performance

size of the motive power unit; unlike a steam or diesel unit, electric locomotives do not have to convert carried fuel into power. It is possible to obtain a greater power output within a given length, weight or space than any other form of traction

freedom from smoke nuisance

favourable reaction from the travelling public leading to stimulation of traffic

greatly improved staff working conditions

A number of possible disadvantages to electrification were considered and noted as follows:

widespread disruption in the event of major power failure. The committee was advised that given suitable sub-station spacing, adequate alternative circuits and inter-switching arrangements, together with regular inspection, maintenance and renewal of cables and electrical gear, the risk of serious failure would be remote.

noisy and rough riding of some multiple unit stock. This arises from the fact that traction motors are mounted directly on the carriage axles and their weight largely unsprung. Main line electrification would however involve the replacement of the steam locomotive with an electrical powered unit and hence the problem would not arise. In addition, developments in multiple unit motor mountings were expected to result in improved riding characteristics.

One other issue would arise; the provision of train heating. This would be resolved by either of two approaches in the committee's view, the provision of boilers on the locomotive or the the inclusion of a steam heating van in the train consist.

Diesel-Electric Traction

Experience with diesel locomotives for train working on main line services in the UK had been confined to two LMSR/English Electric Co. 1,600hp units completed in 1947/8 and two similar units of SR/English Electric Co. design with power uprated to 1,750hp, delivered in 1950/1. An 827hp unit of LMSR/British Thomson-Houston design for secondary services was completed in 1950. The RE (Southern Region) was undertaking development of a third locomotive of a more advanced design, rated at 2,000hp. The potentialities and economics of working this unit under traffic conditions had not then been fully evaluated.

The potential advantages of diesel traction compared with steam are similar to those listed above for electric traction. For the diesel-electric unit, an advantage over electric power is that it is essentially an electric locomotive with its own power plant and thus is not confined to operation on electrified lines. It is however much more complicated and expensive to build and requires more frequent servicing. Comparison of typical first costs in relation to power output may be seen in an exercise conducted in 1950; the results are given in the accompanying table. New maintenance facilities would be required but could be located at or adjacent to existing steam depots. It would be possible to reduce the number of such installations to a minimum, much fewer than for steam servicing.

For branch line working, the use of diesel multiple units and railcars was considered to be equally attractive as alternatives to steam. With dieselisation the need to import oil fuel rather than using indigenous coal production was significant and is addressed below in **Section 2.6**.

Comparison of Typical First Costs in Relation to Power Output

	£. s. d.
BR Standard Cl. 5 4-6-0	13. 6. 0.
	(£13.30)
Co-Co electric unit for Manchester-Sheffield-Wath scheme	17. 12. 10.
	(£17.64)
LMR 1,600hp diesel-electric	65. 0. 0

Diesel Mechanical Traction

The need to interpose a transmission system between diesel engine and driving wheels enabling the unit to provide for flexibility of torque, power and speed essential for railway purposes had been satisfactorily resolved with the electrical transmission system. An alternative system, claimed to be potentially less complicated, was mechanical transmission but which was still in its infancy. A 2,000hp engine, the Fell locomotive, 10100, was on trial on the LMR and little experience had been gained to date. Various technical problems had been encountered and it was not possible to say whether these eventually would be solved. The committee recommended that it was too early to form a sound economic assessment of this form of traction and it should be discounted at that stage awaiting the outcome of further trials.

Gas Turbine Traction

BR operated the only gas turbine locomotive in Europe in 1950, the Western Region (WR) 2,500hp mixed traffic unit, 18000, constructed jointly by the Brown-Boveri Co. and the Swiss Locomotive Works. A second locomotive, again for the WR, a 3,500hp unit, 18100, designed by Metropolitan-Vickers, then was approaching completion. These engines had oil-driven turbines and electric transmission. Experience in operation was lacking with respect to maintenance requirements over a long period and to the probable life of the gas turbine.

A number of technical and economic advantages were claimed based on the fact that the reciprocating diesel engine was replaced by a turbine:

  ability to provide increased horsepower for a given weight and size
  absence of reciprocating parts and consequent elimination of the shock and vibration problems these imposed
  greater simplicity and accessibility with lower maintenance costs
  reduced fuel costs on account of greater thermal efficiency and the ability to use lower grade oil; the gas turbine could burn any kind of liquid fuel, though not with uniform efficiency
  reduced lubricating oil consumption

The testing of the WR unit was still in its early stages and a large number of teething troubles were being experienced. The committee felt that it was much too early to form a view on the performance, reliability and operating costs of the locomotive. Early indications were that at its then state of development, the oil-burning gas turbine system was likely to be so heavy on fuel consumption as to prove uneconomic in the UK. The committee was unable to recommend further experiments with such units at that stage but resolved to monitor progress in the use of coal-fired gas turbine technology being developed in the USA.

2.2 Operating Experience

Railways in Britain had accumulated much experience in the operation of steam power over more than a century. They had little or no experience of operating diesel or electric traction as the principal source of motive power for either passenger or freight working under main-line conditions, although such operations were established in other countries. One main line scheme, the Manchester-Sheffield-Wath route, not then running, was expected to provide useful operating data. Elsewhere electric traction had proved itself both technically and economically feasible over many years of operating under diverse conditions in continental Europe. Similarly the adoption of diesel power on North American railway systems from the 1930s had been an outstanding success. The committee thus proceeded on the basis that these two types of motive power had reached a stage of technical development readily capable of meeting the various requirements of BR as substitutes for steam traction. As noted above, gas turbine-powered units were considered to be at such an early stage of development that they could not at that time be considered viable.

2.3 Future Commercial and Operating Requirements on BR

The trend toward faster, more frequent but shorter passenger trains was apparent. There and back in a day with sufficient time for business and social purposes was the preferred option for many travellers. Suburban traffic was expected to increase, with commuters wishing increasingly to take advantage of living in new towns, examples of which were Welwyn Garden City and Stevenage, whilst still being able to work in large cities. Such traffic was ideal for electrification. For branch line traffic, it was considered likely even at that time that a large number of branch lines would be closed for economic reasons. For the remainder, the use of diesel multiple units was the favoured option.

For freight traffic, the demand for next day deliveries for general merchandise on a greater scale and over longer distances was on the increase and likely would require more frequent trains of smaller size. Vacuum brake-fitted wagons would be necessary for faster schedules to achieve higher degrees of uniformity in train speeds and allow operating economies in scheduling.

2.4 Environmental Factors

It was clear that the travelling public increasingly would demand motive power and coaching stock which were clean, attractive and modern in appearance if BR were to maintain its market share opposite other forms of transport. The steam locomotive rapidly was being outmoded in these respects. Some improvements could be effected regarding cleanliness of steam locomotives but the inherent problems with smoke nuisance would involve considerable expenditure on the cleaning, painting and dealing with the effects of corrosion on infrastructure such as stations, bridges and tunnels as well as rolling stock. Achieving standards of cleanliness with steam power comparable to that with diesels or electric power was regarded as impossible. The cost of dealing with the effects of the smoke problem were put at some £300,000 per year.

Other concerns regarding the smoke and cinders problem were the visibility of signals in tunnels and foggy weather and the incidences of lineside fires. The cost of compensation for the latter were put at £20,000-30,000 per year in an average year but in dry summers, such as that of 1949, the cost was around £150,000. Spark arrestors could be fitted to the more modern designs but for many older locomotives this could not be done without materially affecting steaming capacity.

2.5 Staff Recruitment

The committee considered there were two aspects to the staffing of BR operations,

  working conditions
  economics with particular reference to the size of the workforce

For steam power, there was much heavy manual, even menial, work involved, examples being the clearing of ashpits and the cleaning of locomotives as a result of the inherent smoke nuisance. Footplate and shed areas were not attractive places to work and problems in the recruitment of good quality personnel were anticipated. Experience on the Swiss Federal Railways following conversion from steam operation had shown lower sickness rates and hence the need for fewer staff to cover such absences. The health and working lives of footplate staff in particular had greatly improved with the advent of electric motive power. Morale improvement had been dramatic and both smarter working and the social status of employees had been enhanced. Maintenance depots also were cleaner and fewer staff were required as relatively unskilled labouring jobs disappeared. The smaller number of motive power units required, owing to increased daily mileage and efficiency, reduced significantly the volume of service work necessary.

There was scope also to reduce manning costs using diesel and electric traction. One-man operation was feasible but would require careful negotiations with the trade unions involved and would probably require the extension of Automatic Train Control (ATC) installations. In particular, one-man operation would improve considerably the economic case for the electrifying of many routes.

2.6 Fuel Availability and National Policy

Clearly it was vital that fuel supplies must be assured and economically viable. The two types for railway operation in the UK were coal and oil, either in individual locomotives or for electricity generation in power stations. Hydro-electric power, significant in some continental European countries, was regarded as a non-starter in Great Britain but the development of nuclear power for electricity generation was viewed as likely in the medium and long term. The use of oil as fuel for steam locomotives or power stations was ruled out on economic grounds which left the options of using coal either for steam or electric power or oil for diesel locomotives. Availability and likely long-term price levels for coal and oil then were considered; the case for coal was looked at from the viewpoint of attractiveness for either direct use or in power stations.

Coal

Because of the restrictive loading gauge in Great Britain, the vast majority of steam power was designed around narrow fire-boxes for which large coal was necessary for economic operation. There had been some developments in wide fire-boxes in the UK but these were not applicable to smaller engines and thus large coal would be necessary for many years to come. The National Coal Board (NCB) had indicated that with new mining techniques centred on increased mechanisation, the amount of large coals produced as a proportion of the whole would inevitably reduce.

The 1945 figure of 36.5% was expected to reduce to around 28.0% or less by 1965. Although total production was forecast to increase from 204 million tons in 1950 to 240 million tons in 1965, the NCB was not able to guarantee supply of the forecast large coal requirements for BR over that period. Some lower quality grades might however be possible by 1969 but there was no hope of restoring adequate supplies of pre-WW2 coal quality standards for the foreseeable future. Moreover, prices for large coal had risen some 192% from 17s 0d (£0.85) per ton in 1938 to 49s 7d (£2.48) per ton in 1950 with no prospect of reduction.

The forecast large coal requirement for a BR solely steam powered operation was between 12m and 14m tons per year. This involved a large and costly use of resources in transport and distribution from pitheads to MPDs, resources which the committee felt would be better employed in moving revenue earning freight. It was considered also that reduction in the consumption of coal was likely to be a priority in the coming years for environmental quality reasons. With full conversion to diesel power, no motive power movements for coal would

be required. Fuel oil would of course be substituted for coal but at a much reduced level of 3 million tons per annum and as a fluid would be easier to handle. For full conversion to electric traction, some additional 3-4 million tons of coal would be sufficient for power stations to generate all the current needed for 1951 operation levels and beyond using much inferior grade coal to that required for steam traction.

Electricity

Apart from eliminating the need for premium grade coal, the complete conversion of BR motive power from steam to electricity would result in the absence of standby losses as an electric locomotive simply would be shut down between duties. A further bonus would be the use of regenerative braking on falling gradients. Here the traction motor driven by the force of a descending train would act as a dynamo and the current generated would be fed back into the overhead contact wire for use by ascending trains. The braking effect thus created would steady the train and reduce the wear on brake blocks and wheel tyres of the locomotive and train. Increases in the consumption of electricity would be gradual as the changeover from steam was implemented and the country's electricity generating industry confirmed it would have no difficulty keeping in step. Although the heavy capital expenditure on new power stations then under construction would result in higher prices per electricity unit than those enjoyed by the pre-WW2 railway industry, the grid loads would be better spread over the 24-hour period with much freight being conveyed overnight. This would allow all electricity consumers to benefit.

From the fuel point of view, the case for electrification for intensely used routes was regarded by the committee as very strong. Further, when discussing the economic aspects of electricity and diesel traction, the summer General Meeting of the American Institute of Electrical Engineers in Toronto in June 1951 was of the opinion that:

"When available sources of fuel are restricted, in volume or in kind, electrification will provide an insurance against fuel shortages or adverse prices to a greater degree than any other type of railroad power".

Regarding future developments, there was likely to be substantial progress in three areas of electricity generation:

the advent of large coal-fired gas turbine power stations

progress in high-voltage transmission of direct current and linking the UK electricity supply grid with that of the continental European network which included a contribution from hydro-electric power installations

the possibility of using atomic energy for low-cost electricity generation

Oil

When considering oil as fuel for BR motive power, the committee was aware acutely of the fact that all supplies needed to be imported and paid for in foreign currency. This posed a significant disadvantage compared with coal, which was available within Great Britain and in very large reserves. Hence it was of paramount importance to ensure oil supplies would be available in both peace and war if it were to be used for railway motive power.

The oil requirement at three million tons per year for complete dieselisation of BR's fleet would be approximately one fifth of the tonnage of coal needed for a motive power fleet based solely on steam traction. Worldwide production of crude oil had expanded vastly since 1938 and had kept pace with demand even during the difficult years of WW2. Oil imports to the UK in millions of tons for 1938 and 1950 are noted below:

	1938	1950
Refined Products	8.2	9.3
Crude Oil	2.6	9.5

By 1954, refining capacity was forecast to reach 25m tons per year in the UK compared with 13.5m tons in 1951 and 2.5m tons in 1938. The cost of importing mainly crude oil clearly would be less than for refined products.

For full dieselisation of BR power, the three million tons per annum requirement was envisaged as likely to develop over a period of perhaps 40 or even 50 years into the future, the envisaged lifetime of the steam power then being planned and constructed. The oil industry indicated that it foresaw no difficulty in providing this requirement and would be able to do so very much earlier, given reasonable notice and firm contracts. In the event, UK refining capacity increased dramatically from the 2.5m tons in 1938 (eight refineries) to 112.5m tons (23 refineries) by the end of 1970.

2.7 Effect on the UK Locomotive Building and Engineering Industries

Any changeover from steam to electric and or diesel traction would have profound effects on locomotive construction and repair installations, both for the RE workshops and outside firms. This would apply also to the diesel and electric engineering industry and a wide range of industries supplying raw materials and semi-finished products and components.

BR was almost unique in world railway terms in having its own construction and repair facilities for its locomotives and rolling stock. There were strong grounds for continuing this policy which would mean purchasing electrical equipment and diesel engines from outside industry and erecting the locomotives in RE workshops. These outside companies had developed an international reputation for excellence in design and construction of electric and diesel motive power and the committee was assured that the industry would be able to combine orders for BR with their general production. There was no doubt that British industry and RE engineers and workshops would be able to co-operate to meet all requirements.

In view of the industries' heavy order books, spare capacity would be limited and the RE requirements would in some respects necessitate expansion of production facilities. The industry was prepared to undertake this, subject to guarantees of satisfactory orders over a given period.

RE workshops readily could be modified for erection and maintenance of diesel and electric locomotives. Capacity was unlikely to be an issue as steam construction would be progressively discontinued and a one-by-one facility conversion should present no difficulty.

2.8 Strategic Considerations

While bearing in mind the concerns about security of imported fuel supplies, the committee felt nevertheless it should be looking at the greatest efficiency and reliability in railway motive power operation with minimum labour and materials. For these reasons, there was a strong case for either electrification, dieselisation or a combination of both on economic grounds and undue weight should not be put on strategic considerations regarding fuel supplies. In addition all Royal Navy and Merchant Marine vessels now were using oil-based fuel as were large parts of British industry. The nation was becoming increasingly reliant on electric power and the internal combustion engine and there was no reason why railways should be excluded from this trend.

2.9 Assessment and Conclusions

The committee summarised its deliberations on the different types of motive power as follows.

Steam Traction

Improvements were likely in the development of the steam locomotive but would be confined to details and directed towards increasing availability and economic value of use in traffic. It was unlikely that there would be significant advances to overcome the inherent limitations outlined earlier, i.e. smoke nuisance, low efficiency and poor staff working conditions. Thus any advance in the character of services offered by BR would need to rely on electric or diesel traction. It was acknowledged however that without the allocation of capital resources for changeover from steam, the latter would provide a considerable portion of BR's motive power for many years to come.

Electric Traction

The capital outlay allocation to railway services currently was limited. In view of the national economic situation, including the renewed policy of re-armament, there would be little or no prospect of such resources becoming available in the near future unless there were to be rapid and unexpected changes in circumstances. In view of this and due to lack of experience with electric traction in the UK, it was considered untimely to recommend major investment in wholesale countrywide railway electrification at that stage.

Some local schemes for suburban traffic were ongoing with more to follow. These would not however provide data to test the possibilities and economics of electrified main line operations. The Manchester-Sheffield-Wath electrification project would provide such insights and the committee recommended that resources be allocated as soon as possible for a limited initiative based on this experience. The project having the least capital requirement, since much of its route was on open track through rural areas, was the ex-GN main line from Kings Cross to Grantham. The committee recommended that a team be set up to examine the proposal, which should also include the Hertford loop and the Hitchin-Cambridge branch. From Grantham, electrification could perhaps be extended first to Nottingham and Colwick and then further north to link up with the Manchester-Sheffield route at Rotherwood Junction. As and when capital resources became available, there should be implementation of the project without delay. Other routes such as the West Coast Main Line from Euston and the Midland Main Line from St.

Pancras also would derive great benefits from electrification but such projects would be much more complex, costly and take longer to realise.

Diesel Traction

Setting aside the cost of infrastructure, the case for dieselisation versus electrification is dependent on the relative economics of traffic density. The greater the line occupancy, the more the balance tilts toward electrification. Changeover to diesel traction from steam requires however nothing like the capital expenditure on infrastructure compared with that for electrification. Diesel-electric transmission was regarded as the most technically advanced and reliable compared with the diesel-mechanical system which was still in development for main line units. Diesel-electric locomotives incorporate power generators to drive electric motors and are thus more costly than simple electric locomotives deriving power from either a third rail or an overhead wire. Hence the choice is between costly diesel units with smaller scale investment and cheaper electric locomotives requiring significant amounts of infrastructure capital. Thus diesels could be introduced quite rapidly whereas electrification would take a much longer period to implement.

The two 1,600hp diesel-electric units, 10000/1, had been completed by the LMSR, one prior to and one after nationalisation but performed individually little better than a Class 5 steam locomotive in service. These units were not regarded as offering sufficient scope for wholesale main line dieselisation unless operated in tandem, a very costly option.

However, with the production of 2,000hp units then looking feasible, the outlook would change. The committee recommended a large-scale trial to test the potentialities and economics for main line working as soon as practicable. The cost of around £45,000 per unit for 100 2,000hp units was the estimate for the purchase of components to be assembled in BR workshops. This initiative was to proceed alongside the ordering of a number of smaller scale units or railcars for branch line operation . The dieselisation of shunting work already was taking place and was recommended to be pursued further with all speed in view of its benefits in terms of one man operation and reduced service and standby costs. The project would allow clarification of the economics of operation compared with electrification and could be achieved with the minimum of capital investment for maintenance facilities. Experience with these electrification and diesel projects would then allow clarification of the broader issues of national policy including, for instance, the outlook for the availability of safe and reliable fuel supplies.

The committee acknowledged that the projects would call for considerable capital investment. The expenditure however would be spread over several years. This should be assessed in relation to existing expenditure on steam locomotive renewals which then was about £4.25m per annum. Although the new locomotives would be more efficient and economic than the ones they replaced, the expenditure would be perpetuating the steam locomotive with all its limitations. Equivalent sums spent on the new forms of motive power would make a substantial contribution to realisating of the projects put forward by the committee.

Table 1.1
BR Standard Steam Classes: Revised and Cancelled Building Programmes

Class	Programme								
	1954	1955	1955	1956	1956	1957	1958*	1959*	1960*
	Locos Cancelled	Original	Revised and Implemented	Original	Revised and Implemented	-	-	-	-
9 2-10-0	-	20	-	101	106	WR 18	LMR 40	LMR 35	LMR 35
8 4-6-2	-	-	-	-	-	-	-	-	-
7 4-6-2	-	-	-	LMR/ER/WR 36	-	-	-	-	-
6 4-6-2	SR 5 ScR 10	-	-	NER 20	-	-	-	ScR 17 NER 15	ScR 16 NER 25
5 4-6-0	-	30	35	50	47	-	LMR 15	LMR 45	LMR 46
4 4-6-0	ER 10	-	-	ER/LMR 30	-	-	-	-	-
4 2-6-0	-	-	-	NER/ER 45	40	-	-	ScR 16	ScR 8
3 2-6-0	NER 5	-	-	NER 13	-	-	-	ScR 14	ScR 10
2 2-6-0	-	-	-	LMR 10	10	-	-	LMR 19	LMR 14
4 2-6-4T	-	-	-	WR 20 LMR/ScR 34	24	-	-	-	-
3 2-6-2T	WR 10 NER 8	-	-	WR/NER 10	-	-	-	-	-
2 2-6-2T	-	-	-	LMR 10	-	-	-	-	-
8 2-8-0	-	-	-	WR 5 [1]	WR (18 [2])	-	-	-	-

[1] Locomotives included as 9F 2-10-0s in 1956 Revised Programme. [2] Locomotives included as 9F 2-10-0s in 1957 Programme.

* Programmes projected but not implemented

3. The BR Motive Power Position in 1948

On nationalisation of the four main line companies on 1st January 1948, the Railway Executive inherited some 20,000 locomotives spread over 448 classes. Many of these engines were of old design, some dating back to the nineteenth century whilst others were worn out following the huge demands placed on them, often without proper maintenance, during the difficult years of WW2. Limited investment resources were available as the UK recovered gradually from the disruption of the war years. It was necessary to replace these traction units as quickly as possible at minimum capital cost. The obvious, indeed, only viable option at the time was the perpetuation of steam power built to reliable modern designs. In the meantime, newer forms of motive power could be tested, trialled and developed to allow economic comparison with contemporary steam.

The Dawn of New Forms of Traction

The comprehensive review of the developing modes of motive power alternatives to steam has been summarised in **Section 2**. From that it is clear that as soon as resources were available, a programme devised to replace the steam locomotive with a combination of these modern traction forms would be proposed and implemented. Initially this was expected to be gradual, taking perhaps three or more decades.

In 1953, however, a further reorganisation of management was decreed. The Railway Executive had been perceived, rightly or wrongly, as not being sufficiently proactive in the modernisation of the network and in particular in the development of new traction forms. The Executive was abolished and control of the railways transferred directly to the BTC which had a new chairman, Sir Brian Robertson, with some £1.2 billion of resources allocated for the modernisation of the network over a 15-year period. Current traction costs were regarded as excessive and a determined effort to replace steam was initiated. Dieselisation was regarded as the option offering the quickest returns and, in 1955, the modernisation plan for this traction form, centred on diesel–electric units, was presented. Following developments in West Germany, the acquisition of diesel-hydraulic units, not considered in the 1951 report, was included in the plan for the Western Region.

The Modernisation Plan envisaged also the electrifying of some 1,210 route miles of trunk and suburban lines as well as a 250 route mile extension of the electrified lines of the Southern Region. Following significant advances using alternating current systems for railway electrification projects since the 1951 report, *Electrification of Railways*, the BTC had requested a comparative study of the 1,500V direct current system and a 25KV alternating current system. The subsequent report, *The System of Electrification for British Railways* was published in 1956 and opted for the 25KV alternating current system as standard for main line electrification.

The publication of the Modernisation Plan caused a rethink of the steam locomotive building programmes from 1956 onwards; details are given in **Table 1.1, BR Standard Steam Classes: Revised and Cancelled Building Programmes**. Some 48 locomotives from four classes, still not completed from the 1954 programme, were cancelled in 1956. The original 1956 programme was heavily pruned from a total of 384 to 245 locomotives, 18 of which were deferred to the 1957 programme. The Regions had been invited to make requests for the 1958-1960 steam programmes and the LMR, NER and ScR did so, recommending the building of a further 370 locomotives over the three-year period. None of these programmes was implemented. The reason was simple economics.

A recurrent topic of the politics of the late 1950s and early 1960s was the state of British Railways and in particular its spiralling operating deficit. The result was a call for accelerated modernisation of the network to bring costs under control. The greatly improved operating economics of diesel and electric traction compared with steam resulted in the decision to implement a major acceleration of the dieselisation programme. Steam traction, rather than being phased out over two or three decades, was to be eliminated as soon as possible.

4. BR Standards or Existing Designs?

The BR Standard steam project helped to fulfil the needs of the urgent post-WW2 motive power problem in Great Britain with a series of sturdy, reliable classes incorporating the latest successful developments in design. However, some 1,538 locomotives were built to a number of pre-nationalisation designs between 1948 and 1957 alongside the Standards programmes (for details, see Volume One in this series). In view of this and of the short time between the initiation of the BR Standard steam project and the publication of the BR Modernisation Plan in 1955, it is worth asking whether the project was really necessary. It is arguable that a further 999 engines, the number of Standard units produced, easily could have been built to the pre-nationalisation designs with a significant saving in design and construction costs. Undoubtedly they would have performed adequately in the closing years of steam. It should not go unnoticed that during the swansong of steam in the summer of 1968, it was the ex-LMS class 5 4-6-0s and 8F 2-8-0s which accounted for the majority of the engines then still at work.

Tables 1.2 to 1.6 speculate on how the Standard classes could have been substituted by those earlier designs. For the Standard Cl. 8P Pacific design, a further example of an LMR Princess Coronation class (46258, *City of Perth, Aberdeen, Lincoln?*) no doubt would have been well received in place of 71000 *Duke of Gloucester*. Similarly, the Cl.7MT Britannias could readily have been replaced by Castle Class 4-6-0s (WR), Bulleid light Pacifics (SR) and LMR Patriot/Jubilee 4-6-0 2A

Table 1.2 BR Standard Pacifics – Alternative Motive Power			
Class	**Original Region**	**Allocation number allocated**	**Alternative Motive Power**
Cl.8 *Duke of Gloucester*	LMR	1	LMR Princess Coronation Pacific
Cl.7 *Britannia*	ER	23	LMR Patriot/Jubilee 4-6-0 rebuilt with 2A boiler or SR Bulleid Light Pacific
	SR	2	SR Bulleid Light Pacific
	WR	15	WR Castle Class 4-6-0
	LMR	10	LMR Patriot/Jubilee 4-6-0 rebuilt with 2A boiler
	ScR	5	LMR Patriot/Jubilee 4-6-0 rebuilt with 2A boiler
Cl.6 *Clan*	ScR	10	LMR Patriot/Jubilee 4-6-0 rebuilt with 2A boiler

Table 1.3
BR Standard 4-6-0 Classes - Alternative Motive Power

Class	Original Region	Allocation number allocated	Alternative Motive Power
Cl. 5 73xxx	WR	35	WR Hall or Grange Class 4-6-0
	SR	25	LMR Class 5 4-6-0
	LMR	50	LMR Class 5 4-6-0
	ER	5	ER B1 Class 4-6-0
	NER	12	LMR Class 5 or ER B1 Class 4-6-0
	ScR	45	LMR Class 5 4-6-0
Cl. 4 75xxx	WR	20	WR Manor Class 4-6-0 or LMR Class 4 2-6-0
	LMR	45	LMR Class 4 2-6-0
	SR	15	LMR Class 5 4-6-0

Table 1.4
BR Standard 2-6-0 Classes - Alternative Motive Power

Class	Original Region	Allocation number allocated	Alternative Motive Power
Cl. 4 76xxx	ScR	35	LMR Class 4 2-6-0
	SR	37	LMR Class 4 2-6-4T
	NER	13	LMR Class 4 2-6-0
	LMR	15	LMR Class 4 2-6-0
	ER	15	LMR Class 4 2-6-0
Cl. 3 77xxx	ScR	10	LMR Class 5 4-6-0
	NER	10	LMR Class 2 2-6-0
Cl. 2 78xxx	WR	10	LMR Class 2 2-6-0
	LMR	35	LMR Class 2 2-6-0
	NER	10	LMR Class 2 2-6-0
	ScR	10	LMR Class 2 2-6-0

Table 1.5
BR Standard Tank Classes - Alternative Motive Power

Class	Original Region	Allocation number allocated	Alternative Motive Power
Cl. 4 2-6-4T 80xxx	SR	23	
	LMR	45	All Regions
	ER	36	
	NER	5	LMR Fairburn Class 4 2-6-4T
	ScR	46	
Cl. 3 2-6-2T 82xxx	WR	25	All Regions
	SR	14	LMR Fairburn Class 4 2-6-4T
	LMR	2	or
	NER	4	LMR Ivatt Class 2 2-6-2T
Cl. 2 2-6-2T 84xxx	LMR	13	All Regions
	NER	7	LMR Ivatt Class 2 2-6-2T
	SR	10	

Table 1.6
BR Standard 9F 2-10-0 Class - Alternative Motive Power

Class	Original Region	Allocation number allocated	Alternative Motive Power
Cl. 9F 2-10-0	WR	56	Stanier Class 8F 2-8-0
	LMR	100	Stanier Class 8F 2-8-0
	ER	85	ER Class V2 2-6-2 or ER Class O2 2-8-0
	NER	10	NER Class Q7 0-8-0

boiler rebuilds (LMR/ScR). For the Liverpool St.-Norwich services, ER A1 Pacific or V2 2-6-2 designs would probably have been ruled out on account of weight restrictions on the former GE lines. Again however, the re-boilered Patriot/ Jubilee 4-6-0s would have been suitable, subject perhaps to height clearance work through some of the tunnels; alternatively, the authorities could have persevered with the Bulleid light Pacific trials of 1951.

WR Hall, ER B1 or LMR Cl. 5 4-6-0s would have taken the place of the Standard Cl. 5 4-6-0 whilst WR Manor, LMR Class 4 2-6-0s or Class 5 4-6-0s would have been suitable alternatives for the 75xxx class. The roles of the Standard Cl. 2-6-0s (76xxx, 77xxx and 78xxx) could have been taken by the corresponding LMR 2-6-0 tender or 2-6-4 tank engine classes. The tank engine classes themselves would have been substituted by the LMR Fairburn 2-6-4T class or the LMR Ivatt 2-6-2T class, the 80xxx and 84xxx classes being simply updates of the earlier LMS designs.

For the 9F 2-10-0 class, the LMR 8F, ER O2 2-8-0s or NER Q7 0-8-0 classes would have been suitable for the heavy freight role whereas more ER Class V2 2-6-2s could have carried out the 9F's important fast fitted freight duties on the East Coast Main Line.

Using that most exact of sciences, hindsight, the conclusion must be that, given the subsequent circumstances, the BR Standard Steam Project was indeed redundant. Nevertheless, the words of E. S. Cox, the Executive Officer in charge of the design of the Standard classes, in his book, *Locomotive Panorama Volume 2*, might well summarise the whole endeavour in a single sentence.

"The BR Standard Steam Project could be regarded as an adventurous rearguard action as the steam era drew to its close".

A fitting epitaph.

78048 arriving at Berwick-upon-Tweed with a service from St. Boswells on 1st June 1962.   *Michael Mensing*

APPENDIX 1
Letter dated 13th April 1948 (Reference S.44-1-1 and S.17-1-7) from Sir Cyril Hurcomb, Chairman, British Transport Commission to Sir Eustace Missenden, Chairman, Railway Executive

My dear Missenden,

Future Of Diesel Traction

It seems to me that the question of the future form of traction – whether it is to be steam, electricity. Diesel-electric, Diesel-mechanical, or gas turbine – is probably the most important long-term problem facing the railways today and its, of course, closely linked with the future price ratios and availability of the different fuels.

I presume it is true to say that after more than a century of development, the characteristics and potentialities of the steam locomotive have been exhaustively studied. There is also considerable experience of electric traction for passenger services, and in addition the first large-scale electrification of a main line carrying a heavy freight traffic (i.e. the Manchester-Wath-Sheffield line) is now in hand and will eventually yield much information as a guide to future main line electrification policy.

Equally, there is a vast fund of experience of Diesel-electric traction on main line services available from American sources, which has been extensively studied by British railways, which moreover in recent years have sent several missions of mechanical and electrical engineers to the United States to study the methods and results that have been obtained there over a considerable period of years.

We can , therefore, say that as regards steam, electricity and Diesel-electric, the <u>purely engineering and technical questions</u> can be answered from actual experience.

On the other hand, both gas turbine and Diesel-mechanical traction for main line work must be regarded as in the purely experimental stage and must continue to be so for some considerable time until sufficient experience has been accumulated.

If the foregoing analysis of the present position is correct, it may be useful to consider how far our policy corresponds to it. A large main line electrification scheme is in progress. The Executive also have in hand proposals for prolonged technical trials of both diesel-mechanical and gas turbine main line locomotives. But as regards Diesel-electric traction, there seems to be a disparity. We are still experimenting as though there were no large fund of technical knowledge and experience upon which to draw, and as though our engineers had not been studying the characteristics (as I assume they have been doing) of this form of traction for the past twenty years.

Whilst American practice admittedly requires to be interpreted in the light of smaller loads, shorter average length of haul, and more restricted loading gauge in this country, there should be no major technical questions which are quite unfamiliar.

Where our experience is lacking, is in the true level of maintenance and operating costs under British conditions, and the effects upon operating methods of turning over a complete group of services to Diesel-electric traction. And only a large-scale experiment can give us the answer to these questions.

For this reason, I was disappointed to read in Slim's[1] letter of 23rd March that so limited an experiment as that now in hand in the London Midland Region is all that the Executive apparently contemplate at the moment.

You will remember that in the summer of 1947, the LNER announced that they had prepared a scheme for the dieselisation of the Anglo-Scottish East Coast services, involving the construction of 25 single unit in replacement of 32 Pacific-type express passenger engines. Maintenance facilities were to be provided at London and Edinburgh, entirely separate from the the steam locomotive facilities.

The Commission would, I think, like to know whether it is the fact that this scheme has now been shelved and whether the Executive have come to the conclusions which differ radically from those which were formed by the LNER Board last year. I cannot help feeling, however, that until a major scheme of the kind has been put into operation, we shall not have sufficient actual experience of the capabilities and costs of Diesel-electric traction in relation to steam and other forms of traction.

At the same time, looking even further ahead, I think that we should be considering the question of which prime mover and which type of fuel is likely ultimately to prove the most efficient and economical. I feel that we should appoint a Committee to give us a full report on this most important question, the terms of reference to the proposed Committee, upon which I think a representative of the Commission should sit, with representatives of the Railway Executive, should be to set out the estimated future balance of advantages as between:

1) steam traction
2) electric traction
3) Diesel-electric traction
4) Diesel-mechanical traction
5) gas-turbine traction

The first step of this committee should be to advise on the nature of the experiments to be made in the immediate future.

The approach should be primarily from the economic angle; all scientific and technical advice can be made readily available to the Committee as it may be required by the experts of the Executive or outside advisers.

I suggest we should first have a preliminary talk here on the subject, to which you will probably like to bring Riddles[2] and Barrington-Ward[3] and any other Members or Officers of the Executive who are directly concerned.

Yours sincerely,

(signed) CYRIL HURCOMB

Notes.

1. W. J. (Sir William) Slim, Deputy Chairman, Railway Executive

2. Robert A. Riddles, Member of the Railway Executive for Mechanical and Electrical Engineering

3. V. M. (Sir Michael) Barrington-Ward, Member of the Railway Executive for Operations.

70052 *Firth of Tay* entering the station at Chorleywood on 6th December 1965 on the 8.15am from Nottingham to Marylebone. This photograph was taken about six months before the service from Nottingham was withdrawn. The London Transport infrastructure shown in the picture is of interest.

Martin Gill

73083 ascends Sole Street bank, one of the most demanding sections on the Victoria to Ramsgate line. The climb involves five miles of a 1 in 100 gradient against westbound trains. The curve at the Rochester end of the climb severely restricts a good run at the bank. The train seen here in August 1958 is an inter-regional summer holiday service from Ramsgate to Sheffield.

Kenneth Wightman

2. BRITISH RAILWAYS ENGINE SHEDS HISTORY INCLUDING RECODING AND CLOSING DATES

Introduction

Upon nationalisation, British Railways inherited the locomotives, organisations and infrastructure from the four major companies, GWR, LMS, LNER and SR, that had existed since the grouping a quarter of a century earlier. There were approximately 350 main sheds and a large number of sub-sheds, some of which had their own allocations while most of them used engines provided by their parent sheds. Each company used its own system for the identification and organisation of its engine sheds.

The LMS, the largest of the four companies, had its sheds organised in groups or divisions, each having a main shed. The shed codes comprised a number, which at nationalisation was in the range 1 to 32, followed by a capital letter which was A for the main shed. These codes ranged from 1A for Willesden Junction to 32C for Forres. Engines usually carried the code on an oval shed plate mounted on the smokebox door. Sub-sheds used the same code as the main shed.

The GWR used a series of letter codes, mainly consisting of three capital letters representing the name of the shed, with a few having two letters and the longest being SALOP for the GWR part of Shrewsbury shed. These codes usually were stencilled on the engine's buffer beam but sometimes were carried on the side of the main frame above the cylinders. The GWR used also a system of three digit numerical codes, which related to the divisional structure of the company. These were used for internal administration and in press releases of stock alterations, so that they were used for stock alterations in *The Railway Observer* for a time. The numerical codes were not used on the engines.

The LNER and SR used letter codes also. These were not displayed on the engines. However LNER engines often had the name of the shed stencilled on the buffer beam. These companies also organised their sheds under divisional structures although this was not apparent from the shed codes.

After nationalisation clearly it was necessary to have a unified system for shed codes. One disadvantage of the use of letter codes was that there was some duplication of codes between the constituent companies. It was decided to adopt the LMS system across the whole BR network. At the same time, the railways were reorganised from four major companies to six regions with the formation of the Scottish Region, comprising the Scottish parts of the former LMS and LNER, and the division of the remaining parts of the LNER into the Eastern and North Eastern Regions. LMS sheds in England and Wales retained their existing codes. Sheds in the other regions were allocated two digit codes beginning with three or four for the Eastern Region, five for the North Eastern Region, six for the Scottish Region, seven for the Southern Region and eight for the Western Region. Thus the codes for these regions started with 30A, 50A, 60A and 70A respectively except for the WR which started with 81A.

Recoding was started on 1st January 1949 when the Scottish Region sheds were allocated their numerical codes ranging from 60A Inverness to 68D Beattock. These recodings released codes in the 27 to 32 series for re-use although the 29 series was not used again. The other regions followed with recodings in the rest of 1949 and early 1950, with the Southern Region being the last to change to the new codes in February 1950.

TABLE 2.1
ER Western Section: Provisional Shed Codes – January 1949

40A	Kings Cross		44A	Colwick
40B	Hornsey			Derby Friargate
40C	Hatfield		44B	Annesley
40D	Hitchin		44C	Leicester (G.C.)
40E	Neasden			Leicester (G.N.)
	Aylesbury		44D	Staveley
	Chesham		44E	Woodford Halse
41A	New England		45A	Gorton
	Spalding			Dinting
	Bourne			Hayfield
	Stamford			Macclesfield
41B	Grantham		45B	Sheffield
			45C	Wrexham
42A	Doncaster		45D	Bidston
42B	Mexborough			
42C	Frodingham		46A	Lincoln
42D	Barnsley		46B	Immingham
42E	Retford		46C	Louth
	Newark		46D	Tuxford
			46E	Langwith
43A	Ardsley		46F	Boston
43B	Copley Hill			
43C	Bradford			

It was planned initially that the Eastern Region would use two numerical ranges of codes. The 30 to 33 series was earmarked for the former Great Eastern Railway area plus the London, Tilbury and Southend Railway (LTSR); the latter had passed from LMS to ER control in February 1949 although it continued to use Stanier 2-6-4 tanks until the line was electrified. The former Great Northern and Great Central areas were to be recoded in the second range, the 40-46 series. This plan was not implemented however. Instead codes in the range 30 to 40 were adopted for the ER with the former GN and GC areas now receiving codes ranging from 34A King's Cross to 40F Boston. The former CLC sheds had been transferred to LMR control in November 1948 and were not considered for inclusion in the 40-46 series. Details of the proposed 40-46 codes are given in Table 2.1.

Several recodings took place within the LMR during 1949 and 1950. The original 4 series, with Shrewsbury as its chief shed (see Table 2.2 for details), were transferred to the WR and a new smaller 4 division formed. This consisted of Bletchley 4A with Cambridge, Leighton Buzzard, Oxford, Newport Pagnell and Aylesbury as sub-sheds and Northampton 4B. After the former LTSR sheds (LMR 13 division, see Table 2.3 for details) had been transferred to ER control, a new LMR 13 series was formed from the former CLC sheds with Trafford Park as its main shed; this series was short-lived however, being dispersed to other divisions in April 1950; Table 2.4 gives coding details.

Detailed information about the shed codes, including changes, is presented here covering the period from January 1951, when the first Britannia Pacific entered service, until the end of BR main line steam in August 1968. Many sheds remained in use beyond the end of steam, becoming diesel and/or electric depots, with some still in use, although these have been converted from their original structures to more modern ones to meet the requirements of modern traction. Some sheds continued in use for servicing visiting engines or as

stabling or signing-on points after they had lost their locomotive allocations. The closing dates given in this book are when their allocations were removed.

Detailed information is presented in the form of three tables. Table 2.5 provides a list showing all the main sheds alphabetically with their codes as on 1st January 1951. This table also includes Thornaby, which was opened as a new steam shed in 1958, but does not include depots which were opened after 1951 for diesel and/or electric traction. Table 2.6, organised in order of shed codes at that date, provides the history of any recodings, records the closing dates for steam operation and details any future use. In cases where sheds were transferred to a different region as a result of changes of regional boundaries, new entries have been started under the receiving region. Table 2.7 lists, in alphabetical order, all sheds which had BR Standard engines allocated to them. This table includes the first and last dates for these allocations, but does not include details of any gaps in allocations of BR Standard engines. It also lists which class(es) were allocated to each shed at some time between those dates. These classes have been abbreviated as 70 for Britannias, 71 for Duke of Gloucester, 72 for Clans and so on up to 92 for Cl.9F 2-10-0s.

Finally Table 2.8 lists the codes assigned by the pre-Nationalisation companies to their depots together with their new BR codes and dates of recoding as at 1st January 1948.

Major Reorganisations and Recodings

During the period from January 1951 to August 1968, a number of major reorganisations and recodings took place. The following is a summary of the more significant changes.

October 1951. The 23 Skipton division ceased to exist with the three sheds being absorbed into the 11 Carnforth and 20 Holbeck divisions.

TABLE 2.2 LMS Shrewsbury District Codes From 1935	
4A	Shrewsbury
	Trench
	Coalport
	Ludlow
	Clee Hill
	Craven Arms
4B	Swansea
	Knighton
	Builth Road
	Carmarthen
	Llandovery
4C	Upper Bank
	Gurnos
	Brecon
4D	Abergavenny
	Hereford
4E	Tredegar
	Blaenavon

TABLE 2.3 LMR 13 LTSR Division January 1949	
13A	Plaistow
13B	Devons Road (Bow)
13C	Tilbury
13D	Shoeburyness
13E	Upminster

TABLE 2.4 LMR 13 Trafford Park District February-April 1950	
13A	Trafford Park
13B	Belle Vue
13C	Heaton Mersey
13D	Northwich
13E	Brunswick
	Warrington
	Southport
	Widnes
13F	Walton
13G	Wigan (Lower Ince)

March 1952. There was an internal LMR reorganisation. The 4 Bletchley and 7 Llandudno Junction divisions ceased to exist, Bletchley being taken into the 1 Willesden division and Northampton into the 2 Rugby group while the 7 division sheds were absorbed into the 6 Chester division.

October 1956. The LMR and ER lines in the West Riding of Yorkshire were transferred to the NER. New divisions 55 Holbeck and 56 Wakefield were formed from the previous 20 Holbeck and 25 Wakefield divisions while the former 37 Copley Hill division was abolished. These transfers took place in stages. The transfer of the 37 division was effective in July 1956 giving the somewhat unusual situation that the new 56 division started its existence without an A shed. The Wakefield division sheds were transferred in September 1956 except for 25B Huddersfield which remained as the sole 25 series shed. These transfers were completed in January 1957 with the recoding of the 20 series and Huddersfield to the new 55 series. It should be noted that sources vary slightly in the dates of these recodings.

February 1958. Massive reorganisations took place involving all the regions. The former GCR route, except for the Sheffield area, was transferred to the LMR with the sheds being Annesley, Gorton, Leicester (Central), Neasden and Woodford Halse, each joining a different LMR division. Chester (West) and Wrexham (Rhosddu) exchanged regions between the LMR and WR, also exchanging codes 6E and 84K. The LMR 10 Springs Branch division was abolished with the sheds moving to other divisions in the Liverpool and Manchester areas. The LMR 19 Grimesthorpe division and the ER 35 New England and 38 Colwick divisions ceased to exist with their sheds joining the 34 King's Cross, 40 Lincoln and 41 Darnall divisions. Staveley (Barrow Hill) was moved from the 18 Toton division to the 41 Darnall division. Mexborough and Barnsley were transferred from the 36 Doncaster division while Langwith Junction and Tuxford were transferred from the 40 Lincoln division, all four going to the

41 Darnall division. Some sources give these internal ER changes as taking place in February while other sources give the date as July. The ScR sheds in the northern part of Carlisle, Kingmoor and Canal, moved back to the LMR to join the 12 Carlisle division with Kingmoor replacing Upperby as the A shed and the existing 12 division sheds being recoded within the series; these moves left three Scottish sheds, Dumfries, Stranraer and Beattock in the 68 division which no longer had an A shed. There were also exchanges of some sheds between the SR 71 Eastleigh division and the WR 82 Bristol Bath Road division.

April 1958. There was an internal LMR reorganisation, mostly involving sheds in north west England. The main change was in the 11 Carnforth division. Barrow took over as the chief shed and the series then included Workington 11B, Oxenholm 11C and Tebay 11D; Carnforth was recoded 24L in the Accrington division.

October 1958. The 54 Sunderland division was abolished with the sheds being absorbed into the 52 Gateshead division.

January 1960. The 53 Hull division was abolished with the sheds being absorbed into the 50 York division. At the same time, Neville Hill was transferred from the 50 York division to the 55 Holbeck division.

June 1960. The 3 Bescot and 11 Barrow divisions ceased to exist with their sheds being absorbed in the 21 Saltley and 24 Accrington divisions respectively.

September 1963. There was a major internal LMR reorganisation combined with the transfer of the WR West Midlands and Cambrian Lines sheds to the LMR. Within the LMR the 17 Derby, 18 Toton, 21 Saltley and 27 Bank Hall divisions ceased to exist. The 17 and 18 division sheds were absorbed into the 16 Nottingham division with Toton replacing Nottingham as the A shed while the 27 division sheds were absorbed into the 8 Edge Hill division; the 21 Saltley division was absorbed into the new 2 Tyseley division.

TABLE 2.5
BR Sheds which had an Allocation(s) of Steam Locomotives

This table lists all steam sheds that were open on January 1951 plus Thornaby, which was opened in June 1958, and sub-sheds that had allocations of BR Standard locomotives. They are listed alphabetically with their January 1951 shed codes which can be used to access the more detailed information in Table 2.6.

Aberbeeg	86H	Ardrossan	67D	Barnstaple Jct.	72E
Abercynon	88E	Ardsley	37A	Barrow	11B
Aberdare	86J	Ashford	74A	Barry	88C
Aberdeen (Ferryhill)	61B	Aston	3D	Basingstoke	70D
Abergavenny	86K	Aviemore	60B	Bath (Green Park)	71G
Accrington	24A	Ayr	67C	Bathgate	64F
Agecroft	26B			Beattock	68D
Aintree	27B	Bacup	26E	Bedford	15D
Alnmouth (sub-shed	52D	Balloch	65I	Belle Vue	26G
to Tweedmouth)		Banbury	84C	Bescot	3A
Alsager	5E	Bangor	7B	Bidston	6F
Alston (sub-shed	52C(A)	Bank Hall	27A	Birkenhead	6C
to Blaydon)		Barnsley	36D	Bishops Stortford	30C
Annesley	38B				

Blackpool	28A	Didcot	81E	Hornsey	34B
Blair Atholl	63A	Doncaster	36A	Horsham	75D
(sub-shed to Perth)		Dorchester	71C	Huddersfield	25B
Blaydon	52C	Dover	74C	Hull (Alexandra	53C(A)
Bletchley	4A	Duffryn Yard	87B	Dock)	
Bolton	26C	Dumfries	68B	Hull (Springhead)	53C
Borough Gardens	54C	Dundee (Tay Bridge)	62B	Hurlford	67B
Boston	40F	Dunfermline	62C	Immingham	40B
Botanic Gardens	53B	Eastbourne	75G	Inverness	60A
Bournemouth	71B	Eastfield	65A	Ipswich	32B
Bournville	21B	Eastleigh	71A		
Bradford	37C	Ebbw Jct.	86A	Keith	61C
Brecon	89B	Edge Hill	8A	Kentish Town	14B
Bricklayers Arms	73B	Exeter	83C	Kettering	15B
Bridlington	53D	Exmouth Jct.	72A	Kidderminster	85D
Brighton	75A			King's Cross	34A
Bristol (Barrow Road)	22A	Farnley Jct.	25G	King's Lynn	31C
Bristol (Bath Road)	82A	Faversham	73E	Kipps	65E
Bromsgrove	21C	Feltham	70B	Kirkby-in-Ashfield	16C
Brunswick (Liverpool)	8E	Fleetwood	28B	Kirkby Stephen	51H
Burton-upon-Trent	17B	Forfar	63C	Kittybrewster	61A
Bury	26D	Forres	60E	Laira	83D
Bury St. Edmunds	31E	Fort William	63D	Lancaster	23C
Bushbury	3B	Fratton	71D	Landore	87E
Buxton	9D	Frodingham	36C	Langwith Jct.	40E
				Leamington	84D
Cambridge	31A	Gateshead	52A	Lees	26F
Camden	1B	Gillingham	73D	Leicester (Central)	38C
Canklow	19C	Gloucester (Barnwood)	22B	Leicester (Midland)	15C
Cardiff (Canton)	86C	also known as		Lincoln	40A
Cardiff (Cathays)	88A	Gloucester (Midland)		Llandudno Jct.	7A
Cardiff East Dock	88B	Gloucester (Horton	85B	Llanelly	87F
Carlisle (Canal)	12B	Road)		Llantrisant	86D
Carlisle (Kingmoor)	68A	Goodwick	87J	Longsight	9A
Carlisle (Upperby)	12A	Goole	25C	Lostock Hall	24C
Carmarthen	87G	Gorton	39A	Louth	40C
Carnforth	11A	Grangemouth	65F	Low Moor	25F
Carstairs	64D	Grantham	35B	Lower Darwen	24D
Chester (Midland)	6A	Greenock (Ladyburn)	66D	Lowestoft	32C
Chester (Northgate)	6D	Grimesthorpe, also	19A		
Chester (West)	84K	known as Brightside		Macclesfield	9C
Coalville	17C	in 1950s		Machynlleth	89C
Colchester	30E	Guildford	70C	Malton	50F
Colwick	38A			Manningham	20E
Consett	54D	Hamilton	66C	Mansfield	16D
Copley Hill	37B	Hasland	18C	March	31B
Corkerhill	67A	Hatfield	34C	Market Harborough	2A
Coventry	2D	Haverton Hill	51G	sub-shed to Rugby	
Crewe North	5A	Hawick	64G	Melton Constable	32G
Crewe South	5B	Haymarket	64B	Merthyr	88D
Cricklewood (West)	14A	Heaton	52B	Mexborough	36B
Croes Newydd	84J	Heaton Mersey	9F	Middlesbrough	51D
Cudworth	53E	Helensburgh	65H	Millhouses	19B
		Hellifield	23B	Mirfield	25D
Dairycoates	53A	Helmsdale	60C	Mold Jct.	6B
Dalry Road	64C	Hereford	85C	Monument Lane	3E
Danygraig	87C	Hertford East	30B	Moor Row	12E
Darlington	51A	Highbridge	71J	Motherwell	66B
Darnall	39B	Hitchin	34D		
Dawsholm	65D	Hither Green	73C	Neasden	34E
Derby	17A	Holbeck	20A	Neath (Court Sart)	87A
Devons Road	1D	Holyhead	7C	Neville Hill	50B

Ex-Crosti boilered 92021 storms away from Northampton in the winter of 1960/61 after a crew change with an Irthlingborough to South Wales iron ore train travelling via Bletchley and Oxford. The Northampton coaling tower can be seen in the background. *Brian Denny*

New England	35A	Percy Main	52E	St. Philips Marsh	82B
Newport (IOW)	71E	Perth	63A	St. Rollox	65B
Newport Pill	86B	Peterborough	35C	Salisbury	72B
Newport (Yorkshire)	51B	(Spital Bridge)		Saltburn	51K
Newton Abbot	83A	Plaistow	33A	Saltley	21A
Newton Heath	26A	Plodder Lane	10D	Scarborough	50E
Neyland	87H	Plymouth Friary	72D	Selby	50C
Nine Elms	70A	Polmadie	66A	Severn Tunnel Jct.	86E
Normanton	20D	Polmont	64E	Shoeburyness	33C
Northallerton	51J	Pontypool Road	86G	Shrewsbury	84G
Northampton	4B	Preston	10B	Skipton	23A
North Blyth	52F			Slough	81B
Northwich	9G	Radyr	88A(R)	South Blyth	52F(S)
Norwich	32A	Ramsgate	74B	South Lynn	31D
Norwood Jct.	75C	Reading	81D	Southall	81C
Nottingham	16A	Reading South	70E	Southampton Docks	71I
Nuneaton	2B	Redhill	75B	Southend Victoria	30D
		Retford (GC & GN)	36E	Southport	27C
Oban	63E	Rhyl	7D	Sowerby Bridge	25E
Old Oak Common	81A	Rhymney	88D(R)	Speke Jct.	8C
Oswestry	89A	Rose Grove	24B	Springs Branch	10A
Oxenholme	11C	Rowsley	17D	Stafford	5C
Oxford	81F	Royston	20C	Starbeck	50D
Oxley	84B	Rugby	2A	Staveley (Barrow Hill)	18D
		Ryde (IOW)	71F	Staveley (Central)	38D
Parkeston Quay	30F			Stewarts Lane	73A
Parkhead	65C	St. Albans	14C	Stirling	63B
Patricroft	10C	St. Blazey	83E	Stockport (Edgeley)	9B
Penrith	12C	St. Leonards	74E	Stockton	51E
Penzance	83G	St. Margarets	64A	Stoke	5D

78050 of Motherwell shunts the yard at Chapelhall station in a typical North Lanarkshire industrial scene on a wintery day in March 1962. The Caledonian branch from Coatbridge to Newhouse closed to passengers on 1st December 1930 but freight traffic survived to serve the heavy iron and steel industries of this area for another 36 years, until closed completely on 4th April 1966.   *Douglas Hume*

Stourbridge Jct.	84F		Trafford Park	9E		Westhouses	18B
Stourton	20B		Tredegar	86K(T)		Weymouth	82F
Stranraer	68C		Treherbert	88F		Whitby	50G
Stratford	30A		Truro	83F		Wick	60D
Stratford-on-Avon	21D		Tunbridge Wells West	75F		Widnes	8D
Sunderland	54A		Tuxford	40D		Wigan (Central)	27D
Sutton Oak	10E		Tweedmouth	52D		Wigan (Lower Ince)	10F
Swansea East Dock	87D		Tyne Dock	54B		Willesden	1A
Swansea (Paxton	87K		Tyseley	84E		Wolverhampton	84A
Street), also known						(Stafford Road)	
as Swansea (Victoria)			Uttoxeter	5F		Woodford Halse	38E
Swindon	82C		Wadebridge	72F		Worcester	85A
			Wakefield	25A		Workington	12D
Taunton	83B		Walsall (Ryecroft)	3C		Wrexham (Rhosddu)	6E
Tebay	11D		Walton-on-the-Hill	27E			
Templecombe	71H		Warrington (Dallam)	8B		Yarmouth Beach	32F
Thornaby	51L		Warwick	2C		Yarmouth South Town	32D
Thornton Jct.	62A		Watford	1C		Yarmouth Vauxhall	32E
Three Bridges	75E		Wellingborough	15A		Yeovil (Pen Mill)	82E
Tilbury	33B		Wellington	84H		Yeovil Town	72C
Tonbridge	74D		West Auckland	51F		Yoker	65G
Tondu	86F		West Hartlepool	51C		York	50A
Toton	18A		Westbury	82D			

TABLE 2.6

BR Sheds which had an Allocation(s) of Steam Locomotives, in Shed Code order

Information on each shed is limited to the period from January 1951 to August 1968 or until the shed was closed or steam locomotives removed. Later dates when sheds had diesel allocations have been omitted as have cases where a closed shed later re-opened for modern traction. In some cases closed only meant that the shed no longer had locomotives allocated but remained open as a signing-on or stabling point. Where sheds became sub-sheds their closing dates have not been included since they lost their allocations when they became sub-sheds. Sheds which never had steam locomotives allocated are not included in this table.

In some cases locomotives were allocated to sub-sheds. Only those sub-sheds which had an allocation of BR Standard Locomotive(s), or were main sheds for part of the period from January 1951 to August 1968, are included.

Entries for sub-sheds and for sheds transferred from other regions have been inset slightly to distinguish them from the other entries.

LONDON MIDLAND REGION

Willesden	1A, steam removed 9/65
Camden	1B, steam removed 9/63
Watford	1C, closed 3/65
Devons Road	1D, steam removed 8/58.
Rugby	2A, recoded 1F 9/63, steam removed 5/65

    Market Harborough a sub-shed to Rugby 2A, recoded 2F 10/55 (becoming a main shed), recoded 15F 4/58, closed 10/60

Nuneaton	2B, recoded 5E 9/63, closed 6/66
Warwick	2C, to WR (code not changed so not listed under WR) 2/58, closed 11/58
Coventry	2D, steam removed 11/58

    Tyseley transferred from WR as 2A 9/63, steam removed 11/66

    Oxley transferred from WR as 2B 9/63, steam removed 3/67

    Stourbridge Jct. transferred from WR as 2C 9/63, steam removed 7/66

    Banbury transferred from WR as 2D 9/63, closed 10/66

    Woodford Halse transferred from ER as 2G 2/58, recoded 2F 4/58, recoded 1G 9/63, closed 6/65

    Leamington transferred from WR as 2L 9/63, closed 6/65

    Wellington transferred from WR as 2M 9/63, closed 8/64

    Kidderminster transferred from WR as 2P 9/63, closed 8/64.

Bescot	3A, recoded 21B 6/60, recoded 2F 9/63, steam removed 3/66
Bushbury	3B, recoded 21C 6/60, recoded 2K 9/63, closed 4/65
Walsall (Ryecroft)	3C, steam removed 6/58
Aston	3D, recoded 21D 6/60, recoded 2J 9/63, closed 10/65
Monument Lane	3E, recoded 21E 6/60, steam removed 2/62.
Bletchley	4A, recoded 1E 3/52, steam removed 7/65
Northampton	4B, recoded 2E 3/52, recoded 1H 9/63, closed 9/65.
Crewe North	5A, closed 5/65
Crewe South	5B, closed 11/67
Stafford	5C, closed 7/65
Stoke	5D, steam removed 8/67

Alsager	5E, closed 6/62
Uttoxeter	5F, closed 12/64
Chester (Midland)	6A, steam removed 6/67
Mold Jct.	6B, closed 4/66
Birkenhead	6C, recoded 8H 9/63, steam removed 11/67
Chester (Northgate)	6D, steam removed 1/60
Wrexham (Rhosddu)	6E, transferred to WR as 84K 2/58
Bidston	6F, closed 2/63

    Croes Newydd transferred from WR as 6C 9/63, closed 6/67

    Shrewsbury transferred from WR as 6D 9/63, steam removed 3/67

    Chester (West) transferred from WR as 6E 2/58, closed 4/60

    Oswestry transferred from WR as 6E 9/63, closed 1/65

    Machynlleth transferred from WR as 6F 9/63, closed 12/66.

Llandudno Jct.	7A, recoded 6G 3/52, steam removed 10/66
Bangor	7B, recoded 6H 3/52, closed 6/65
Holyhead	7C, recoded 6J 3/52, steam removed 12/66
Rhyl	7D, recoded 6K 3/52, closed 2/63.
Edge Hill	8A, closed 5/68
Warrington (Dallam)	8B, closed 10/67
Speke Jct.	8C, closed 5/68
Widnes	8D, closed 4/64
Brunswick (Liverpool)	8E, recoded 27F 4/58, locomotives removed 9/61, closed 11/61.
Longsight	9A, steam removed 2/65
Stockport (Edgeley)	9B, closed 5/68
Macclesfield	9C, closed 6/61
Buxton	9D, recoded 9L 9/63, locomotives removed 3/68, closed 4/68
Trafford Park	9E, recoded 17F 1/57, recoded 9E 4/58, closed 3/68
Heaton Mersey	9F, recoded 17E 1/57, recoded 9F 4/58, closed 5/68
Northwich	9G, recoded 8E 4/58, closed 3/68

    Gorton transferred from ER as 9H 2/58, recoded 9G 4/58, closed 6/65.

Springs Branch	10A, recoded 8F 4/58, steam removed 12/67
Preston	10B, recoded 24K 2/58, closed 9/61
Patricroft	10C, recoded 26F 2/58, recoded 9H 9/63, closed 7/68
Plodder Lane	10D, closed 10/54
Sutton Oak	10E, recoded 10D 10/55, recoded 8G 4/58, closed 6/67
Wigan (Lower Ince)	10F, closed 3/52.
Carnforth	11A, recoded 24L 4/58, recoded 10A 9/63, closed 8/68
Barrow	11B, recoded 11A 4/58, recoded 12E 6/60, recoded 12C 9/63, steam removed 12/66
Oxenholme	11C, recoded 12G 6/60, closed 6/62
Tebay	11D, recoded 12H 6/60, recoded 12E 9/63, closed 1/68.
Carlisle (Upperby)	12A, recoded 12B 1/58, steam removed 12/66
Carlisle (Canal)	12B, transferred to ScR as 68E 7/51, transferred from ScR as 12D 2/58, recoded 12C 4/58, closed 6/63
Penrith	12C, recoded 12B 10/55, closed 12/55
Workington	12D, recoded 12C 10/55, recoded 11B 4/58, recoded 12F 6/60, recoded 12D 9/63, closed 1/68
Moor Row	12E, closed 7/54

Carlisle (Kingmoor) transferred from ScR as 12A 2/58, steam removed 1/68

Kirkby Stephen transferred from NER as 12E 2/58, recoded 12D 4/58, closed 11/61.

Cricklewood (West)	14A, recoded 14B 9/63, steam removed 12/64
Kentish Town	14B, closed 4/63
St. Albans	14C, closed 1/60

Neasden transferred from ER as 14D 2/58, closed 6/62.

Wellingborough	15A, recoded 15B 9/63, steam removed 6/65, steam reintroduced 4/66, steam removed 6/66
Kettering	15B, recoded 15C 9/63, closed 6/65
Leicester (Midland)	15C, recoded 15A 9/63, steam removed 6/66
Bedford	15D, recoded 14E 4/58, recoded 14C 9/63, steam removed 9/63

Leicester (Central) transferred from ER as 15E 2/58, recoded 15D 9/63, closed 7/64.

Nottingham	16A, recoded 16D 9/63, steam removed 4/65
Kirkby-in-Ashfield	16C, recoded 16B 10/55, recoded 16E 9/63, steam removed 10/66
Mansfield	16D, recoded 16C 10/55, steam removed 2/60

Colwick transferred from ER as 16B 1/66, steam removed 12/66, steam reintroduced (stationary boiler only) 6/67, steam removed 7/67

Annesley transferred from ER as 16D 2/58, recoded 16B 9/63, closed 1/66.

Derby	17A, recoded 16C 9/63, steam removed 10/66
Burton-upon-Trent	17B, recoded 16F 9/63, steam removed 9/66
Coalville	17C, recoded 15D 4/58, recoded 15E 9/63, closed 10/65
Rowsley	17D, recoded 17C 4/58, recoded 16J 9/63, closed 4/64.
Toton	18A, recoded 16A 9/63, steam removed 11/66
Westhouses	18B, recoded 16G 9/63, closed 10/66
Hasland	18C, recoded 16H 9/63, closed 9/64
Staveley (Barrow Hill)	18D, transferred to ER as 41E 2/58.
Grimesthorpe, also known as Brightside in 1950s	19A, transferred to ER as 41B 2/58
Millhouses	19B, transferred to ER as 41C 2/58
Canklow	19C, transferred to ER as 41D 2/58.
Holbeck	20A, transferred to NER as 55A 2/57
Stourton	20B, transferred to NER as 55B 2/57
Royston	20C, transferred to NER as 55D 2/57
Normanton	20D, transferred to NER as 55E 2/57
Manningham	20E, transferred to NER as 55F 2/57.
Saltley	21A, recoded 2E 9/63, steam removed 3/67
Bournville	21B, closed 2/60
Bromsgrove	21C, transferred to WR as 85F 2/58
Stratford-on-Avon	21D, closed 2/53.
Bristol (Barrow Road)	22A, transferred to WR as 82E 2/58
Gloucester (Midland)	22B, transferred to WR as 85E 2/58, also known as Gloucester (Barnwood).
Skipton	23A, recoded 20F 10/51, recoded 24G 2/57, recoded 10G 9/63, steam removed 2/67
Hellifield	23B, recoded 20G 10/51, recoded 24H 2/57, closed 6/63
Lancaster	23C, recoded 11E 10/51, recoded 24J 2/57, recoded 10J 9/63, closed 4/66.
Accrington	24A, steam removed 3/61
Rose Grove	24B, recoded 10F 9/63, closed 8/68
Lostock Hall	24C, recoded 10D 9/63, steam removed 8/68
Lower Darwen	24D, recoded 10H 9/63, closed 2/66.
Wakefield	25A, transferred to NER as 56A 9/56
Huddersfield	25B, transferred to NER as 55G 2/57
Goole	25C, transferred to NER as 53E 9/56
Mirfield	25D, transferred to NER as 56D 9/56
Sowerby Bridge	25E, transferred to NER as 56E 9/56
Low Moor	25F, transferred to NER as 56F 9/56
Farnley Jct.	25G, transferred to NER as 55C 9/56.
Newton Heath	26A, recoded 9D 9/63, closed 7/68
Agecroft	26B, recoded 9J 9/63, closed 10/66
Bolton	26C, recoded 9K 9/63, closed 7/68
Bury	26D, recoded 9M 9/63, closed 4/65
Bacup	26E, closed 10/54

Lees	26F, recoded 26E 10/55, recoded 9P 9/63, closed 4/64
Belle Vue	26G, recoded 26F 10/55, closed 4/56.
Bank Hall	27A, recoded 8K 9/63, closed 10/66
Aintree	27B, recoded 8L 9/63, closed 6/67
Southport	27C, recoded 8M 9/63, closed 6/66
Wigan (Central)	27D, recoded 8P 9/63, closed 4/64
Walton-on-the-Hill	27E, recoded 8R 9/63, closed 12/63.
Blackpool	28A, recoded 24E 4/52, recoded 10B 9/63, closed 11/64
Fleetwood	28B, recoded 24F 4/52, recoded 10C 9/63, closed 2/66.

EASTERN REGION

Stratford	30A, steam removed 9/62
Hertford East	30B, closed 11/60
Bishops Stortford	30C, closed 2/59
Southend Victoria	30D, became sub-shed to Stratford 30A 12/56
Colchester	30E, closed 11/59
Parkeston Quay	30F, steam removed 1/61.
Cambridge	31A, steam removed 6/62
March	31B, steam removed 12/63
King's Lynn	31C, steam removed 4/59
South Lynn	31D, closed 3/59
Bury St. Edmunds	31E, closed 1/59.

Norwich	32A, steam removed 4/62
Ipswich	32B, steam removed 11/59
Lowestoft	32C, steam removed 9/60.
Yarmouth South Town	32D, steam removed 11/59
Yarmouth Vauxhall	32E, closed 1/59
Yarmouth Beach	32F, closed 2/59
Melton Constable	32G, closed 2/59.
Plaistow	33A, closed 11/59
Tilbury	33B, closed 6/62
Shoeburyness	33C, closed 6/62.
King's Cross	34A, closed 6/63
Hornsey	34B, steam removed 7/61
Hatfield	34C, closed 1/61
Hitchin	34D, steam removed 6/61
Neasden	34E, transferred to LMR as 14D 2/58.
New England	35A, recoded 34E 7/58, steam removed 1/65
Grantham	35B, recoded 34F 7/58, closed 9/63
Peterborough (Spital Bridge)	35C, recoded 31F 7/58, closed 2/60.
Doncaster	36A, steam removed 4/66
Mexborough	36B, recoded 41F 7/58, closed 3/64
Frodingham	36C, steam removed 2/66
Barnsley	36D, recoded 41G 7/58, closed 1/60
Retford (GC & GN)	36E, GC shed closed 1/65, GN shed closed 6/65.

Immingham shed did not spend much time cleaning its express engines as illustrated by 70041 *Sir John Moore*. The working is the 09.33am Cleethorpes-King Cross seen passing through Oakleigh Park station on the ECML on 12th August 1961. Considering the state of the locomotive is it surprising that it survived until April 1967? *K. L. Cook*

Ardsley	37A, transferred to NER as 56B 7/56
Copley Hill	37B, transferred to NER as 56C 7/56
Bradford	37C, transferred to NER as 56G 7/56.
Colwick	38A, recoded 40E 7/58, transferred to LMR as 16B 1/66
Annesley	38B, transferred to LMR as 16D 2/58
Leicester (Central)	38C, transferred to LMR as 15E 2/58
Staveley (Central)	38D, recoded 41H 7/58, closed 6/65
Woodford Halse	38E, transferred to LMR as 2G 2/58.
Gorton	39A, transferred to LMR as 9H 2/58
Darnall	39B, recoded 41A 6/55 (possibly implemented later, 41A shed plates came into general use about 4/56 or 5/56), steam removed 6/63.
Lincoln	40A, steam removed 1/64
Immingham	40B, steam removed 2/66
Louth	40C, closed 12/56
Tuxford	40D, recoded 41K 7/58, closed 2/59
Langwith Jct.	40E, recoded 41J 7/58, closed 2/66
Boston	40F, closed 1/64

Grimesthorpe transferred from LMR as 41B 2/58, closed 9/61

Millhouses transferred from LMR as 41C 2/58, closed 12/61

Canklow transferred from LMR as 41D 2/58, steam removed 6/65

Staveley (Barrow Hill) transferred from LMR as 41E 2/58, steam removed 10/65.

NORTH EASTERN REGION

York	50A, steam removed 6/67
Neville Hill	50B, recoded 55H 1/60, steam removed 6/66
Selby	50C, closed 9/59
Starbeck	50D, closed 9/59
Scarborough	50E, closed 4/63
Malton	50F, closed 4/63
Whitby	50G, closed 4/59.
Darlington	51A, steam removed 3/66
Newport (Yorkshire)	51B, closed 6/58 (replaced by nearby new shed Thornaby)
West Hartlepool	51C, closed 9/67
Middlesbrough	51D, closed 5/58 (replaced by nearby new shed Thornaby)
Stockton	51E, closed 6/59
West Auckland	51F, closed 2/64
Haverton Hill	51G, closed 6/59
Kirkby Stephen	51H, transferred to LMR as 12E 2/58
Northallerton	51J, closed 3/63
Saltburn	51K, closed 1/58
Thornaby	51L, opened 6/58, steam removed 12/64.
Gateshead	52A, steam removed 3/65
Heaton	52B, closed 6/63
Blaydon	52C, closed 6/63
Alston (sub-shed to Blaydon)	52C(A), closed 9/59

Tweedmouth	52D, steam removed 6/66
Alnmouth (sub-shed to Tweedmouth)	52D(A), closed 6/66
Percy Main	52E, steam removed 2/65
North Blyth	52F, sometimes referred to as 52F(N), closed 9/67
South Blyth	52F(S), closed 5/67.
Dairycoates	53A, recoded 50B 1/60, steam removed 6/67
Botanic Gardens	53B, steam removed 6/59
Hull (Springhead)	53C, steam removed 12/58
Hull (Alexandra Dock)	53C(A) sub-shed to Hull (Springhead), recoded 53C 12/58, recoded 50B(A) 1/60 sub-shed to Dairycoates 50B 1/60, steam removed 11/60
Bridlington	53D, closed 12/58
Cudworth	53E, closed 7/51

Goole transferred from LMR as 53E 9/56, recoded 50D 1/60, steam removed 5/67.

Sunderland	54A, recoded 52G 10/58, closed 9/67
Tyne Dock	54B, recoded 52H 10/58, closed 9/67
Borough Gardens	54C, recoded 52J 10/58, closed 6/59
Consett	54D, recoded 52K 10/58, closed 5/65.

Holbeck transferred from LMR as 55A 2/57, steam removed 10/67

Stourton transferred from LMR as 55B 2/57, steam removed 1/67

Farnley Jct. transferred from LMR as 55C 9/56, closed 11/66

Royston transferred from LMR as 55D 2/57, steam removed 11/67

Normanton transferred from LMR as 55E 2/57, steam removed 9/67

Manningham transferred from LMR as 55F 2/57, closed 4/67

Huddersfield transferred from LMR as 55G 2/57, closed 1/67.

Wakefield transferred from LMR as 56A 9/56, closed 6/67
Ardsley transferred from ER as 56B 7/56, closed 10/65
Copley Hill transferred from ER as 56C 7/56, closed 9/64
Mirfield transferred from LMR as 56D 9/56, closed 1/67
Sowerby Bridge transferred from LMR as 56E 9/56, closed 1/64
Low Moor transferred from LMR as 56F 9/56, recoded 55J 8/67, closed 10/67
Bradford transferred from ER as 56G 7/56, steam removed 1/58.

SCOTTISH REGION

Inverness	60A, steam removed 6/62
Aviemore	60B, steam removed 7/62
Helmsdale	60C, closed 7/61
Wick	60D, closed 7/62
Forres	60E, steam removed 5/59.
Kittybrewster	61A, steam removed 6/61
Aberdeen (Ferryhill)	61B, closed 3/67
Keith	61C, closed 6/61.

Thornton Jct.	62A, steam removed 6/67
Dundee (Tay Bridge)	62B, closed 5/67
Dunfermline	62C, steam removed 5/67.
Perth	63A, steam removed 5/67
Blair Atholl (sub-shed to Perth)	63A, closed 6/62
Stirling	63B, recoded 65J 6/60, steam removed 6/66, steam reintroduced 11/66, closed 12/66
Forfar	63C, became sub-shed to Perth 63A 11/59, closed 7/64
Fort William	63D, recoded 65J 5/55, recoded 63B 6/60, steam removed 6/62
Oban	63E, recoded 63D 5/55, recoded 63C 11/59, steam removed 3/62.
St. Margarets	64A, closed 4/67
Haymarket	64B, steam removed 9/63
Dalry Road	64C, closed 10/65
Carstairs	64D, recoded 66E 6/60, steam removed 2/67
Polmont	64E, recoded 65K 6/60, closed 5/64
Bathgate	64F, closed 8/66
Hawick	64G, closed 1/66.
Eastfield	65A, steam removed 11/66
St. Rollox	65B, closed 11/66
Parkhead	65C, closed 12/62
Dawsholm	65D, closed 10/64
Kipps	65E, closed 1/63
Grangemouth	65F, steam removed 10/65
Yoker	65G, steam removed 3/61
Helensburgh	65H, closed 11/60
Balloch	65I, steam removed 11/60.
Polmadie	66A, steam removed 5/67
Motherwell	66B, closed 5/67
Hamilton	66C, steam removed 11/62
Greenock (Ladyburn)	66D, steam removed 11/66.
Corkerhill	67A, steam removed 5/67
Hurlford	67B, closed 12/66
Ayr	67C, steam removed 10/66
Ardrossan	67D, closed 2/65.
Carlisle (Kingmoor)	68A, transferred to LMR as 12A 2/58
Dumfries	68B, recoded 67E 7/62, steam removed 5/66
Stranraer	68C, recoded 67F 7/62, steam removed 11/66
Beattock	68D, recoded 66F 7/62, closed 5/67
Carlisle (Canal) transferred from ScR as 68E 7/51, transferred to LMR as 12D 2/58.	

SOUTHERN REGION

Nine Elms	70A, closed 7/67
Feltham	70B, steam removed 7/67
Guildford	70C, closed 7/67
Basingstoke	70D, closed 3/63
Reading South	70E, closed 12/62 but lost engine allocation earlier, probably in 1959.

Eastleigh	71A, recoded 70D 9/63, steam removed 7/67
Bournemouth	71B, recoded 70F 9/63, steam removed 7/67
Dorchester	71C, closed 3/55
Fratton	71D, recoded 70F 9/54, closed 11/59
Newport (IOW)	71E, recoded 70G 9/54, closed 11/57
Ryde (IOW)	71F, recoded 70H 9/54, steam removed 12/66
Bath (Green Park)	71G, transferred to WR as 82F 2/58
Templecombe	71H, transferred to WR as 82G 2/58
Southampton Docks	71I, steam removed 7/63
Highbridge	71J, transferred to WR and became sub-shed to Bath (Green Park) 82F 2/58
Weymouth transferred from WR as 71G 2/58, recoded 70G 9/63, steam removed 3/67	
Yeovil (Pen Mill) transferred from WR as 71H 2/58, closed 1/59.	
Exmouth Jct.	72A, transferred to WR as 83D 9/63
Salisbury	72B, recoded 70E 12/62, closed 7/67
Yeovil Town	72C, transferred to WR as 83E 9/63
Plymouth Friary	72D, transferred to WR as 83H 2/58
Barnstaple Jct.	72E, transferred to WR as 83F 9/63
Wadebridge	72F, transferred to WR as 84E 9/63.
Stewarts Lane	73A, recoded 75D 6/62, steam removed 9/63
Bricklayers Arms	73B, closed 6/62
Hither Green	73C, steam removed 10/61
Gillingham	73D, closed 6/59
Faversham	73E, steam removed 6/59.
Ashford	74A, recoded 73F 10/58, steam removed 6/62
Ramsgate	74B, recoded 73G 10/58, closed 6/59
Dover	74C, recoded 73H 10/58, closed 6/61
Tonbridge	74D, recoded 73J 10/58, closed 6/62
St. Leonards	74E, closed 6/58.
Brighton	75A, steam removed 6/64
Redhill	75B, closed 1/65
Norwood Jct.	75C, closed 6/64
Horsham	75D, closed 7/59
Three Bridges	75E, closed 1/64
Tunbridge Wells West	75F, closed 9/63
Eastbourne	75G, became sub-shed to Brighton 10/52.

WESTERN REGION

Old Oak Common	81A, steam removed 3/65
Slough	81B, closed 6/64
Southall	81C, steam removed 1/66
Reading	81D, steam removed 1/65
Didcot	81E, steam removed 4/65
Oxford	81F, steam removed 1/66.
Bristol (Bath Road)	82A, steam removed 9/60
St. Philips Marsh	82B, closed 6/64
Swindon	82C, steam removed 10/64
Westbury	82D, recoded 83C 10/63, steam removed 9/65

21

Yeovil (Pen Mill)	82E, transferred to SR as 71H 2/58
Weymouth	82F, transferred to SR as 71G 2/58

Bristol (Barrow Road) transferred from LMR as 82E 2/58, closed 11/65

Bath (Green Park) transferred from SR as 82F 2/58, closed 3/66

Templecombe transferred from SR as 82G 2/58, recoded 83G 10/63, closed 3/66.

Newton Abbot	83A, steam removed 9/62
Taunton	83B, steam removed 10/64
Exeter	83C, closed 10/63
Laira	83D, recoded 84A 9/63, steam removed 4/64
St. Blazey	83E, steam removed 4/62
Truro	83F, steam removed 3/62
Penzance	83G, steam removed 9/62

Exmouth Jct. transferred from SR as 83D 9/63, steam removed 5/65

Yeovil Town transferred from SR as 83E 9/63, closed 6/65

Barnstaple Jct. transferred from SR as 83F 9/63, closed 9/64

Plymouth Friary transferred from SR as 83H 2/58, closed 5/63.

Wolverhampton (Stafford Road)	84A, closed 9/63
Oxley	84B, transferred to LMR as 2B 9/63
Banbury	84C, transferred to LMR as 2D 9/63
Leamington	84D, transferred to LMR as 2L 9/63
Tyseley	84E, transferred to LMR as 2A 9/63

Stourbridge Jct.	84F, transferred to LMR as 2C 9/63
Shrewsbury	84G, recoded 89A 1/61, transferred to LMR as 6D 9/63
Wellington	84H, transferred to LMR as 2M 9/63
Croes Newydd	84J, recoded 89B 1/61, transferred to LMR as 6C 9/63
Chester (West)	84K, transferred to LMR as 6E 2/58

Wadebridge transferred from SR as 84E 9/63, closed 10/64

Wrexham (Rhosddu) transferred from LMR as 84K 2/58, closed 1/60.

Worcester	85A, steam removed 12/65
Gloucester (Horton Road)	85B, steam removed 1/66
Hereford	85C, recoded 86C 1/61, steam removed 10/64
Kidderminster	85D, recoded 84G 1/61, transferred to LMR as 2P 9/63

Gloucester (Barnwood) transferred from LMR as 85E 2/58, recoded 85C 1/61, closed 5/64

Bromsgrove transferred from LMR as 85F 2/58, recoded 85D 1/61, closed 9/64.

Ebbw Jct.	86A, recoded 86B 9/63, steam removed 10/65
Newport Pill	86B, closed 6/63
Cardiff (Canton)	86C, recoded 88A 1/61, steam removed 9/62
Llantrisant	86D, recoded 88G 1/61, closed 10/64
Severn Tunnel Jct.	86E, steam removed 11/65.

Having emerged from Twerton long tunnel, 264 yards in length, with its attractive Tudor Gothic semi-elliptical arch and flanking towers, 82007 in unlined green livery, is passing the closed Twerton Tunnel signal box on 22nd June 1963. The train is the Saturdays only 1.12pm from Calne to Weston-super-Mare, an unusual working which ran only during the summers of 1962 and 1963. Note on this occasion the engine is displaying class A headlamps, a rare sight on the Calne branch!

Hugh Ballantyne

Tondu	86F, recoded 88H 1/61, closed 3/64	Cardiff (Cathays)	88A, steam removed 12/57
Pontypool Road	86G, steam removed 5/65	Radyr	88A(R) sub-shed to Cardiff Cathays, recoded 88A (becoming a main shed) 12/57, recoded 88B 1/61, steam removed 7/65
Aberbeeg	86H, recoded 86F 1/61, closed 12/64		
Aberdare	86J, recoded 88J 1/61, closed 3/65		
Abergavenny	86K, closed 11/54	Cardiff East Dock	88B, steam removed 3/58, steam reintroduced 9/62 when code was 88L, recoded 88A 9/63, closed 8/65
Tredegar	86K(T) sub-shed to Abergavenny 86K, recoded 86K 11/54, closed 6/60.		
		Barry	88C, closed 9/64
Neath (Court Sart)	87A, closed 6/65	Merthyr	88D, closed 11/64
Duffryn Yard	87B, closed 3/64	Rhymney	88D(R) sub-shed to Merthyr 88D, recoded 88D 11/64, closed 4/65
Danygraig	87C, steam removed 1/60		
Swansea East Dock	87D, closed 7/64	Abercynon	88E, closed 11/64
Landore	87E, steam removed 6/61	Treherbert	88F, closed 3/65.
Llanelly	87F, closed 10/65		
Carmarthen	87G, steam removed 3/64	Oswestry	89A, recoded 89D 1/61, transferred to LMR as 6E 9/63
Neyland	87H, closed 9/63		
Goodwick	87J, closed 9/63	Brecon	89B, closed 11/59
Swansea (Paxton Street), also known as Swansea (Victoria).	87K, closed 8/59	Machynlleth	89C, transferred to LMR as 6F 9/63.

TABLE 2.7
Sheds which had Allocation(s) of BR Standard Locomotives

This list gives the dates when BR Standard locomotives were first allocated and last removed from each shed (in some cases BR Standard locomotives were not allocated to a shed for the whole of this period), and indicates which class(es) were at each shed for some or all of this period. It includes Crewe Works and Horwich Works, which had BR Standard locomotives allocated as works shunters, but excludes works allocations when locomotives were there only for test purposes.

	First Standard Allocated A	Last Standard Removed B	Standard Class(es) Allocated C		First Standard Allocated A	Last Standard Removed B	Standard Class(es) Allocated C
Abercynon	6/56	7/56	82	Bescot	11/54	3/66	76, 78
Aberdeen (Ferryhill)	10/56	9/65	73, 76, 78, 80	Bidston	8/55	2/63	92
				Birkenhead	7/56	11/67	73, 80, 84, 92
Accrington	9/53	8/56	75	Blackpool	11/51	3/60	73, 80
Agecroft	4/66	10/66	73	Blair Atholl (sub-shed to Perth)	4/54	12/54	77
Aintree	11/56	6/67	75, 78				
Alnmouth (sub-shed to Tweedmouth)	4/53	4/54	76	Blaydon	2/53	9/59	73, 76, 77
				Bletchley	6/52	6/65	73, 75, 80, 84
Alston (sub-shed to Blaydon)	4/54	9/59	76, 77	Bolton	4/58	4/68	73, 78, 84, 92
				Botanic Gardens	9/54	6/59	77, 82
Annesley	1/57	12/65	70, 84, 92	Bournemouth	7/53	7/67	75, 76, 80, 82
Ardrossan	10/58	2/65	76, 80	Bricklayers Arms	12/59	6/62	80, 84
Ardsley	12/62	11/63	80	Brighton	1/52	6/64	75, 76, 80, 84
Ashford	3/57	5/62	80, 84	Bristol (Barrow Road)	5/57	11/65	73, 75, 80, 82, 92
Aston	9/61	10/65	70, 75, 76	Bristol (Bath Road)	6/51★	10/60	75★, 82
Aviemore	11/58	7/62	78				
Ayr	2/52	12/66	73, 76, 78, 80.				

★ This was an allocation that was changed before the new locomotive was delivered from Swindon Works, although it did carry a 82A shed plate while running-in. The first normal allocation was in 3/58.

Banbury	5/58	10/66	70, 73, 92				
Bangor	8/56	6/65	75, 78, 80, 82	Bromsgrove	5/56	8/64	92
Bank Hall	12/54	10/66	75, 78, 84	Burton-upon-Trent	8/53	1/66	84, 92
Barrow	12/62	5/63	78	Bury	10/53	9/56	80, 84.
Barry	7/53	7/58	82				
Basingstoke	6/56	3/63	75	Cambridge	6/60	9/60	76
Bath (Green Park)	6/54	12/65	73, 75, 80, 82, 92	Camden	6/51	1/60	70
				Canklow	6/54	11/62	73, 78
Bathgate	11/63	9/66	76, 78	Cardiff (Canton)	10/52	9/62	70, 73, 75, 92
Beattock	6/61	5/67	76, 80	Cardiff East Dock	9/62	8/65	92
Bedford	9/52	8/63	73, 75, 80, 84	Carlisle (Canal)	9/61	6/63	70

	A	B	C		A	B	C
Carlisle (Kingmoor)	2/52	1/68	70, 72, 73, 92	Haymarket	11/57	3/60	72
Carlisle (Upperby)	12/63	12/66	70	Heaton	11/59	7/60	76
Carmarthen	12/53	6/62	73, 82	Heaton Mersey	1/57	4/66	73, 75, 76
Carnforth	11/66	8/68	70, 73, 75, 92	Helmsdale	2/57	9/58	78
Carstairs	5/60	12/66	73, 76, 77, 80	Hereford	6/57	1/64	78, 82
Chester (Midland)	10/51	6/67	70, 73, 75, 76, 78, 80, 82	Hitchin	3/55	6/55	76
Chester (Northgate)	10/55	1/60	75, 78, 84	Holbeck	6/51	10/63	70, 73, 80
Chester (West)	9/53	4/60	73, 75, 82	Holyhead	11/52	7/66	70, 73, 75, 78
Coalville	12/63	9/64	78	Horwich Works	5/63	12/63	84
Colwick	6/63	7/67	75, 76, 92	Huddersfield	10/58	8/64	73
Copley Hill	3/63	9/63	82	Hull (Springhead)	1/58	12/58	77
Corkerhill	12/51	5/67	70, 73, 76, 78, 80	Hurlford	7/54	12/66	76, 77, 80.
Crewe North	5/52	5/65	70, 71, 78, 80, 84				
Crewe South	4/62	11/66	70, 76, 78	Immingham	2/59	2/66	70, 92
Crewe Works	7/62	9/64	84	Inverness	11/56	10/57	73, 78
Cricklewood (West)	11/56	12/64	73, 76, 92	Ipswich	9/58	1/59	70.
Croes Newydd	7/62	6/67	73, 75, 76, 80, 84, 92.				
				Keith	11/55	6/61	76, 78, 80
Dairycoates	12/52	12/65	76, 77, 84	Kentish Town	10/52	1/63	70, 80, 84
Dalry Road	5/60	3/64	76, 80	Kettering	4/54	3/65	78, 92
Darlington	12/52	5/64	76, 77, 78, 82	Kidderminster	8/55	7/59	82
Darnall	4/58	12/58	73, 92	King's Cross	2/56	10/58	73, 80
Dawsholm	3/54	10/64	76, 77, 78, 80	Kirkby-in-Ashfield	6/60	6/66	78, 92
Derby	4/51	10/66	73, 75, 78, 80, 92	Kirkby Stephen	3/54	6/60	76, 78, 82
Doncaster	12/55	4/66	78, 92	Kittybrewster	10/51	6/61	76, 78, 80.
Dorchester	5/54	2/55	76				
Dover	5/53	2/60	70, 75, 80	Laira	8/51	10/60	70, 75, 82, 92
Dumfries	10/56	6/66	76, 78, 80	Lancaster	10/54	2/62	76, 78, 84
Dundee (Tay Bridge)	9/55	12/65	80	Landore	12/53	1/54	73
Dunfermline	1/60	12/66	76	Langwith Jct.	1/65	10/65	92
				Leamington	5/58	6/65	73, 75, 80, 82
Eastbourne	3/52	10/52	80	Lees	9/54	4/59	84
Eastfield	5/55	11/66	73, 76, 80	Leicester (Central)	9/59	3/63	73
Eastleigh	8/52	7/67	73, 75, 76, 80, 82, 84, 92	Leicester (Midland)	6/51	7/66	73, 75, 76, 78, 84, 92
Ebbw Jct.	1/54	10/65	92	Llandudno Jct.	10/53	9/66	70, 73, 75, 78, 84
Edge Hill	6/65	4/66	75	Llanelly	5/60	8/64	73, 78, 80
Exmouth Jct.	6/52	7/65	70, 73, 75, 80, 82, 84.	Longsight	12/52	9/62	70, 80
				Lostock Hall	9/61	6/67	75, 78, 80
Farnley Jct.	11/63	12/64	77, 78	Low Moor	9/53	3/63	82, 84
Feltham	5/63	10/66	73, 76, 80, 92	Lower Darwen	2/57	3/65	76, 84.
Fleetwood	5/54	12/65	84				
Fort William	6/60	8/62	76	Machynlleth	4/53	12/66	75, 76, 78, 80, 82
Frodingham	1/59	1/65	92.	Malton	5/53	4/63	76, 82
				Manningham	4/64	11/65	77, 78
Gateshead	1/53	9/60	73, 76, 77	March	4/54	12/63	70, 76, 78, 80, 92
Gloucester (Barnwood)	8/58	4/64	73, 75, 78	Mexborough	3/58	4/58	92
Gloucester (Horton Road)	11/54	12/65	73, 75, 78, 82, 92	Millhouses	8/51	1/62	73, 78
Goole	12/65	3/66	77	Mold Jct.	4/60	4/62	75
Gorton	12/64	6/65	78	Motherwell	10/52	5/67	73, 76, 77, 78, 80.
Grangemouth	10/61	10/65	73, 76, 77				
Grantham	6/58	9/58	92	Neasden	5/54	7/62	70, 73, 76, 80, 84
Greenock (Ladyburn)	1/63	12/66	76, 80	Neath (Court Sart)	3/63	9/64	80, 92
Grimesthorpe	9/51	4/61	73, 78, 92	Neville Hill	2/53	10/63	73, 76, 77, 80
Guildford	12/62	7/67	73, 76, 77, 80, 82.	New England	11/54	1/65	92
				Newton Abbot	6/51	12/56	70, 82
				Newton Heath	11/52	6/67	70, 80, 84, 92
				Neyland	9/61	10/61	82
Hamilton	3/54	11/62	73, 77, 80	Nine Elms	5/51	7/67	70, 73, 75, 80, 82
Hawick	3/55	1/66	76, 78, 80	Normanton	9/57	4/64	73
				Northallerton	3/55	3/63	78
				Northampton	7/65	9/65	92
				Northwich	11/59	3/66	77, 78

	A	B	C
Norwich	4/51	11/61	70, 76
Norwood Jct.	7/63	12/63	75
Nottingham	9/51	4/65	73, 75, 78
Nuneaton	9/54	6/66	73, 75, 76, 78, 82.
Oban	5/60	6/60	76
Old Oak Common	6/51	9/63	70, 73, 80, 92
Oswestry	12/52	1/65	75, 78, 80, 84
Oxford	9/54	12/65	73, 75, 92
Oxley	10/56	3/67	70, 73, 76, 78
Parkhead	6/57	12/61	76
Patricroft	11/51	7/68	73, 75, 82
Percy Main	3/53	4/53	76
Perth	4/51	11/66	73, 76, 77, 78, 80
Plaistow	9/53	10/59	80
Plodder Lane	8/53	10/54	84
Polmadie	11/51	5/67	70, 72, 73, 76, 77, 78, 80
Pontypool Road	8/58	1/59	92
Preston	9/54	9/61	78.
Radyr	3/58	4/58	82
Ramsgate	4/57	6/59	84
Reading	9/54	4/56	73, 75
Redhill	10/52	6/65	76, 80
Rhyl	9/54	2/63	75, 78, 84
Rose Grove	5/55	6/57	84
Rowsley	11/59	4/64	73, 92
Royston	9/53	9/63	73, 84
Rugby	1/55	2/63	70, 80.
St. Albans	11/54	9/56	80
St. Margarets	10/55	12/66	72, 76, 78, 80
St. Philips Marsh	9/53	10/62	73, 82, 92
St. Rollox	1/57	11/66	73, 76, 80
Salisbury	5/53	4/67	70, 76, 80
Saltley	5/53	12/66	76, 80, 92
Scarborough	2/56	4/63	73, 77, 80, 82
Selby	3/53	9/59	76, 77
Severn Tunnel Jct.	1/59	10/65	92
Shoeburyness	10/59	by 6/62★	80

* Probably just a short trial with 80133 and then moved to Tilbury as an unrecorded transfer. All the other engines at Shoeburyness were Stanier 3-cylinder 2-6-4Ts.

	A	B	C
Shrewsbury	8/51	3/67	73, 75, 78, 80, 82
Skipton	1/55	4/67	75, 76, 78, 84
South Blyth	4/61	4/66	77
Southall	2/60	9/65	92
Southport	12/51	6/64	75, 84
Speke Jct.	6/64	5/68	92
Springs Branch	4/60	12/67	75, 76, 78
Staveley (Barrow Hill)	9/64	1/65	92
Stewarts Lane	7/51★	9/63	70, 73, 75, 80, 84

★70014 given in Vol. 1 as 9/51 but should probably be 7/51

	A	B	C
Stirling	10/55	12/66	73, 78, 80
Stockport (Edgeley)	12/64	6/67	70, 84
Stoke	4/62	8/67	75, 76, 78
Stourbridge Jct.	4/52★	5/66	76, 82

* Allocations for 82000/1 were not included in Vol. 3

	A	B	C
Stourton	9/63	12/66	77
Stranraer	12/57	8/66	76, 78, 80
Stratford	1/51	9/62	70, 72, 73, 76, 78, 80, 92
Sunderland	12/52	9/61	76
Sutton Oak	12/56	6/67	76
Swansea East Dock	7/62	3/64	80
Swansea (Paxton St. or Victoria)	4/55	7/57	75, 82
Swindon	5/51	2/64	70, 73, 75, 78.
Taunton	10/61	6/64	82
Tebay	4/67	1/68	75
Templecombe	2/59	3/66	75, 80, 82
Thornaby	4/62	10/63	76, 77
Thornton Jct.	8/57	11/64	76
Three Bridges	1/59	1/63	75, 80
Tilbury	1/54	7/62	80
Tonbridge	6/61	6/62	80
Toton	9/53	11/66	70, 78, 92
Trafford Park	5/57	11/66	70, 73, 76, 78
Treherbert	9/53	5/58	82
Tunbridge Wells West	7/51	9/63	80
Tweedmouth	10/63	6/66	77, 78
Tyne Dock	11/55	11/66	77, 92
Tyseley	4/52	12/66	73, 75, 82, 92.
Uttoxeter	10/63	12/64	76.
Wakefield	6/63	6/67	73, 92
Walton	11/63	12/63	75
Warrington (Dallam)	6/61	10/67	84, 92
Watford	5/52	4/65	78, 80
Wellingborough	3/54	9/64	84, 92
Wellington	7/56	1/60	82
West Auckland	12/53	2/64	76, 77, 78
West Hartlepool	6/55	9/58	76, 82
Westbury	9/60	7/61	92
Westhouses	2/56	7/65	92
Weymouth	9/58	4/67	73, 80
Whitby	5/55	4/59	77, 80
Widnes	5/56	5/63	78, 84
Wigan (Central)	10/56	4/64	78
Willesden	9/52	10/65	70, 73, 75, 76, 78, 80, 92
Wolverhampton (Stafford Road)	7/51★	9/63	75★, 78

★ This was an allocation that was changed before the new locomotive was delivered from Swindon Works, although it did carry a 84A shed plate while running-in. The first normal allocation was in 3/62.

	A	B	C
Woodford Halse	6/55	1/65	73, 76, 92
Worcester	7/53	12/65	75, 78, 82
Workington	4/60	9/62	75, 78
Wrexham (Rhosddu)	3/54	1/60	82, 84.
Yarmouth South Town	9/58	2/59	70
Yeovil Town	9/58	7/65	73, 75, 76, 80, 82
York	12/52	6/67	73, 76, 77, 80, 82, 92.

Notes:

Sub-sheds are listed under their main depot, offset slightly to the right.

All main entries in this list are from reference British Railway Locomotives.

Recoding information is from reference *Railway Locomotives* (various issues in 1949 and 1950).

Ex-GWR Engine Depots and Codes

Shed Code	Location	Comments
ABDR	Aberdare	Recoded to 86J in 2/50
ABEEG	Aberbeeg	ABG also used. Recoded to 86H in 2/50
ABH	Aberystwyth	Main shed until 2/50, then sub-shed to Machynlleth
AYN	Abercynon	Recoded to 88E in 2/50
BAN	Banbury	Recoded to 84C in 2/50
BCN	Brecon	Recoded to 89B in 2/50
	Builth Wells	
BHD	Birkenhead	Shared with LMS depot. Became one LMR depot in 2/50, recoded to 6C
BRD	Bristol Bath Road	Recoded to 82A in 2/50
	Bath	
	Wells	
	Weston-Super-Mare	
	Yatton	
BRY	Barry	Recoded to 88C in 2/50
CARM	Carmarthen	Recoded to 87G in 2/50
	Newcastle Emlyn	
CDF	Cardiff Canton	Recoded to 86C in 2/50
CED	Cardiff East Dock	Recoded to 88B in 2/50
CH	Cae Harris	Main shed until 2/50, then sub-shed to Merthyr
CHEL	Cheltenham (Malvern Road)	Main shed until 2/50, then sub-shed to Gloucester
	Brimscombe	
	Chalford	
	Cirencester	
CHR	Chester West	Recoded to 84K in 2/50
CHYS	Cardiff Cathays	CYS also used. Recoded to 88A in 2/50
CNYD	Croes Newydd	Recoded to 84J in 2/50
	Bala	
	Trawsfynydd	
	Penmaenpool	
DG	Danygraig	Recoded to 87C in 2/50
DID	Didcot	Recoded to 81E in 2/50
	Newbury	
	Wallingford	
	Winchester	
DYD	Duffryn Yard	PT also used. Recoded to 87B in 2/50
EXE	Exeter	Recoded to 83C in 2/50
	Tiverton Junction	
FDL	Ferndale, Cardiff Valleys	Main shed until 2/50, then sub-shed to Treherbert
FGD	Fishguard	Also known as Goodwick.

Shed Code	Location	Comments
		Recoded to 87J in 2/50
GLO	Gloucester	
	Horton Road	Recoded to 85B in 2/50
HFD	Hereford	Recoded to 85C in 2/50
	Kington	
	Ledbury	
	Leominster	
	Ross-on-Wye	
KDR	Kidderminster	Recoded to 85D in 2/50
LA	Laira	Recoded to 83D in 2/50
	Launceston	
	Princetown	
LDR	Landore	Recoded to 87E in 2/50
LLY	Llanelly	Recoded to 87F in 2/50
	Burry Port	
	Pantyffynnon	
LMTN	Leamington Spa	Recoded to 84D in 2/50
LTS	Llantrisant	Recoded to 86D in 2/50
LYD	Lydney	Main shed until 2/50, then sub-shed to Gloucester
	Tetbury	
MCH	Machynlleth	Recoded to 89C in 2/50
	Aberayron	
	Portmadoc	
	Pwllheli	
MTHR	Merthyr	Recoded to 88D in 2/50
NA	Newton Abbot	Recoded to 83A in 2/50
	Ashburton	
	Kingsbridge	
NEA	Neath	Recoded to 87A in 2/50
	Glyn Neath	
	Neath N&B	
NEY	Neyland	Recoded to 87H in 2/50
	Milford Haven	
NPT	Newport	
	Ebbw Junction	Recoded to 86A in 2/50
OSW	Oswestry	Recoded to 89A in 2/50
	Llanfyllin	
	Llanidloes	
	Moat Lane	
	Welshpool	
OXF	Oxford	Recoded to 81F in 2/50
	Abingdon	
	Fairford	
OXY	Oxley	Recoded to 84B in 2/50
PDN	Old Oak Common	Recoded to 81A in 2/50
PILL	Newport Pill	Recoded to 86B in 2/50
PPRD	Pontypool Road	Recoded to 86G in 2/50
	Branches Fork	
	Pontrilas	
PZ	Penzance	Recoded to 83G in 2/50
	Helston	
	St. Ives	
RDG	Reading	Recoded to 81D in 2/50
	Basingstoke	
	Henley	
RHY	Rhymney	Main shed until 2/50, then sub-shed to Merthyr
	Dowlais Central	

75053 and 75063 attack the final mile of 1 in 56 to Talerddig summit on the up "Cambrian Coast Express" from Aberystwyth on 28th December 1965. The very frosty conditions must have made the 1 in 52 climb from Llanbrynmair and the final two miles of 1 in 56 to the summit hard work for the crews. In the later days of this working the headboard was not in use.   *Trevor Owen*

RYR	Radyr	Main shed until 2/50, then sub-shed to Cardiff Cathays SLP also used. Shared with LMS depot. Recoded to 84G in 2/50
SALOP	Shrewsbury	
	Ludlow	
SBZ	St. Blazey	Recoded to 83E in 2/50
	Bodmin	
	Moorswater	
SDN	Swindon	Recoded to 82C in 2/50
	Andover Jct.	
	Chippenham	
	Malmesbury	
SED	Swansea East Dock	Recoded to 87D in 2/50
SHL	Southall	Recoded to 81C in 2/50
	Staines	
SLO	Slough	Recoded to 81B in 2/50
	Aylesbury	
	Marlow	
	Watlington	
SPM	St. Philip's Marsh	Recoded to 82B in 2/50
SRD	Wolverhampton (Stafford Road)	Recoded to 84A in 2/50
STB	Stourbridge Jct.	Recoded to 84F in 2/50
STJ	Severn Tunnel Jct.	Recoded to 86E in 2/50
TDU	Tondu	Recoded to 86F in 2/50
	Bridgend	
THT	Treherbert	TRT also used. Recoded to 88F in 2/50
	Pwllrhebog	
TN	Taunton	Recoded to 83B in 2/50

	Barnstaple	
	Bridgwater	
	Minehead	
TR	Truro	Recoded to 83F in 2/50
TYS	Tyseley	Recoded to 84E in 2/50
	Stratford-on-Avon	
WES	Westbury	Recoded to 82D in 2/50
	Frome	
	Salisbury	
WEY	Weymouth	Recoded to 82F in 2/50
	Bridport	
WLN	Wellington	Recoded to 84H in 2/50
	Crewe Gresty Lane	
	Much Wenlock	
WOS	Worcester	Recoded to 85A in 2/50
	Evesham	
	Kingham	
WTD	Whitland	Main shed until 2/50, then sub-shed to Neyland
	Cardigan	
	Pembroke Dock	
YEO	Yeovil Pen Mill	Recoded to 82E in 2/50

Ex-Southern Railway Engine Depots and Codes

Note: Sub-sheds are listed under their main depot, offset slightly to the right.

These sub-sheds had their own codes, which are also offset slightly to the right of the main codes.

AFD	Ashford	Recoded to 74A in 2/50
CAN	Canterbury West	

BA	Bricklayers Arms	Recoded to 73B in 2/50
NX	New Cross Gate	Main shed until 6/47, then sub-shed to BA
BAS	Basingstoke	Recoded to 70D in 2/50
BAT	Stewarts Lane	Recoded to 73A in 2/50
BM	Bournemouth	Recoded to 71B in 2/50
HAM	Hamworthy Jct.	
SWE	Swanage	
BPL	Barnstaple	Recoded to 72E in 2/50
ILF	Ilfracombe	
TOR	Torrington	
BTN	Brighton	Recoded to 75A in 2/50
NHN	Newhaven	
DOR	Dorchester	Recoded to 71C in 2/50
WEY	Weymouth	
DOV	Dover Marine	Recoded to 74C in 2/50
FOL	Folkestone Jct.	
EBN	Eastbourne	Recoded to 75G in 2/50
ELH	Eastleigh	Recoded to 71A in 2/50
AND	Andover Jct.	
LYM	Lymington	
WIN	Winchester	
EXJ	Exmouth Jct.	Recoded to 72A in 2/50
BUD	Bude	
EXM	Exmouth	
LCN	Launceston	
LR	Lyme Regis	
OKE	Okehampton	
SEA	Seaton	
FAV	Faversham	Recoded to 73E in 2/50
FEL	Feltham	Recoded to 70B in 2/50
FRA	Fratton	Recoded to 71D in 2/50
GOS	Gosport	
MID	Midhurst	
GFD	Guildford	Recoded to 70C in 2/50
ASH	Ash	
BOR	Bordon	
GIL	Gillingham	Recoded to 73D in 2/50
HIT	Hither Green	Recoded to 73C in 2/50
HOR	Horsham	Recoded to 75D in 2/50
BOG	Bognor Regis	
9E	Nine Elms	Recoded to 70A in 2/50
NOR	Norwood Jct.	Recoded to 75C in 2/50
PLY	Plymouth Friary	Recoded to 72D in 2/50
CAL	Callington	
RAM	Ramsgate	Recoded to 74B in 2/50
RED	Redhill	Recoded to 75B in 2/50
RDG	Reading	Recoded to 70E in 2/50
SAL	Salisbury	Recoded to 72B in 2/50
SOT	Southampton Docks	Recoded to 71I in 2/50
STL	St. Leonards	Recoded to 74E in 2/50
3B	Three Bridges	Recoded to 75E in 2/50
TON	Tonbridge	Recoded to 74D in 2/50
TWW	Tunbridge Wells West	Recoded to 75F in 2/50
WAD	Wadebridge	Recoded to 72F in 2/50
YEO	Yeovil Town	Recoded to 72C in 2/50
TEM	Templecombe Upper	

Isle of Wight

NPT	Newport	Recoded 71E in 2/50
RYD	Ryde	Recoded 71F in 2/50

Ex-LMS Engine Depots and Codes

Note: Sub-sheds are listed under their main depot, offset slightly to the right.

1A	Willesden	
1B	Camden	
1C	Watford	
2A	Rugby	
	Market Harborough	
	Seaton	
2B	Bletchley	Recoded to 4A in 2/50
	Aylesbury	
	Cambridge	
	Leighton Buzzard	
	Oxford	
	Newport Pagnell	
2C	Northampton	Recoded to 4B in 2/50
2D	Nuneaton	Recoded to 2B in 2/50
2E	Warwick	Recoded to 2C in 2/50
2F	Coventry	Recoded to 2D in 2/50
3A	Bescot	
3B	Bushbury	
3C	Walsall	
3D	Aston	
3E	Monument Lane	
4A	Shrewsbury	Shared with WR depot. Became one WR depot in 2/50, recoded to 84G
	Builth Road	
	Clee Hill	
	Coalport	
	Craven Arms	
	Kinghton	
	Ludlow	
4B	Swansea Victoria	Recoded to 87K in 2/50
	Llandovery	
4C	Upper Bank	Main shed until 2/50, then sub-shed to Swansea Victoria
	Brecon	
	Gurnos	
4D	Abergavenny	Recoded to 86K in 2/50
4E	Tredegar	Main shed until 2/50, then sub-shed to Abergavenny
5A	Crewe North	
	Whitchurch	
5B	Crewe South	
5C	Stafford	
5D	Stoke	
5E	Alsager	
5F	Uttoxeter	
6A	Chester Midland	
6B	Mold Jct.	
6C	Birkenhead	
7A	Llandudno Jct.	
7B	Bangor	
7C	Holyhead	
7D	Rhyl	
	Denbigh	
8A	Edge Hill	
8B	Warrington Dallam	
	Arpley	
	Over and Wharton	
8C	Speke Junction	
8D	Widnes	

Code	Shed	Notes
9A	Longsight	
9B	Stockport Edgeley	
9C	Macclesfield	
9D	Buxton	
	Cromford	
	Middleton	
	Sheep Pasture	
10A	Springs Branch	
10B	Preston	
10C	Patricroft	
10D	Plodder Lane	
10E	Sutton Oak	
11A	Carnforth	
11B	Barrow	
	Coniston	
	Lakeside	

There was no shed coded 11C in 1948

Code	Shed	Notes
11D	Oxenholme	Recoded to 11C in 2/50
11E	Tebay	Recoded to 11D in 2/50
12A	Kingmoor	Recoded to 68A in 1/49
12B	Upperby	Recoded to 12A in 2/50
12C	Penrith	
12D	Workington	
12E	Moor Row	
12F	Beattock	Recoded to 68D in 1/49
12G	Dumfries	Recoded to 68B in 1/49
	Kirkcudbright	
12H	Stranraer	Recoded to 68C in 1/49
	Newton Stewart	
13A	Plaistow	Recoded to 33A in 2/50
13B	Devons Road	Recoded to 1D in 4/49
13C	Tilbury	Recoded to 33B in 2/50
13D	Shoeburyness	Recoded to 33C in 2/50
13E	Upminster	Main shed until 2/50, then sub-shed to Plaistow
14A	Cricklewood	
14B	Kentish Town	
14C	St. Albans	
15A	Wellingborough	
15B	Kettering	
15C	Leicester Midland	
15D	Bedford	
16A	Nottingham	
	Lincoln	
	Southwell	
16B	Peterborough Spital Bridge	
16C	Kirkby-in-Ashfield	
16D	Mansfield	
17A	Derby	
17B	Burton-on-Trent	
	Overseal	
17C	Coalville	
17D	Rowsley	
18A	Toton	
18B	Westhouses	
18C	Hasland	
18D	Staveley Barrow Hill	
	Sheepbridge	
19A	Grimesthorpe	
	Also known as Sheffield Brightside in 1950s	
19B	Millhouses	
19C	Canklow	
19D	Heaton Mersey	Recoded to 13C in 2/50, then to 9F in 4/50

Code	Shed	Notes
19E	Belle Vue	Recoded to 13B in 2/50, then to 26G in 4/50

There was no 19F; maybe this code was allocated for Northwich but not used

Code	Shed	Notes
19G	Trafford Park	Recoded to 13A in 2/50, then to 9E in 4/50
20A	Holbeck	
20B	Stourton	
20C	Royston	
20D	Normanton	
20E	Manningham	
	Ilkley	
20F	Skipton	Recoded to 23A in 2/50
	Ingleton	
	Keighley	
20G	Hellifield	Recoded to 23B in 2/50
20H	Lancaster	Recoded to 23C in 2/50
21A	Saltley	
21B	Bournville	
	Redditch	
21C	Bromsgrove	
21D	Stratford-on-Avon	
22A	Bristol Barrow Road	
22B	Gloucester Barnwood	
	Dursley	
	Tewkesbury	
22C	Bath Green Park	Recoded to 71G in 2/50
	Branksome	
	Radstock	
22D	Templecombe	Recoded to 71H in 2/50
22E	Highbridge	Main shed to 2/50, then sub-shed to Templecombe
	Wells	
23A	Bank Hall	Recoded to 27A in 2/50
23B	Aintree	Recoded to 27B in 2/50
23C	Southport	Recoded to 27C in 2/50
23D	Wigan Central (L&Y)	Recoded to 27D in 2/50
24A	Accrington	
24B	Rose Grove	
24C	Lostock Hall	
24D	Lower Darwen	
24E	Blackpool	Recoded to 28A in 2/50
24F	Fleetwood	Recoded to 28B in 2/50
25A	Wakefield	
25B	Huddersfield	
25C	Goole	
25D	Mirfield	
25E	Sowerby Bridge	
25F	Low Moor	
25G	Farnley Junction	
26A	Newton Heath	
26B	Agecroft	
26C	Bolton	
26D	Bury	
26E	Bacup	
26F	Lees	
27A	Polmadie	Recoded to 66A in 1/49
27B	Greenock Ladyburn	Recoded to 66D in 1/49
	Greenock Princes Pier	
27C	Hamilton	Recoded to 66C in 1/49
28A	Motherwell	Recoded to 66B in 1/49
28B	Dalry Road	Recoded to 64C in 1/49
28C	Carstairs	Recoded to 64D in 1/49

29A	Perth	Recoded to 63A in 1/49
	Aberfeldy	
	Blair Atholl	
	Crieff	
29B	Aberdeen Ferryhill	Shared with LNER depot. Became one ScR depot in 1/49, recoded 61B
29C	Dundee West	Main shed to 1/49, then sub-shed to Dundee (Tay Bridge)
29D	Forfar	Recoded to 63C in 1/49
	Arbroath	
	Brechin	
	Killin	
30A	Corkerhill	Recoded to 67A in 1/49
30B	Hurlford	Recoded to 67B in 1/49
	Beith	
	Muirkirk	
30C	Ardrossan	Recoded to 67D in 1/49
30D	Ayr	Recoded to 67C in 1/49
31A	St. Rollox	Recoded to 65B in 1/49
31B	Stirling	Recoded to 63B in 1/49
31C	Oban	Recoded to 63E in 1/49
	Ballachulish	
31D	Grangemouth	Recoded to 65F in 1/49
31E	Dawsholm	Recoded to 65D in 1/49
	Dumbarton	
	Yoker	Became main shed in 1/49 and recoded 65G
32A	Inverness	Recoded to 60A in 1/49
	Dingwall	
	Dornoch	
	Fortrose	
	Helmsdale	Became main shed in 1/49 and recoded 60C
	Kyle of Lochalsh	
	Tain	
	Thurso	
	Wick	Became main shed in 1/49 and recoded 60D
32B	Aviemore	Recoded to 60B in 1/49
32C	Forres	Recoded to 60E in 1/49
CW	Crewe Works	
HW	Horwich Works	

Ex-LNER Engine Depots and Codes

Note: Some ex-LNER sheds had alternative versions of their letter codes.

For example ARD or ARDS, which is listed below as ARD(S) to indicate both versions.

Southern Area

Note: Sub-sheds are listed under their main depot, offset slightly to the right

ANN	Annesley	Recoded to 44B in 2/49, then to 38B in 2/50
ARD(S)	Ardsley	Recoded to 43A in 2/49, then to 37A in 2/50
BFD	Bradford	Recoded to 43C in 2/49, then to 37C in 2/50

The much photographed station at Killin usually depicts an ex-Caledonian McIntosh 0-4-4T working the one-coach branch train from Killin Jct. on the Caledonian line to Oban. Shown here in February 1964, heavyweight motive power has been introduced with 80028 waiting to return to Killin Jct. The branch closed, with the Dunblane to Crianlarich section of the Oban line on 28th September 1965 after the Glenogle landslide.

Douglas Hume

Code	Depot	Recoding
BID	Bidston (CLC)	Recoded to 45D in 2/49, then to 6F in 2/50
BOS	Boston	Recoded to 46F in 2/49, then to 40F in 2/50
BRN	Barnsley	Recoded to 42D in 2/49, then to 36D in 2/50
BSE	Bury St Edmunds	Recoded to 31E in 2/49
	Sudbury	
CAM	Cambridge	Recoded to 31A in 2/49
	Ely	
	Huntingdon East	
	Saffron Walden	
	Thaxted	
CHR	Chester Northgate (CLC)	Recoded to 6D in 2/50
CLK	Colwick	Recoded to 44A in 2/49, then to 38A in 2/50
	Derby Friargate	
COL	Colchester	Recoded to 30B in 2/49, then to 30E in 2/50
	Braintree	
	Clacton	
	Kelvedon	
	Maldon	
	Walton-on-Naze	
COP	Copley Hill	Recoded to 43B in 2/49, then to 37B in 2/50
DON	Doncaster	Recoded to 42A in 2/49, then to 36A in 2/50
FRO(D)	Frodingham	Recoded to 42C in 2/49, then to 36C in 2/50
GOR	Gorton	Recoded to 45A in 2/49, then to 39A in 2/50
	Dinting	
	Hayfield	
	Macclesfield	
GRA	Grantham	Recoded to 41B in 2/49, then to 35B in 2/50
	Newark	
HAT	Hatfield	Recoded to 40C in 2/49, then to 34C in 2/50
HIT	Hitchin	Recoded to 40D in 2/49, then to 34D in 2/50
HSY	Hornsey	Recoded to 40B in 2/49, then to 34B in 2/50
IMM	Immingham	Recoded to 46B in 2/49, then to 40B in 2/50
IPS	Ipswich	Recoded to 32B in 2/49
	Aldeburgh	
	Felixstowe Beach	
	Framlingham	
	Laxfield	
	Stowmarket	
KL	King's Lynn	Recoded to 31C in 2/49
	Hunstanton	
	Wisbech	
KX	King's Cross	Recoded to 40A in 2/49, then to 34A in 2/50
LEI	Leicester Central	Recoded to 44C in 2/49, then to 38C in 2/50
	Leicester Belgrave Road	
LIN	Lincoln	Recoded to 46A in 2/49, then to 40A in 2/50
LIV	Brunswick (CLC)	Recoded 13E in 2/50, then to 8E in 4/50
	Southport	
	Warrington	
	Widnes	
LNG	Langwith Junction	Recoded to 46E in 2/49, then to 40E in 2/50
LOW	Lowestoft	Recoded to 32C in 2/49
LTH	Louth	Recoded to 46C in 2/49, then to 40C in 2/50
MAR	March	Recoded to 31B in 2/49
MC	Melton Constable	MEL also used later. Recoded to 32E in 2/49, then to 32G in 2/50
	Cromer Beach	
	Norwich City	
MEX	Mexborough	Recoded to 42B in 2/49, then to 36B in 2/50
NEA	Neasden	Recoded to 40E in 2/49, then to 34E in 2/50
	Aylesbury	
	Chesham	
NOR	Norwich	Recoded to 32A in 2/49
	Cromer Beach	
	Dereham	
	Swaffham	
	Wells	
	Wymondham	
NTH	Northwich (CLC)	Recoded 13D in 2/50, then to 9G in 4/50
NWE	New England	Recoded to 41A in 2/49, then to 35A in 2/50
	Bourne	
	Spalding	
	Stamford	
PKS	Parkeston	Recoded to 30C in 2/49, then to 30F in 2/50
RET	Retford (GC & GN)	Recoded to 42E in 2/49, then to 36E in 2/50
SHF	Darnall	Recoded to 45B in 2/49, then to 39B in 2/50
SL	South Lynn	Recoded to 31D in 2/49
STP	Heaton Mersey (CLC)	Shared with LMS depot. Became one LMR depot in 2/50 recoded 13C, then to 9F in 4/50
STR	Stratford	Recoded to 30A in 2/49
	Bishop's Stortford	Became main shed in 2/50 and recoded 30C
	Brentwood	
	Buntingford	
	Chelmsford	
	Enfield Town	
	Epping	
	Hertford East	Became main shed in 2/50 and recoded 30B
	Palace Gates	
	Southend Victoria	Became main shed in 2/50 and recoded 30D
	Southminster	
	Spitalfields	
	Ware	
	Wickford	
	Walthamstow Wood Street	

STV	Staveley Central	Recoded to 44D in 2/49, then to 38D in 2/50
TFD	Trafford Park (CLC)	Shared with LMS depot. Became one LMR depot in 2/50 recoded 13A, then to 9E in 4/50
TUX	Tuxford	Recoded to 46D in 2/49, then to 40D in 2/50
WAL	Walton-on-the-Hill (CLC)	Recoded 13F in 2/50, then to 27E in 4/50
WFD	Woodford Halse	Recoded to 44E in 2/49, then to 38E in 2/50
WIG	Wigan Lower Ince (CLC)	Recoded to 13G in 2/50, then to 10F in 4/50
WRX	Wrexham Rhosddu (CLC)	Recoded to 45C in 2/49, then to 6E in 2/50
YAR	Yarmouth South Town	Recoded to 32D in 2/49
	Yarmouth Vauxhall	Became main shed in 2/50 and recoded 32E
YB	Yarmouth Beach	Recoded to 32F in 2/49

Departmental Stock

BOSE	Boston Engineering Works
DONW	Doncaster Works
LOWS	Lowestoft Sleeper Works
STRW	Stratford Works

North East Area

Note: Sub-sheds are listed under their main depot, offset slightly to the right

These sub-sheds had their own codes, which are also offset slightly to the right of the main codes

The ones marked ★ had their own allocations of locomotives

AUK	West Auckland	Recoded to 51F in 2/49
WHD★	Wearhead	
WVJ	Wear Valley Junction	
BLA	Blaydon	Recoded to 52C in 2/49
ALS★	Alston	
HEX★	Hexham	
RMH★	Reedsmouth	
BOR(O)	Borough Gardens	Recoded to 54C in 2/49
BRI(D)	Bridlington	Recoded to 53D in 2/49
CON	Consett	Recoded to 54D in 2/49
BLK	Blackhill	
WAS	Waskerley	
CUD	Cudworth	Recoded to 53E in 2/49
DAR	Darlington	Recoded to 51A in 2/49
MIT★	Middleton-in-Teesdale	
GHD	Gateshead	Recoded to 52A in 2/49
BOW★	Bowes Bridge	
GOS	Gosforth	
HAV	Haverton Hill	Recoded to 51G in 2/49
HLB	Hull Botanic Gardens	Recoded to 53B in 2/49

Following the opening of the new Tyne Dock iron ore quay and the construction of the 13,000 ton capacity bunker in 1953, BR supplied 30 56 ton side discharge bogie wagons for the iron ore traffic to Consett. Trains ran when an ore cargo arrived at Tyne Dock and ran continuously until all of the ore had been moved to Consett as there was little storage space at Tyne Dock. In the days of 9F haulage, it took almost five days to move a 30,000 ton shipment. 92065 with the hard work done coasts down the bank past Stanley, heading for Tyne Dock bottom yard on 14th August 1963.

Howard Forster

HLD	Hull Dairycoates	Recoded to 53A in 2/49
HLS	Hull Springhead	Recoded to 53C in 2/49
HLA★	Hull Alexandra Dock	
HTN	Heaton	Recoded to 52B in 2/49
KBY	Kirkby Stephen	Recoded to 51H in 2/49
PEN	Penrith	Probably same as LMR shed
MAL	Malton	Recoded to 50F in 2/49
PKG★	Pickering	
MID	Middlesbrough	Recoded to 51D in 2/49
GUI(S)★	Guisborough	
NBH	North Blyth	Recoded to 52F in 2/49
SBH★	South Blyth	
RBY★	Rothbury	
NEV	Neville Hill	Recoded to 50B in 2/49
ILK★	Ilkley	
NLN	Northallerton	Recoded to 51I in 2/49, then to 51J in 2/50
LEY★	Leyburn	
NPT	Newport (Teesside)	Recoded to 51B in 2/49
PMN	Percy Main	Recoded to 52E in 2/49
SAL	Saltburn	Recoded to 51K in 2/49
SBK	Starbeck	Recoded to 50D in 2/49
PAT★	Pateley Bridge	
SCA(R)	Scarborough	Recoded to 50E in 2/49
SEL	Selby	Recoded to 50C in 2/49
SKN	Stockton-on-Tees	Recoded to 51E in 2/49
SUN	Sunderland	Recoded to 54A in 2/49
ANP	Annfield Plain	
DUR★	Durham	
SEA	Seaham	
TDK	Tyne Dock	Recoded to 54B in 2/49
PEL★	Pelton Level	
TWD	Tweedmouth	Recoded to 52D in 2/49
ALN★	Alnmouth	
WBY	Whitby	Recoded to 50G in 2/49
WHL	West Hartlepool	Recoded to 51C in 2/49
YK	York	Recoded to 50A in 2/49
NMN	Normanton	Shared with LMS depot. Recoded to 20D in 2/49

Also HAW Hawes Junction was sub-shed to Hellifield (LMR)

Departmental Stock

DARF	Darlington Faverdale Works
DARG	Darlington Geneva PW Depot
YKE	York Engineering Yard

Scottish Area

Note: Sub-sheds are listed under their main depot, offset slightly to the right

ABD	Aberdeen Ferryhill	Recoded to 61B in 1/49
BGT	Bathgate	Recoded to 64F in 1/49
	Morningside	
CAR	Carlisle Canal	Recoded to 12B in 2/50
DEE	Dundee Tay Bridge	Recoded to 62B in 1/49
	Arbroath	
	Montrose	
	St. Andrews	
	Tayport	
DFU	Dunfermline Upper	Recoded to 62C in 1/49
	Loch Leven	
	Kelty	
EFD	Eastfield	Recoded to 65A in 1/49
	Aberfoyle	
	Arrochar	
	Balloch	Became main shed in 1/49 and recoded 65I
	Kilsyth	
	Lennoxtown	
	Stobcross	
FW(L)	Fort William	Recoded to 63D in 1/49
	Mallaig	
HAY	Haymarket	Recoded to 64B in 1/49
HAW	Hawick	Recoded to 64G in 1/49
	Jedburgh	
	Kelso	
	Riccarton Junction	
	St. Boswells	
KEI	Keith	Recoded to 61C in 1/49
	Banff	
	Boat of Garten	
	Elgin	
KIT	Kittybrewster	Recoded to 61A in 1/49
	Ballater	
	Fraserburgh	
	Macduff	
	Peterhead	
KPS	Kipps	Recoded to 65E in 1/49
PKD	Parkhead	Recoded to 65C in 1/49
	Helensburgh	Became main shed in 1/49 and recoded 65H
POL	Polmont	Recoded to 64E in 1/49
	Kinneil	
PTH	Perth	Same as LMS shed? Recoded to 63A in 1/49
STG	Stirling (Shore Road)	Main shed until 1/49, then sub-shed to Stirling
	Alloa	
STM	St. Margarets	Recoded to 64A in 1/49
	Dunbar	
	Galashiels	
	Hardengreen	
	Longniddry	
	North Berwick	
	Peebles	
	Penicuik	
	Polton	
	Seafield	
THJ	Thornton Junction	Recoded to 62A in 1/49
	Anstruther	
	Burntisland	
	Ladybank	
	Methil	

3. ORGANISATION AND CONTROL OF WORKS REPAIRS FOR LOCOMOTIVES ON BR

The main sources for this section are papers from the Roland C. Bond Collection at the National Railway Museum at York. R. C. Bond was appointed as the Chief Officer (Locomotive Construction and Maintenance) on the Railway Executive at its formation in 1948. Some of the material was delivered as a lecture to the Institution of Locomotive Engineers at several locations in the spring of 1953. The paper was published in the *Journal* of the institution in 1953, Vol.43, pp.175-216. The description is based on R. C. Bond's experiences at Crewe Works on the LMR. Similar procedures would be carried out at the works of the other regions.

Introduction

The main activity of locomotive workshops is the repair and maintenance of the current stock. The building of new locomotives also is an important part of the works role, allowing full economic advantage to be taken of the greater thermal efficiency, higher availability and increased mileage between repairs in more modern designs when replacing life-expired stock. The accompanying Table 3.1 shows the division of activity in a typical large works.

For the first four years of operation, the Railway Executive recorded considerable progress in rationalising the locomotive fleet inherited at Nationalisation; details are given in Table 3.2. A reduction in the net operating stock of locomotives of some 4.5% was accompanied by a net reduction in the number of classes of over 17% over the period from the beginning of 1948 to the end of 1951. There are two aspects to the objective of attaining the highest possible standard of mechanical efficiency, reliability and safety of the fleet for the lowest level of expenditure:

a) day-to-day servicing, examination and categorised as running shed repairs
b) the more comprehensive repairs undertaken at the locomotive Works

Works Repairs

The decision on when it is no longer economical to retain a locomotive in service by day-to-day attention at the running shed is influenced by three considerations:

1) the time the locomotive will be out of service
2) the general condition to which the locomotive can be restored without resorting to works repairs
3) the mileage and time the locomotive will be expected to run before requiring further repair.

Works repairs broadly fall into three categories:

1) periodical repairs at which the boiler is changed for a complete overhaul, classified as the so-called 'General' repair
2) periodical repairs without the need for the boiler to be removed from the frame, classified as the Intermediate repair and
3) casualty repairs of various classifications.

With due regard to the standard equipment normally available at running sheds and the relatively short distances of sheds from works locations, classified repairs other than boiler tube changing and buffer beam repairs were not generally undertaken at running sheds; repairs carried out at sheds were usually covered by the terms 'Non Classified' or 'Unclassified'. The statutory requirement for the reporting of locomotive repairs set out by the Ministry of Transport categorised the repairs as either 'Heavy' or 'Light' and was taken as the basis for the BR classification. It was supplemented for management purposes by a more detailed description, details of which are given in the accompanying Table 3.3, previously included as Table 8.3, p.184 in Volume 4 of this series, *The 9F 2-10-0 Class*, and reproduced here for convenience.

The standard classification of locomotive repairs used on BR from 1949 gave details of the work done annually as shown:

a) number of repairs in the specified categories
b) output in relation to mileage run and cost of repairs
c) forecasts of the number, type and cost of repairs likely in subsequent years.

The average mileage between consecutive periodical repairs for each Region's principal locomotives out-shopped in 1951 is as listed in Table 3.4. The figure of 100,000 miles between repairs was closely approached by a handful of classes including Stanier class 5 4-6-0s with Manganese steel axle box liners and the Peppercorn class A1 Pacifics; in the case of the Ivatt class 2 2-6-0s, the figure was exceeded. The 100,000 mile target between major overhauls was thus considered feasible and was adopted for the new Standard classes.

Locomotive design, materials used, together with other aspects such as boiler feed water quality and the type of duties on which the various classes were employed are significant factors in the mileages obtained. The major determinant however is the standard of maintenance in the motive power depots. It is this which influences the time and mileage which the locomotives can be run between visits to works.

Locomotive Availability

For minimising capital cost and depreciation charges, it is clear that for a given amount of traffic, the number of locomotives employed should be as low as possible. A high proportion of the total stock should be available for service and these units should be used in useful work for as many

TABLE 3.1
Typical Division of Activities in a Large Locomotive Works

Activity	% Man-Hours
Maintenance and Repair of Steam Locomotives	42.4
Stock Orders, new and repair	
Foundries and Forge	5.2
Boiler repairs	4.9
Other shops	19.4
New boilers for other works	3.8
Miscellaneous work for outdoor machinery and other departments	14.6
Total Maintenance and Repair	90.2
New Building Programme	9.8
Grand Total	

TABLE 3.2
British Railways Workshops
Locomotive Repairs, New Building and Breaking Up

Year	1948	1949	1950	1951
No. of Classified Repairs	10,750	10,725	10,047	10,057
Locos on Works at Year End				
No.	1,214	990	979	952
% of Operating Stock	6.2	5.1	5.1	5.1
New Locomotives	314	301	311	278
New Boilers (excluding for new locos)	355	325	375	264
Locos Withdrawn for Breaking Up	772	818	591	792
Loco Stock at Year End				
Owned ('000s)	20.3	19.9	19.7	19.3
Net Operating ('000s)	19.8	19.4	19.1	18.9
No. of Classes	435	417	402	360
Engine Mileage Run ('000s)	493.3	503.2	499.8	492.3

hours per day as traffic conditions permit. For comparable levels of traffic, Table 3.5 shows a reduction of almost 20% in the size of the locomotive stock at 31st December 1951 compared with that on the the last day of 1923, the year of Grouping into the Big Four.

In the early 1950s, the aim was to achieve an average availability of 85% for the operating stock; of the remaining 15%, 10% would be stopped at shed for various reasons and 5% would be on works or awaiting repairs there. For the 19,000 or so locomotives in BR stock, some 16,150 would thus be available for work. If the availability deteriorated to 80%, there would be around 950 fewer locomotives for working the given amount of traffic, requiring some 1,187 more additions to stock. Alternatively, if availability could be increased to 90%, the fleet could be reduced by some 1,050 units. Paradoxically, an increase in mileage run on a time basis would tend to reduce the overall availability of a locomotive due to increased amount of time required for servicing. There would however be a net saving in the number of units required for a given volume of traffic.

Non availability of locomotives can be grouped under a small number of headings:

Motive Power Depots

Under or awaiting shed repairs
Under or awaiting examinations
Awaiting material
Awaiting repair decision

Works

On works undergoing repairs
Awaiting works repairs

A summary of the position at each motive power depot was prepared weekly and an example for a week in early 1951 is displayed in Table 3.6. In such a detailed analysis, the source of any availability problems can readily be identified and suitable action authorised. Particular attention is given to controlling

with the aim of reducing the number of locomotives under or awaiting repairs in works. Resources such as increased shop capacity, improved handling equipment or skilled supervision were given the highest priority.

System for Controlling the Locomotive Repair Process
Basis for Selection

It would seem obvious that the criteria for selecting locomotives for repair should be either time elapsed or mileage run between repairs. This is not as clear cut as it appears however. Boiler and firebox wear depends more on the number of hours in steam rather than mileage run whereas wear and tear on mechanical parts is almost entirely a function of mileage. Bearing in mind the significant variation in the rate of mileage run by locomotives of the same class for a given time period, experience indicates that the only criterion by which the need for repairs is judged is the actual physical condition of the locomotive. This is subject to regular examination at the running shed as outlined earlier. A decision then is made whether the locomotive is fit to continue working or is likely to need major repairs in the near future. In this way, repair shops have an indication of the amount of work outstanding and can devise a suitable programme to deal with it. The trend, up or down, of the number of locomotives scheduled for repairs on a week to week basis is thus a good indicator of how well the system is meeting requirements.

General Principles and Procedures

Controlling the flow to the works of locomotives requiring repairs was one of the first issues to be dealt with by the Railway Executive in 1948. The methods developed by the pre-nationalisation companies were examined and the best practices adopted; conditions were established as follows:

a) decisions on whether a locomotive should be sent to works were to be made by the Regional Mechanical Engineer's headquarters organisation.
b) such decisions should be made only on the actual condition of each individual locomotive.

TABLE 3.3
British Railways Steam Locomotive Repair Classification

Repair Type	Designation	Description of Work Carried Out	Status
General (G) †	Heavy (H)	Boiler Change All mechanical parts stripped, repaired or renewed as necessary to enable the engine to run to the next Intermediate or General Overhaul	Mileage 'made good'
Intermediate (I)	Heavy (H) or Light (L) depending on work done as defined in Ministry of Transport Classification (see below)	Boiler not changed but such repairs to be carried out to it and to all mechanical parts as will ensure mileage approx. equal to average for the class between consecutive General and Intermediate repairs will be attained before next scheduled General or Intermediate repair	Mileage 'made good'
Casual (C)	Heavy (H) or Light (L) depending on work done as defined in Ministry of Transport Classification (see below)	Repair or replace those parts which have become defective due to failure or mishap making engine unserviceable No work carried out on other components	Mileage NOT 'made good'
Non-Classified (NC)	–	Repairs necessary as defined for Casual repairs but not covered by Ministry of Transport Heavy (H) or Light (L) classification No work carried out on other components	Mileage NOT 'made good'

Key: † General: Darlington Works appears in some cases to have classified Heavy General Overhaul as 'G' rather than 'HG'

Ministry of Transport Classification of Heavy and Light Repairs

Heavy Repairs
1. Engine re-boilered
2. Boiler taken out of frame for repair

or

any two of the following:

3. Fitting of new tyres to four or more wheels
4. Fitting new cylinders
5. Fitting new axle or axles on engine or tender
6. Re-tubing of boiler
7. Turning up wheels or refitting axle boxes; or motion and brake-work stripped and overhauled
8. Repairing of boiler on frame with not less than 50 stays renewed

Note: the two items in 7 would not, taken together, constitute a Heavy repair

Light Repairs
1. Fitting new axle or axles on engine or tender
2. Taking out and replacing 50 or more boiler tubes
3. Taking out and replacing four or more superheater tubes
4. Taking down and replacing superheater header
5. Renewal of piston valve liners or piston valves
6. Fitting new tyres to one or more wheels
7. Turning up four or more wheels and refitting axle boxes
8. Complete overhaul of one or more valve gears
9. Fitting patch on boiler or firebox
10. Renewing 30 or more firebox stays
11. Fitting four or more new axleboxes or engine axlebox brasses
12. Welding, patching or straightening frame or renewing buffer beam
13. Re-boring cylinders and re-facing ports
14. Taking off and repairing tanks

Note on Mileage 'made good'

It will be noted that in the work specified in the Ministry of Transport Classification table above, constituting a Heavy or Light repair, no indication is given of the extent to which mileage run in traffic has been 'made good'.

A locomotive, for example, which has its boiler lifted for attention to some leaking rivets behind the frames or for any other reason, however incidental, is automatically classified as having had a Heavy repair, although no work may have been done on the tyres, axleboxes, frames or motion.

In such circumstances, the mileage run by the locomotive since previous repairs has not been 'made good' and it is not necessarily fit for a further a further full average period in traffic until the next Heavy or Intermediate repair.

c) the stock of all locomotives at all times was to be maintained in a first class mechanical condition.

Expenditure incurred in the maintenance of locomotives was to be the minimum consistent with condition c above.

The resources of each Region and between various Regions should be used to the best advantage of British Railways as a whole.

To facilitate this, there was set up at each of the regional head-quarters of the mechanical engineer's department a 'locomotive shopping bureau'. The principal functions of these bureaux were:

a) to control the acceptance and stopping of locomotives for works

b) to distribute locomotives for repairs to each works within the Region in accordance with capacity

c) to arrange for periodical examination of locomotive boilers at MPDs

For each locomotive class, a period in months since previous major repairs was to elapse before individual class members were to be considered for works repairs. For the BR Standard classes, these periods are as shown:

Class	Period in Months
Class 8 4-6-2	12
Class 7 4-6-2	15
Class 6 4-6-2	18
Class 5 4-6-0	24
Class 4 4-6-0	28
Class 4 2-6-0	30
Class 3 2-6-0	32
Class 2 2-6-0	36
Class 4 2-6-4T	28
Class 3 2-6-2T	33
Class 2 2-6-2T.	36
Class 9 2-10-0	36★

★ WR period 34 months

Six weeks before the elapse of the specified period since its last shop repair, and preferably while the locomotive was still running, a proposal form was generated giving details of its general condition, mileage run and time since last in works. The proposal was forwarded to the shopping bureau of the Region responsible for its maintenance where arrangements were made for an independent boiler inspection. Based on these findings of these two reports, the locomotive would either be accepted for works repair or returned to service for a further specified period and subject to a later re-proposal process. The criteria for taking into shops were two-fold:

1) the locomotive was already out of traffic due to mechanical or boiler defects which could not be easily remedied at the MPD or the local concentration depot ('A' shed) where appropriate.

2) its condition was judged to be such that unless repaired, it would no longer be suitable for its booked work and would have to be taken out of traffic within a few weeks unless alternative duties could be found.

In the re-proposal system, the opportunity to identify alternative work reinforced the point that a locomotive does

On one of the rare occasions when a Clan was used on a RCTS rail tour, 72007 *Clan Mackintosh* takes water at Hellifield when working the Ribble Lune tour on 23rd May 1964. The tour commenced at Preston and visited Blackburn, Hellifield, Lancaster Green Ayre, Morecambe and Lancaster Goods before returning to Preston (see also p.109). *Gavin Morrison*

TABLE 3.4
Average Mileage Between Periodical
Repairs of Principal Regional Types of
Locomotives in the Year 1951

Region	Class of Locomotive	Average Mileage Between Periodical Repairs ('000s)
LM	4-6-2 Coronation	73.2
	4-6-0 Royal Scot Taper Boiler & 5X conversions	70.5
	4-6-0 Cl. 5	57.0
	4-6-0 Cl. 5 ★ Mn steel liners	97.3
	2-8-0 Cl. 8	50.4
	2-6-4T Cl. 4	55.6
	2-6-4T Cl. 4 ★ Mn steel liners	79.4
	2-6-0 Cl. 4	90.7
	2-6-0 Cl. 2	104.3
	2-6-2T Cl. 2	83.2
ER	4-6-2 A1	93.4
	4-6-2 A2	85.7
	4-6-2 A3	83.6
	4-6-2 A4	86.6
	4-6-0 B1	78.4
	2-8-0 O1	55.6
	2-8-0 WD	62.6
	2-6-2 V2	77.9
	2-6-2T V1	66.2
	2-6-2T V3	66.8
	2-6-4T L1	67.2
WR	4-6-0 King	79.0
	4-6-0 Castle	87.4
	4-6-0 Hall	87.9
	4-6-0 County	87.6
	2-8-0 28xx	87.0
	2-6-2T 3150-81xx	71.7
SR	4-6-2 Merchant Navy	75.7
	4-6-2 West Country & Battle of Britain	74.7
	4-6-0 Lord Nelson	81.6
	4-6-0 King Arthur	71.0
	4-4-0 Schools	69.9
	2-6-0 N	53.9
	2-6-0 U	68.9
	★ Mn: Manganese	

not necessarily have the right to a works repair simply because the minimum period since the last shop repair had elapsed; actual condition was the only criterion for taking the locomotive into shops and it was possible that there would be more than one re-proposal exercise for any individual locomotive.

To function properly, the system was dependent on the accuracy of the MPD and boiler inspectors' reports together with the experience and sound judgement of the shopping bureau technical staff. Time rather than mileage was used for the shopping periods as supervision of the system was more easily controlled. It also fitted in with the statutory boiler inspection requirements which were also based on specified time intervals in service.

The pool of engines agreed for a works visit was aimed to be equal to three to four weeks' work. If greater than this, some locomotives could be idle out of service before the works were in a position to accept them, whereas if the pool were smaller, there would be insufficient time for the shops to plan their work programmes efficiently.

Allocation for Maintenance

For economic and efficiency reasons, for example in the provision of spare boilers and other renewable parts, maintenance of the Standard classes operating on more than one division or Region initially was confined to a limited number of works. The principles used were as follows, modified for practical and operating reasons:

a) maintenance for each class should be limited both in numbers or Regions and works within those regions. Ideally one class was to be maintained by one nominated works.

b) locomotives were to be allocated to those works which had built them or to one which already maintained locomotives of the same class.

c) taking the above into account, locomotives should be maintained in the same Region on which they operated. As the numbers in the Standard classes in traffic increase, the opportunity should taken to allocate classes to other works so that experience of repair performance was gained with the aim of taking over routine maintenance.

Table 3.7 shows the maintenance allocation for the BR Standard classes authorised to be built to the end of 1952. Later, the policy was changed to have Regions maintain the locomotives allocated to them wherever possible. Towards the end of steam, the policy was again reversed, for example with the 9F 2-10-0 class, where maintenance was concentrated at Crewe Works in the latter years before the end of steam on BR.

If the pool of locomotives stopped awaiting works was exhausted, the works' weekly quotas were made up from the list of those agreed for repairs but still in traffic. Teleconferences were made on a regular basis to ensure that all stopped engines were taken into works within the operating Region or elsewhere rather than use the 'agreed but still running' list.

The general position of works throughput was reviewed on a day to day basis using data from the respective MPDs and shopping bureaux. The position was easily and accurately established by use of the following simple formula.

$\star = A + B - C + D \pm E$ where

$\star$ = the difference between the number of locomotives agreed for shops at any two dates
A = the number of locomotives agreed for repairs between the two dates
B = locomotives sent to the works between the two dates without prior agreement
C = the number of locomotives turned out of the shops after repairs
D = locomotives taken out of traffic between the two dates
E = the difference between the number of locomotives in works at the the two dates

Operating System Checks

Bearing in mind that the interests of the works and the MPDs do not necessarily coincide, careful supervision is required in operating the system to its full advantage. Some problems which arise are:

a) as noted earlier, mileage targets between repairs are a guide only. The works are not obliged to take in locomotives in good working order even after such mileage has been achieved; a possible area of conflict could be when an engine is found to be 'running rough' even though it is still considered safe to operate.

b) the aim should be to achieve the highest number of running miles between repairs. Hence MPD day to day maintenance is essential on all engines, whether recently ex-works or due for shops where the amount of attention would likely be much higher.

c) the objective is to have the lowest number of locomotives either under or awaiting repairs, again best achieved by strict adherence to scheduled maintenance.

d) the decision as to whether to send to works should not be influenced by traffic requirements. The practice of recommending engines for shops during the winter period so that they will be ready for the busy summer season was not condoned.

e) stopped engines have priority over those 'agreed for repairs but still running'. 'Good runners' must take their turn for forwarding to shops.

Organisation of Repairs at Works

Focus was on the need to reduce the amount of time a locomotive spent on works. Work carried out on individual engines was strictly controlled and costed. Examiners independent of foremen and chargehands decided the amount of work to be carried out according to limits of wear specified by the Mechanical Engineers' department. They monitored progress paying great attention to delays and cost over-runs during the completion of the various stages; these were analysed rigorously and recommendations made for for remedial action.

To minimise a locomotive's stay stay on works, careful attention was given to the following:

a) a timetable was laid down for the whole repair sequence for each locomotive, from arrival on works to return to traffic. The rate-determining step for completion of an overhaul had in the past been the availability of the repaired boiler, which always took longer to refurbish than any other component. To reduce an engine's dwell time on works, spare boilers, ready mounted, tubed and tested were provided so that there would be no delay in completing the repair.

b) scheduled times were set up and adhered to for each stage in the process, the principle being to employ the maximum number of men for the minimum number of hours.

c) the main erecting shop schedule required a strict timetable for new or repaired components to be made available at specified times to facilitate re-assembly.

d) in addition to spare boilers, a small 'float' of other components such as cylinders and wheels was to be available at all times

The Progressive Repair System

During a locomotive overhaul, the process of stripping, frame repair and re-assembly is divided into various stages. The

TABLE 3.5
Stock of Locomotives

At Year End	Owned Stock of Steam, Diesel and other Locomotives
1923	23,894
1928	23,316
1933	20,823
1938	19,627
1943	19,938
1947	20,101
1948	20,302
1949	19,914
1950	19,741
1951	19,289

TABLE 3.6
Steam, Diesel or Electric Locomotives Awaiting Repair:
Typical Weekly Average for the year 1951

Operating Stock		Total BR	%
Total Operating Stock	A	19,249	-
No. Stored in Serviceable Condition	B	400	-
Net Operating Stock	C	18,849	-
Mechanical Engineers Workshops			
Number in Works	D	823	4.37
No. Stopped Awaiting Works	E	129	0.68
Total Stopped for Works (D+E)	F	952	5.05
MPDs			
Number not Available at MPDs throughout 24 Hours Midnight to Midnight			
Stopped at MPD Awaiting Repair Decision	G	43	0.23
Awaiting Repair Material	H	310	1.64
Under or Awaiting Repair.	J	681	3.61
Under Examination	K	323	1.72
Total Under Repair or Examination (J+K)	L	1,004	5.33
Availability for Traffic			
Total Not Available for Whole 24 Hours (F+G+H+L)	M	2,309	12.25
Number Available for Whole or Some Part of 24 Hours Midnight to Midnight (C−M)	N	16,540	87.75
Number Available by 18.00 hours after Shed Attention which could not be used.	P	693	3.68
Number Available during 24 Hours (N−P)	Q	15,847	84.07

Prior to 1953 when the new iron ore quay was opened at Tyne Dock, ore trains consisted of 22 21 ton capacity bottom discharge wagons which were hauled by either Q7 or O1 locomotives from Tyne Dock shed. Following the introduction of 56 ton capacity wagons in 1953, trains were made up of eight wagons, which was increased to nine wagons when the 9Fs took over the haulage in 1956. Banking took place up the hill from the ore quay and on the 1 in 50 climb from South Pelaw usually to South Medomsley box, which is situated between Annfield Plain and Leadgate. 92098 was pictured passing Stanley banked by WD 90016 on 29th May 1963. *Howard Forster*

previous approach whereby a team was given several locomotives to repair throughout at any one time was replaced by 'progressing' the locomotive, moving it (more often than not) by overhead crane to the next stage. Here a dedicated team specialising in that stage continued the overhaul. As a result, specialised equipment was not being constantly moved around the shops, the risk of potential damage thus being significantly reduced. The system also allowed material from other parts of the works always to be delivered to the same area, maximising efficiency. Handing an engine over on time from one team to another encouraged higher standards of workmanship and helped to keep the repair on schedule.

To enable the 'Progressive System' to work well, a great deal of initial planning was necessary. It was essential to:

a) assess the man-hours required for the completion of each repair stage and to arrange the sequence in which stages were undertaken
b) build in flexibility to take account of the varying amounts of work required for individual locomotives by grouping the tasks within the different stages and assigning them to separate gangs

In this way, modified in the light of experience, it was possible to establish the number of days in which various types of repair could be completed for each class of locomotive. A preferred mix of classes and extent of repairs thus could be identified for a particular repair shop and used to summon particular locomotives from the 'agreed for repairs' pool with

the aim of minimising the number of engines under repair at any one time and maximising efficient throughput.

Provision of Spares

Boilers

As a general rule, repairs to virtually all parts of a locomotive can be completed within the timetable laid down. The major exception to this is repairs to boilers. In some cases, depending on the nature of the work to be done, it is possible to rectify the problem whilst the boiler is still on the frames. Where a boiler requires remedial attention taking a longer time than allocated for the overhaul however, it is essential to have a fully functioning spare boiler on hand and available for fitting. The economic stock of spare boilers for each class can be calculated based on:

a) the average running time in months between boiler changes for each class
b) the average and maximum number of locomotives of each class to be repaired each week
c) the difference between the time when a replacement boiler is required to be fitted, usually from two to three days after the locomotive enters the erecting shop and the time needed to complete heavy boiler repairs, usually from 20 to 30 days on average.

Stock of Other Spare Parts

For newly built locomotives, there will be less of a need to

40

carry a readily available stock of spare parts for possibly up to the first ten years of their lives. Depending on running experience however, it may be necessary in due course to have certain parts available as spares, namely wheels, tyres, axles and frames including cylinders, dragboxes and stretchers; bunkers and tanks for non-tender engines also would be likely to be an economic investment.

Control and Supervision of Locomotive Maintenance

Regular scrutiny of accurate statistics and records relating to cost and expenditure, volume of work in relation to requirements and the levels of efficiency within the maintenance activities is essential. Overall, the statistics by which the efficiency of the organisation was judged related to the following factors:

1) number and percentage of locomotives under or awaiting repairs
2) number of days on works under repairs
3) number of days out of traffic for repairs
4) mileage run in relation to the various classified repairs carried out
5) number and percentage of casual repairs (other than casualties) in relation to general and intermediate repairs
6) number of mechanical failures in service in relation to mileage run

Such statistics were collated on quarterly and annual bases. Table 3.8 makes a comparison of the positions for the years 1950 and 1951 and shows steady progress being made in virtually all categories. This trend was continued in subsequent years.

TABLE 3.7
BR Standard types authorised to the end of 1952

Class of Locomotive	Total Number Authorised for Building		Operating Region		Maintaining Region
	Number	Building Works	Number	Region	Works
4-6-2 Cl. 7 Britannia	45	Crewe	5	London Midland	Crewe
			25	Eastern	Crewe
			15	Western	Crewe
4-6-2 Cl. 6 Clan	10	Crewe	10	Scottish	Crewe
4-6-0 Cl. 5	50	Derby	35	London Midland	Derby
			15	Scottish	St. Rollox
4-6-0 Cl. 4	50	Swindon	30	London Midland	Derby
			20	Western	Swindon
2-6-0 Cl. 4	20	Horwich	15	Southern	Eastleigh
			5	Scottish	Doncaster
	5	Doncaster	5	North Eastern	Doncaster
2-6-0 Cl. 2	10	Darlington	10	Western	Swindon
2-6-4T Cl. 4	54	Brighton	30	London Midland	Derby
			13	Southern	Eastleigh
			11	Scottish	St. Rollox
	15	Derby	15	Scottish	St. Rollox
2-6-2T Cl. 3	35	Swindon	15	Western	Swindon
			20	Southern	Swindon

TABLE 3.8
Works repair statistics comparison for 1950 and 1951

	1950	1951
Locomotives under and Awaiting Repair		
Number	979	952
% of Net Operating Stock	5.14	5.05
Weekdays Out of Service		
Average no. of days on Works	25	24
Average no. of days out of service	32	31
Mileage Run with respect to Classified Repairs		
All Classified Repairs	41,751	42,218
Generals and Intermediates Only	66,457	65,244
Casual Repairs		
Number	2,527	2,512
% with respect to General and Intermediate repairs	33.60	33.29
Mechanical Casualties in Service		
Miles per Casualty	20,757	27,083

In the mid-1950s West Auckland shed had a batch of 76000s and 77000s within its allocation to work all the remaining duties on the Stainmore line together with Standard class locomotives from Kirkby Stephen shed. On summer Saturdays there were several extra passenger workings from the north east, mainly to Blackpool, as well as other west coast destinations. These ran right up to the last summer of operations on the line, as seen here with 76050 passing Stainmore summit (1,370 feet) with a return working from Blackpool to Newcastle on 5th August 1961.

Gavin Morrison

73080 on a Victoria to Ramsgate holiday working passes Ravensbourne on the Catford Loop line. In a scene that has changed totally, the semaphore signals were swept away in 1959 when the whole area was converted to colour light control. The site of the sidings behind the down platform is now covered with houses. The observant reader will have noticed the London, Chatham & Dover Railway finial on top of the signal at the exit from the sidings. The exact date of the photograph is not known but it is thought to be in the summer of 1958. *Kenneth Wightman*

84002 stands in the platform at Buckingham awaiting to depart on the service to Bletchley on 24th August 1956. 84002 was one of a small class of 30, the first 20 built at Crewe and the remaining ten at Darlington. The last of the class, 84029, has the distinction of being the last tank engine to be built for British Railways and the very last locomotive to be built at Darlington North Road Works. *John Edgington*

43

78001 heads a short freight towards Dursley on 12th May 1965 nearly three years after closure to passenger traffic in September 1962. Opened in September 1856 this branch, off the Bristol to Gloucester line, finally closed to all traffic in June 1968 after which it was operated as a private siding until 1970. The alternate black and white bands on the distant signal post were a London Midland Region initiative designed to improve signal sighting against a sky background.

Bill Potter

82023 departs from Bude on the 18-mile journey to Halwill Jct. on 16th June 1962. The line climbed at 1 in 73 from two miles outside Bude to Whitstone & Bridgerule. This gradient was one of a number of climbs of more than 1 in 100 on the line to Halwill Jct. The line was opened in August 1898 and closed to freight traffic on September 1964. The last passenger trains ran from Okehampton to Bude and Wadebridge on 1st October 1966. The line from Meldon Jct. to Bude and Wadebridge closed completely on 3rd October 1966.

R. C. Riley

80041 in open countryside west of Tresmeer on the 3.10pm Padstow to Okehampton working on 22nd August 1964. 80041 was built at Brighton and entered traffic in July 1955. Brighton Works built 130 examples of the class with 15 built at Derby and 10 at Doncaster. The locomotive illustrated was withdrawn in March 1966 and scrapped by J. Cashmore, Newport in June 1966. *Peter Gray*

92245 on Midford Viaduct with the 7.43am Bradford to Bournemouth West crossing the Limpley Stoke to Camerton branch on 25th August 1962. The branch being crossed was used for the making of the 1953 Ealing comedy "The Titfield Thunderbolt" using the Liverpool & Manchester preserved *Lion* locomotive which was renamed *Thunderbolt* for the purpose of the story. *Roy Hobbs*

73152 leaves the down side yard at Beattock station on 6th September 1962, with much needed banking assistance at the rear of the train to tackle the gradients of the fearsome Beattock bank which vary from 1 in 69 to 1 in 88 over a distance of some ten miles. The motive power depot for the banking engines can be seen in the background with several locomotives in steam awaiting their call of duty. *Ken Falconer*

Coming down the south side of Beattock's 1 in 76 incline passing Greskine signal box up outer starting signal on 30th May 1966 is 92071 taking empty limestone wagons from Ravenscraig steel works back to Hardendale quarry, near Shap. 92071 was one of a batch of Class 9Fs allocated to Carlisle Kingmoor shed primarily for these workings, this engine arriving at Kingmoor in December 1965 and remaining there until withdrawal in November 1967. *Hugh Ballantyne*

78048 on the 4.00pm ECS working from St. Boswells drawing out of Berwick-upon-Tweed station on 24th May 1962. The locomotive was delivered new to St. Margarets in October 1955 and remained in Scotland all its working life. Four of the class were allocated to Hawick to work the St. Boswells to Berwick branch, until the service was withdrawn in June 1964, and local passenger trains from Carlisle and Galashiels on the Waverley route.

Michael Mensing

92006 was allocated to Bath Green Park shed for only three months to work the summer Saturday extra trains between June and September 1961. The engine is seen leaving one of the short single bore tunnels at Chilcompton on a hot summer day, 12th August 1961, heading the 7.43am Bradford Forster Square-Bournemouth West.

Gavin Morrison

Five Clans were delivered new to Polmadie in 1951 and 1952 primarily for working the Glasgow Central to Liverpool and Manchester expresses which often proved too heavy for 6MTs. One of these, 72003 *Clan Fraser*, makes slow progress up Shap, near the summit, on a summer Saturdays only express from Liverpool Exchange on 6th August 1960. By 1954 the Clans were replaced by Britannias, 70050 to 70054, on these duties.

Gavin Morrison

In glorious summer weather 70052 *Firth of Tay* with the later BR1D tender nears Beattock summit with W157 the 10.05am Euston-Perth in June 1956. The train is of early BR Mk.1 coaches with a LMS Stanier Port Hole 3rd added to the front displaying the early BR corporate image colours.

David Kelso

78045 of Keith stands at bay platform 3 at the east end of Elgin station on 13th May 1961 waiting to depart with the 12.30pm Saturdays only coast line train to Buckie. The coast line between Cairnie Jct. and Elgin closed to all traffic seven years later, on 6th May 1968.

Douglas Hume

78048 runs tender first on the 11.30am St. Boswells-Kelso, passing Heiton siding, half a mile east of Roxburgh, on 30th May 1962. The locomotive spent all its working life in Scotland, being withdrawn from Hawick in July 1964 and scrapped by Motherwell Machinery & Scrap Co., Wishaw in April 1965.

Michael Mensing

70028 *Royal Star* makes a smokey approach to Birkett tunnel on a southbound freight from Carlisle to Leeds, in June 1965. 70028 was new in December 1952 and allocated to the Western Region until moved to the London Midland Region in late 1961 where it remained until withdrawal in September 1967. In later years the Britannias were relegated to freight duties hence 70028 is in very poor condition. *Derek Cross*

A very clean 92234 was based at Bromsgrove for over two months to replace the usual banker, 92079, which was away at Wolverhampton Stafford Road Works for heavy repair. 92234 assists an express from Bristol to the north hauled by Royal Scot 46147 up the 1 in 37 climb from Bromsgrove to Blackwell on 2nd September 1961.
Rodney Lissenden

On 10th December 1964 the line to Consett was completely blocked by a derailment of a Q6-hauled coal train near Beamish which had suffered a runaway the previous day. The dozen or so daily loaded and empty ore trains therefore were diverted via Ouston Jct., the ECML, Relly Mill Jct. and Lanchester. Here we see 92065 passing through the cutting south of the viaduct at Durham on the ECML with a standard nine-wagon set of specially designed 56ton bogie wagons in tow. The air pumps used to operate the air-powered discharge doors, and fitted exclusively to the ten 9Fs allocated to this work, clearly can be seen.

Mike Robinson

Derby-based 73137 pilots Holbeck Jubilee 45565 *Victoria* with the 10.37am Bradford Forster Square-St. Pancras on 9th May 1959 through Elstree on the Midland main line. Both locomotives survived the cutters torch until 1967.

K. L. Cook

77012 departs northbound from York past what was York MPD and is now the NRM with a Gresley Third compartment coach transferred to Departmental stock in the late 1950s/early 1960s and branded "Mobile Instruction Coach". 77012 is displaying Class 1 headlamps as officers' inspection trains were classified as Class 1 workings.

Alan Sainty collection

70044 *Earl Haig* with the summer seasonal Saturdays only 1L59 Glasgow Central-Morecambe service at Hest bank crossing from the up main line to the single branch leading to Bare Lane (opened in August 1864) on 13th July 1963. Note the LNWR coach converted for camping use (in 1952) in the old goods yard adjoining the shore of Morecambe Bay. 70044 entered traffic in June 1953 but was not named until March 1957; it was withdrawn from traffic from Stockport in October 1966 and scrapped by T. W. Ward, Beighton in February 1967. *Noel Machell*

80082 passes Millbrook on a westbound train for Bournmouth on 20th March 1966. The leading coach is a rare example of a British Railways Mk.2 design in all over Southern Region green, an all first class vehicle denoted by the yellow band. For the forthcoming electrification of the Bournemouth main line conductor rails have been unloaded and await installation.

Roy Hobbs

80096 on a northbound train approaching Aberdovey from Penhelig on 2nd September 1963. The front coach is an ex-LMS corridor third brake followed by two ex-GWR coaches. The line at the base of the picture is the Aberdovey Harbour branch opened on 24th October 1863, built to convey passengers to the harbour, then to be taken by steamship across the Dovey estuary to Ynyslas; this was prior to the opening of Aberdovey to Dovey Jct. The branch closed to passengers on 14th August 1867 and to freight on 14th May 1964.

Martin Gill

80043 pulls away from Penshurst station on a service from Tonbridge to Reading via Guildford in the summer of 1959. The locomotive was delivered new to Bletchley in July 1952, moving to the Southern Region in December 1959, spending three years on the Eastern section of the Southern before being moved to Exmouth Junction in 1962. Withdrawn from service in March 1966 and scrapped by J. Cashmore, Newport in July 1966.

Kenneth Wightman

73026 departs the yard at Banbury on an up freight on 12th October 1963. The class of 172 locomotives was built between 1951-57, the work being shared between the BR works at Derby and Doncaster. The final batch cost increased by 28% from that built in 1951. Interesting how inflation was also rampant between 1951-57 when the final batch cost increased from £17,603 to £28,075 per locomotive.

R. C. Riley

Birkenhead-based 92102 near Stenson Jct. with an iron ore empty working on 16th October 1965. Stenson Junction is situated on the line from Derby to Burton-on-Trent; passenger traffic between Stenson Jct. and Sheet Stores Jct., Trent was withdrawn in 1930 closing two stations on the line, Weston-on-Trent and Castle Donnington & Shardlow.

Roy Hobbs

73099 at Edinburgh Princes Street waits to leave on the 6.12pm (SO) to Glasgow Central on 28th April 1962. The station was constructed by the Caledonian Railway between 1890 and 1893, replacing a temporary station opened on the site in 1870 which was a replacement of an earlier building known as Lothian Road. After a long decline and gradual withdrawal of traffic following nationalisation Princes Street station closed in September 1965. The buildings were demolished in 1970.

Ken Falconer

92206 of York is a long way from home, on the up relief line near milepost 150 on the Western Region main line at the western approaches to the extensive marshalling yard at Severn Tunnel Junction with a train of iron ore empties heading to the east Midlands from one of the South Wales steel plants on 14th May 1965. Note that Undy water troughs were situated only in the up and down fast lines. *Hugh Ballantyne*

Following the demise of the ex-Cambrian 0-6-0s, Standard Class 2s were stationed at Portmadoc to work local trains. 78007 pulls away from Llanbadarn crossing working the 10.20am Aberystwyth all stations to Shrewsbury. This train supplemented the 10.00am up limited stop "Cambrian Coast Express". The location was about two miles from Aberystwyth climbing the 1 in 75 out of the Rheidol valley. *Trevor Owen*

At the iron and coal town of Muirkirk in East Ayrshire the G&SW Railway from Auchinleck and Ayr and the Caledonian Railway from Lanark met head on. The G&SW section closed to passengers in 1951 and altogether in 1969. The Caledonian section to Lanark closed to passengers and freight in 1964. Until the closure of the G&SW section this station boasted two signal boxes and an overbridge. 77018 stands at Muirkirk in May 1962 with a train for Lanark.

Douglas Hume

Carlisle Kingmoor Britannia 70003 *John Bunyan* is ready to depart from Bradford Valley Road goods yard with the 7.40pm freight to Carlisle on 29th June 1966. The locomotive spent nearly 13 years on the Great Eastern section before being moved to Kingmoor in December 1963, where it remained until withdrawal in March 1967.

Gavin Morrison

80104 on an early afternoon northbound train, seen between Abertafol and Penhelig on 2nd September 1963. Road and rail hug the estuary coast at this point; the observant reader will have noticed the red triangle road sign at the top of the picture. 80104 was delivered new to the London, Tilbury & Southend section of British Railways in March 1955, later displaced by electrification, withdrawn from service in July 1965 and now preserved on the Swanage Railway.
Martin Gill

70043 *Lord Kitchener* breasts Shap summit after the five-mile climb of 1 in 75 from Tebay on 1S91 from Birmingham New St. to Glasgow Central on a very hot sunny day on 27th July 1963. *Lord Kitchener* entered traffic in June 1953 and was withdrawn in August 1965 after only twelve years in service.
Rodney Lissenden

In the original 1956 locomotive building programme proposed in February 1955 a further 36 Britannias, 70055-90, for the LMR, ER and WR, were pencilled in. These were later cancelled when the programme was pruned as a result of the large number of locomotives already outstanding from previous programmes. The introduction of the BR Modernisation and Re-Equipment Plan in 1955 with its focus on non-steam traction meant that no further building of Britannias was sanctioned.

The following article was first published in *Steam World*, No.251 of May 2008, pp.8-14 where the process for selecting the names for the Britannia class was discussed in some detail. The author, Mr. Andrew Dow, has kindly given permission to reproduce the article in full. It would be interesting to speculate which, if any, of the 'Britannias That Never Were' would have been named and whether the names would have been chosen from the many listed in Mr. Dow's article

Mr. Andrew Dow wrote:

What Was Wrong with 70047?

Despite many meetings, memos, and suggestions one Britannia Pacific was never named. Andrew Dow reveals for the first time the detailed process of selecting names for BR''s Standard Britannia Pacific class and how the class nearly became known as 'Hurcombs' or Great Britons

"The reappearance of 70013 *Oliver Cromwell* on the main line later this year (2008) may prompt some people to wonder how this locomotive got its name and why such a person who, warts and all, overthrew the monarchy, should be commemorated on a passenger locomotive. Well it is a long story, starting in March 1948, three years before the locomotive was built. The newly created Railway Executive (RE) decided that the business of naming locomotives was something that they and not the Regions should decide. The RE inherited substantial locomotive building programmes from the 'Big Four' companies and were to build rather more than 1,000 locomotives before doing much about building standard British Railways designs.

Many of these locomotives were eligible for naming. The Southern Region was still manufacturing Bulleid Pacifics, the Great Western Region (as it was known to many) was still turning out Castles and Halls at Swindon and the Eastern and North Eastern Regions were yet to build Peppercorn Class A1 Pacifics.

If the RE was to take responsibility for naming locomotives, it had to have a means of doing it. And so they established the British Railways Locomotive Naming Committee, to which mouthful I will refer to as the LNC. The Chairman of the committee who represented the RE was Derek Barrie, who had joined the LMS before World War II, to work in public relations. The Chief Mechanical Engineer (CME) was represented by E. S. Cox, ex-LMS, who was to play a leading role in the design of the Standard locomotives. The Regions were represented by George Dow, who had been public relations chief of the LNER for nearly nine years and was then in charge of public relations on the Eastern and North Eastern Regions. In March 1949, he was to move to the same job on the London Midland Region.

The committee soon set themselves up and gave themselves a few rules and terms of reference. These included looking at existing naming practices and recommending the principles that they would adopt. Their rules included not 'overdoing it', using euphonious names, avoiding slavish adherence to class names and not allowing with names already in use. 'Overdoing it' was avoided by naming only the principal passenger classes; the desire to avoid slavish class names was prompted by the 330-strong Hall class, which included several halls far from GWR territory.

The first task in front of the LNC was the naming of 49 class A1 Pacifics coming out of Doncaster and Darlington Works These were given names from a wide variety of sources, including racehorses, characters from Sir Walter Scott's novels, pre-grouping constituent companies of the LNER, former CMEs of the Great Northern and North Eastern Railways and names used on North British Railway Locomotives.

Next came the Britannias. The committee was aware that the Britannias were to be used by all of the Regions and that individual engines would move between Regions; there would therefore be a great diversity of ideas as to suitable names for them. This, together with the committee's own rule that class names (meaning names for a whole class on a single theme) were not to be used slavishly prompted them to think in terms of small groups of names.

The first batch of Britannias was of 25 locomotives, these being 15 for the Eastern Region and 10 for the Western. Proposals were invited. The first suggested list was put together by George Dow on 15th March 1949, nearly two years before the first engine appeared.

It was a long list of 60 names, and was divided into six sections, covering William Shakespeare and nine characters from his plays; Charles Dickens and nine of his characters; 10 famous British authors and playwrights including John Bunyan; 10 famous British statesmen including Oliver Cromwell; 10 famous British women including Boadicea and finally 10 famous British poets including Geoffrey Chaucer, Lord Byron, John Milton, Lord Tennyson and William Wordsworth. The 10 names mentioned specifically are those that survived all the debate and discussion at LNC to appear on locomotives of one batch or another. The other 50 names were not successful in being selected.

The full list, spelled as they appear in the files, follows (names eventually selected are shown in bold).

4.1 Shakespeare Characters

William Shakespeare	*Julius Caesar*
Mark Anthony	*Cleopatra*
Coriolanus	*Cymbeline*
Hamlet	*King Lear*
Macbeth	*Pericles*

4.2 Charles Dickens Characters

Charles Dickens	*Oliver Twist*
David Copperfield	*Nicholas Nickleby*
Mr Pickwick	*Sam Weller*
Sidney Carton	*Betsy Trotwood*
Mr Micawber	*Paul Dombey*

70018 *Flying Dutchman* heads the up "Capitals Limited Express" through Sonning cutting en route to Paddington. The Western Region introduced this title to the 8.00am Cardiff-Paddington in 1956 after Cardiff became the Welsh capital in December 1955. *Flying Dutchman* was delivered new to the Western Region in the summer of 1951, allocated to Old Oak Common depot, moving to Cardiff in late 1956 before being transferred to the London Midland Region in 1961. The locomotive was withdrawn from Carlisle Kingmoor in December 1966 and scrapped by Motherwell Machinery & Scrap Co. at Wishaw in May 1967.   *Kenneth Wightman*

4.3 Authors and Playwrights

John Bunyan	*William Thackeray*
Richard Sheridan	*Oliver Goldsmith*
John Galsworthy	*Joseph Conrad*
G. K. Chesterton	*H. G. Wells*
Conan Doyle	*George Bernard Shaw*

4.4 British Statesmen

Cardinal Wolsey	*Edward Hyde*
Oliver Cromwell	*William Pitt*
Charles Fox	*Robert Walpole*
Lord Beaconsfield	*William Gladstone*
Robert Peel	*Joseph Chamberlain*

4.5 British Women

Boadicea	*Nell Gwynne*
Sarah Siddons	*Lady Hamilton*
Elizabeth Barrett	*Jane Austen*
Charlotte Bronte	*Florence Nightingale*
Elizabeth Fry	*Edith Cavell*

4.6 Poets

Geoffrey Chaucer	*Edmund Spenser*
Ben Jonson	*William Dryden*
Lord Byron	**John Milton**
Thomas Grey	*John Keats*
Lord Tennyson	**William Wordsworth**

Of all the names, the one that George Dow regretted not seeing on a locomotive was *Betsy Trotwood*. For some reason, this name conjured up, in his mind, the sight of Walschaert's valve gear in motion!

Once this list was before the LNC, a great debate ensued. As a result, Derek Barrie prepared a new list of no fewer than 99 names to record their thoughts for their further consideration. Remember, this was for only 25 locomotives.

The 99 names encompassed Empire and Royalty, Saints George, Andrew, Patrick and David, kinds of dogs, birds, famous British women, poets and playwrights, British heroes and a variety of classical names. The list was (names eventually selected in bold):

4.7 Empire Group

British Empire	*Empire Festival*
Emperor	*Empress*
Prince Charles	*Duke of Edinburgh*

4.8 Saints Group

Saint George	*Saint Andrew*
Saint David	*Saint Patrick*

4.9 National Names ending in 'ia'

Anglia	**Britannia**
Cambria	*Hibernia*
Scotia	

4.10 Dogs

Bloodhound	*Bulldog*
Boarhound	*Beagle*
Foxhound	*Greyhound*

4.11 Birds

Albatross	*Bittern*
Eagle	*Falcon*
Hawk	*Kingfisher*

4.12 British Women

*Queen **Boadicea***	*Mary Queen of Scots*
Flora MacDonald	*Florence Nightingale*
Elizabeth Fry	*Edith Cavell*

4.13 Poets and Playwrights

Geoffrey Chaucer	*Edmund Spenser*
Ben Jonson	*William Dryden*
Lord Byron	***John Milton***
Thomas Grey	*John Keats*
Lord Tennyson	***William Wordsworth***
John Bunyan	*William Thackeray*
Richard Brinsley Sheridan	*Oliver Goldsmith*

4.14 British Heroes

Caractacus	***Alfred the Great***
Edmund Ironside	*Thomas a Becket*
John O' Gaunt	***The Black Prince***
Coeur de Lion	***Owen Glendower***
Hotspur	*Robert Bruce*
Robin Hood	*William Wallace*
Iron Duke	*Bonnie Prince Charlie*
Sir Walter Scott	

4.15 Classical Names & Miscellaneous Others

Aeolus	***Ariel***
Apollo	*Cavalier*
Centaur	*Challenger*
Champion	*Conqueror*
Centurion	*Cerberus*
Columbine	*Crusader*
Enchantress	*Fire Queen*
Gladiator	*Harlequin*
Hercules	*Hyperion*
Lightning	*Marathon*
Mars	*Merlin*
Mercury	*Meteor*
Minerva	*Oberon*
Perseus	*Perseverance*
Pathfinder	*Pegasus*
Quicksilver	*Sirocco*
Swiftsure	*Thunderbolt*
Tornado	***Vulcan***

The personal preferences of the committee members then started to emerge. Stewart Cox made very few contributions but Derek Barrie felt obliged to represent the Western Region's interests and proposed a number of names that had once been used on broad gauge locomotives. He seemed quite averse to original thought where names were concerned. He also proposed the name Great Western. George Dow preferred the animate names such as people. He anticipated the needs of the Eastern Region by speaking up for the names of people associated with the eastern side of the country, including Oliver Cromwell.

For the first name of the class, the LNC chose *Great Britain*, which was very much in line with the Festival of Britain, to be celebrated in the same year that the locomotives were to appear. Although *Britannia* had come out of the discussions, it was not selected because it duplicated the name on a Jubilee class 4-6-0.

On 23rd August 1948, a Railway Executive *Memorandum of Decision* required that the first BR Standard Main Line Passenger locomotive to be produced under the aegis of RE was to be named *Sir Cyril Hurcomb*, after the British Transport Commission's chairman.

The names for the Britannias that were actually recommended were listed in a report covering the A1s and the Britannias. In the case of the latter, the report ignored the instruction on Hurcomb and included *Great Britain* instead. The report said; *"The class-name of GREAT BRITAIN for the first engine of the larger 4-6-2 type has been selected as being appropriate to the Festival of Britain, while the ensuing 14 names continue this conception along patriotic and traditional lines"*.

This was carefully worded to put the notion before the chairman of the BTC; the committee did not want the engines to be known as 'Hurcombs'. The names chosen for the Western Region were noted as perpetuating historic and euphonious names of early GWR engines.

The whole report, including these recommendations, was well received by the RE but it was still a whole year before the engines were due to appear. The RE approved all of the report, including the names for the Britannias, except that they now required that the first two locomotives be named *Great Britain* and *Sir Cyril Hurcomb*; the latter to be substituted for one of the other recommendations.

Nothing further happened for nearly a year, except of course that the engines were being built, and then in September 1950, Derek Barrie set about finishing the list. He had to delete a name to make room for *Sir Cyril Hurcomb* and a couple of duplications had been discovered, one of them because Swindon had used the name *Great Western* without the naming committee being told.

The plan to avoid using Hurcomb's name had not wholly succeeded but at least the LNC had stopped the name being used for the first of the class. There feelings were summed up in a memo from George Dow; *"It is my regret that such a little man should have been included amongst the big names. I was hoping that the joint machinations of B, C and D (Barrie, Cox and Dow) had scotched this idea but apparently it is not to be"*.

Table 4.1 lists the names for the first 25 engines as they appeared in the last draft of the LNC report. On this final list, the authors and playwrights were given precedence over the heroes of the past. Why this change was made, I do not know; it hardly seems of consequence either way.

The committee did not expect that *Great Britain* would be ousted. But Riddles, the CME, was a Crewe man; I suspect that he was therefore very interested in locomotive names and possibly he thought that *Great Britain* sounded too much like Webb's failure *Greater Britain* of 1891. What he did like was the name *Britannia*, which some people associate with the LNWR because of her appearance on their coat of arms.

In fact the name had been used by the Sirhowy Valley Railway as early as 1825 and then by the LSWR a good 10 years before the 'Premier Line' applied it to a Ramsbottom 2-4-0. But no doubt Riddles gave the South Western not a thought when, as a member of the RE, he was able to influence the choice of names once they had been recommended by the committee. The fact that a Jubilee 4-6-0 already had the name did not deter him.

The LNC then, to follow its own rule of no duplications, had to find a new name for Jubilee 4-6-0 45700. Both Barrie and George Dow frequently received suggestions, one way or another, of names for locomotives from members of the public. George Grigs of the RCTS had suggested 45700 be named *Amethyst* after the warship of that name. This ship had had a contretemps with the Chinese in the Yangtze river and the name was very much in the public mind. This suggestion was made to the Chief Regional Officer of the London Midland, who asked for comments or other suggestions from his Commercial Superintendent, a man called Hammett and the Public Relations and Publicity officer, George Dow, (who by now had moved to the LM from Kings Cross).

The two discussed it and decided that they didn't care for the name because it was thought too ephemeral. I quote: *"In a few years, most of the public, who have short memories, will have forgotten that 'Amethyst' was a ship and will wonder why a locomotive has been named after a precious stone"*.

So they made three other suggestions. *Festival*, to commemorate the Festival of Britain that year, *Lord Stamp*, who had been Chairman of the LMS and *Sir Henry Fowler*, whose period of office as CME of the LMS was second only to that of Stanier. And then the Chief Regional Officer (CRO) of the London Midland put these ideas to the RE, who rushed off, got Admiralty concurrence to the name *Amethyst* and ruled that this name should be applied to 45700. No doubt George Grigs was delighted!

The locomotive building programme for 1952 included 20 more Britannias and in August 1951 Barrie wrote to Dow and Cox to ask if they could get together to discuss names for them. These were to go on a further five for the Western (70025-29), five for the London Midland (70030-34) and 10 for the ER (70035-44). Out of this came the idea that the engines for the LM be given classical names beginning with the letter 'A'.

The initial work on these engines was done by George Dow at home, using the family copy of **Brewer's Dictionary of Phrase and Fable**. They were a bit of a mixture. *Aphrodite* was the Greek equivalent of Venus, *Atalanta* was a swift runner, *Amazons* were a tribe of female warriors who had their right breasts burned off to make it better to draw a bow, *Aurora* is early morning, *Ariadne* was the daughter of King Minos, *Aeolus* was the Roman god of the winds, *Alecto* was one of the three Greek goddesses of vengeance, equivalent of the Roman Furies, *Amphion* was so good on his lute that stones danced into walls and houses of their own accord, *Andromeda* was extraordinarily beautiful and generally a 'bit of all right' and *Antaeus* was a gigantic wrestler.

George Dow's memo concludes: *"My own choice for the five names is: APHRODITE, ATALANTA, AURORA,*

ARIADNE, ANDROMEDA, all of which besides being euphonious, are names of Goddesses it would have been rather pleasant to know".

The next meeting of Barrie, Cox and Dow led to a first draft of their recommendations. These recommended the names of Stars for the Western Region locomotives and this idea survived later drafts, although the particular names and their order was changed before it was finalised. The idea of names beginning with 'A' was chopped around a lot before being dropped altogether. The following further 'A's were considered: *Althea, Amaryllis, Amphitrite, Aspasia,* and *Athene*. All these were rejected, in particular, *Aspasia*, who was a woman of easy virtue and whose name was thought to be totally inappropriate for a locomotive. This resulted in the use of names of famous Britons being used for the LM locomotives as well as for the Eastern Region locomotives.

A late draft of the recommendations (see Table 4.1) for this second batch of locomotives shows a comparison with the names as allocated to the locomotives. Shortly after this, the reorganisations and lack of unity among regional managers resulted in the Locomotive Naming Committee ceasing to work. A decision was made that in future the Regions could do their own naming and would only have to seek permission for the use of names of royalty. The LNC was called back to name the first generation of diesels but that is another story.

The third and last batch of Britannias provided five locomotives each for the Scottish and London Midland Regions. The Scottish Region decided very quickly to name these after firths, thus:

70050	*Firth of Clyde*
70051	*Firth of Forth*
70052	*Firth of Tay*
70053	*Moray Firth*
70054	*Dornoch Firth*

The London Midland did not have such an easy time. The proposals were handled by George Dow, London Midland CME Freddie Harrison, and Motive Power Superintendent S. T. Clayton. George Dow proposed personal names again, with seven to choose from for five locomotives: *Nell Gwynne, Lady Hamilton, Jane Austen, Robert Peel, Cardinal Wolesy, George Bernard Shaw* and *William Gladstone*. Freddie Harrison proposed the names of the five principal pre-grouping constituent companies of the LMS, Midland, London & North Western, Lancashire & Yorkshire, Furness and North Staffordshire.

His reaction to the five proposed by George Dow was: *"...so far as GEORGE BERNARD SHAW is concerned, the answer is quite definitely 'not pygmalion likely'. So far as ROBERT PEEL, JANE AUSTEN and CARDINAL WOLSEY are concerned, I don't mind but certainly not NELL GWYNNE. What connection NELL GWYNNE can have with a locomotive either remotely or otherwise, I can't imagine."*

It is interesting that Harrison's views echo those he had expressed earlier on one of the 'A's, *Aspasia*: gentlemen don't name locomotives after ladies of easy virtue. Clayton chipped in with the general suggestions of the names of Dukes and of famous sportsmen, although he did not propose any particular names. George Dow responded positively: *"I am quite happy to eliminate GEORGE BERNARD SHAW from the list"*.

He went on:"...neither *NELL GWYNNE* nor any of the other names had anything to do with locomotives; after all, we are not naming locomotives after locomotive men but after national characters and characters which are not ephemeral at that. I would however observe in passing that the former Great Western Railway thought differently, for they named an engine after Nell Gwynne's paramour, and others were named *KING HENRY VIII* (who could hardly be regarded as chaste), *KING GEORGE III* (who died an imbecile) and *KING JAMES I* (who was described as the wisest fool in Christendom). It is because we must, I think, avoid ephemeral names that we should not adopt the suggestion made by Mr Clayton that names of famous sportsmen should be included and there is another danger in this connection. If two or three engines were named after footballers or cricketers we should get all sorts of requests from the public for engines to be named after leaders in other sports, such as hockey or tennis and before we knew where we were, table tennis".

He appended a revised list, giving the names of *William Thackeray, Robert Peel, Jane Austen, Cardinal Wolsey* and *Lord Beaconsfield*. The other two agreed to this list and also agreed to shoot down a suggestion which came down from the CRO that locomotives be named after football clubs. Clayton thought the suggestion most undignified!

This was in April 1954 and nothing further was heard until July when the CRO (J. W. Watkins) telephoned George Dow and asked for five further names. The written reply is marked 'Personal' and so no doubt Dow felt he need not consult Clayton and Harrison. He offered these former locomotive engineers: *John Ramsbottom, Samuel W. Johnson, Sir John Aspinall, George Hughes* and *Sir Henry Fowler*. He also offered one alternate, *H. G. Ivatt*, who unlike all the others was still alive. Watkins liked this idea and so did Harrison when he was asked. So Watkins formally approved the names and instructed Harrison to go ahead and put the names on the engines.

According to the RCTS history of these locomotives, the patterns for the nameplates for the first three of the names were found in later years. I have not been able to establish where they are now (but I would dearly love to know, as they were my father's suggestion). Clearly Watkin's instruction was acted upon quickly before he was advised by the British Transport Commission (BTC) that the names would mean nothing to the general public and they should not be used.

And so, in direct response to the charge that engineers' names would not be recognised, Freddie Harrison and George Dow agreed to propose five more: *Sir Edmund Hillary, Sir John Hunt, Roger Bannister, Chris Chataway* and *Sir Gordon Richards*. The names of mountaineers came from a hotelier who wrote in to suggest them but five Irish names (for use on the 'Irish Mail'), suggested by H. C. Casserley, were not adopted.

A year later, in October 1955, George Dow was asked for yet another set of five names. He set down a memo which recounted the unhappy history of names for these five engines and some manuscript notes in George Dow's file clearly show that he briefly contemplated suggesting the names of Queens but found that all the best were already in use, primarily on Stanier Pacifics. In his memo he then noted that Clayton and members of the public had suggested the use of names of Dukes. By now it was known that the BR Standard Class 8 Pacific, *Duke of Gloucester*, was not going to be built in numbers, for the dieselisation programme was about to start.

And so he offered the *Dukes of York, Lancaster, Kent, Norfolk* and *Westminster*. He added "*I have not included the Duke of Edinburgh because our solitary Class 8 locomotive – being bigger and better than a Class 7 – is already named Duke of Gloucester*".

This didn't work either. Two weeks later the Director of Traffic Services, Edward Arkle, for whom George Dow now worked, asked for yet another list and five horses were submitted to the CRO, Watkins, on 20th October 1955. I mention the date because this submission, which failed as surely as had all the others, marked the end of any formal effort to name these five Britannias as a group. They were *Pegasus*, the mythical winged horse, *Bucephalus*, the horse of Alexander the Great, *Rosabella*, the favourite horse of Mary Queen of Scots, *Orelia*, the war-horse of Roderick, the last King of the Goths and *Xanthus*, the horse of Achilles. He added *Black Bess* and *Black Saladin*.

Quite separately from any work done by the naming committee and after the locomotives had entered service, 70045 was named *Lord Rowallan*, after the Chief Scout in 1957 and 70048 was named *The Territorial Army 1908-1958* in the fiftieth anniversary year of that army, the locomotive selected because it was the next due for a full overhaul.

Then a relief stationmaster popped up and suggested four names for 70046-70049: *Sir Edmund Hillary, Dr Vivian Fuchs, Sir Lennard (sic) Hutton*, and *Stanley Matthews*. The first two were thought to be of appeal, for they were modern-day heroes but once again the sportsmen were not favoured. There was a suggestion that T. S. Eliot be used instead of one of them but none of them floated and the idea was turned down.

And then Anthony Cox, of Stone, suggested the name of John Axon, a driver who had been awarded a posthumous George Cross in 1957 should be perpetuated. This was thought an excellent idea by all consulted except the public relations man, by now a man called Crawshaw, who was not a railwayman by inclination; he had just joined BR from one of the London evening newspapers. He thought that to agree with the suggestion would be to oblige BR to name engines after all of the railwaymen who had been awarded the George Cross. And for goodness' sake, why not? George Dow wrote to the Central Chancery of the Orders of Knighthood and established that three other railway GCs had been awarded. They were Benjamin Gimbert, James Nightall and Norman Tunna. He passed the names to Crawshaw but nothing came of it.

Eventually, 70046 was named *Anzac* in late 1959 and later still 70049 was named *Solway Firth* which fitted in very well with the five Scottish Britannias named after firths and which followed 70049 in numerical order.

The whole process of naming, one of the few for which records survive, shows that British Railways in the 1950s was prepared to take great care in naming its locomotives. A small and effective committee of intelligent and well-educated men spent much time trying to get it right, with names that were not ephemeral. Generally they were successful in producing fine-sounding names, even if they included that of the man who overthrew the Monarchy.

But after all this effort and long hours with reference books and in debate, 70047 was never named. If you have ever wondered why, you may rest assured it was not for want of trying!

TABLE 4.1
BRITANNIA PACIFICS
PROPOSED NAMES AND NAMES ACTUALLY CARRIED

No.	Proposed Name	Name Actually Carried	No.	Proposed Name	Name Actually Carried
70000	Great Britain	Britannia	70028	Royal Star	Royal Star
70001	Lord Hurcomb	Lord Hurcomb	70029	Shooting Star	Shooting Star
70002	Alfred the Great	Geoffrey Chaucer	70030	Albion	William Wordsworth
70003	Coeur-de-Lion	John Bunyan	70031	Andromeda	Byron
70004	Black Prince	William Shakespeare	70032	Ariadne	Tennyson
70005	Owen Glendower	John Milton	70033	Atalanta	Charles Dickens
70006	Hotspur	Robert Burns	70034	Aurora	Thomas Hardy
70007	John O'Gaunt	Coeur-de-Lion	70035	Boadicea	Rudyard Kipling
70008	Oliver Cromwell	Black Prince	70036	Hereward the Wake	Boadicea
70009	Iron Duke	Alfred the Great	70037	Robin Hood	Hereward the Wake
70010	Geoffrey Chaucer	Owen Glendower	70038	Ben Jonson	Robin Hood
70011	John Bunyan	Hotspur	70039	John Dryden	Sir Christopher Wren
70012	William Shakespeare	John of Gaunt	70040	Sir Christopher Wren	Clive of India
70013	John Milton	Oliver Cromwell	70041	Lord Byron	Sir John Moore
70014	Robert Burns	Iron Duke	70042	William Wordsworth	Lord Roberts
70015	Apollo	Apollo	70043	Charles Dickens	Lord Kitchener
70016	Ariel	Ariel	70044	Lord Tennyson	Earl Haig
70017	Arrow	Arrow	70045 [1]	Midland	Lord Rowallan
70018	Flying Dutchman	Flying Dutchman	70046	London & North Western	Anzac
70019	Lightning	Lightning	70047	Lancashire & Yorkshire	–
70020	Mercury	Mercury	70048 [2]	The Territorial Army 1908–1958	The Territorial Army 1908–1958
70021	North Star	Morning Star			
70022	Tornado	Tornado	70049 [3]	Furness	Solway Firth
70023	Venus	Venus	70050	North Stafford	Firth of Clyde
70024	Vulcan	Vulcan	70051	Firth of Forth	Firth of Forth
70025	Western Star	Western Star	70052	Firth of Tay	Firth of Tay
70026	Polar Star	Polar Star	70053	Moray Firth	Moray Firth
70027	Rising Star	Rising Star	70054	Dornoch Firth	Dornoch Firth

Other names proposed were   [1] John Ramsbottom   [2] George Hughes   [3] Sir Henry Fowler

92064 passing Stanley with a loaded coal train from Monckton washery formed by a rake of 21 ton mineral wagons on 19th January 1965.

Howard Forster

5. BR STANDARD STEAM CLASSES - PERFORMANCE IN SERVICE

5.1 Performance Logs

Since the publication of the earlier volumes in the BR Standards series, further examples of fine performances involving the Standard classes have come to light and a number of logs are reproduced in this section. Where possible, comparisons with non-steam traction have been included.

In Table 5.1, a comparison is made between a BR Standard Cl. 5 4-6-0, a Britannia Pacific and a B1 4-6-0 on the Ipswich-Liverpool St. section of the ER. The Britannia Pacifics had made a very successful debut on this route during 1951 but had been withdrawn temporarily towards the end of that year amid reports of the driving wheels moving on their axles whilst in service. During the absence of the Standard Pacifics, a number of different types shared the workings on the Liverpool St.-Norwich line. Two BR Class 5 4-6-0s were loaned from the LMR at this time and a run behind 73000, timed by Mr. M. Hedges, was recorded in the *Railway Magazine* by Mr. Cecil J. Allen in his celebrated *British Locomotive Practice and Performance* columns.

The engine gave a very creditable account of itself with seven bogies, 240 tons gross a load equal to that of the pre-WW2 *East Anglian* service and on a booking three minutes faster than that of the latter from Ipswich.

The speed restriction over the Stour bridge at Manningtree greatly had been eased by this time and 73000 passed the latter point punctually, the only loss of time being on the very sharp eight-minute allowance from there to Colchester. From there to Shenfield, the performance was noteworthy, two minutes being gained on the schedule with a time of 29min. 6sec. for the 31.5 miles, including some substantial gradients against the engine. Of special note was the rise in speed from 74 to 76mph on the level between Kelvedon and Witham, the maximum of no less than 67mph on the rising grades after Chelmsford and the speed of 61mph maintained up the bank as far as Shenfield. The frequent checks and a stop spoiled the conclusion of the run but the net time was calculated at no more than 75 minutes.

TABLE 5.1
ER Ipswich–Liverpool Street

Date Locomotive Class:		Late 1951 Cl.5 4-6-0			Early 1952 Britannia 4-6-2		Early 1952 ? B1 4-6-0		1958 Cl. 40 2,000 hp Diesel Electric			1958 Cl. 31 1,250 hp Diesel Electric		
No. Name Shed Load Recorder(s)		73000 - Stratford 7 coaches 228 tons tare 240 tons gross Mr. M. Hedges			70015 *Apollo* Stratford 8 coaches 263 tons tare 280 tons gross Mr. J. W. Turner		61050 - Norwich 8 coaches 283 tons tare 305 tons gross Mr. J. W. Turner		D205 (40005) - Norwich 9 coaches 310 tons tare 330 tons gross Mr. B. I Nathan			D5513 (31013) - Stratford 9 coaches 309 tons tare 330 tons gross Mr. F. G. Cockman		
Dist. Miles		Sched. min.	Actual min. sec.	Speed mph	Actual min. sec.	Speed mph	Actual min. sec.	Speed mph	Sched. min.	Actual min. sec.	Speed mph	Sched. min.	Actual min. sec.	Speed mph
00.0	IPSWICH	0	00 00	-	00 00	-	00 00	-	0	00 00	-	0	00 00	-
03.7	Milepost 65		07 07	39/38	06 48	43½	07 04	40½		06 00	47½		06 11	43
05.5	Bentley	8	09 07	65	08 39	76	09 03	-	8	07 53	66	9½	08 14	62
			p.w.s	*40	p.w.s	-	p.w.s	-		-	-		-	-
09.2	MANNINGTREE	13	12 57	44	12 18	-	13 10	-	11½	10 56	74	12½	11 38	68
12.7	Ardleigh		17 26	45/43	16 35	52	18 17	43		14 00	61½/71½		15 15	57/65
14.6	Parsons Heath		19 36	70	18 22	73	20 09	70½						
17.0	COLCHESTER	21	21 51	*44	20 29	-	22 26	*42	19½	17 42	*44	20½	19 24	*50
22.1	Marks Tey		27 46	-	25 41	-	28 28	-	25	22 02	66	26	24 46	64
26.5	Kelvedon		31 29	74	29 21	78	32 34	71		26 55	79		28 58	67
			-	-	p.w.s	35	-	-		-	-		-	-
30.1	WITHAM	34	34 24	76	33 35	-	35 29	75½	32	29 39	81	33	32 12	66
32.8	Hatfield Peverel		36 47	63	36 13	-	37 50	64		31 45	73_		34 44	61
36.6	New Hall		39 53	72	39 14	80½	41 06	74		34 33	80		38 09	67
			-	-	-	-	-	-		p.w.s	*28		-	-
39.0	CHELMSFORD	42	41 57	*64	41 12	*62	43 16	*61	40	37 59	*57	41	40 24	*60
45.1	Ingatestone		47 44	67/60	46 36	71	48 53	68		43 51	67/69		46 22	61
48.5	SHENFIELD	52	50 57	64/61	49 39	-	52 03	-	49	46 55	61	52	50 01	58
			-	-	-	-	-	-		-	-		sigs.	*43
49.5	Milepost 19_		-	-	50 34	64½	53 04	58½		47 50	59_		-	*41
			p.w.s	*30	p.w.s	-	p.w.s	-		-	-		sigs.	
53.7	Harold Wood		57 54	58	56 03	-	58 35	-		51 25	75		56 34	61½
58.7	Chadwell Heath	62	62 42	68	60 27	-	63 18	-	59	55 42	69	62	61 24	68
			p.w.s	*32	p.w.s	-	p.w.s	-		-	-		-	*60
61.4	Ilford		-	-	63 34	-	66 27	-		58 04	*63/68_		64 05	*60
			-	-	-	-	-	-		-	-		sigs.	*31
64.7	STRATFORD	69	70 59	-	67 39	-	70 37	-	65	61 09	*46	69	68 20	-
			sig.stop	-	-	-	-	-		sigs.	-		-	-
68.7	LIVERPOOL ST.	77	81 37	-	74 46	-	78 03	-	73	69 18	-	77	75 46	-
Net time min.		75			67¾		74		66½			72¼		

First published in *Railway Magazine*, Vol.98 No.610, Feb. 1952, p.116

First published in *Railway Magazine*, Vol.98, No.612, April 1952, p.261

First published in *Trains Illustrated*, Vol. XII, No.126, March 1959, p.134

First published in *Trains Illustrated*, Vol. XII, No.126, March 1959, p.134

* speed reduced by brakes

Following the return of the Britannia Pacifics to the route early in 1952, a run timed by Mr. J. W. Turner with 70015 *Apollo* is recorded in Table 5.1. The Pacific, with an eight-coach train of 280 tons gross, had a net time of 67¾ minutes for the 68.7 miles. After a relatively slow start, with 43½mph at Belstead, 76mph before the Manningtree slack, a recovery to 52mph up Dedham bank and 73mph after Parsons Heath, *Apollo* reached 78mph at Kelvedon only to be slowed to 35mph for permanent way repairs before Witham. Then came 80½mph at New Hall, an easing of 62mph through Chelmsford, a most energetic 71mph after Ingatestone and a grand 64½mph minimum at Ingrave. A string of checks followed but with a fast and unchecked finish from Stratford there was a gain of 2¼ min. on schedule to Liverpool St.

In column three, Table 5.1, a B1 4-6-0 made a creditable showing with an eight-coach train of some 305 tons gross. The 4-6-0 was doing 40½mph at Belstead summit but could not get above 43mph on Dedham bank after a more than usual slowing at Manningtree. Then followed 70½ after Parsons Heath, a slowing of 42 through Colchester, 71 at Kelvedon, 75½ at Witham, 64 up Blunts Hall bank, 74 at New Hall, 61 through Chelmsford, 68 after Ingatestone and 58½ at Ingrave, giving a time of 24min. 36sec. for the 27.4 miles from Marks Tey to Ingrave and getting the train through Shenfield on schedule. The numerous subsequent checks resulted in a loss of one minute but the net time for the run was no more than 74 minutes; this run was also timed by Mr. J. W. Turner.

Two runs with diesel power are the subject of the final two columns in Table 5.1, one with an English Electric Type 4, D205 (Cl.40) and the other with a Brush Type 2, D5513 (Cl.31). The performance of D205 was of a rousing description throughout. By Colchester, 1¾ minutes had been gained; then followed the good time over the 14½ miles from Marks Tey to New Hall. Despite the permanent way check before Chelmsford, the train was still two minutes early at Shenfield and four minutes early by Stratford. The terminus was reached in an actual time of 69min. 18sec. and a net time of 66½ minutes.

The run with the 1,250hp Brush diesel D5513 indicated that the 73-minute schedule could be kept with a nine-coach load but only provided that no checks were experienced. The actual time of 75min. 46sec. (net time 72½ minutes), was achieved by taking some liberties with the speed restrictions through both Colchester and Chelmsford.

Table 5.2 sets out three runs on the ex-MR Peak Forest section between Derby Midland and Manchester Central, now sadly no more; comparisons are between a Jubilee 4-6-0, a Britannia Pacific and a pair of Metrovick Type 2 diesel-electric units on the "XL Limit" timings introduced in 1957. From Derby as far as Rowsley, the line gradually rises mostly on slight gradients, the steepest being the 1½ miles up at 1 in 177 from Cromford. After Rowsley, however, the going became much tougher. Except for the three short ¼ mile descents before Bakewell, Monsal Dale and Miller's Dale, the ruling gradient from Rowsley almost to Miller's Dale was around 1 in 100. From the latter, point the three miles to Peak Forest summit rose even more steeply at 1 in 90. On such upgrades, a class 6 engine such as a Jubilee 4-6-0 had little to spare on the "XL limit" timings.

On the run with Jubilee 4-6-0 45616 *Malta GC*, time was kept to Matlock, with the usual 30mph Ambergate slack, at no higher speed than 60mph. Up the 1 in 100 from Rowsley, speed did not fall below 47mph and again time was kept despite a permanent way slowing before Rowsley. From Miller's Dale, excellent work ensued up the 1 in 90 with the attainment of 45mph at Peak Forest. Following the usual restrained speed down to Chinley, two maxima of over 80mph were noted between there and Cheadle Heath. Manchester Central was reached three minutes early against schedule and in a net time of around 32¼ minutes for the 30 miles from Miller's Dale.

The superior performance in the run with Britannia Pacific 70014 *Iron Duke* is apparent. A speed of 70mph was attained at Belper before the Ambergate slack and over 1½ min was gained to Matlock. From the standing start at Miller's Dale, the Britannia accelerated up the 1 in 90 to Peak Forest to 53mph. The final stretch of this run had a net time of of 31½ minutes for the 30 miles from Miller's Dale to Central which gave a net gain on schedule of 9½ minutes on schedule and an arrival 1½ minutes early.

Also included in Table 5.2 for interest is a run with a pair of Metrovick Type 2s, D5710/4, on the 12.25pm St. Pancras-Manchester, another "XL Limit" timing. On leaving Derby, the controller position was gradually advanced to eight notches out of a maximum of ten but eased back to seven after about one mile. Speed rose to 67mph at Belper but great respect was shown to the slack at Ambergate as were the various restrictions between there and Matlock. From Rowsley, the two locomotives were driven all out and speed was sustained at 55½ – 56mph up the long 1 in 100 gradients Signal checks after Miller's Dale, Chinley South Junction, Hazel Grove and Chorlton-cum-Hardy meant the run ended disappointingly although a maximum of 82mph was recorded at Hazel Grove.

Table 5.3 gives four runs in the the southbound direction on the Peak Forest route between Manchester Central and Derby Midland. The climb began at Cheadle Heath but was more varied than the ascent from the south. It began with the 1¼ miles at 1 in 100, easing to 1¾ miles at 1 in 142 to Milepost 178, Bramhall Moor Lane, steepened to 1 in 100-110 to the north portal of Disley tunnel, easing again to 1 in 132 and then ¾ mile level to just short of New Mills South Jct. After this, there is a practically unbroken nine miles at 1 in 90 past Chinley to Peak Forest; this is followed by a downhill run all the way to Derby.

The first three runs in Table 5.3 with the eight-coach "Palatine" compares the work of a Standard Cl. 5 4-6-0, a Class 6 Jubilee 4-6-0 and a Britannia Pacific; the last run details the return run with the Metrovick Type 2s, D5710/4 featured in Table 5.2. The Jubilee 4-6-0, 45589 *Gwalior*, was away with the smartest start but with the help of a higher than usual speed over Throstle Nest Jct. speed was 50mph at the south end of Disley tunnel and 37mph was maintained up the 1 in 90 before the Chinley stop, reached in 1½ minutes inside schedule. From Chinley, there was an acceleration up the 1 in 90 to 39mph at Peak Forest giving a net gain of 1½ minutes to Miller's Dale although a signal check made the actual time ¾ more. Another two minutes was gained down to Matlock and the net time of 19 minutes from Matlock to Derby gave the crew a total credit of 5½ minutes on the run.

With Britannia Pacific 70014 *Iron Duke*, more caution was shown over the Throstle Nest curve and, from this slack

73080 passes through Bromley South on the down "Kentish Belle" from Victoria to Ramsgate in the summer of 1958. The locomotive attacks the climb of 1 in 95 to Bickley Jct. in the final year of the all Pullman "Kentish Belle". This train ceased to operate in September 1958 prior to the Kent Coast electrification in the following year.

Kenneth Wightman

Now the preserve of Cl.60 and 66 diesels with bogie hopper mineral wagons, a very filthy unidentified Britannia coasts downhill past Peak Forest North signal box and the Buxton Lime Firms Company loading hoppers with a Manchester Central to St. Pancras express in August 1958.

David Kelso

TABLE 5.2
LMR Derby Midland–Manchester Central

				mid-1959 7.55 am St. Pancras–Manchester (*The Palatine*) Britannia Pacific 70014 *Iron Duke* Trafford Park 8 coaches 282 tons tare 300 tons gross H. Edwards/B. Thomas Mr. Malcolm R. Palmer		mid-1959 12.25 pm St. Pancras–Manchester Type 2 Metrovick DE D5710 and D5714 Derby 6 coaches 198 tons tare 210 tons gross Lane/not recorded Mr. O. S. Nock		mid-1959 7.55 am St. Pancras–Manchester (*The Palatine*) Jubilee 4-6-0 45616 *Malta G.C.* Kentish Town 8 coaches 273 tons tare 290 tons gross H. Edwards/B. Thomas Mr. Malcolm R. Palmer	

Date / Train / Locomotive Class / No. / Shed / Load / Driver/Fireman / Recorder(s)

Dist. Miles		Sched. min.	Actual min. sec.	Speed mph	Actual min. sec.	Speed mph	Actual min. sec.	Speed mph
00.0	DERBY MIDLAND	0	00 00	–	00 00	–	00 00	–
00.7	Nottingham Road		02 05	43	–	–	02 20	36
03.2	*Little Eaton Jct.*		05 18	55	–	–	05 49	53
05.2	Duffield		07 15	64	07 11	64	08 02	56
07.8	Belper		09 35	70	09 31	67	10 42	58
10.3	Ambergate	13	12 28	★28	12 40	★20	13 37	★30
12.3	Whatstandwell		15 18	62	–		16 05	54
15.2	Cromford		18 08	66	18 52	55(max)	19 04	60
16.0	Matlock Bath		18 50	60	–	–	19 50	56
17.1	MATLOCK	22	20 20	–	21 27	–	21 24	–
02.2	Darley Dale		03 03	58/61	03 37	66	03 58	★
04.5	Rowsley	6	05 28	★50/44	05 55	★45	07 10	28
07.8	Bakewell		09 43	51	10 07	56	11 30	48/44
10.2	Great Longstone		12 42	47	12 37	55½	14 33	49
11.6	Monsal Dale		14 23	53½	14 00	64/57	16 14	47
14.3	MILLERS DALE	20	17 54	–	17 23	–	19 42	55
01.8	*Peak Forest Jct.*		03 50	39	sigs	–	04 05	37
04.6	Peak Forest	8	07 28	53	08 38	50	08 02	45
08.2	Chapel-en-le-Frith		–	–	sig. stop	–	–	–
10.2	CHINLEY	14	11 38	60	–	–	12 12	65
			13 30	64/58	16 58	–	13 53	72/★54
12.9	*New Mills South Jct*	16½	15 45	78	19 27	–	16 08	81
14.7	*Disley Box*		–	–	20 49	–	–	–
18.0	*Hazel Grove*		–	85	23 21	82	–	–
18.7	*Milepost 178*		20 12	82	–	–	20 44	76/82
			p.w.s.	★26	sigs.	–	sigs.	★50
22.0	CHEADLE HEATH	24½	23 52	50	27 09	–	23 40	50
24.3	Didsbury		–	–	29 17	75	–	–
24.9	Withington		26 40	75	–	–	26 30	69
26.4	*Chorlton Junction*	29	27 52	75	–	–	27 48	68
			sigs.	–	–	–	–	–
26.9	Chorlton-cum-Hardy		–	–	31 13	76	–	–
			–	–	sigs.	★10	–	–
28.5	*Throstle Nest E. Jct.*	32	31 00	★	34 53	–	30 00	★
30.0	MANCHESTER C.	36	34 30	–	38 49	–	33 02	–

★ Speed restriction

First published in *Trains Illustrated*, Vol. XIII, No.138, March 1960 p.178	First published in *Railway Magazine*, Vol. 106, No.715, November 1960, p.791	First published in *Trains Illustrated*, Vol. XIII, No.138, March 1960 p.178

TABLE 5.3
Manchester Central-LMR Derby Midland

Date	mid-1959	mid-1959	mid-1959	mid-1959
Train	2.25pm Manchester Central - St. Pancras *(The Palatine)*	2.25pm Manchester Central - St. Pancras *(The Palatine)*	2.25pm Manchester Central - St. Pancras *(The Palatine)*	5.55pm Manchester Central - St. Pancras
Locomotive Class	Jubilee 4-6-0	Britannia Pacific	BR 5 4-6-0	Type 2 Metrovick DE
No.	45589 *Gwalior*	70014 *Iron Duke*	73073	D5714+D5710
Shed	Leeds Holbeck	Trafford Park	Sheffield Millhouses	Derby
Load	8 coaches 272 tons tare 290 tons gross	8 coaches 274 tons 290 tons gross	8 coaches 276 tons tare 295 tons gross	9 coaches 299 tons tare 320 tons gross
Driver/Fireman	H. Edwards/B. Thomas	H. Edwards/B. Thomas	H. Edwards/B. Thomas	C. Stokes
Recorder(s)	Mr Malcolm R. Palmer	Mr. Malcolm R. Palmer	Mr Malcolm R. Palmer	Mr. O. S. Nock

Dist. Miles		Sched. min.	Actual min. sec.	Speed mph	Actual min. sec.	Speed mph	Actual min. sec.	Speed mph	Actual min. sec.	Speed mph
00.0	MANCHESTER CENTRAL	0	00 00	-	00 00	-	00 00	-	00 00	-
01.5	*Throstlenest E. Jct.*	4	03 16	48	04 30	31	03 47	43	03 30	*15
03.6	*Chorlton Jct.*	7	05 50	50	07 45	40	06 30	51	06 35	54
05.8	Didsbury		08 08	58	10 32	50	08 48	55½	-	-
			-	-	p.w.s.	*27	p.w.s.	-	-	62½/60
08.0	CHEADLE HEATH	12	10 42	60/62	14 30	47	12 42	46	10 52	62
11.3	*Milepost* 178		14 34	50/57	18 50	51/60	16 57	49/56	-	-
12.0	*Hazel Grove*		-	-	-	-	-	-	15 07	54
15.0	*Disley Box*		-	-	-	-	-	-	19 10	43
17.1	*New Mills South Jct.*	23	22 08	46	25 20	53	24 09	52	21 30	46½
18.9	Buxworth		24 34	37	27 22	51	26 30	43	24 10	39
			-	-	-	-	-	-	sigs.	-
19.8	CHINLEY	28	26 22	-	28 53	-	28 15	-	26 35	-
02.0	Chapel-en-le Frith		04 28	37	03 55	45	04 35	37	04 15	37
			-	-	-	-	-	-	p.w.s.	*20
05.6	Peak Forest	11	10 28	39/57	09 22	43/68	10 29	36/68	11 50	34/60
			sigs.	*40	-	-	-	-	-	-
08.4	*Peak Forest Jct.*		13 50	*40	12 05	*40	13 18	*42	-	-
10.2	MILLERS DALE	17	16 15	-	14 22	-	15 41	-	17 12	-
02.7	Monsal Dale		04 12	68	04 12	69	04 18	67	-	-
04.1	Great Longstone		05 28	66½/72	05 23	69/75	05 30	68½/72	-	-
06.5	Bakewell		07 28	*48/75	07 22	*56/80	07 28	*54/76	07 48	66(max)
09.8	Rowsley	11½	10 16	*50	10 01	*45	10 10	*52	11 12	*45
12.1	Darley Dale		12 10	72½	12 01	71	12 22	62	13 31	60
14.3	MATLOCK	16½	14 38	-	14 23	-	14 58	-	16 15	-
01.9	Cromford		03 30	56	03 41	56	03 48	53	03 07	-
04.8	Whatstandwell		06 22	65	06 35	65	06 50	62	-	-
06.7	AMBERGATE	9	08 25	*28	08 53	*28	09 04	*20	09 12	*20
			p.w.s.	*22	-	-	-	-	-	-
09.3	Belper		11 45	54	12 07	66	12 18	64	12 48	62
11.9	Duffield		14 20	70½	14 17	78	14 34	75/83	15 00	70
13.9	*Little Eaton Jct.*		16 00	*76	15 47	82	15 59	81	16 43	70
			sigs.	*36	sigs.	*36	sigs.	*39	-	-
16.4	Nottingham Road		18 22	-	18 12	-	19 03	-	-	-
17.1	DERBY MIDLAND	19½	20 08	-	19 50	-	20 41	-	21 12	-
* Speed restriction			First published in *Trains Illustrated*, Vol. XIII, No. 138, March 1960 p.178		First published in *Trains Illustrated*, Vol. XIII, No. 138, March 1960 p.178		First published in *Trains Illustrated*, Vol. XIII, No. 138, March 1960 p.178		First published in *Railway Magazine*, Vol. 106, No.715, Nov. 1960, p.794	

recovery was slow and hampered by a permanent way check at Heaton Mersey. A very vigorous effort was put in from Disley onwards, speed up the 1 in 90 still over 50mph before steam was shut off for the Chinley stop; net time to this point was 27 minutes. From Chinley, 45mph was attained on the 1 in 90 and a minimum of 43mph at Peak Forest, leading to a gain of over 2½ minutes to Miller's Dale. There was a further two-minute gain on the next stretch including an 80mph maximum before the Rowsley curve slack. An 82mph maximum was achieved before Derby, cut short by a signal check before Nottingham Road. Despite the 82mph maximum, the net time for this part of the run was 19¼ minutes, indicating this easily was the tightest part of the schedule.

In the third column, a creditable performance by Standard Cl. 5 4-6-0 73073 is recorded. After the Heaton Mersey check, the Cl. 5 did well to accelerate to 49mph by Bramhall Moor Lane and thence to 56mph on the short Disley level. The minimum at Buxworth was also well above *Gwalior's* 37mph; net time to Chinley was $26\frac{3}{4}$ minutes. Up the 1 in 90 to Peak Forest, a sustained 37-36mph was enough to achieve a gain of $1\frac{1}{4}$ min to Miller's Dale. The most outstanding feat of the 4-6-0 was the 81-83mph maintained from Duffield to Little Eaton Jct., although even so, the Derby arrival was one minute late.

The final run in Table 5.3 with the Metrovick Type 2 diesel-electric units was on the 5.55pm Manchester-St. Pancras. From Throstle Nest Jct., where the 15mph speed restriction was carefully observed, the controller positions were at the maximum 10 to Chorlton Jct., eight from Didsbury, nine at Heaton Mersey and 10 once again from Cheadle Heath. Speed was held at 54mph over the easier stretch leading to Hazel Grove station but by now the train was well ahead of time and the controller was eased back to notch seven for the passage through Disley tunnel. On this occasion, there was a permanent way slack to 20mph extending about halfway through Dove Holes tunnel but time was kept, nevertheless. After this, it was a case of observing speed restrictions rather than obtaining high power output from the locomotives. Some smart running was needed at the finish down the line from Ambergate to Derby. Notch 10 was used to Belper and nine thence to Duffield; after that notch seven kept the train running steadily at 70mph on the gradual descent to Derby.

Table 5.4 gives details of a run with a Standard Cl. 2MT 2-6-0, 78041, on the 3.25pm Liverpool Exchange-Preston, sometime in 1957. Although the train was a three-coach affair weighing less than 100 tons, a speed of 70mph was achieved at

Maghull on the first leg to Ormskirk enabling the train to arrive comfortably within schedule. Further speeds in the upper 60s were noted at Croston and Midge Hall during the subsequent run to Preston. The recorder, '45671' also known as Mr. A. J. Powell, was of the opinion that, given a suitable road, the engine with its small 5ft. diameter wheels could have kept up a speed of 65-70mph all day.

The cross-country service from Salisbury to Portsmouth was still steam-hauled in 1963 and is featured in Table 5.5. Although the line as far as Southampton is fairly straightforward, the road from there to Fareham, winds around the shores of Southampton Water with a number of severe curves and sharp changes of gradient. The log describes a run with Standard Cl.4 2-6-0 76005 on the 10.30am Cardiff-Portsmouth and Southsea between Salisbury and Cosham. From a start of four minutes late, 76005 recovered all the lost time and more to reach Fareham three minutes early. Proceeding towards Romsey, the start from Salisbury is difficult. There are slacks at Tunnel Jct. where the route diverges from the main line to Waterloo and, again at Milford Jct., before the 1 in 150 climb can be attempted. Nevertheless, 76005 had attained 56mph at Alderbury Jct., after which there is an unbroken descent through Dean and Dunbridge to Romsey and a speed of 72mph was recorded at the latter point. From Romsey, a further fast getaway was made to achieve 66mph at Nursling. On to Fareham, 76005 had little difficulty in gaining over three minutes on schedule and a speed of 45mph on the climb to Swanwick was impressive.

Table 5.6 details a series of runs made in the autumn of 1962 over a route rarely worked by steam at that time. Because of heavy engineering work in progress at Swaythling, some Sunday Bournemouth expresses were diverted via the Portsmouth Direct Line. Three runs between Havant and

TABLE 5.4
LMR Liverpool Exchange-Preston

Date	1957?
Train	3.25 pm Liverpool Exchange-Preston
Locomotive Class	Cl. 2MT 2-6-0
No.	78041
Shed	Bank Hall (Liverpool)
Load	3 coaches
	84 tons tare
	95 tons gross
Driver/Fireman	Wood (Bank Hall)/not recorded

Dist. Miles		Sched. min.	Actual Time min. sec.	Speed mph	Regulator	Cut-off %
00.0	LIVERPOOL Exchange dep.	0	00 00		$\frac{1}{2}$	25
			sigs.		-	-
01.5	Sandhills	3	03 33	42/40	$\frac{1}{2}$	22
			p.w.s.	-	-	-
03.6	Walton Jct.	6	07 14	44/13	$\frac{1}{2}$	45/35
04.9	Aintree	8	09 26	38/51	$\frac{1}{2}$	25
			sigs.	-	-	-
07.4	Maghull		12 04	70/50	$\frac{1}{2}$	35/30
10.2	Town Green		14 58	58/60	$\frac{1}{2}$	30
12.2	ORMSKIRK arr.	18	17 30	-	-	-
00.0	ORMSKIRK dep.	0	00 00	-	First Valve	40/25
02.6	Burscough Jct.	4	03 31	61	Shut	-
05.5	Rufford		06 25	58	First Valve	25
08.1	Croston		08 50	66/62	First Valve	25
10.9	Midge Hall		11 25	67/58	Shut	-
12.6	Moss Lane Jct.	15	13 45	40/45	First Valve	40/27
13.7	Lostock Hall		15 22	32	Shut	-
			sigs.	-	-	-
14.6	Todd Lane Jct.	18	17 34	24/50	First Valve	30
			sigs.	-	-	-
16.6	PRESTON arr.	21	21 05	-	-	-

First Published in *Trains Illustrated*, Vol.XI, No.118, July 1958, p.352.

TABLE 5.5
SR Salisbury-Cosham

Date	Saturday 11th May 1963
Train	10.30 am Cardiff-Portsmouth and Southsea
Locomotive Class	Cl. 4MT 2-6-0
No.	76005
Shed	Salisbury
Load	6 coaches
	190 tons tare
	210 tons gross
Recorder	Mr. N. Harvey

Dist. Miles		Sched. min.	Actual Time min. sec.	Speed mph
00.0	SALISBURY	0	00 00	-
01.1	Tunnel Jct.		03 30	Slack
05.0	Alderbury Jct.		09 30	56
09.0	Dean		13 20	68/70 max.
12.8	Dunbridge		16 47	68/72 max.
16.5	ROMSEY	25	20 33	
03.6	Nursling		05 25	66 max/slack
05.4	Redbridge		07 15	35
07.2	Millbrook		10 15	-
08.1	SOUTHAMPTON CENTRAL	16	11 53	-
01.1	Northam Jct.		03 25	-
01.9	St. Denys		05 40	-
02.7	Bitterne		07 08	Slack/20
05.0	Sholin		10 45	-
06.8	Netley		13 15	54
08.9	Burlesdon		15 35	53
10.9	Swanwick		18 00	45 min.
14.6	FAREHAM	27	23 36	
03.2	Portchester		05 15	54/56
05.8	COSHAM	9	08 40	-

First published in *Railway World*, Vol. 24, No.279, August 1963, p.302.

70

Guildford, recorded by Mr. I. J. Turnbull, compared the work of West Country Pacifics, both rebuilt and unrebuilt, with that of a Standard Cl.5 4-6-0; also included for interest is a log of an SR Maunsell Schools 4-4-0 on a Portsmouth-Waterloo service in the pre-electrification days of the mid-1930s, timed by Mr. O. S. Nock.

The route traverses some heavy gradients. There is a continuous ascent from Havant to the summit just south of Buriton tunnel. At first the incline varies from 1 in 147 and 1 in 120 to Rowlands Castle. After Idsworth crossing, there is almost a mile at 1 in 100 followed by 1¾ miles at 1 in 80. Then comes a fast descent through Petersfield and a further steep downgrade near Liss. Next is the climb to the flanks of the Hindhead ridge, near Haslemere, including two miles at 1 in 80 just after Liss, four miles of a more gradual rise past Liphook and a final two miles at 1 in 100 to the summit.

The first run with unrebuilt West Country Pacific 34102 *Lapford* was from a dead start at Havant. Good work was done up to Buriton tunnel with the 400ton gross load but a slight signal check preceded the approach to Petersfield. After that, no higher speed than 60mph was attained on the racing descent to Stodham crossing and as a result, speed dropped to a minimum of 40mph on the sharp ascent at 1 in 80 after Liss. *Lapford* was not pressed on the easier stretch past Liphook but speed did not fall below 40mph on the pull up to Haslemere summit. The descent to Guildford includes much curvature and required copious brake applications.

In Column 2, the rebuilt West Country Pacific 34021 *Dartmoor* did not do so well in the uphill work and there was some restrained running between Buriton tunnel and Liss. Both drivers were however improving on the point-to-point times laid down for these diverted services.

The third run had the advantage of passing Havant without stopping, albeit at very slow speed. As a result, Standard Cl.5 4-6-0 73087 *Linette* gained some two minutes on the Pacifics to Rowlands Castle. 73087 remained about this much ahead of *Dartmoor* throughout to Haslemere and in consideration of the moderate speed between Petersfield and Liss the final climb was creditable. The engine also had a clear road through to Guildford and without exceeding 72mph managed to gain seven minutes on the special schedule over the 36.1 miles from Havant.

TABLE 5.6
SR/Southern Railway Havant-Guildford

Date Train Locomotive Class No. Name Shed Load Recorder(s)		SR Autumn 1962 Bournemouth- Waterloo Service (Diverted) WC Pacific Unrebuilt 34102 *Lapford* Bournemouth 370 tons tare 400 tons gross Mr. I. J. Turnbull		SR Autumn 1962 Bournemouth- Waterloo Service (Diverted) WC Pacific Rebuilt 34021 *Dartmoor* Eastleigh 367 tons tare 395 tons gross Mr. I. J. Turnbull		SR Autumn 1962 Bournemouth- Waterloo Service (Diverted) BR Cl. 5 4-6-0 73087 *Linette* Nine Elms 363 tons tare 395 tons gross Mr. I. J. Turnbull		Southern Railway 1930s Portsmouth-Waterloo Pre-Electric Service Schools 4-4-0 925 *Cheltenham* Fratton 360 tons tare 395 tons gross Mr. O. S. Nock		
Dist. Miles		Sched. min.†	Actual min. sec.	Speed mph	Actual min. sec.	Speed mph	Actual min. sec.	Speed mph	Sched. min	Actual min. sec.	Speed mph
00.0	HAVANT	0	00 00	–	00 00	–	★00 00	–	0	★00 00	–
03.1	Rowlands Castle		06 53	38½	07 08	38	04 50	45		05 20	41
05.2	*Idsworth Crossing*		09 41	47	10 12	44	07 48	47		08 10	45
08.1	*Milepost 58¼*		14 02	29	15 21	25	12 58	25		13 16	24½
			sigs	–		65	–	–		–	–
11.5	PETERSFIELD	20	18 44	52	19 19	61	16 59	64	18	17 13	75
14.9	Liss		22 10	60/57	22 44	61	20 21	58		19 51	83½/74
17.1	*Milepost 49¼*		24 51	40	25 19	41½	23 11	36		21 55	52½
19.5	Liphook		28 02	47	28 21	56	26 25	60		24 24	64½
23.6	HASLEMERE	35	33 08	40	32 59	35	30 52	39	31½	28 25	48½
			–	71 max	–	69 max	–	72		p.w.s.	74 max
27.9	Witley		38 10	–	38 13	–	35 36	69		32 48	30
			–	–	sigs.	–	–	–		–	65 max
31.9	Godalming		42 45	–	44 09	–	39 23	60		37 18	–
			–	–	sigs.	–	–	–		p.w.s.	–
36.1	GUILDFORD	52	49 07	–	53 04	–	44 57	–	45½	★43 02	–

★ Passing times
† Schedule of diverted Bournemouth trains

First published in *Railway Magazine*, Vol. 110, No. 760, August 1964, p.626.

70023 *Venus* at Shap Wells on 16th June 1963 with a Manchester to Glasgow working, assisted at the rear up to Shap summit by a long standing resident of Tebay depot, LMS Fowler side-windowed cab 2-6-4T 42424. This location was very popular with photographers in the latter years of the steam era due to the peace and quiet, broken only by the call of the curlews. Northbound trains whistled for banking assistance as they approached Tebay from the south. Trains generally laboured slowly up the 1 in 75 incline, an added bonus to good photography. The location is now changed completely and apart from the railway it is now a conifer plantation with the M6 motorway in the background.

Noel Machell

The fourth run, on the pre-electrification service was in a different class. It was made by a crack driver working over his regular route with an engine in first-class order, Maunsell Schools 925 *Cheltenham*. The 4-4-0 was surpassed only by the unrebuilt West Country Pacific on the ascent to Buriton. The point-to-point times of the 90 minute Portsmouth non-stop services were 18 minutes to Petersfield, $31\frac{1}{2}$ minutes to Haslemere and $45\frac{1}{2}$ minutes to Guildford, which timing was kept by the 4-6-0 *Linette*.

The Schools run was made on a Sunday however and because of the signal checks at the early stages, Havant had been passed $4\frac{1}{2}$ minutes late .With three permanent way checks to come, the driver was going hard to make up some of the lost time. One of the features of the run was his method of working the engine. Throughout from Portsmouth to Waterloo, the cut-off was unchanged at 29%; all variations in power output were made by adjusting the regulator, yet nothing more than the first valve was used. This method of working seemed to suit the engine to perfection and once through Buriton tunnel some tremendous running began. Petersfield was passed at 75mph, and a top speed of $83\frac{1}{2}$mph was reached at Stodham crossing. This resulted in a minimum of $52\frac{1}{2}$mph up the sharp rise beyond Liss. There was a final acceleration to $64\frac{1}{2}$ mph beyond Liphook and the final climb to Haslemere did not lower the speed below $48\frac{1}{2}$mph. By this time, 925 had gained $2\frac{1}{2}$ minutes on the BR5 4-6-0 but the permanent way checks before Guildford reduced the advantage to less than two minutes from Havant.

The series of logs in Table 5.7 gives details of runs on the former London Tilbury & Southend line. Comparisons are made between three Cl.4 2-6-4 Tank engine classes, the Stanier three-cylinder class specifically designed for the route and introduced in 1934, the Fairburn two-cylinder class introduced in 1945 and the BR Standard class design of 1951; also included is a run behind a Brush Type 2 diesel-electric Cl.31. The logs were first published in an article by Mr. P. I. Paton in the April 1962 issue of *Railway World*. All were timed on the 9.05am up 'flyer' with a 46-minute booking from Westcliffe-on-Sea to Fenchurch St.

From Westcliffe-on-Sea, the gradient is downhill through to Chalkwell at 1 in 94 making for a fast start. The line levels through Leigh-on-Sea followed by a short stretch at 1 in 150 to Benfleet. From Pitsea up to Laindon, the line climbs for some three miles at 1 in 110/132 after which it is downgrade at similar inclines through West Horndon followed by another rise to Upminster at 1 in 198/165/132. From there, the line is mainly downgrade before a level stretch to Barking followed by almost level track or rising gently to Fenchurch St. apart from a short 1 in 105 from Bromley to Gas Factory Jct.

The first run in Table 5.7 features Stanier 3-cylinder tank engine 42507. The train had an excellent start from Westcliffe down the 1 in 90 to Chalkwell where speed usually was around 50mph. 42507 made to the best start of the four, attaining 53 by Chalkwell, 64 at Pitsea, and a good minimum of 50mph to Laindon. Thereafter, the engine ran fast to Upney before easing for Barking with maxima of 78mph at West

Horndon and 75mph at Dagenham East. A good recovery was made from the Barking slack with 60mph after Plaistow and despite a concluding check, 42507 was into Fenchurch St. 5½ minutes ahead of time.

Run No.2 was the best of four made by Mr. Harry Blackshaw in Whit week 1958. The run was all the more remarkable for having to contend with no less than six temporary speed restrictions .After attaining 67mph before and passing Pitsea in the fast time of 9min. 19sec., two slowings were encountered on Laindon bank. Recovering from these, 78mph was reached at West Horndon and speed had not dropped below 70mph on the rise to Upminster when the train was braked for the next slack. The acceleration from 67mph at Dagenham East to 73mph after Becontree was notable. Two more slowings in the Barking area and another beyond Stepney did not prevent a 4½ minute early arrival in a net time of 38 minutes.

Run No. 3 with BR Standard Cl.4 80133 running in reverse was the only one Mr. Paton ever recorded where even time was attained, despite a slowing, between Laindon and West Horndon. The initial start was not unduly fast but 71mph

before Pitsea was another record for Mr. Paton. The slowing beyond Laindon prevented a fast descent to West Horndon but to fall to only 70mph at Upminster after passing West Horndon at 71mph was good work. Even time was attained by Dagenham East, passed at 78mph, 23.5 miles in 23min. 25sec. A severe check followed just after Becontree, not surprisingly as the train was running seven minutes ahead of time in the path of the preceding train. On this fine run, the 24.4 miles from Chalkwell to Becontree were reeled off in 22min. 38sec. at average speed of 64½mph.

The Brush Type 2 diesel-electric D5501 run in column 4 was comparable in performance to those of the 2-6-4 tank engines and gave a net time to Fenchurch St. of 39½ minutes, equivalent to the first run with the three-cylinder 42507. A speed of 75mph at West Horndon was preceded by a more than usual drop in speed on the climb to Laindon. The time of 9min. 5sec. from West Horndon to Upney with a maximum of 77mph was again a near tie with that of 42507.

The authors are indebted to Mr. D. Landau for runs in Table 5.8 from his collection featuring Standard Cl.4 2-6-4 tank

TABLE 5.7

ER Westcliff on Sea-Fenchurch Street
Four runs with the 9.05am Southend on Sea-Fenchurch Street (late 1950s/early 1960s)

Locomotive Class			Stanier 3-cylinder 2-6-4 Tank Engine		Fairburn 2-cylinder 2-6-4 Tank Engine		BR Cl. 4 2-cylinder 2-6-4 Tank Engine		Brush Type 2 A1A-A1A DE	
No.			42507		42679		80133		D5501	
Shed			Shoeburyness		Shoeburyness		Shoeburyness		Stratford	
Load			8 coaches		8 coaches		8 coaches		8 coaches	
			229 tons tare		229 tons tare		229 tons tare		229 tons tare	
			260 tons gross		260 tons gross		260 tons gross		260 tons gross	
Recorder(s)			Mr. P. I. Paton		Mr. H. Blackshaw		Mr. P. I. Paton		Mr. P. I. Paton	

		Sch. min.	Actual min. sec.	Speed mph	Actual min. sec.	Speed mph	Actual min. sec.	Speed mph	Actual min. sec.	Speed mph
00.00	WESTCLIFF-ON-SEA	0	00 00	–	00 00	–	00 00	–	00 00	–
00.95	Chalkwell		01 54	53	02 00	53	02 08	50	01 56	51
02.30	Leigh-on-Sea		03 30	58	03 30	61	03 45	58	03 42	54
05.70	Benfleet		06 56	62	06 47	65/66	07 04	65/66	07 15	61/62
08.30	PITSEA		09 36	64	09 19	62/67	09 32	71/55	09 55	66
			–	–	p.w.s.	★38			–	–
12.00	Laindon		14 04	50	14 15	47	13 28	58	14 29	50
			–	–	–	–	p.w.s	★–	–	–
15.70	West Horndon		17 33	78	17 41	78	16 49	71	17 57	75
19.60	UPMINSTER		20 48	68	20 59	70	20 09	73/70	21 17	66
			–	–	p.w.s.	★41			–	–
21.15	Hornchurch		22 12	70/73	23 07	53/61	21 31	72/74	22 41	71/74
23.50	Dagenham East		24 13	75	25 27	67	23 25	78	24 39	77
25.25	Becontree		25 36	74	26 53	71/73	24 46	75	26 01	74
			–	–	–	–	sigs. severe	★	–	–
26.40	Upney		26 36	–	27 52	–	26 48	–	27 02	–
			p.w.s.	–	p.w.s.	★25	–	–	p.w.s.	39
27.30	BARKING		28 21	28	29 41	–	29 18	37	28 22	–
			–	–	p.w.s.	★30	p.w.s.	25	sigs.	–
28.60	East Ham		30 33	47	32 07	46	31 48	37	31 13	31
30.30	Plaistow		32 30	58/60	34 01	59	34 10	52	33 50	51/53
			–	–	–	–	sigs.	44	–	–
31.80	Bromley		33 57	–	35 30	–	36 09	–	35 26	–
32.10	Gas Factory Jct.	40	34 45	–	36 21	–	37 05	–	36 24	–
									p.w.s.	–
33.10	Stepney (East)	42	36 29	41	37 44	44	38 58	–	39 22	–
			–	–	p.w.s	–	p.w.s.	–	p.w.s.	–
34.85	FENCHURCH STREET	46	40 40	–	41 29	–	44 06	–	45 07	–
34.85	Net time (minutes)	46	39½	–	38	–	38	–	39½	–

First published in *Railway World*, Vol.23, No.263, April 1962, p.117.

TABLE 5.8

LMR/ER Potton–Cambridge

Date		3rd January 1953			30th May 1953		
Train		Oxford–Bletchley–Cambridge			Oxford–Bletchley–Cambridge		
Locomotive Class		BR Class 4 2-6-4 Tank			BR Class 4 2-6-4 Tank		
No.		80043			80042		
Shed		Bletchley			Bletchley		
Load: coaches/tons tare/tons gross		4 + horsebox/127/132			4/118/125		
Recorder		Mr. D. Twibell			Mr. D. Twibell		

Dist. Miles		Sched. min.	Actual Min. sec.	Speed mph	Sched. min.	Actual min. sec.	Speed mph
00.0	POTTON	0	00 00	–	0	00 00	–
02.6	Gamlingay		03 55	56 $\frac{1}{2}$/60		04 40	–
			–	59$\frac{1}{2}$/51$\frac{1}{2}$		05 40	–
			–			06 07	–
07.2	Old North Road		08 55	68_/82		13 31	–
			–	–		15 00	sig. stop
			–			19 43	–
12.5	Lords Bridge		13 12	72$\frac{1}{2}$/74$\frac{1}{2}$		25 15	79/78
			18 22	sig. stop		30 30	sig. stop
			18 40	–		31 48	–
	Cambridge Goods Yard		20 20	–		–	–
17.9	CAMBRIDGE	27	22 50	–	27	34 25	–

SR Tonbridge–Redhill

Date		22nd February 1964			27th October 2008		
Train		2.15 pm Tonbridge – Redhill			Composite of three runs		
Locomotive Class		BR Class 4 2-6-4 Tank			Cl.508 three-car EMU with GEC 310 traction motors		
No.		80085			508207+205+211¶		
Shed		Redhill			–		
Load: coaches/tons tare/tons gross		3/101/105			3/99/105		
Recorder		Mr. D. Landau			Mr. D. Landau		

		Sched. min.	Actual min. sec.	Speed mph	Sched. min.	Actual min. sec.	Speed mph
00.00	TONBRIDGE	0	00 00	–	0	00 00	–
01.16	Milepost 41		02 36	53		02 25	64
02.55	LEIGH	4.5	04 27	–	3.5	04 04	–
00.61	Milepost 39		01 42	47		01 09	59
01.61	PENSHURST	3.5	03 18	–	3.5	02 36	–
01.00	Milepost 37		01 40	58		01 29	63$\frac{1}{2}$
02.00	Milepost 36		02 39	64$\frac{1}{2}$		02 21	72
03.00	Milepost 35		03 31	73		03 10	74$\frac{1}{2}$
04.00	Milepost 34		04 19	78		–	★36/59
05.00	EDENBRIDGE	7.5	05 33	–	5.5	05 46	–
01.00	Milepost 32		01 36	62		01 44	61
02.00	Milepost 31		02 32	71$\frac{1}{2}$		02 38	70$\frac{1}{2}$
03.00	Milepost 30		03 19	79		03 27	76
04.00	Milepost 29		04 03	83		04 16	★64
04.88	GODSTONE	7.5	05 04	–	6.5	05 35	–
00.87	Milepost 27$\frac{1}{4}$		01 30	56		01 27	60
02.12	Milepost 26		02 39	73		02 35	71$\frac{1}{2}$
03.12	Milepost 25		03 27	77		–	★
03.57	NUFFIELD	6.5	04 10	–	4.5	04 35	–
00.55	Milepost 24		01 07	53		sigs.	★
02.09	REDHILL	5.0	04 02	–	5.0	05 04	–

¶ 508207: Tonbridge–Edenbridge; 508205: Edenbridge–Godstone, 508211: Godstone–Redhill.

★ Brakes or speed restriction

engines. The first logs were timed by Mr. D. Twibell in 1953 and were made on the Bletchley-Cambridge service with 80043 and 80042 respectively. The loads were comparatively light at 132 and 125 tons gross but both engines showed they were capable of speeds of around 80mph on the falling gradients at between 1 in 100 and 1 in 115 through Old North Road and on to the gentler grades through Lords Bridge.

Table 5.8 also shows a comparison of a 2-6-4 tank engine (80085) run in 1964 with the recent (2008) timing of a three-car EMU (Cl.508) on the Tonbridge-Redhill line. 80085, again with a light load of 105 tons gross, was able to attain a speed of over 80mph on the 1 in 270 rising gradient towards Godstone; the engine appeared quite capable of keeping to the EMU's schedule throughout.

From Mr. D. Landau's archive also is the run with another 2-6-4 tank engine, 80067, on the 4.56pm commuter service from Euston to Watford and Tring sometime in the mid-1950s: details are given in Table 5.9. The engine sustained a speed in the mid-60s on the long 1 in 339 from Wembley to Hatch End and despite a signal check at Headstone Lane and a PW slowing after Bushey was only just over half a minute behind time at Watford on the tight schedule.

The 23-minute timing from Euston was the same as that for one of the two-hour Euston-Birmingham services in 1953. A comparison is made with LMR Jubilee 4-6-0 45676 *Codrington* with ten coaches of the 8.50am from Euston. Again a speed of 60mph was maintained on the climb through Hatch End. Earlier, in the mid-1930s, the crack 5.50pm

Birmingham service was booked for Compound 4-4-0s and a log from Mr. R. A. H. Weight's collection is included for interest. Here the schedule from Euston to Watford was sharp with a passing time of 22 minutes. Nevertheless, 1053 was inside this with a 280ton load despite a 35mph signal check before Watford and a subsequent PW slowing.

Logs of runs with the BR Cl. 3 2-6-0s are few and far between but again Mr. D. Landau came to the rescue with a run behind 77018 on an Ayr-Kilmarnock local timed by Mr. G. M. Foss in 1965; details are given in Table 5.10. The route is generally on a level from Ayr through to Barassie and 77018 was able to achieve a speed of 53½ on the Prestwick-Troon section; after this a maximum of 45½ was reached at St. Marnock Box.

Table 5.11 details two runs on the WR Westbury-Exeter route, comparing Britannia Pacific 70021 *Morning Star* with one of the new forms of motive power being examined as possible alternatives to steam traction on BR; this featured gas turbine electric locomotive, 18000, brought into service on the WR in 1951.

Although the Britannias embodied many features which would be considered alien to GWR practice, the new charges were clearly being given a chance to show their worth. The log with 70021 was first published in *Four Thousand Miles on the Footplate* by Mr. O.S. Nock (Ian Allan, 1952) and Mr. Nock, an engineer of great experience with GWR express running, noted immediately that the fire was built up in characteristic 'haycock' formation but horizontally rather than longitudinally as was usual in the narrow firebox Swindon-

TABLE 5.9

LMS/LMR Euston–Watford Junction

Date	mid/late–1950s	1953	mid–1930s
Train	4.56pm Euston-Watford-Tring	8.50am Euston-Birmingham	5.50pm Euston-Birmingham
Locomotive Class	4MT 2-6-4 Tank	Jubilee 4-6-0	LMS Compound 4-4-0
No.	80067	45676	1053
Name		*Codrington*	-
Shed	Watford	Camden	Camden
Load	7 coaches	10 coaches	9 coaches
	201 tons tare	322 tons tare	-
	225 tons gross	345 tons gross	280 tons gross
Driver/Fireman	Atkinson/not recorded	not recorded	not recorded
	Willesden	-	
Recorder	Mr. D. Landau	Mr. A. P. Sinkinson	Mr. R. A. H. Weight

Dist. Miles		Sched. min.	Actual min. sec.	Speed mph	Sched. min.	Actual min. sec.	Speed mph	Sched. min.	Actual min. sec.	Speed mph
00.0	EUSTON	0	00 00	-	0	00 00	-	0	00 00	-
01.1	*Camden No. 1*		02 58	-		p.w.s.	-		-	-
03.7	Queens Park		06 35	56		-	-		-	-
05.4	WILLESDEN	9	08 38	35	10	11 20	-		09 00	59
08.1	Wembley		11 57	53		14 20	-		-	-
08.9	North Wembley		12 48	54		-	-		-	-
09.4	South Kenton		13 25	56		-	-		-	-
10.3	Kenton		14 20	66		-	-		-	-
11.4	Harrow		15 23	64		17 55	-		15 00	62/61
12.6	Headstone Lane		16 35	64		-	-		-	-
			sigs.	*30		-	-		-	-
13.3	Hatch End		17 34	-		19 55	60		-	-
14.6	Carpenders Park		19 21	-		-	-		-	-
15.9	Bushey		20 47	58		-	-		-	sigs. 35
			p.w.s.	*20		-	-		-	p.w.s. 25
17.5	WATFORD Jct.	23	23 35		23	24 18	-	22	21 35†	

* speed reduced by brakes	Previously unpublished	First published in *Railway Magazine*, Vol.99, No.629, September 1953, p.610	First published in *Railway World*, Vol.21, No.239 April 1960, p.100
† passing time			

TABLE 5.10			
ScR 17.08 Ayr-Prestwick-Kilmarnock			
Date	26th March 1965		
Locomotive Class	BR 3MT 2-6-0		
No.	77018		
Shed	Hurlford (Kilmarnock)		
Coaches/tons tare/tons full	5/154/160		
Driver/Fireman	not recorded		
Recorder	Mr. G. M. Foss		

Dist. Miles		Actual min. sec.	Speed mph
00.00	AYR	00 00	–
00.55	*Milepost 40*	01 39	33½
01.20	NEWTON-ON-AYR	02 55	–
00.30	*Milepost 39*	01 17	33
01.30	*Milepost 38*	02 49	45
01.95	PRESTWICK	03 53	–
00.40	*Milepost 37*	01 15	35
01.40	*Milepost 36*	02 40	46/56
02.40	*Milepost 35*	03 50	53½
02.80	*Milepost 12/2*	04 16	53½
03.30	TROON	05 12	–
00.20	*Milepost 1*	00 50	38
01.30	BARASSIE	02 53	–
00.70	*Milepost 7*	01 50	–
01.70	*Milepost 6*	03 12	47
02.70	*Milepost 5*	04 23	46½
03.00	DRYBRIDGE	05 04	–
00.70	*Milepost 4*	01 52	39
01.40	*Milepost 3*	03 22	31½
02.10	Gatehead	04 19	sig.stop
02.70	*Milepost 2*	06 01	32
03.85	St. Marnock Box	–	45½/44
04.70	KILMARNOCK	10 39	

built engines. The firing practice was the traditional GWR 'little and often' approach and boiler pressure was maintained in the 230-235 p.s.i. range. On the uphill section to Milepost 122¾, cut-offs were 22% from Fairwood Jct., 30% on the tough climb to Clink Road, back to 20% over the Frome cut-off and then 24% from Blatchbridge Jct. to the summit. The 12.8 miles generally rising gradient from Westbury to that point had been covered in a little under 17 minutes; the steam chest pressure was kept at 200-215lb p.s.i. during the ascent. On the rest of the run to Taunton, speed averaged 65.3mph over the 22.8 miles from Castle Cary to Cogload box. *Morning Star* had used a modest 1,200 gallons of water from Westbury to Taunton, an average of 26 gallons per mile with coal consumption of between 32 and 33lb per mile with a 380-ton train at a start-to-stop average of 56.3mph.

The overall allowance of 44 minutes for the 30.8 miles from Taunton to Exeter was fairly easy and included five minutes of recovery time inserted from Whiteball down to Exeter. 70021 was smartly away from Taunton and continued with 25% cut-off to Norton Fitzwarren. From there this was increased to 30%. *Morning Star* did well on the bank with cut-off being increased to 32% at Milepost 17½ and to 36% at 172¼. In the 2½ miles at 1 in 90/86/80 to the tunnel entrance, speed fell from 50 to 36½mph. Boiler pressure was comfortably maintained and the engine obviously had a great deal in reserve. The five-minute recovery allowance was not required and under clear signals, Exeter was reached well ahead of time.

The run with the gas turbine electric locomotive, 18000, was first published in *Railway Magazine*, Vol.96, No.596, December

77015 with a local train stands at the north end of Kilmarnock's island platform 4/5 in June 1961. Platform 4 was the main southbound face and the train is standing in platform 5. It is possible the train has arrived from Ayr or may be about to depart with a service to Ardrossan or Glasgow St. Enoch. In the background stands the Johnny Walker whisky bottling plant. This later was enlarged and incorporated the site of the old locoshed, behind 77015 in this picture.

Alan Sainty collection

TABLE 5.11
WR Westbury-Exeter

Date		1951			1950		
Train		1.30pm Paddington-Penzance			3.30pm Paddington-Plymouth		
Locomotive Class		Britannia Pacific			Gas Turbine Electric		
No.		70021 *Morning Star*			18000		
Shed		Laira (Plymouth)			Old Oak Common		
Load		11 coaches			13 coaches		
		356 tons tare			430 tons tare		
		380 tons gross			470 tons gross		
Driver/Fireman		Green/Higgins			not recorded		
		(Old Oak Common)					
Recorder		Mr. O. S. Nock			Lieut. C. H. H. Harwood		

Dist. Miles		Sched. min.	Actual min. sec.	Speed mph	Sched. min.	Actual min. sec.	Speed mph
00.0	WESTBURY	0	00 00	-	0	00 00	-
01.5	*Fairwood Jct.*		03 15	43		03 35	-
04.8	*Clink Road Jct.*		08 03	41		-	-
06.8	*Blatchbridge Jct.*	10	10 22	60		09 44	62
10.9	Witham		14 44	54		13 54	56
12.6	Brewham		-	-		15 51	53
12.8	*Milepost 122_*		16 58	50		-	-
16.2	Bruton		20 06	68		-	78
19.7	Castle Cary	23	23 18	60		22 08	*61
24.5	Keinton Mandeville		27 48	68/59½		27 06	53
26.7	Charlton Mackrell		29 56	61¼		-	-
30.0	Somerton		32 56	70½/64		32 53	63/56
34.3	Langport East		-	-		37 00	71
35.3	*Curry Rivel Jct.*		37 32	71½		-	-
39.2	Athelney		41 08	63½/60		-	-
42.3	*Cogload*		-	-		44 48	58
44.8	*Creech Jct.*		46 32	63		sigs.	-
47.2	TAUNTON	51	50 16	-	59	52 48	-
02.0	Norton Fitzwarren		03 57	-		04 00	45
04.9	*Milepost 168*		07 26	50		-	-
07.1	Wellington		10 16	47/50		09 50	56
07.9	*Milepost 171*		11 11	47		-	-
08.9	*Milepost 172*		12 34	41½		-	-
09.9	*Milepost 173*		14 09	36½		-	-
10.9	*Whiteball Box*	17	15 48	-		14 54	34
15.9	*Tiverton Jct.*		20 55	67/58		20 00	70/64
18.2	Cullompton		23 05	66		22 03	70
23.6	Silverton		28 15	eased		27 03	61/64
27.4	Stoke Canon		31 54	-		-	-
29.5	*Cowley Bridge Jct.*		34 04	-		33 03	54
30.8	EXETER	44¶	36 57	-	40	35 55	-

* Speed reduced by brakes	First published in *Four Thousand Miles on the Footplate*, O. S. Nock, Ian Allan, 1952, p.45	First published in *Railway Magazine*, Vol.96, No.596 December 1950, p.836
¶ Includes five minutes recovery time		

1950 and is again taken from one of the articles by Mr. Cecil J. Allen, *British Locomotive Practice and Performance*. The run was timed by Lieut. C. H. H. Harwood with the Sunday 3.30pm from Paddington. This service had an easier schedule from Westbury to Taunton than the one with 70021, although similar timings were evident.

Speeds on the Westbury-Taunton section were broadly similar to those of *Morning Star* but with a load of around 90 tons more. A minimum of 53mph at Brewham and a time of 22min. 8sec. to Castle Cary were good. Taunton was reached in 52min. 48sec. for the 47.2 miles from Westbury or a calculated 50-minute net against the schedule of 59 minutes. Again a good start was made from Taunton and the 10.9 miles to Whiteball box was breasted in 14min. 54sec., a fine achievement with 470tons gross and no banking assistance. Exeter was reached in a little less than 36 minutes, a further gain of four minutes on the schedule.

For interest, Table 5.12 gives a comparison between *Morning Star's* run and timings made with several other engines on the climb up to Whiteball. These include a Saint class 4-6-0, 2923 *Saint George* with 320 tons, Castle class 4-6-0, 5029 *Nunney Castle* (355 tons), another run behind gas turbine 18000 (375 tons), King class 4-6-0, 6022 *King Edward III* (375 tons), County class 4-6-0, 1015 *County of Gloucester* (380 tons) and

stretch to Totnes after which another good climb ensued to Tigley box. Again 37% cut-off and full regulator were employed; successive half miles up to Tigley box were run at 46.2, 43.9, 37.5, 34 and 29mph. From Tigley to Rattery, the gradient eases from 1 in 47/56/52 to 1 in 90/95/65 resulting in a slow acceleration towards Rattery. 70021 had gained on the schedule by this time and Brent was passed some four minutes early. The run down to Plymouth from Wrangaton was uneventful and the four minutes recovery time was not required; arrival was almost eight minutes ahead of time.

The comparison run with 7036 *Taunton Castle* was outstanding. Delayed running west of Exeter was anticipated as the late-running "Devonian" (Bradford-Paignton) had left only a few minutes ahead and was due to call at Dawlish and Teignmouth. In addition, there were PW slowings. In the event, the "Devonian" was put into the loop at Dawlish and 7036 was given its head. Once over Aller Jct., the regulator was fully opened out at 25% cut-off. Speed

TABLE 5.12
GWR/WR: Taunton-Whiteball Summit

Locomotive Class No. Name		Saint 4-6-0 2923★ *Saint George*	Castle 4-6-0 5029 *Nunney Castle*	Gas Turbine 18000	King 4-6-0 6022 *King Edward III*	County 4-6-0 1015 *County of Gloucester*	Britannia 4-6-2 70021 *Morning Star*	Castle 4-6-0 7019 *Fowey Castle*
Load tons gross		320	355	375	375	380	380	405
Dist. Miles		Actual min. sec.	Actual min. sec.	Actual min. sec.	Actual min. sec.	Actual min. sec.	Actual min. sec.	Actual min. sec.
00.0	TAUNTON	00 00	00 00†	00 00	00 00	00 00	00 00	00 00
02.0	Norton Fitzwarren	03 47	02 00	04 50	03 50	04 02	03 57	03 53
03.9	*Milepost 167*	05 58	–	06 51	06 05	–	06 15	06 15
05.9	*Milepost 169*	08 13	–	08 52	08 19	–	08 41	08 49
07.1	Wellington	09 31	07 38	10 07	09 44	09 35	10 16	10 28
07.9	*Milepost 171*	10 26	08 30	10 51	10 32	–	11 11	11 25
08.9	*Milepost 172*	11 40	09 48	11 55	11 43	–	12 34	12 57
09.9	*Milepost 173*	13 02	11 23	13 07	13 05	12 53	14 09	14 53
10.9	*Whiteball Box pass*	14 27	13 09	14 28	14 30	14 24	15 48	16 55

★ non-superheater engine
† times from passing Taunton at 35mph

First published in *Four Thousand Miles on the Footplate*, O. S. Nock, Ian Allan, 1952, p.46.

Castle 7019 *Fowey Castle* (405 tons). Perhaps the most impressive performance here was that of one of the relatively unsung County 4-6-0s, a class not always given its full credit over the years. A time of 14min. 24sec. on this climb cannot be regarded as other than excellent and was not far off $1\frac{1}{2}$ minutes faster from Taunton than 70021 with the same load.

Table 5.13 details a later section of the run with 70021 *Morning Star* described in Table 5.11. Here a comparison is made with a Castle class 4-6-0, 7036 *Taunton Castle* between Newton Abbot and Plymouth North Road. For 70021, the load had been reduced to seven coaches, 232 tons tare. The fresh crew apparently had not driven a Pacific before but evidently relished the challenge. A speed of 46mph was reached at the foot of the climb to Dainton and the engine with full regulator and 37% cut-off was still doing 40mph at Milepost $217\frac{1}{4}$. Cut-off was then advanced to 45% and the last three quarter-miles were run at 35.3, 31.6 and 32.7mph respectively, allowing a start-to-pass time of 6min. 49sec. to Dainton box. *Morning Star* then coasted down the winding

fractionally exceeded the 45mph on the bank and from milepost 216, successive half-miles were run at 46, 44.4 and 33.6mph. Cut-off had been advanced 35% at milepost $216\frac{1}{2}$ and at $217\frac{1}{2}$ further increased to 40%. Speed fell to a minimum of $27\frac{1}{2}$ at Dainton summit but the time from Newton Abbot was an extraordinary 5min. 45sec., a gain of almost two minutes on booked time. Totnes was passed at 62mph. and Rattery was topped at 33mph a speed of 25mph having been sustained on the incline with 35% cut-off. The road is all downhill to Plymouth from Hemerdon which was passed at 68mph after adherence to the restrictions through Bittaford, Ivybridge and Cornwood. Then one quarter mile was clocked at $77\frac{1}{2}$mph before the brakes were applied for the curves through Plympton station, Tavistock Jct. and Laira Jct. resulting in an on-time arrival at North Road.

The performance of 70021 *Morning Star* is compared with several other classes on the Newton Abbot–Plymouth route in Table 5.14. These timings were first published in *Trains Illustrated*, Vol.X, No.104, May 1957, pp.244-5 in one of the

TABLE 5.13
WR Newton Abbot–Plymouth

Date		1951			1951		
Train		3.30pm ex-Paddington			1.30pm ex-Paddington		
Locomotive Class		Castle 4-6-0			Britannia 4-6-2		
No.		7036			70021		
Name		*Taunton Castle*			*Morning Star*		
Load		7 coaches			7 coaches		
		241 tons tare			232 tons tare		
		260 tons gross			250 tons gross		
Driver/Fireman		Cook/not recorded			Lee/not recorded		

Dist. Miles		Sched. min.	Actual min. sec.	Speed mph	Sched. min.	Actual min. sec.	Speed mph
00.0	NEWTON ABBOT	0	00 00*	c 30	0	00 00	–
01.1	Aller Jct.		01 33	–		02 45	–
02.0	Milepost 216		02 28	46		03 48	46
03.0	Milepost 217		03 47	–		05 05	40
03.5	Milepost 217_		04 41	29		05 53	–
04.0	Milepost 218 (Dainton)	7½	05 45	27½		06 49	–
08.8	TOTNES	14½	11 29	62	15½	12 54	50
10.1	Milepost 224		12 50	–		14 22	–
11.1	Milepost 225		14 24	–		15 51	–
12.1	Milepost 226		16 47	–		17 47	–
13.3	Rattery Box	24	19 29	33	25	20 20	–
15.6	Brent	27	22 39	55½	28	23 35	–
			p.w.s.	15 †		–	–
17.8	Wrangaton		26 18	–		26 25	–
21.1	Ivybridge		30 22	40 †		30 15	–
25.2	Hemerden Box	39	34 37	68	41	35 40	–
27.9	Plympton		36 50	–		38 44	–
30.4	Lipson Jct.	46	39 42	–	50	42 11	–
31.9	PLYMOUTH	50	42 50	–	54	46 10	–

★ Times from passing Newton Abbot at around 30mph

First published in *Four Thousand Miles on the Footplate*, O. S. Nock, Ian Allan, 1952, p.212.

† Speed reduced by brakes

'Locomotive Running Past and Present' series by Mr. Cecil J. Allen. Run No.1 was with a City class 4-4-0, 3433 *City of Bath* with a five-coach train which included three Royal saloons on the occasion of the visit of the then Prince and Princess of Wales, later King George V and Queen Mary to Plymouth. After leaving Paddington, the train had averaged 69.8mph for just over 157 miles from Ealing to Taunton and had topped Whiteball summit at 50mph. In the log quoted here, Dainton summit was breasted at 30mph and the lowest speed recorded on the climb to Rattery was 36mph followed by a minimum of 51½mph over Wrangaton. Some very lively running from there to Plymouth resulted in an arrival 37 minutes ahead of time, no doubt to the great consternation of the Royal reception party at North Road.

Run no.2 again features the 3.30pm from Paddington with gas turbine 18000 in charge. The load was only six coaches and 18000 made light work of the duty, managing 41mph at Dainton summit, 49½ at Rattery and 43 at Wrangaton. The engine was then eased for the remainder of the run as the train was now well ahead of the 50-minute schedule which also applied to most of the other runs in the table.

Run no.4 with Castle 5085 was timed by Mr. C. W. Herbert. No point speeds were quoted but *Evesham Abbey* had a similar time to Dainton as that for 18000, probably one of the fastest ascents of this bank with steam ever recorded. Run no.5 was with Star class 4-6-0, 4003 *Lode Star* on the "Cornish Riviera Express" in 1921. This outstanding performance came at the end of four hours of very hard steaming from Paddington.

King 4-6-0 6005 *King George II* is the subject of run no.6 made in 1927. The 27½mph minimum at Dainton was achieved with a cut-off lengthened progressively from 20% to

35% with full regulator. The same cut-off gave 28½mph at Tigley and 43½ at Rattery. In this case, the Newton Abbot–Plymouth schedule was only 4½ minutes so the time gained was only 2¼ minutes.

The 1948 locomotive exchange produced a number of strangers on this route. Run no.7 gives details of a trip with LMR Royal Scot 4-6-0 46162 *Queen's Westminster Rifleman*. The engine was not seen at its best here. The maximum cut-off on the ascents of both Dainton and Rattery was not allowed to exceed 30% and although the main port of the regulator was in use, it was not fully open, resulting in the relatively low minima of 20 and 23mph respectively on the climbs. It is likely that the main objective during the trials was the achievement of the most economical operation of the engine rather than any attempt at spectacular running performance.

Run No.8 was made in the 1925 exchanges with an LNER Gresley A1 Pacific 4474 *Victor Wild* in the time before the first modification to class A3 occurred featuring improved valve setting and 220p.s.i. boiler pressure. The performance was excellent with a speed of 40mph at Rattery only surpassed by 18000 (run no.3) and 6005 (run no.6) with lesser loads. The 27½ at Tigley and 54 through Brent were impressive.

Castle class 4-6-0, 4074 *Caldicot Castle* was the GWR representative in the 1925 trials and details are given in run no.9. No records were traced of the speeds on this section; the 4-6-0 was faster than the Britannia Pacific down from Dainton through Totnes and had a similar point-to-point time from there to Rattery. Further fast work resulted in an impressive time of just over 41½ minutes to the Plymouth stop.

The work of a King class 4-6-0, modified with double chimney, 6017 *King Edward IV* is shown in run no.10. This was timed by Mr. J. A. Crittenden on the "Cornish Riviera Express". The climbs over Dainton and Rattery were not outstanding but nevertheless were good enough to recover a two minute loss on schedule.

Runs 11 and 12 were recorded during the 1948 exchanges with an ER double chimney A4 Pacific, 60033 *Seagull* and an LMR Duchess Pacific, 46236 *City of Bradford*. The performance of the A4 was disappointing, with a 35% cut-off and full regulator resulting in a minimum of 19mph over Dainton whereas *City of Bradford* managed 27mph with 30% cut-off and the main regulator half open. Up to Rattery, 60033 was worked at a maximum of 35% with full regulator and the Duchess at the same figure with half regulator. Speeds were 25 and 31½mph at Tigley and 32 and 37mph at Rattery respectively. By Wrangaton, the LMR Pacific was over two minutes ahead. Both Pacifics were well behind the equally loaded 6017 in run no.10, although both were working well within schedule.

Run no.13 is included as an example of a really heavy load that had to be double-headed, with 6012 *King Edward VI* piloted by Bulldog 4-4-0, 3401 *Vancouver*, just after the end of World War II. The pair managed to keep time despite a signal stop between Brent and Ivybridge.

Table 5.15 compares the work of Britannia Pacific 70019 *Lightning* with three former GWR 4-6-0s from the County, Castle and Hall classes on the up "Cornish Riviera Express" from Penzance to Plymouth. The Britannia trip was made in

TABLE 5.14
WR Newton Abbot–Plymouth

Run No.			1	2	3	4	5	6	7	8	9	10	11	12	13
Locomotive Class			Britannia # 4-6-2	City 4-4-0	G.T.E A1A-A1A	Castle 4-6-0	Star 4-6-0	King 4-6-0	Royal Scot 4-6-0	A1 4-6-2	Castle 4-6-0	King 4-6-0	A4 4-6-2	Duchess 4-6-2	King 4-6-0
No. (for Names, see below)			70021	3433	18000	5085	4003	6005	·46162	4474	4074	6017 ‡	60033	46236	6012 †
Load tons tare/tons gross			232/250	-/130	201/215	241/255	249/260	253/270	253/270	281/305	292/310	327/350	328/350	329/350	450/495
Dist. Miles		Sched min.	Actual min. sec.	Actual min. sec.	Actual min. sec.	Actual min. sec.	Actual min. sec.	Actual min. sec.	Actual min. sec.	Actual min. sec.	Actual min. sec.	Actual min. sec.	Actual min. sec.	Actual min. sec.	Actual min. sec.
00.0	NEWTON ABBOT	0	00 00	00 00*	00 00*	00 00*	00 00*	00 00*	00 00	00 00*	00 00*	00 00*	00 00	00 00	00 00
01.1	Aller Jct.	–	02 45	–	–	–	–	–	–	p.w.s.	p.w.s.	p.w.s.	–	–	–
03.9	Dainton	–	06 49	05 37	04 56	05 02	06 00	06 05	07 54	07 15	07 15	05 20	08 24	07 22	08 30
08.8	TOTNES	15½	12 54	10 55	10 45	11 30	11 20	11 25	14 29	13 10	12 35	11 32	15 19	14 25	14 50
11.4	Tigley	–	–	–	14 28	15 50	15 05	15 35	19 04	17 35	16 30	15 57	20 19	18 40	19 48
13.3	Rattery	25	20 20	–	16 55	19 02	18 05	18 40	22 48	20 50	20 00	19 22	23 57	21 55	23 59
15.6	Brent	28	23 35	20 21	19 51	22 02	21 10	21 25	26 10	23 50	23 03	22 32	27 15	25 05	27 24
17.8	Wrangaton	–	26 25	22 54	22 37	24 30	23 40	23 55	29 36	26 05	25 15	25 17	30 08	27 59	30 38 (sigs.)
21.1	Ivybridge	–	30 15	26 20	26 34	27 55	27 00	27 35	33 47	29 55	28 45	28 56	34 18	31 54	37 15 (sig. stop)
25.2	Hemerden Box	41	35 40	30 34	31 22	32 30	31 10	31 40	38 26	34 15	32 45	33 16	39 32	37 28	41 41
27.9	Plympton	–	38 44	33 03	34 09	35 40	33 40	34 25	40 46	37 05	35 16	36 07	42 49	39 59	44 17
					sigs.	p.w.s.	sigs.		–	p.w.s.	p.w.s.	p.w.s.	p.w.s.	p.w.s.	p.w.s.
31.9	PLYMOUTH NORTH ROAD	54	46 10	·37 44	44 17	42 20	42 30	39 10	49 20	43 30	41 33	42 05	52 44	50 04	50 27
	Net time (minutes)	–	–	39¾	41¼	39¼	39¼	45¶	41½	39¾	41½	47¶	44¼¶	45¾¶	
Speeds (mph) at:	Newton Abbot		–	–	35	–	35	30	0	25	–	44	0	0	–
	Milepost 216		46	–	60	–	–	49	48	44½	–	60	45½	51	–
	Dainton Summit		32	30	41	–	30½	27½	20	24½	–	24	19	27	18
	Tigley		–	–	39½	–	32½	28½	23	27½	–	27	25	31½	24½
	Rattery		–	36	49½	–	37	43½	36	40	–	38	32	37	31½
	Wrangaton		–	51½	43	–	52½	49	47½	49½	–	–	47	47½	–

First published in *Trains Illustrated*, Vol.X, No.104, May 1957 pp.244-245.

Locomotive Names: 70021 *Morning Star*, 3433 *City of Bath*, 5085 *Evesham Abbey*, 4003 *Lode Star*, 6005 *King George II*, 46162 *Queen's Westminster Rifleman*, 4474 *Victor Wild*, 4074 *Caldicot Castle*, 6017 *King Edward IV*, 60033 *Seagull*, 46236 *City of Bradford*, 6012 *King Edward VI*.

* Times from passing Newton Abbot at around 30mph   ‡ double chimney   † piloted by 4-4-0 3401 *Vancouver*   ¶ Calculated on pass to stop basis
\# Log first published in *Four Thousand Miles on the Footplate*, O. S. Nock, Ian Allan 1952, p.212.

October 1951 and timed by Mr. O. S. Nock. A heavy dew had made the rails slippery and the engine lost its footing briefly on getting away from Penzance. But 30% cut-off and full regulator rapidly increased the speed to 51½mph on the level past Marazion. Two miles of gradients rising at 1 in 127 up to 1 in 85 meant that the somewhat unrealistic schedule to St. Erth was exceeded by one minute. More slipping occurred on restarting and a speed of only 34mph rather than the usual 40-45mph was achieved on the sharp fall of 1 in 70 for the first half mile. The 1 in 61 incline up to Gwinear Road was worked at between 45 and 54% cut-off continuously. Speed did not fall below 26½mph but the slow start cost a further minute to Gwinear Road. The starts from Gwinear Road, Truro and Par were then made without a trace of slipping. From Gwinear Road, 70019 took the 1 in 61 to Cambourne with 42% cut-off at first, followed by 45, 48 and 50% all the time with full regulator and the two-minute loss had been retrieved by the time Truro was reached. On the undulating road to Par *Lightning* proved to have complete mastery of the job and arrival at Par was three minutes before schedule. The restart up the the 1 in 84/109/62 to Treverrin tunnel was perhaps the most impressive of the whole trip. The first quarter mile on the 1 in 84 was taken at 26mph and then with cut-off varying between 47 and 50%, the subsequent quarter miles were run at 28, 27½, 30, 31, 29 and 29mph at which speed the summit was topped.

On the long bank up to Doublebois, much of which is at 1 in 58/70/90, cut-offs varied between 38 and 43%, with boiler pressure steady at 232-5psi. Liskeard was passed three minutes early and the rest of the trip down to Plymouth was taken quietly with speed at no time exceeding 52mph; arrival was four minutes ahead of schedule.

The ride with County class 4-6-0 1006 *County of Cornwall* was timed by Mr. Cecil J. Allen on a perfect September morning. Leaving Penzance, the first port of the regulator was used with full 75% cut-off brought back almost immediately to 45% and then by stages to 23% three quarters of a mile out of Penzance. Again time was lost on the over-optimistic schedule to St. Erth. The tough ascent to Gwinear Road was tackled at 27-33% cut-off with speed falling first to 34½mph above Hayle and later to 25½mph. From Gwinear Road, speed fell to 25mph up the 1 in 61/55 to Cambourne, with cut-off advanced from 30 to 35%. Truro was reached just under 1½ minutes early. Further good work on the inclines to Par resulted in a further 1¾ gain to the credit of the engine and crew on arrival. The ascent from Par to Treverrin tunnel brought speed down to 22½mph. This was followed by a long and severe permanent way check which cost some 2½ minutes. Speed at the Doublebois summit was 28mph with cut-offs on the ascent varying between 23 and 35%. The run downhill to Plymouth was again taken quietly with speeds not exceeding 60mph.

Also included in Table 5.15 are two runs timed by Mr. O. S. Nock featuring Castle class 4-6-0, 5079 *Lysander* (oil-fired) and Hall class 4-6-0 5915 *Trentham Hall*. The Castle performance was similar to that detailed above for *Lightning* and *County of Cornwall*. The run behind 5915 was impressive. A Penzance engine, it was probably being used as a substitute for a failed Laira Castle or County 4-6-0. With a Cl.5MT power rating, the engine nevertheless gave an excellent performance with some 355 tons behind the tender.

The Exeter-Bristol line is the subject of the runs in Table 5.16. Here the work of a Britannia Pacific, 70022 *Tornado*, is compared with that of a County class 4-6-0, 1022 *County of*

TABLE 5.15
GWR/WR Cornish Riviera Limited

	1951	c.1947	1947	1948
Date	1951	c.1947	1947	1948
Locomotive Class	Britannia Pacific	County 4-6-0	Castle 4-6-0	Hall 4-6-0
No.	70019	1006	5079 ¶	5915
Name	*Lightning*	*County of Cornwall*	*Lysander*	*Trentham Hall*
Shed	Laira (Plymouth)	Laira (Plymouth)	Laira (Plymouth)	Penzance
Load: Coaches/tons tare/tons gross	12/389/410 †	9/293/315	10/324/350	10/325/355
Driver/Fireman	Hammet/Courtney	Hocking/Rogers	not recorded	not recorded
Recorder	Laira (Plymouth) Mr. O. S. Nock	Laira (Plymouth) Mr. C. J. Allen	- Mr. O. S. Nock	- Mr. O. S. Nock

Dist. Miles		Sched. min.	Actual min. sec.	Speed mph	Sched. min.	Actual min. sec.	Speed mph	Sched. min.	Actual min. sec.	Speed mph	Sched. min.	Actual min. sec.	Speed mph
00.0	PENZANCE	0	00 00	-	0	00 00	-	0	00 00	-	0	00 00	-
01.9	Marazion.		04 27	51½		04 20	43½		03 57	50½		04 23	47
04.8	*Milepost 321¾*		08 08	43½			34½		07 45	42		08 28	39
05.6	ST. ERTH	9	10 00	-	9	10 12	-	9	09 07	-	9	09 55	-
01.6	Hayle		03 35	34		02 58	40		02 54	44		02 54	45
03.0	*Milepost 318*		06 24	29/31			-		05 20	27		05 15	33½
04.5	*Milepost 316½*		09 36	26½			24½		09 00	22½		08 20	25
05.0	GWINEAR ROAD	10	11 10	-	10	09 51	-	10	10 27	-	10	09 42	-
01.0	*Milepost 315*		02 21	47½			41		02 08	45		02 08	46
02.5	Camborne		04 42	28		05 08	25		04 52	26		04 55	25
04.1	Carn Brea	8	07 31	50		08 07	50		p.w.s	-		-	-
06.2	Redruth		10 11	slack*		10 53	*35		11 13	-		10 43	-
08.3	Scorrier		13 26	59		13 53	56½		-	-		-	-
10.0	Chacewater	16	15 24	60 max	16	15 52	*45	15	17 46	57	15	15 44	-
14.6	*Penwithers Jct.*		-	-	22	21 20	61		-	-		sigs.	-
15.2	TRURO	24	21 54	-	24	22 34	-	23	24 53	-	23	22 56	-
00.8	*Milepost 300*		02 02	36		-	-		01 48	33		02 22	30
01.3	*Milepost 299½*		-	-		-	-		02 49	-		03 29	26
01.8	*Milepost 299*		02 57	33		04 17	24½		-	-		-	-
-				51½		-	-		-	-		-	-
-	*Polperro Tunnel Exit*		-	50		-	-		-	-		-	-
05.3	Probus		07 48	60		08 23	57		08 28	27		08 00	62
07.7	Grampound Road	12	11 02	33½	12	12 11	27	12	12 53	60½	12	11 22	30
09.8	*Milepost 291*		13 52	55		-	-		16 11	21		14 15	55½
12.1	Burngullow		16 53	33		18 39	36		20 08	51½		17 31	30
			-	-		-	-		-	-		p.w.s.	-
14.5	ST. AUSTELL	22½	20 02	-	22_	21 39	-	23	23 47	-	23	22 24	15
19.0	PAR	29	26 05	-	29	27 13	-	30	29 25	-	30	27 52	-
00.8	*Milepost 281*		02 18	28		-	-		02 13	28		02 21	25
01.8	*Milepost 280*		04 18	31		-	-		04 15	31		04 34	30
02.8	*Milepost 279*		06 16	29		-	-		06 29	24		06 41	26
			-	*39		p.w.s.	-		p.w.s.	-		-	-
04.3	Lostwithiel		08 35	44½		09 41	*25		09 07	-		08 39	slack
07.8	BODMIN ROAD	13	13 23	41	13	15 18	44	13	14 39	-	13	13 14	41
09.3	*Milepost 272½*		15 33	42		17 40	39		16 53	39		15 26	45
10.8	*Milepost 271*		18 08	32		20 31	28		19 48	25		18 02	30
11.8	*Milepost 270*		20 15	26½		22 55	24½		22 24	22½		20 16	25
12.8	*Milepost 269*		22 16	30/29		25 11	27		-	-		-	-
13.6	Doublebois		23 56	32		26 54	28		26 17	30		24 27	26½
			-	-		-	-		-	-		p.w.s.	15
16.9	LISKEARD	31	28 38	-	29	31 18	56	29	30 53	-	29	30 15	-
20.0	Menheniot		32 56	easy		35 27	-		35 04	60		34 50	60
25.4	St. Germans		39 28	52 max		41 44	*45		41 22	-		40 31	-
			-	-		-	*25		p.w.s.	-		p.w.s	-
30.5	Saltash	47	46 18	-	48	49 05	*15	48	49 12	-	48	48 40	-
31.6	St. Budeaux		-	-		52 08	-		-	-		-	-
32.5	Keyham		50 30	48		-	-		53 02	-		52 30	-
34.2	*Devonport Jct.*		53 48	-		sigs.	-		-	-		-	-
34.7	PLYMOUTH NORTH ROAD	56	55 43	-	57	58 00	-	57	57 25	-	57	56 32	-

* speed reduced by brakes

¶ Oil fired

† 420 tons gross from Truro

First published in *Four Thousand Miles on the Footplate*, O. S. Nock, Ian Allan, 1952, p.222.	First published in *Railway Magazine*, Vol.93, No.572 November & December 1947, p.391.	Published in *Sixty Years of Western Express Running*, O. S. Nock, Ian Allan, 1973, p.290.	Published in *Sixty Years of Western Express Running*, O. S. Nock, Ian Allan, 1973, p.290.

70027 *Rising Star* passes West Ealing on the 3.45pm Paddington-Swansea on 1st June 1957. The line on the left of the picture is the branch to Greenford. Note the milk depot in the centre containing six-wheeled milk tanks used on the daily service from the West Country.

R. C. Riley

Eastfield-based 73108 departs from Gleneagles with a failed railbus en route to Stirling on 6th August 1962. The railbuses served the branch from Gleneagles to Crieff until the service was withdrawn in 1964.

Ken Falconer

TABLE 5.16
GWR/WR Exeter–Bristol

	1951	1947?	1955
Date			
Train	1.00pm Plymouth – Liverpool	8.45am Plymouth – Liverpool and Manchester	7.30am Penzance-Manchester London Road
Locomotive Class	Britannia Pacific	County 4-6-0	Star 4-6-0
No.	70022 *Tornado*	1022 *County of Northampton*	4056 *Princess Margaret*
Shed	Laira (Plymouth)	Shrewsbury	Bristol Bath Road
Load	10 coaches	13 coaches	11 coaches
	318 tons tare	408 tons tare	350 tons tare
	345 tons gross	440 tons gross	375 tons gross
Driver/Fireman	Williams/Bolt	Waters/Wheeler	Iles/not recorded
	Newton Abbot	Shrewsbury	Bristol Bath Road
Recorder	Mr. O. S. Nock	Mr. C. J. Allen	Mr. O. S. Nock

Dist. Miles		Sched. min.	Actual min. sec.	Speed mph	Sched. min.	Actual min. sec.	Speed mph	Sched. min.	Actual min. sec.	Speed mph
00.0	EXETER ST DAVIDS	0	00 00	-	0	00 00	-	0	00 00	-
01.3	*Cowley Bridge Jct.*		03 17	-		-	-		-	-
03.4	Stoke Canon		06 12	49		07 11	43½		06 07	48
07.2	Silverton		10 41	53½/50		12 08	53		10 16	56½
08.4	Hele		12 06	56		-	-		-	-
12.6	Cullompton		16 22	64		18 04	57½		15 37	63
14.8	*Tiverton Jct.*		18 38	56/64		20 44	48/55		17 56	54½/61
16.6	Sampford Peverell		20 21	62		-	-		-	-
18.9	*Milepost 175*		22 43	54		-	-		-	-
19.2	Burlescombe		-	-		25 59	44		-	-
19.9	*Whiteball Box*	26	23 56	46		27 06	37½	26	23 29	44½
			-	69		-	-		p.w.s.	30
23.7	Wellington		27 45	60 slack		30 58	77½		29 12	72
28.8	Norton Fitzwarren		32 18	74		35 02	76½		p.w.s.	30
30.8	TAUNTON	37	35 02	-	38	38 11	-	37	37 13	-
02.4	*Creech Jct.*		-	-	4	04 25	-		03 55	55
04.7	*Cogload Jct.*		06 31	62½/66		07 01	57		06 20	60
08.0	Fordgate		-	-		10 16	66		09 21	67
10.3	*Meads Crossing*		-	-		12 31	-		-	-
11.5	BRIDGWATER	16	13 47	-	15	14 22 †	-	15	13 05 †	-
			p.w.s.	15						
02.5	Dunball		05 47	-						
			p.w.s.	40						
06.3	HIGHBRIDGE		12 37	58						
09.1	Brent Knoll		15 15	69½						
13.6	*Uphill Jct.*		18 59	76½						
16.5	*Worle Jct.*	19½	21 11	80						
21.3	Yatton	24½	25 37	61/64						
27.4	Flax Bourton		31 40	58						
			-	54						
31.4	Parson Street		36 05	-						
33.3	BRISTOL TEMPLE MEADS	43*	40 25	-						

* Includes four minutes recovery time
† Train continued to Bristol Temple Meads via Weston-Super-Mare.

First published in *Four Thousand Miles on the Footplate*, O. S. Nock, Ian Allan, 1952, p.49.

First published in *Railway Magazine*, Vol.93, No. 572, November/December 1947, p.394.

First published in *The GWR Stars, Castles and Kings, Part 2*, O. S. Nock, David & Charles, 1970/1973 p.228.

Northampton and a Star class 4-6-0, 4056 *Princess Margaret*. The Britannia run was timed by Mr. O. S. Nock on the 'Liverpool Diner', the 1.00pm Plymouth-Liverpool Lime St.; the commentary is taken up from Exeter. Departure was at 25% cut-off with the regulator eased twice to maintain boiler pressure during the first stages. With the boiler eventually settling down, the ascent to Whiteball was made at a minimum speed of 46mph after two maxima at Cullompton and Tiverton Junction of 64mph. A permanent way slack through Wellington kept speed down to 60mph there but Taunton was reached at almost two minutes ahead of time. On the level stretch from there to Bridgwater, a maximum of 66mph was made at Cogload Jct. Bridgwater was left on time but a long permanent way slack followed costing several minutes. It was necessary to make up time before Bristol as this was a busy Saturday with a potential for conflicting train movements from Worle Jct. onwards. With cut-off at 25% and regulator almost full open *Tornado* achieved 58mph at Highbridge, 69½ at Brent Knoll, 72 at Brean Road, 76½ at Bleadon and 80mph at Worle Jct. Time had been regained by then and the engine was eased through to Bristol without the need for the full four minutes recovery time in the schedule.

Run no.2 in Table 5.16 was with County class 4-6-0 1022 *County of Northampton* of Shrewsbury shed working the long Newton Abbot turn on the 8.45am Plymouth-Liverpool and Manchester. Full cut-off was used on the start from Exeter, reducing to 35% almost straight away and then gradually to 25% by the end of the second mile. On the level, the small port of the regulator was used with some recourse to the main valve, partly open for the faster work. Up the 1 in 155 after Cullompton a minimum speed of 48½mph was sustained which reduced to 37½ over Whiteball summit. Downhill to Taunton, speeds in the mid-70s were maintained. On the short stretch from there to Bridgwater, a maximum of 66mph was attained at Fordgate. From Bridgwater, the train ran to Bristol via Weston-Super-Mare and further comparison with *Tornado's* work was not possible.

Star class 4-6-0 4056 *Princess Margaret* was employed on express work as late as November 1955 and a run on the 7.30am Penzance-Manchester London Road timed by Mr. O. S. Nock is detailed here. From Exeter, full regulator and 25% cut-off was used from Cowley Bridge Jct. and 21% from Stoke Canon. After this the working was unchanged until Whiteball summit was passed at 44½mph. The mainly level running from Taunton was made on 15% cut-off and mostly full open regulator with a maximum speed of 67mph at Fordgate. Again, this service was routed via Weston-Super-Mare.

The last two tables compare performances of Stewarts Lane-based Britannia Pacific 70004 *William Shakespeare* with other classes on the boat train traffic between London Victoria and Dover Marine. Four down runs are detailed in Table 5.17, featuring the work of unrebuilt West Country Light Pacific 34104 *Bere Alston*, diesel-electric 2,000hp 1Co-Co1, 10203 and DC electric 2,500hp E5015 in comparison with the Britannia. Four up runs are laid out in Table 5.18 where *William Shakespeare's* efforts are displayed opposite runs with West Country Light Pacific 34102 *Lapford*, rebuilt Merchant Navy Pacific 35015 *Rotterdam Lloyd* and unrebuilt Merchant Navy Pacific 35029 *Ellerman Lines*.

The run with 70004 in Table 5.17 was timed by Mr. O. S. Nock on the "Golden Arrow" in 1951, shortly after the engine

had been released from the exhibition on the South Bank celebrating the Festival of Britain event. The train was banked out of Victoria up the 1 in 64 to Grosvenor Road bridge during which 70004's cut-off was initially 45%, reducing to 40% before the bridge was reached. Here the cut-off was reduced to 35% and the boiler pressure had fallen from 235 to 180psi, as a big fire with small coals had not properly burned through. As a result, progress was indifferent through the suburban area with speed falling to 26½mph at Sydenham Hill and 30mph at Bickley Jct. Things were then taken steadily up to Knockholt, speed falling to 30mph on the 1 in 120.

The fire was now beginning to burn through and speed reached 65½mph at Dunton Green, falling back to 55½ on the subsequent rise. A maximum of 72½mph was achieved near Hildenborough and despite the slow start, Tonbridge was passed only 2¼ minutes late. Cut-off was now at 31% in accelerating from the Tonbridge slack and reduced to 25% in Tudeley cutting where the gradient changes from 1 in 258 up to 1 in 285 down. Boiler pressure was then steady at 240psi. The short descent from Staplehurst brought speed up to 64mph, followed by 69 on the level at Headcorn. The three and a half mile rise to Pluckley on gradients varying between 1 in 499 and 1 in 244 was cleared at 66mph and reached 71mph through the station. Ashford was passed at 73½mph falling to 60 at Westenhanger. Lateness was still 2½ minutes at Sandling Jct. but this had been reduced to just under 1¾ minutes on arrival. Net time from Victoria was 9½ minutes, an average of 51.2mph on a road which involves the need to thread through heavy suburban traffic with awkward gradients in its early stages.

The second run in Table 5.17 was with unrebuilt West Country Light Pacific 34104 *Bere Alston*, with a heavily loaded 11.00am boat express from Victoria. The train was banked out of Victoria by Standard Cl.4-6-0 73086 and things were taken easily over the early stages, with a minimum of 30mph up the 1 in 101 to Sydenham Hill. A permanent way slack through Beckenham and a slow recovery up the 1 in 95 past Bromley South led to a 3½ minute deficit on schedule at Bickley Jct. From then on a clear road allowed 34104 to pick up over 4½ minutes to Folkestone Junction, keeping an average of 68½mph over the 49.3 miles from the north end of Sevenoaks tunnel to Folkestone Warren. Over the 21.3 miles from Paddock Wood to Ashford, the average with this heavy train was as high as 72½mph; the net time from Victoria was no more than 87 minutes.

Run no.3 in Table 5.17 gives performance details of one of the SR diesel-electric units, 10203 (2,000hp) on the heavily loaded "Night Ferry". The service was very popular at the time, frequently requiring the inclusion of seven Wagon-Lits which with five SR coaches and two SNCF (French National Railways) vans made up a total of 591 tons tare, 615 tons gross in this case. The SR diesel took this load without the pilot that a Merchant Navy Pacific would have required. A 30mph slack through Brixton was followed by a steady 33mph up the 1 in 101 to Sydenham Hill. But the train then suffered a signal stop of 32 seconds at Bickley Jct. The usual rear-end assistance had been provided out of Victoria and full power was used to Sydenham Hill but the controller was well back from there to the signal stop. Full power was again used from Bickley Jct. to

TABLE 5.17
SR London Victoria–Dover Marine

Date	1951	1956	c1955	c1962
Train	The "Golden Arrow"	11.00am Boat Express	The "Night Ferry"	The "Golden Arrow"
Locomotive Class	Britannia Pacific	Unrebuilt West Country Light Pacific	Diesel Electric 2,000hp 1Co-Co1	DC Electric 2,500hp (TOPS Cl.71, later Cl.74)
No.	70004	34104	10203	E5015
Name	*William Shakespeare*	*Bere Alston*	–	–
Shed	Stewarts Lane	Stewarts Lane	Nine Elms ‡	Stewarts Lane
Load	9 Pullmans, 2 vans 379 tons tare 395 tons gross	14 coaches 444 tons tare 475 tons gross	14 coaches 591 tons tare 615 tons gross	11 coaches 366 tons tare 380 tons gross
Driver/Fireman	J. Durrant/E. Blackwell (Dover)	not recorded	not recorded	W. Mills (Dover)
Recorder(s)	Mr. O. S. Nock	"Adam of Usk"	Mr. A. T. H. Tayler	Mr. O. S. Nock

Dist. Miles		Sched. min.	Actual min. sec.	Speed mph	Sched. min.	Actual min. sec.	Speed mph	Sched. min.	Actual min. sec.	Speed mph	Sched. min.	Actual min. sec.	Speed mph
00.0	LONDON VICTORIA	0	00 00	–	0	00 00	–	0	00 00	–	0	00 00	–
00.7	*Grosvenor Road Box Site*		02 50	–		–	–		–	–		–	–
01.9	Wandsworth Road		05 30	–		05 44	36½		–	–		sigs.	–
04.0	HERNE HILL	8½	09 28	–	8½	08 50	40½	8½	07 59	33	6½	07 15	–
05.0	Dulwich		11 32	34½		–	–		–	–		–	–
05.7	Sydenham Hill		13 12	26½		11 58	30		11 13	33		09 32	54
			–	–		p.w.s.	*17		–	–		–	66
08.7	Beckenham Jct.	16½	17 40	47	16	17 32	23	16½	15 13	49/44	12	12 37	–
10.0	Shortlands		–	–		20 41	40/44		17 03	–	13½	13 50	60
			–	–		–	–		20 46	–		–	
10.9	BROMLEY SOUTH		20 40	–		23 14	29		–	–		14 37	64½
			–	--		–	–		stop	–		sigs.	*20
12.6	*Bickley Jct.*	22	23 47	30	22	25 10	37½	23	21 18	–	16½	17 00	–
13.4	*Petts Wood Jct.*		–	–		26 29	32		24 02	28		–	–
14.9	Orpington	27	28 01	40½	27	29 01	42	28	26 44	42	19	20 10	53
16.4	Chelsfield		30 18	34½		–	–		–	–		–	–
17.7	Knockholt		32 40	30		33 26	31½		30 51	37		23 08	58½
			p.w.s.	*15		–	–		–	–		–	–
21.7	Dunton Green		38 37	65½		37 59	68		35 20	64		26 35	77½
23.2	Sevenoaks	37½	40 06	55½	37	39 33	56	39	36 54	55/53	27	28 01	60
28.1	Hildenborough		44 57	72½		44 11	80		–	71		32 20	(slack)
30.6	TONBRIDGE	45½	47 45	*39	44½	46 27	*	47	44 22	*45	34	34 43	75
35.9	Paddock Wood	51½	53 42	64½	50	51 27	76	53	49 50	72	39½	39 54	50
			p.w.s.	*30		–			–	–		p.w.s.	(slack)
40.5	Marden		59 44	53		55 07	75		53 42	70		45 31	69
43.0	Staplehurst		62 20	64½		57 10	76		55 48	73/75		47 30	*20
46.3	Headcorn		65 17	69		59 50	74		58 21	74		50 06	70
51.5	Pluckley		69 54	66/71		64 11	73		62 55	68		54 17	70/80½
55.0	*Chart Siding*		72 56	67		67 21	66		–	72		–	76/72
			–	–		–	–		sigs.	–		sigs.	78
57.2	ASHFORD	72	74 48	73½	69½	69 07	72	74	68 38	56	59½	59 25	–
61.5	Smeeth		78 37	66½		72 49	67		–	–		63 14	50
65.3	Westenhanger		82 14	60		76 27	59½		76 46	60		66 15	64
66.5	Sandling Jct.	81	83 27	69	81	77 42	64½		77 59	64/70		–	78
71.0	FOLKESTONE CENTRAL		87 33	–		81 33	73		82 13	*60		–	72
72.0	Folkestone Jct.	87½	88 29	–	84	82 23	70	90	83 26	57	73	72 00	–
			–	–		p.w.s.	40		eased	–		sigs.	–
78.0	DOVER MARINE	95	96 40	–	92	90 47	–	100	94 11	–	82	81 10	eased
													–

* Speed restriction ‡ On loan to Stewarts Lane	First published in *Four Thousand Miles on the Footplate,* O. S. Nock, Ian Allan, 1952, p.196.	First published in *Trains Illustrated,* Vol.X, No.101, February 1957, p.85.	First published in *Railway Magazine,* Vol.101, No.650, June 1955, p.413.	First published in *Railway Magazine,* Vol.108, No.739, November 1962, p.780.

Knockholt, the engine accelerating to 28mph up the 1 in 100 to Petts Wood and further to 42mph on the 1 in 310 up to Orpington, finally falling to 37 on the climb to Knockholt. Maximum speed through Hildenborough was 71mph, after which full power was again applied along the Paddock Wood to Ashford stretch with speeds between 70 and 75mph until the eight-mile ascent from Headcorn to Chart mostly at 1 in 346/268 where it fell to 68mph. After a signal check through Ashford, a steady 60mph was kept up to Westenhanger, followed by easy running from Folkestone Jct. leading to an arrival at Dover Marine almost six minutes ahead of schedule.

The last run timed in Table 5.17 again featured the "Golden Arrow" this time with a 2,500hp DC electric in charge. The train was away fairly smartly from Victoria but traffic congestion in the Brixton area brought speed down to 20mph. For a steam-powered "Golden Arrow", this would have made

TABLE 5.18
SR Dover Marine–London Victoria

Date	c.1955	c.1956	c.1959	1951
Train	The "Golden Arrow"	The "Golden Arrow"	The "Golden Arrow"	The "Night Ferry"
Locomotive Class	Britannia Pacific	Unrebuilt West Country Light Pacific	Rebuilt Merchant Navy Pacific	Unrebuilt Merchant Navy Pacific
No.	70004	34102	35015	35029
Name	*William Shakespeare*	*Lapford*	*Rotterdam Lloyd*	*Ellerman Lines*
Shed	Stewarts Lane	Stewarts Lane	Stewarts Lane	Dover
Load	9 Pullmans, 2 vans, 1 truck	7 Pullmans, 3 vans	7 Pullmans, 2 coaches, 3 vans	12 coaches
	375 tons tare 390 tons gross	326 tons tare, 345 tons gross	404 tons tare 425 tons gross	477 tons tare 510 tons gross
Driver/Fireman	J. White/B. Smith Stewarts Lane	J. Brewer/C. Watson Stewarts Lane	not recorded	J. Durrant/E. Blackwell Dover
Recorder(s)	Dr. P. Ransome-Wallis	Mr. N. Harvey	Mr. O.S. Nock	Mr. O.S. Nock

Dist. Miles		Sched. min.	Actual min. sec.	Speed mph	Sched. min.	Actual min. sec.	Speed mph	Sched. min.	Actual min. sec.	Speed mph	Sched. min.	Actual min. sec.	Speed mph
00.0	DOVER MARINE	0	00 00	–	0	00 00	–	0	00 00	–	0	00 00	–
00.4	*Archcliffe Jct.*		–	–		p.w.s.	–		–	–		03 28	–
–	Shakespeare Cliff Halt		–	–		06 10	–		–	–		09 12	–
04.9	Warren Halt		–	–		–	–		–	–		14 49	–
06.0	Folkestone Junction		11 15	46	12	12 25	44		–	–	12	16 29	41½
07.0	FOLKESTONE CENTRAL		12 31	51		13 47	–		13 12	49		17 53	44
07.7	Shorncliffe		–	–		14 40	47		–	–		–	–
08.8	*Cheriton Jct.*		14 30	55		–	–		–	–		20 16	46½
11.5	*Sandling Jct.*		17 28	53		18 55	54		18 35	53	20	23 42	49
12.7	Westenhanger		18 46	56/74		–	–		19 56	–		25 08	50
			sigs.	–		–	–		–	–		–	–
16.5	Smeeth		23 15	★20		–	–		23 20	75		28 52	66/62
			p.w.s.	★40					–	–			
20.8	ASHFORD	26½	29 30	54	27	27 25	72max	26½	26 55	eased	30	32 49	74
						p.w.s.							
23.0	*Chart Siding*		–	–		29 20	★20		–	–		34 43	67
						p.w.s.	–						
26.5	Pluckley		35 07	75		35 15	48		31 17	82		37 44	75/70
31.7	Headcorn		39 10	79/85		39 39	84		35 00	88		42 06	75
35.0	Staplehurst		41 35	82		41 58	84		37 17	86/81		44 44	74
37.5	Marden		43 30	76		43 50	80		39 06	85		46 54	69/75
												stop	brakes
42.1	Paddock Wood	44½	46 58	79	46½	47 05	86	44½	42 25	80	53	55 26	–
47.4	TONBRIDGE	49½	51 25	★44/39	51½	51 40	★40	49½	46 50	slack	58	62 31	45/50
49.9	Hildenborough		54 55	42		55 05	48/46		49 43	50		65 48	44
51.8	*Weald Intermediate Box*		–	–		57 50	48/40		52 22	39		68 44	36½
54.2	*Sevenoaks Tunnel Exit*		–	–		–	–		56 08	38		73 28	slipping
54.8	SEVENOAKS	60½	61 45	51	63	62 00	44	60½	56 52	–	71	74 31	–
56.3	Dunton Green		63 20	56		63 25	50		58 26	65		76 18	57½
			sigs.	★10		sigs.			–	–		–	–
60.3	Knockholt		71 12	47/70		67 50	40/42		62 51	44		81 06	41½
			–	–		sigs.	–		–	–		–	–
63.1	Orpington	69	74 00	60	72	71 35	58/28	69	65 51	62	81	83 53	67
65.4	*Bickley Jct.*	72½	76 59	43	75½	76 05	–	72½	68 35	slack	84½	86 46	slack
67.1	BROMLEY SOUTH		–	–		78 50	54/42		70 46	–		89 28	–
69.3	Beckenham Jct.	78	82 30	47	81	81 35	50	78	73 38	–	92	93 11	★10
												sigs.	
70.2	Kent House		83 41	–		–	–		74 28	–		94 46	–
			p.w.s.	15									
70.8	Penge		–	–		83 30	46		–	–		97 56	–
												sigs.	
72.3	Sydenham Hill		88 10	41		85 25	48		76 55	–		–	–
74.0	HERNE HILL	85	89 40	–	88	87 40	★slack	85	80 05	–	103	104 43	–
						sigs.	–						
74.8	Brixton		–	–		89 05	–		–	–		–	–
76.1	Wandsworth Road		–	–		–	–		–	–		108 04	–
78.0	LONDON VICTORIA	92	95 50	–	95	95 33	–	92	87 05	–	110	111 46	–

★ speed reduced by brakes

First published in *On Engines in Britain and France,* P. Ransome-Wallis, Ian Allan, 1957, p.198.

First published in *Railway World,* Vol.18, No.208 September 1957, p.232.

First published in *Railway Magazine,* Vol.105, No.702, October 1959, p.705.

First published in *Four Thousand Miles on the Footplate,* O. S. Nock, Ian Allan, 1952, p.192.

for a very bad start but the electric locomotive accelerated swiftly to 54mph on the ascent to Sydenham Hill. Despite the delay at Brixton and the speed constraints at Kent House, Beckenham and Shortlands and the relatively tight schedule, the train was virtually on time at Shortlands. A further severe check to 20mph occurred at Bickley Jct. On practically full power speed rose to 58mph on the climb to Knockholt and by Paddock Wood the train was less than half a minute behind time. A permanent way check to 20mph preceded the fastest sustained period of running, with $80\frac{1}{2}$mph on the level nearing Headcorn and 78mph at Smeeth; arrival at Dover Marine was almost one minute early.

In Table 5.18, runs with the "Golden Arrow" and the "Night Ferry" from Dover Marine to London Victoria are compared. The first timing was by Dr. P. Ransome-Wallis with Britannia Pacific 70004 *William Shakespeare* about 1955. Shortly after starting away from Dover, cut-off was set at 27% with the regulator almost fully open. Folkestone Jct. was passed at 46mph. Later an increase to 32% resulted in the climb to Westenhanger mainly at 1 in 250/270 being taken at around 55mph. After the summit, speed rose to 74mph before a signal check at Smeeth reduced speed to 20mph. There followed a permanent way slack of 40mph but after this, with a clear road, the regulator was fully opened. Ashford was passed at 54mph with cut-off down to 25% some three minutes behind schedule. 70004 was then opened up and a speed of 85mph was attained through Headcorn. Tonbridge was passed only two minutes behind time and with full regulator and 25% cut-off, Hildenborough bank, six miles at 1 in 122/114, was breasted at 39mph, with the regulator eased to about three quarters open, probably to avoid slipping on the wet rails through Sevenoaks tunnel. The ascent to Knockholt was severely hampered by a 10mph signal check at Polhill. Accelerating on the 1 in 143 gradient through Polhill tunnel was a challenge and at 30% cut-off, the regulator had to be eased in order to reduce the risk of slipping. Nevertheless, a speed of 47mph was attained through Knockholt station. A brief 70mph at Chelsfield, with a brake application to 60mph through Orpington reduced lateness there to five minutes. There was then a clear road into Victoria resulting in an arrival less than four minutes late, despite a 15mph permanent way slack after Kent House.

Run no.2 in Table 5.18 was made by Mr. N. Harvey with West Country Light Pacific 34102 *Lapford* on the "Golden Arrow". Apart from a 20mph speed restriction between Chart and Pluckley, no other out-of-course slowings were expected apart from the permanent way slacks normally in force. The uphill work was of an equally fine order with 54mph maintained from Sandling Jct. to Westenhanger, despite the slowing before Pluckley, the 10.4 miles from Headcorn to Paddock Wood were reeled off in just under $7\frac{1}{2}$ minutes with 20% cut-off on the second valve of the regulator. On the ascent from Tonbridge to the north portal of Sevenoaks tunnel a minimum speed of 40mph was sustained. Signal checks on the approach to Victoria meant arrival was just over half a minute behind schedule.

Another run with the up "Golden Arrow" is detailed in Run No.3, on this occasion with rebuilt Merchant Navy Pacific 35015 *Rotterdam Lloyd* with a load of 425 tons gross.

After a moderate start up to Westenhanger and a somewhat restrained descent to Ashford, the engine was opened out,

making an average speed of 84mph over the 15.6 miles from Pluckley to Paddock Wood. The late start had been recovered by Tonbridge which was passed in well under "even time". Although the run was made on a Whitsun Tuesday with heavy traffic bound for London, the train had a virtually clear road, arriving almost five minutes ahead of schedule.

The last run in Table 5.18 was with the "Night Ferry" hauled by unrebuilt Merchant Navy Pacific 35029 *Ellerman Lines*. With over 500 tons behind the tender 35029 repeatedly engaged in bouts of slipping on the climb to Shakespeare's Cliff tunnel, the first three quarters of a mile taking over six and a half minutes. Folkestone Jct. was eventually passed around four and a half minutes late at $41\frac{1}{2}$mph. Acceleration on the climb to Westenhanger however resulted in a speed of 50mph there after which 35029 got into its stride. The speed passing Ashford was 74mph, falling away to 67 on the approach to Chart siding, then reaching maxima of 75mph at both Pluckley and Headcorn. Progress was then halted by a curious incident. The vacuum hose on the front of the engine slipped off the dummy coupling and the train was brought to a stand very quickly. The stoppage lasted little over a minute however but a permanent way slack followed, hampering the climb past Tudeley box. The stoppage and engineers' slack cost all of seven minutes but Tonbridge was passed only four and a half minutes down. On the ascent to Knockholt, 20% cut-off was used and Hildenborough was passed at 44mph but speed then fell to 35mph at the entrance to Sevenoaks tunnel. A further bout of slipping then took place and 35029 took nearly four and a quarter minutes over the $2\frac{1}{2}$ miles from Weald box to the north portal. Speed increased to $57\frac{1}{2}$mph on the downgrade through Dunton Green and cut-off was increased to 20% for the remainder of the ascent to Knockholt passed at $41\frac{1}{2}$mph following another bout of slipping in Polhill tunnel. On the downgrade through Orpington, speed touched 67mph. Progress was sedate through the suburbs approaching Victoria with yet another slipping incident on the 1 in 101 up to Penge following a signal check. Despite all the problems, *Ellerman Lines* drew into Victoria less than two minutes late, having experienced some 11-12 minutes delay on the road.

5.2 Performance in Service

From 1950, BR produced annual performance statistics for its locomotive fleet. The data summarised details of the operating stock, average annual mileage and average amount of time spent under repair for individual locomotives of each class. The figures were referred to as the 'Miles and Days' statistics and were used as a general guide to productivity of the various classes. Availability was defined as the number of days in service in a year compared with a notional maximum which in 1953 was 315 days (314 for the ScR), later reduced to 309 days (310 for the ScR) beginning in 1954.

A brief synopsis for each BR Standard Class for the years 1953 (tender classes only), 1954, 1956 and 1958 follows. After the latter year, the collection of data was much reduced, in line with the increasing focus on alternative modes of traction.

5.2.1. Britannia Class 7 Pacifics - 70000-70054

The high mileage and availability associated with the ER allocation in 1953 (Table 5.19) reflected its intensive use on the Liverpool St.-Norwich services; two of the ER contingent on loan to the LMR in that year showed even higher mileage and availability. This was higher than the LMR's own allocation of five locomotives, although one of their number, 70043, was involved in the Westinghouse brake trials from October onwards and was thus unavailable for operational service.

The two SR engines, 70004/14, were very poorly utilised, averaging less than 10,000 miles each and, moreover, were apparently 'not required' for 35 days each during the year. The availability of a large number of Bulleid Pacifics to the SR authorities was certainly a factor here.

Data for the WR stud of 15 locomotives has not been traced for 1953 but, based on statistics from subsequent years, it would be surprising if the figures had indicated mileage in excess of 50,000 and availability of more than 60%.

In the following year, 1954 (Table 5.20), the ER allocation still held the 'Blue Riband' for both mileage and availability. The LMR contingent, now increased to ten locomotives were on a par with other Class 7 power on the Region whilst the SR couple showed a doubling of mileage compared with the previous year, albeit with a significant increase in time out for classified repairs. The 15 WR locomotives had a similar mileage to that of the main Class 7 power on the Region, the Castle Class 4-6-0s, but again with considerably more time out for repairs. The ScR allocation, 70050-4, was delivered during the latter half of 1954 and no data was generated by the Region for the class until the following year.

The situation was similar for the Britannia class during 1956 (Table 5.21) but the SR utilisation continued to disappoint and there must have been questions posed 'on high' about the economics of leaving the locomotives with the Region.

In 1958 (Table 5.22), the main operational change was the transfer of six of the class to the LMR Midland Division. The accelerated timings on the London St. Pancras-Manchester route introduced in 1957 were proving too much for the Jubilee Class 4-6-0s, the staple express power on the route. Timekeeping had suffered and double-heading was not uncommon. The Britannias arrived in the middle of the year, the choice of candidates being fairly straightforward. The SR pair, 70004/14 under-utilised for years, was obvious. From the WR, where the class was not universally appreciated, 70015/7/21 were released and with the arrival of the new English Electric Type 4 diesels (later designated Cl.40), D200 (40122), D202-205 (40002-5) for the Liverpool St.-Norwich services, 70042 was also included in the move.

From 1958 the delivery of more Type 4 diesel classes to the ER, LMR and WR accelerated, after which express steam power, including the Britannia class, was gradually eased out of its previous role.

5.2.2. Class 8 Pacific 71000 *Duke of Gloucester*

The sole member of the class, introduced in 1954, was well established on the LMR by 1956 (Table 5.23) and was a regular performer on the down "Mid-Day Scot", Euston-Glasgow. Compared with other Class 8 power on the LMR, however, 71000's mileage was lower, much lower indeed than that of the two roller bearing-fitted Duchess Pacifics, 46256/7. Only the SR's Merchant Navy Pacifics and the WR's King Class 4-6-0s had lower productivity for the year. There was no improvement in 1958, when only the ER's W1 4-6-2-2 (rebuilt from Gresley's 'Hush-Hush' locomotive 1000) and

the A1/1 4-6-2 60113 *Great Northern* had lower overall productivity. The significant improvement in the Merchant Navy Pacifics performance could be attributed to the fact that around half of the class had been rebuilt with Walschaerts valve gear and with air-smoothed casing removed by the end of the year.

5.2.3. Clan Class 6 Pacifics 72000-72009

The ScR was the only Region to receive this class on introduction in 1952. Performance in terms of mileage and availability was broadly similar to that of the Jubilee 4-6-0s, with which they shared some duties. In early 1958, Carlisle Kingmoor depot was transferred from the ScR to the LMR, along with its allocation of the class (72005-9). Again, the overall productivity of the Clans and the LMR's Jubilee Class was similar. It will be noted that 72009 spent a few weeks operating from the ER's Stratford depot from mid-October.

5.2.4. Class 5 4-6-0 73000-73171

In 1953, the ScR allocation achieved high mileage as a result of their intensive use on the Glasgow-Aberdeen services. The figure was significantly higher than that of both the Stanier and B1 4-6-0 classes on the ScR with similar availability. This continued through 1954 but with the total number operating in the Region in 1956 having increased to 35 and then 45 in 1958, allocated to other sheds and routes, the mileage figure was lower, approaching that of the ScR-based Stanier Class 5 4-6-0s.

For the initial LMR allocation, the 1953 mileage was similar to that of the Stanier 4-6-0s but availability was lower due to the apparent need for many more days out of action under repair. In the following year, the Standard Class 5 4-6-0 productivity improved and this continued through to 1958.

The 1953 data for the WR has not been traced but in 1956, the WR was operating some 25 Standard Class 5 4-6-0s. Productivity was lower than that of other Class 5 power on the Region, a situation which showed no improvement to 1958. Lower utilisation of the ER batch was also a feature of the 1956 statistics but showed improvement by 1958. The ER and NER figures were reported separately in 1958 and the Region's Standard 5s were on a par with the Stanier 5s for mileage and availability.

Although the SR received four of the Standard 5 class during 1954, no statistics on mileage and availability were issued. The figures for 1956 and 1958 show the Region's Standard 5s averaging over 40,000 miles each per year with over 70% availability which was similar to the two Stanier 5s remaining on the S&D line and represented an improvement on the productivity of other Cl. 5 power on the Region.

5.2.5. Class 4 4-6-0 75000-75079

The allocation of the class for all three Regions, LMR, WR and SR showed respectable availabilities with average annual mileages in excess of 30,000. Despite the fact that during the debate on which designs should be included in the building programme the LMR saw no role for such a locomotive, the Region nevertheless had over 60% of the class on its books by the end of 1958.

Taking into account the tendency of Swindon Works to spend more time on the repair of the Standard classes compared with the WR 'native' types, the WR allocation of Class 4 4-6-0s nevertheless had overall a similar productivity to that of the Region's 43xx 2-6-0s. On the SR, the productivity of the class was similar to that of the Region's Class 4 2-6-0s.

5.2.6. Class 4 2-6-0 76000-76114

The BR Class 4 2-6-0 design was similar to that of the LM Class 4 2-6-0 introduced just prior to Nationalisation, so overall performances on the ER, NER and LMR were similar. On the SR, the class demonstrated improved productivity compared with that of the established N, N1, U and U1 2-6-0s with whom they shared some duties.

5.2.7. Class 3 2-6-0 77000-77019

The class was allocated initially to only two Regions, ScR and NER. Their productivity on the ScR was similar to that of the Standard Class 4 2-6-0s in 1956 and 1958 with annual average mileages approaching 30,000. On the NER their branch line work was soon to be taken over by diesel multiple units and by 1958, the engines were officially 'not required' for almost two months each.

5.2.8. Class 2 2-6-0s 78000-78064

The Standard Class 2 2-6-0s introduced in 1953 were a virtual copy of the LMS Class 2 2-6-0s of 1946. Productivities were similar but annual mileages for the Standard Class 2s had fallen to little more than 20,000 on the LMR, ScR and WR in 1958. In the case of the ER/NER allocation the equivalent figure was as low as 15,700 and 13,300 respectively as their traditional work either dried up or was taken over by diesels.

5.2.9. Class 4 2-6-4T 80000-80154

In 1954, (Table 5.24) the ER allocation continued to be employed on the intensive former LT&SR commuter service alongside LM three-cylinder Class 4 2-6-4Ts and also LM two-cylinder Class 4 2-6-4Ts of which they were a development. High mileages and availability characterised the 2-6-4 tank classes on this section. Later deliveries to the ER in 1956 (Table 5.25) were to Neasden for similar duties on the ex-GCR routes from Marylebone, again with a high productivity. In 1958 (Table 5.26), the NER allocation was at Whitby until June when much of their work was taken over by diesel multiple units; utilisation was significantly lower than that of their stablemates on the ER.

The ScR and SR locomotives also achieved high productivity on commuter services, the BR and LM 2-6-4T classes showing similar performance, although on the SR, the BR class had the the edge. On the LMR, the class was not so intensively used. Availability was high but average mileage did not exceed 30,000; again performance was on a par with that of the Region's LM 2-6-4Ts.

5.2.10. Class 3 2-6-2T 82000-82044

In 1956, the NER allocation achieved high productivity on the Darlington-Penrith trains via the Stainmore route. At the beginning of 1958 however, the service was given over to diesel multiple units. The reassignment of the class in that year

resulted in a halving of the annual average mileage with each locomotive officially recorded as 'not required' for almost one month each.

On the SR, the class was based at Exmouth Junction and Eastleigh on delivery showing good mileage and availability, which continued through 1956 and 1958. The WR engines returned similar mileage figures to those on the SR but with lower utilisation; average mileages declined as dieselisation gained pace.

The LMR which had not seen a need for the class, never-the-less had seven examples on its books by the end of 1958, achieving a modest average mileage of 25,000 each. Productivity was an improvement over the LM Class 3 2-6-2Ts operating on other parts of the Region.

5.2.11. Class 2 2-6-2T 84000-84029

The 84xxx class was based on the LM Ivatt Class 2-6-2 design and was used on similar duties, including branch line 'push and pull' services. As these routes were gradually dieselised, utilisation of the class was lower until by 1958, the number of "not required' days had increased to an average of 40 per locomotive.

The SR allocation was delivered in the first half of 1957 and was initially based at Ramsgate and Ashford, where productivity was good, the average mileage achieved being in excess of 35,000 per locomotive. Again the number of 'not required' days had increased to almost one month by 1958.

5.2.12. Class 9F 2-10-0 92000-92250

Mileage and availability for this class was covered in Volume Four of this series on page 225.

5.2.13. Non-Steam Traction

Statistics for the small number of diesel, electric and gas turbine locomotives operating on BR have been traced for the years 1956 and 1958 (Table 5.27).

In 1956, productivity of the six main line diesels in service on the LMR was low, with many days out of action under repair. In contrast, figures for the Co-Co 1,470hp dc electric units 20001-3 which were well established on the SR's Victoria-Newhaven route showed high productivity for the class, 72,000 miles in the year with an availability of 84%.

For 1958, the data for the LMR diesels showed considerable improvement in both mileage and availability for the year, although the productivity of the Bo-Bo unit 10800 was still low with no less than 160 days recorded as under repair. The SR Co-Co units had even greater productivity than in 1956.

Statistics for the Manchester-Sheffield-Wath electrics in 1958 indicated excellent productivity with the EMI Bo-Bo units showing 94% availability.

The WR gas turbine unit, 18000, had an overall availability of only 41% in 1958 but the mileage for that year, at 45,600, compared well with the figures for the WR Britannia Pacific and the Castle class 4-6-0 allocation at 46,600 and 48,900 respectively.

70004 *William Shakespeare,* one of three of the class that were allocated originally to the Southern Region, breasts the climb of 1 in 100 from Beckenham Jct. to Shortlands Jct. on the down "Golden Arrow" on 3rd August 1957. The locomotive was built at Crewe Works and delivered directly to the Festival of Britain in London before being allocated together with 70014 *Iron Duke* to Stewarts Lane depot for work on the "Golden Arrow" and "Night Ferry" services. 70009 *Alfred the Great* spent a short time on the south western section of the Southern Region before being moved to the Great Eastern section.   *Kenneth Wightman*

84007 at Castle Ashby on the 10.25am Northampton–Wellingborough train on 18th March 1961. This class was introduced in 1953 to replace many ageing 0-4-4, 0-4-2, 2-4-2 and 0-6-2 tank engines that were coming to the end of their useful lives. The class of 30 did not last long; 84000 had the longest life of 12 years 3 months and 84027 the shortest, lasting only just over 6 years 11 months.   *Alan Sainty collection*

Loco Class	Operating Stock at 31.12.53	Average Annual Miles ('000s)	Weekdays Out Of Service (WOOS)				Total WOOS	In Service	
			Repairs					No. of Days	% of Total Possible (315 days)
			Classified Shop & Shed	Running & Exams	Total Repairs	Not Re-quired			
ER/NER									
BR Cl.7 4-6-2	21	71.8	31	30	61	2	63	252	80
BR Cl.7 4-6-2	2	77.0	5	27	32	3	35	280	89
(on loan to LMR)									
A3 Cl. 4-6-2	59	48.2	26	64	90	2	92	223	71
A2 Cl. 4-6-2	4	61.5	23	43	66	3	69	246	78
A2/2 Cl. 4-6-2	6	39.5	37	79	116	3	119	196	62
A2/3 Cl. 4-6-2	14	52.1	20	71	91	2	93	222	71
A2/1 Cl. 4-6-2	1	46.4	80	30	110	1	111	204	65
V2 Cl. 2-6-2	141	39.8	21	57	78	3	81	234	74
B1 Cl. 4-6-0	326	39.0	23	35	58	4	62	253	80
B16/1 Cl.4-6-0	45	26.5	19	53	72	8	80	235	75
BR Cl.4 2-6-0	10	28.5	2	44	46	5	51	264	84
LM Cl.4 2-6-0	97	24.8	23	30	53	4	57	258	82
K2 Cl. 2-6-0	45	24.6	23	35	58	11	69	246	78
LMR									
BR Cl.7 4-6-2	5	67.3	7	76	83	3	86	229	73
Scot 4-6-0	1	68.3	29	62	91	nil	91	224	71
Scot Par 4-6-0	3	46.4	8	91	99	nil	99	216	79
Scot Con 4-6-0	62	61.7	35	53	88	1	89	226	72
5X Con 4-6-0	20	60.2	34	53	87	1	88	227	72
LM Jub 4-6-0	159	53.7	27	51	78	2	80	235	75
LM Pat 4-6-0	34	41.9	21	58	79	1	80	235	75
BR Cl.5 4-6-0	18	43.2	37	63	100	nil	100	215	68
LM Cl.5 4-6-0	507	40.3	20	37	57	3	60	255	81
BR Cl.4 4-6-0	30	31.6	9	55	64	4	68	247	78
ScR									
BR Cl.6 4-6-2	10	57.6	19	67	86	1	87	227	72★
LM Jub 4-6-0	29	50.4	30	52	82	1	83	231	74★
ER V2 Cl. 2-6-2	43	39.3	27	69	96	1	97	217	69★
BR Cl.5 4-6-0	5	65.2	24	57	81	1	82	232	74★
LM Cl.5 4-6-0	238	44.6	33	39	72	2	74	240	76★
B1 Cl. 4-6-0	70	38.6	20	50	70	1	71	243	77★
BR Cl.4 2-6-0	5	31.6	10	29	39	5	44	270	86★
LM Cl.4 2-6-0	10	28.5	19	43	62	3	65	249	79★
LM Cpd 4-4-0	43	14.3	25	53	78	113	191	123	39★
SR									
BR Cl.7 4-6-2	2	9.9	15	82	97	35	132	183	58
SR Light 4-6-2	110	42.4	27	61	88	20	108	207	66
LN Cl. 4-6-0	16	43.7	22	47	69	10	79	236	75
N15/X 4-6-0	7	26.3	11	49	60	39	99	216	69
N15 4-6-0	73	30.9	18	42	60	54	114	201	64
V Cl. 4-4-0	40	37.6	32	31	63	31	94	221	70
LM Cl.5 4-6-0	3	46.9	16	45	61	2	63	252	80
(S&D Line)									
BR Cl.4 2-6-0	20	37.1	nil	35	35	6	41	274	87
N Cl. 2-6-0	80	27.7	29	30	58	8	66	249	79
U Cl. 2-6-0	50	29.5	32	36	68	9	77	237	79
WR	–	–	–	–	–	–	–	–	–

Note: WR data not traced   ★ ScR adopted 314 days as total possible

Key for Tables 5.19 – 5.23

Engine Classes

Scot 4-6-0	Royal Scot Conversion of High Pressure steam locomotive 6399
Scot Par. 4-6-0	Royal Scot with Parallel Boiler
Scot Con. 4-6-0	Royal Scot Rebuilt with 2A Taper Boiler
5X Con. 4-6-0	Jubilee or Patriot Cl. Rebuilt with 2A Taper Boiler
LM Jub 4-6-0	Jubilee Cl. 6P/5F
LM Pat 4-6-0	Patriot Cl. 6P/5F
F. Crab 2-6-0	Fowler Crab 2-6-0
S. Crab 2-6-0	Stanier Crab 2-6-0
LM Cpd 4-4-0	LM Compound Cl. 4-4-0

TABLE 5.20

BR Standard Tender Engine Classes
Comparison of Average Annual Mileage and Availability with Other Classes for the Year 1954

| Loco Class | Operating Stock @ 31.12.54 | Average Annual Miles ('000s) | Weekdays Out Of Service (WOOS) | | | | | In Service | |
| | | | Repairs | | | | | | |
			Classified Shop & Shed	Running & Exams	Total Repairs	Not Required	Total WOOS	No. of Days	% of Total Possible (309 days)
ER/NER									
BR Cl.7 4-6-2	23	74.6	40	35	75	1	76	233	75
A3 Cl. 4-6-2	59	51.1	28	56	84	2	86	223	72
A2 Cl. 4-6-2	4	64.2	23	42	65	1	66	243	79
A2/2 Cl. 4-6-2	6	37.9	46	73	119	1	120	189	61
A2/3 Cl. 4-6-2	14	53.0	34	55	89	1	90	219	71
A2/1 Cl. 4-6-2	1	57.5	4	57	61	nil	61	248	80
V2 Cl. 2-6-2	141	41.2	23	52	75	1	76	233	75
B1 Cl. 4-6-0	326	38.6	27	32	59	4	63	246	80
B16/1 Cl.4-6-0	45	26.9	26	51	77	7	84	225	73
BR Cl.4 2-6-0	20	23.0	4	27	31	4	35	274	89
LM Cl.4 2-6-0	97	23.5	23	25	48	4	52	257	83
K2 Cl. 2-6-0	45	23.7	35	29	64	3	67	242	78
BR Cl.2 2-6-0	10	28.0	nil	45	45	8	53	256	83
LM Cl.2 2-6-0	18	27.3	14	41	55	12	67	242	78
LMR									
BR Cl.7 4-6-2	10	55.4	8	79	87	nil	87	222	72
Scot 4-6-0	1	46.1	84	62	146	nil	146	163	53
Scot Con 4-6-0	64	60.6	30	54	84	1	85	224	72
Scot Par 4-6-0	1	47.1	40	49	89	1	90	219	71
5X Conv. 4-6-0	20	61.8	24	56	80	1	81	228	74
LM Jub 4-6-0	159	54.3	23	53	76	2	78	231	75
LM Pat 4-6-0	34	40.4	27	50	77	2	79	230	74
BR Cl.5 4-6-0	30	41.4	10	47	57	2	59	250	81
LM Cl.5 4-6-0	507	40.2	17	37	54	3	57	252	82
F. Crab 2-6-0	179	25.7	19	41	60	5	65	244	79
S. Crab 2-6-0	40	26.1	24	35	59	3	62	247	80
BR Cl.4 4-6-0	30	35.7	10	34	44	7	51	258	83
ScR									
BR Cl.7 4-6-2 †	5	–	–	–	–	–	–	–	–
BR Cl.6 4-6-2	10	54.1	28	51	79	4	83	228	73★
LM Jub 4-6-0	29	51.9	24	44	68	1	69	242	78★
BR Cl.5 4-6-0	15	67.9	26	48	74	nil	74	237	76★
LM Cl.5 4-6-0	238	44.9	27	40	67	1	68	243	78★
B1 4-6-0	70	37.9	22	46	68	1	69	242	78★
BR Cl.4 2-6-0	5	29.5	nil	45	45	5	50	261	84★
LM Cl.4 4-6-0	10	26.3	18	48	66	2	68	243	78★
SR									
BR Cl. 7 4-6-2	2	23.1	72	78	150	36	186	123	40
SR Light 4-6-2	110	42.7	30	55	85	24	109	200	65
LN Cl. 4-6-0	16	41.9	31	43	74	10	84	225	73
LM Cl.5 4-6-0 #	2	38.8	9	41	50	11	61	248	80
BR Cl.4 2-6-0	20	37.4	4	45	49	8	57	252	82
U Cl. 2-6-0	50	31.1	16	40	56	17	73	236	77
N Cl. 2-6-0	80	28.7	21	29	50	9	59	250	81
WR									
BR Cl.7 4-6-2	15	48.3	26	104	130	4	134	175	57
Castle Cl. 4-6-0	167	49.0	36	49	85	3	88	221	72
County Cl. 4-6-0	30	40.4	32	58	90	3	93	216	70
BR Cl.5 4-6-0 (LMR owners)	17	29.1	16	71	87	5	92	217	70
BR Cl.5 4-6-0 (ScR owners)	8	38.1	nil	62	62	4	66	243	79
LM Cl.5 4-6-0	8	43.8	15	46	61	3	64	245	79
Star Cl.4-6-0	3	41.4	14	58	72	2	74	235	76
Hall Cl.4-6-0	329	42.0	15	42	57	3	60	249	81
Grange Cl.4-6-0	76	38.1	18	43	61	3	64	245	79
BR Cl.4 4-6-0	20	35.0	24	38	62	5	67	242	78
Manor Cl. 4-6-0	30	35.5	9	40	49	3	52	257	83
43XX Cl. 2-6-0	212	30.1	18	39	57	4	61	248	80
BR Cl.2 2-6-0	10	26.4	2	62	64	8	72	237	77
LM Cl.2 2-6-0	25	27.9	3	48	51	8	59	250	81

* ScR adopted 311 days as total possible   # S&D line   † No data, new during 1954

TABLE 5.21
BR Standard Tender Engine Classes
Comparison of Average Annual Mileage and Availability with Other Classes for the Year 1956

| Loco Class | Operating Stock @ 31.12.56 | Average Annual Miles ('000s) | Weekdays Out Of Service (WOOS) | | | | | In Service | |
| | | | Repairs | | | | | | |
			Classified Shop & Shed	Running & Exams	Total Repairs	Not Required	Total WOOS	No. of Days	% of Total Possible (309 days)
ER/NER									
BR Cl.7 4-6-2	23	74.0	47	46	93	2	95	214	69
A3 Cl. 4-6-2	59	51.2	32	52	84	10	94	215	70
A2 Cl. 4-6-2	4	59.0	28	58	86	4	90	219	71
A2/2 Cl.4-6-2	6	40.3	43	61	104	2	106	203	66
A2/3 Cl. 4-6-2	14	52.4	29	54	83	2	85	224	72
A2/1 Cl. 4-6-2	1	44.7	16	64	80	4	84	225	73
V2 Cl. 2-6-2	141	43.1	22	46	68	2	70	239	77
BR Cl.5 4-6-0	5	30.5	21	106	127	13	140	169	55
LM Cl.5 4-6-0	1	29.8	16	76	92	13	105	204	66
BR Cl.4 2-6-0	28	30.0	12	32	44	6	50	259	84
LM Cl.4 2-6-0	97	22.4	17	39	56	7	63	246	80
BR Cl.3 2-6-0	10	23.6	16	44	60	37	97	212	69
BR Cl.2 2-6-0	10	19.5	19	40	59	22	81	228	74
LM Cl.2 2-6-0	18	18.4	17	39	56	15	71	238	77
LMR									
BR Cl.7 4-6-2	10	57.6	40	56	96	nil	96	213	69
Scot 4-6-0	1	48.2	70	72	142	nil	142	167	54
Scot Con. 4-6-0	65	59.1	38	52	90	1	91	218	71
5X Con 4-6-0	20	57.9	33	58	91	1	92	217	70
BR Cl.5 4-6-0	39	40.4	18	50	68	2	70	239	77
LM Cl.5 4-6-0	513	40.6	22	34	56	4	60	249	81
F. Crab 2-6-0	180	26.1	20	41	61	7	68	241	78
S. Crab 2-6-0	40	26.5	23	38	61	3	64	245	79
BR Cl.4 4-6-0	33	33.9	24	38	62	9	71	238	77
BR Cl.2 2-6-0	35	22.7	2	49	51	11	62	247	80
LM Cl.2 2-6-0	80	25.4	10	30	40	10	50	259	84
ScR									
BR Cl.7 4-6-2	5	57.4	33	72	105	6	111	199	64★
Scot Con. 4-6-0	5	53.2	28	72	100	2	102	208	67★
BR Cl.6 4-6-2	10	53.5	32	44	76	2	78	232	75★
LM Jub 4-6-0	29	50.0	28	43	71	1	72	238	77★
BR Cl.5 4-6-0	35	49.1	15	45	60	2	62	248	80★
LM Cl.5 4-6-0	238	42.7	24	46	70	3	73	237	76★
F. Crab 2-6-0	65	28.9	21	48	69	9	78	232	75★
B1 Cl. 4-6-0	83	36.1	18	50	68	2	70	240	77★
BR Cl.4 2-6-0	10	28.9	nil	28	28	10	38	272	88★
LM Cl. 4 4-6-0	10	23.9	11	50	61	2	63	247	80★
BR Cl.3 2-6-0	10	28.8	4	39	43	8	51	259	84★
BR Cl.2 2-6-0	10	26.5	nil	18	18	5	23	287	93★
LM Cl.2 2-6-0	5	17.4	25	57	82	6	88	222	71★
SR									
BR Cl.7 4-6-2	2	29.6	2	88	90	65	155	154	50
SR Light 4-6-2	110	44.0	33	50	83	25	108	201	65
LN Cl. 4-6-0	16	35.5	16	53	69	19	88	221	72
BR Cl.5 4-6-0	25	42.1	13	54	67	19	85	223	72
LM Cl.5 4-6-0 †	2	39.7	12	45	57	28	85	224	73
N15 Cl. 4-6-0	63	28.9	13	50	63	56	119	190	62
V Cl. 4-4-0	40	36.6	32	37	69	31	100	209	68
BR Cl.4 4-6-0	15	32.7	nil	38	38	43	81	228	74
BR Cl.4 2-6-0	37	36.9	21	41	62	10	72	237	77
U Cl. 2-6-0	50	28.8	22	35	57	18	75	234	76
N Cl. 2-6-0	80	28.3	19	31	50	12	62	247	80
WR									
BR Cl.7 4-6-2	15	46.6	40	89	129	nil	129	180	58
Castle Cl. 4-6-0	167	45.6	56	47	103	1	104	205	66
Star Cl. 4-6-0	2	40.3	nil	58	58	2	60	249	81
County Cl.4-6-0	30	40.5	43	48	91	3	94	215	70
BR Cl.5 4-6-0	35	25.3	18	63	81	4	85	224	72
LM Cl.5 4-6-0	8	40.4	21	37	58	1	59	250	81
Hall Cl. 4-6-0	329	41.5	18	41	59	3	62	247	80
Grange Cl. 4-6-0	76	38.4	14	45	59	3	62	249	80
BR Cl.4 4-6-0	20	31.7	44	42	86	7	93	216	70
Manor Cl. 4-6-0	30	32.7	20	37	57	3	60	250	81
43XX Cl. 2-6-0	206	29.7	21	38	59	3	62	247	80
BR Cl.2 2-6-0	10	20.1	35	38	73	11	84	225	73
LM Cl.2 2-6-0	25	24.7	46	27	73	5	78	231	75

* ScR adopted 310 days as total   † S&D line

TABLE 5.22
BR Standard Tender Engine Classes
Comparison of Average Annual Mileage and Availability with Other Classes for the Year 1958

Loco Class	Operating Stock @ 31.12.58	Average Annual Miles ('000s)	Classified Shop & Shed	Running & Exams	Total Repairs	Not Required	Total WOOS	No. of Days	% of Total Possible (309 days)
ER									
BR Cl.7 4-6-2	22	61.2	41	29	70	4	74	235	76
A3 Cl.4-6-2	29	54.6	30	60	90	3	93	216	70
V2 Cl.2-6-2	57	38.7	24	60	84	2	86	223	72
BR.Cl.5 4-6-0	14	37.9	23	63	86	14	100	209	68
B1 Cl. 4-6-0	207	36.6	23	39	62	5	67	242	78
BR Cl.4 2-6-0	5	20.3	21	39	60	6	66	243	79
LM Cl.4 2-6-0	56	24.2	17	33	50	10	60	249	81
BR Cl. 2 2-6-0	6	15.7	33	48	81	3	84	225	73
LM Cl.2 2-6-0	9	24.3	19	35	54	5	59	250	81
NER									
BR Cl.7 4-6-2	3	56.3	17	73	90	1	91	218	71
Scot Con. 4-6-0	5	69.6	37	37	74	nil	74	235	76
A3 Cl.4-6-2	30	57.7	35	51	86	16	102	207	67
V2 Cl. 2-6-2	76	38.8	29	67	96	3	99	210	68
LM Jub 4-6-0	22	57.5	32	45	77	1	78	231	75
BR Cl.5 4-6-0	17	39.0	5	53	58	1	59	250	81
LM Cl.5 4-6-0	35	43.3	21	38	59	2	61	248	80
B1 Cl. 4-6-0	96	32.6	25	37	62	6	68	241	78
F. Crab 2-6-0	15	22.8	44	45	89	6	95	214	69
BR Cl.4 2-6-0	6	21.5	17	54	71	10	81	228	74
LM Cl.4 2-6-0	47	20.0	11	46	57	6	63	246	80
BR Cl.3 2-6-0	10	16.2	14	33	47	58	105	204	66
BR Cl.2 2-6-0	6	13.3	7	31	38	60	98	211	68
LM Cl.2 2-6-0	22	15.6	10	34	44	16	60	249	81
LMR									
BR Cl.7 4-6-2	15	51.6	25	79	104	3	107	202	65
A3 Cl. 4-6-2	4	52.9	19	71	90	nil	90	219	71
Scot 4-6-0	1	63.8	42	45	87	nil	87	222	72
Scot Con. 4-6-0	60	57.0	33	53	86	2	88	221	72
5X Con 4-6-0	20	58.1	33	52	85	1	86	223	72
BR Cl.6 4-6-2	5	46.0	52	55	107	2	109	200	65
LM Jub 4-6-0	134	49.7	25	51	76	3	79	230	74
LM Pat 4-6-0	31	38.2	38	45	83	2	85	224	72
BR Cl.5 4-6-0	16	30.8	25	63	88	4	92	217	70
BR Cl.5 4-6-0 [1]	20	36.2	nil	68	68	3	71	238	77
LM Cl.5 4-6-0	533	39.4	22	39	61	3	64	245	79
F. Crab 2-6-0	188	26.2	15	46	61	6	67	242	78
S. Crab 2-6-0	40	26.0	18	43	61	3	64	245	79
BR Cl.4 4-6-0	50	35.0	21	38	59	10	69	240	78
BR Cl. 4 4-6-0 [2]	1	29.4	55	31	86	22	108	201	65
BR Cl.4 2-6-0	32	27.3	15	53	68	10	78	231	75
LM Cl.4 2-6-0	50	23.1	18	46	64	8	72	237	77
BR Cl.2 2-6-0	33	20.9	11	31	42	23	65	244	79
LM Cl.2 2-6-0	66	22.7	7	31	38	17	55	254	82
ScR									
BR Cl.7 4-6-2	3	43.0	39	85	124	3	127	183	59*
Scot Con 4-6-0	5	52.4	31	75	106	1	107	203	65*
BR Cl.6 4-6-2	5	44.0	22	53	75	2	77	233	75*
LM Jub 4-6-0	11	38.1	24	55	79	24	103	207	67*
BR Cl.5 4-6-0	45	47.3	16	53	69	1	70	240	77*
LM Cl.5 4-6-0	194	40.6	27	51	78	3	81	229	74*
B1 Cl. 4-6-0	75	34.7	17	50	67	2	69	241	78*
F. Crab 2-6-0	39	26.6	19	52	71	10	81	229	74*
BR Cl.4 2-6-0	35	35.7	4	35	39	3	42	268	86*
LM Cl.4 2-6-0	9	23.3	3	59	62	11	73	237	76*
K2/2 Cl.2-6-0	23	23.0	13	40	53	9	62	248	80*
BR Cl.3 2-6-0	10	28.5	6	42	48	3	51	259	84*
BR Cl.2 2-6-0	10	20.3	15	32	47	16	63	247	80*
LM Cl.2 2-6-0	5	21.5	nil	39	39	1	40	270	87*
SR									
BR Cl.5 4-6-0	27	41.0	19	38	57	26	83	226	73
LN Cl. 4-6-0	16	31.2	33	40	73	25	98	211	68
SR Light 4-6-2	110	46.4	25	48	73	21	94	215	70
N15 Cl. 4-6-0	52	25.9	19	51	70	62	132	177	57
V Cl. 4-4-0	40	31.1	27	47	74	39	113	196	63
BR Cl.4 4-6-0	12	35.6	24	37	61	32	93	216	70
BR Cl.4 2-6-0	37	35.4	23	48	71	8	79	230	74
N Cl. 2-6-0	80	28.9	16	28	44	11	55	254	82
U Cl. 2-6-0	50	26.6	22	32	54	26	80	229	74
U1 Cl. 2-6-0	21	27.2	21	47	68	31	99	210	68
WR									
BR Cl.7 4-6-2	12	45.6	44	69	113	1	114	195	63
Castle Cl. 4-6-0	165	48.9	37	51	88	1	89	220	71
BR Cl.5 4-6-0	27	30.8	31	57	88	8	96	213	69
LM Cl.5 4-6-0	8	42.8	12	55	67	1	68	241	78
County Cl. 4-6-0	30	36.5	71	36	107	2	109	200	65
LM Jub 4-6-0	9	62.3	21	47	68	1	69	240	78
LM Pat 4-6-0	3	35.1	35	54	89	2	91	218	71
Manor Cl. 4-6-0	30	32.4	15	39	54	5	59	250	81
Grange Cl. 4-6-0	80	37.7	21	39	60	9	69	240	78
Hall Cl. 4-6-0	329	38.5	23	40	63	6	69	240	78
BR Cl.4 4-6-0	17	29.3	24	46	70	8	78	231	75
43XX Cl. 2-6-0	178	27.6	18	39	57	15	72	237	77
BR Cl.2 2-6-0	10	19.8	23	41	64	18	82	227	73
LM Cl.2 2-6-0	25	26.8	1	40	41	10	51	258	83

* ScR adopted 310 days as total possible   [1] Caprotti valve gear   [2] On loan to WR

TABLE 5.23
BR Standard LMR-based Class 8 4-6-2, 71000 *Duke of Gloucester*
Comparison of Annual Mileage and Availability with Other Class 8 Locomotives for the Years 1956 and 1958

Loco Class	Opera-ting Stock @ year end	Average Annual Miles ('000s)	Weekdays Out Of Service (WOOS)					In Service	
			Repairs					No. of Days	% of Total Possible (309 days)
			Classified Shop & Shed	Running & Exams	Total Repairs	Not Re-quired	Total WOOS		
1956									
ER/NER									
W1 Cl. 4-6-2-2	1	60.4	3	61	64	5	69	240	78
A1 Cl. 4-6-2	45	67.0	27	43	70	3	73	236	76
A4 Cl. 4-6-2	27	65.8	23	62	85	3	88	221	72
LMR									
BR Cl. 8 4-6-2 71000	1	53.1	32	78	110	1	111	198	64
Duchess Cl. 4-6-2	24	68.4	58	55	113	2	115	200	63
Duchess Cl. 4-6-2 (RB Expt.)	3	70.3	50	61	111	4	115	200	63
Duchess Cl. 4-6-2 RB	2	81.5	39	57	96	nil	96	219	70
Princess Cl. 4-6-2	12	58.4	55	74	129	1	130	185	59
ScR									
Duchess Cl. 4-6-2	9	53.8	35	61	96	1	97	213	69★
A1 Cl. 4-6-2	5	76.4	13	21	34	nil	34	276	89★
A4 Cl. 4-6-2	5	62.8	45	44	89	nil	89	221	71★
A4/1 Cl. 4-6-2	2	72.9	20	31	51	nil	51	259	84★
SR									
MN Cl. 4-6-2	30	50.5	45	64	109	22	131	178	58
WR									
King Cl. 4-6-0	30	50.3	73	64	137	1	138	171	55
1958									
ER									
W1 Cl. 4-6-2-2	1	43.0	12	121	133	nil	133	176	57
A1 Cl. 4-6-2	12	66.0	28	65	93	3	96	213	69
A1/1 Cl. 4-6-2	1	44.3	63	84	147	5	152	157	51
A4 Cl. 4-6-2	19	61.2	27	69	96	3	99	210	68
NER									
A1 Cl. 4-6-2	32	64.2	27	60	87	2	89	220	71
A4 Cl. 4-6-2	8	60.2	35	70	105	2	107	202	65
LMR									
BR Cl.8 4-6-2 71000	1	43.5	24	105	129	nil	129	180	58
Duchess Cl. 4-6-2	26	72.0	35	60	95	1	96	213	69
Duchess Cl. 4-6-2 (RB Expt.)	3	69.0	40	59	99	1	100	209	68
Duchess Cl. 4-6-2 RB	2	78.9	37	56	93	1	94	215	70
Princess Cl. 4-6-2	10	52.2	77	53	130	nil	130	179	58
ScR									
Princess Cl. 4-6-2	2	54.1	81	56	137	nil	137	173	56★
Duchess Cl. 4-6-2	7	54.7	27	70	97	2	99	211	68★
A1 Cl. 4-6-2	5	72.3	25	41	66	nil	66	244	79★
A4 Cl. 4-6-2	5	70.4	25	55	80	1	81	229	74★
A4/1 Cl. 4-6-2	2	71.9	54	43	97	nil	97	213	68★
SR									
MN Cl. 4-6-2	30	59.7	31	63	94	18	112	197	64
WR									
King Cl. 4-6-0	30	55.3	47	71	118	1	119	190	61

Key

RB: Roller bearing fitted, RB (Expt.): Experimental roller bearings fitted, A4/1 engines fitted with smaller inside cylinder.

71000 *Duke of Gloucester* with an up Liverpool Lime St. to Euston service at Northchurch tunnel on 9th September 1952. Here the up and down fast lines are nearest the camera and the up and down slow lines are beyond the train, unlike the layout on the West Coast Main Line north of Nuneaton where the slow lines lie outside the fast lines.

Alan Sainty collection

A combination only found on the Somerset & Dorset section with the pairing of 75009 piloting 7F 53806 as they approach the points at Bath Jct. with the summer Saturday trans-England holiday train, 7.00am Cleethorpes-Exmouth on 25th August 1962. Both engines would be detached at Templecombe and replaced by Southern Region locomotives for the remainder of the journey. This train had only two more weeks to be routed via the S&D route before the summer Saturday trains were redirected off the line.

Hugh Ballantyne

TABLE 5.24
BR Standard Tank Engine Classes
Comparison of Average Annual Mileage and Availability with Other Classes for the Year 1954

Loco Class	Operating Stock @ 31.12.54	Average Annual Miles ('000s)	Weekdays Out Of Service (WOOS)					In Service	
			Repairs						% of Total Possible (309 days)
			Classified Shop & Shed	Running & Exams	Total Repairs	Not Required	Total WOOS	No. of Days	
ER									
BR Cl.4 2-6-4T	15	43.9	35	15	50	4	54	255	83
ER Cl.L1 2-6-4T	100	34.0	24	41	65	5	70	239	77
LM Cl.4 2-6-4T	7	33.7	35	49	84	11	95	214	69
LM Cl.4 2-6-4T (Parallel Boiler)	2	27.1	nil	69	69	9	78	231	75
LM Cl.4 2-6-4T (2-cylinder)	28	35.5	39	21	60	3	63	246	80
LM Cl.4 2-6-4T (3-cylinder)	37	37.2	45	14	59	3	62	247	80
ER Cl.V3 2-6-2T	16	32.8	23	35	58	3	61	248	80
LMR									
BR Cl.4 2-6-4T	45	29.9	6	55	61	9	70	239	77
LM Cl.4 2-6-4T (Taper Boiler)	308	32.3	15	35	50	6	56	253	77
LM Cl.4 2-6-4T (Parallel Boiler)	116	28.1	17	43	60	6	66	243	79
BR Cl.2 2-6-2T	20	31.0	3	37	40	7	47	262	85
LM Cl.2 2-6-2T	91	29.6	12	32	44	11	55	254	82
51xx 2-6-2T	10	21.1	20	73	93	3	96	213	69
ScR									
BR Cl.4 2-6-4T (Taper Boiler)	35	38.2	16	31	47	2	49	262	84★
LM Cl.4 2-6-4T	106	34.8	11	36	47	2	49	262	84★
ER Cl.V3 2-6-2T	17	30.4	15	31	46	1	47	264	85★
SR									
BR Cl.4 2-6-4T	13	37.6	19	45	64	5	69	240	78
LM Cl.4 2-6-4T	34	34.6	21	59	80	12	92	217	70
BR Cl.3 2-6-2T	14	34.2	24	26	50	3	53	256	83
BR Cl.2 2-6-2T	5	26.8	7	31	38	2	40	269	87
LM Cl.2 2-6-2T	30	28.5	21	39	60	4	64	245	79
WR									
BR Cl.3 2-6-2T	12	33.1	52	39	91	6	97	212	69
LM Cl.3 2-6-2T	12	18.2	17	35	52	27	79	230	74
45xx 2-6-2T	153	26.0	28	35	63	5	68	241	78
44xx 2-6-2T	3	20.5	7	30	37	4	41	268	87

* ScR adopted 311 days as total possible

TABLE 5.25
BR Standard Tank Engine Classes
Comparison of Average Annual Mileage and Availability with Other Classes for the Year 1956

Loco Class	Operating Stock @ 31.12.56	Average Annual Miles ('000s)	Weekdays Out Of Service (WOOS)					In Service	
			Repairs			Not Required	Total WOOS	No. of Days	% of Total Possible (309 days
			Classified Shop & Shed	Running & Exams	Total Repairs				
ER/NER									
BR Cl.4 2-6-4T	41	35.3	25	36	61	10	71	238	77
ER Cl.L1 2-6-4T	100	29.7	26	40	66	9	75	234	76
LM Cl.4 2-6-4T	7	18.5	1	62	63	55	118	191	62
LM Cl.4 2-6-4T (Parallel Boiler)	2	21.1	18	62	80	30	110	199	64
LM Cl.4 2-6-4T (2-cylinder)	28	35.0	25	38	63	4	67	242	78
LM Cl.4 2-6-4T (3-cylinder)	37	36.3	42	19	61	4	65	244	79
BR Cl.3 2-6-2T	4	43.5	16	30	46	7	53	256	83
ER Cl.V1 2-6-2T	11	22.0	19	26	45	4	49	260	84
ER Cl.V3 2-6-2T	21	30.3	27	27	54	4	58	251	81
LMR									
BR Cl.4 2-6-4T	45	28.6	10	50	60	10	70	239	77
LM Cl.4 2-6-4T (Taper Boiler)	308	32.1	16	32	48	8	56	253	82
LM Cl.4 2-6-4T (Parallel Boiler)	116	29.1	15	38	53	6	59	250	81
BR Cl.3 2-6-2T	2	27.0	nil	46	46	4	50	259	84
BR Cl.2 2-6-2T	20	24.9	11	46	57	28	85	224	72
LM Cl.2 2-6-2T	91	30.1	12	33	45	16	61	248	80
51xx 2-6-2T	10	16.6	3	34	37	75	112	197	64
ScR									
BR Cl.4 2-6-4T (Taper Boiler)	46	37.2	7	33	40	3	43	267	86★
LM Cl.4 2-6-4T	106	35.0	12	36	48	3	51	259	84★
ER Cl.V3 2-6-2T	23	30.1	24	30	54	1	55	255	82★
SR									
BR Cl.4 2-6-4T	19	40.0	31	47	78	10	88	221	72
LM Cl.4 2-6-4T	34	36.0	23	51	74	13	87	222	72
BR Cl.3 2-6-2T	14	37.7	16	22	38	7	45	264	85
WR									
BR Cl.3 2-6-2T	25	34.8	7	49	56	10	66	243	79
LM Cl.3 2-6-2T	12	14.3	12	34	46	58	104	205	66
45xx 2-6-2T	137	25.5	24	38	62	8	70	239	77

* ScR adopted 310 days as total possible.

TABLE 5.26
BR Standard Tank Engine Classes
Comparison of Average Annual Mileage and Availability with Other Classes for the Year 1958

| Loco Class | Operating Stock @ 31.12.58 | Average Annual Miles ('000s) | Weekdays Out Of Service (WOOS) | | | | | In Service | |
| | | | Repairs | | | | | | |
			Classified Shop & Shed	Running & Exams	Total Repairs	Not Re-quired	Total WOOS	No. of Days	% of Total Possible (309 days)
ER									
BR Cl.4 2-6-4T	28	36.8	35	28	63	1	64	245	79
ER Cl.L1 2-6-4T	74	24.9	31	46	77	9	86	223	72
LM Cl.4 2-6-4T (2-cylinder)	16	35.9	26	32	58	4	62	247	80
LM Cl.4 2-6-4T (3-cylinder)	37	35.0	36	24	60	5	65	244	79
NER									
BR Cl.4 2-6-4T	5	30.8	33	53	86	13	99	210	68
LM Cl.4 2-6-4T	45	27.7	14	46	60	16	76	233	75
ER Cl.L1 2-6-4T	10	19.4	17	37	54	32	86	223	72
ER Cl.V3 2-6-2T	22	17.4	17	36	53	21	74	235	76
BR Cl.3 2-6-2T	4	20.6	nil	35	35	26	61	248	80
LM Cl.3 2-6-2T	16	21.1	9	48	57	17	74	235	76
BR Cl.2 2-6-2T	1	12.1	63	89	152	45	197	112	36
LM Cl.2 2-6-2T	23	25.8	2	40	42	20	62	247	80
ER Cl.N1 0-6-2T	7	9.8	nil	40	40	47	87	222	72
LMR									
BR Cl.4 2-6-4T	53	29.0	22	41	63	8	71	238	77
LM Cl.4 2-6-4T (Taper Boiler)	299	28.5	18	36	54	12	67¶	242	78
LM Cl.4 2-6-4T (Parallel Boiler)	101	22.4	18	39	57	9	69¶	240	78
ER Cl.L1 2-6-4T	16	29.3	28	62	90	4	108¶	201	65
BR Cl.3 2-6-2T	7	25.0	49	20	69	2	71	238	77
LM Cl.3 2-6-2T (Taper Boiler)	97	17.6	11	34	45	30	86¶	223	72
LM Cl.3 2-6-2T (Parallel Boiler)	66	10.9	10	37	47	16	134¶	175	57
BR Cl.2 2-6-2T	19	20.9	16	38	54	40	94	215	70
LM Cl.2 2-6-2T	57	27.0	7	32	39	23	67¶	242	78
ScR									
BR Cl.4 2-6-4T	46	32.3	14	48	62	2	64	246	79★
LM Cl.4 2-6-4T (Taper Boiler)	106	34.0	13	42	55	3	58	252	81★
ER Cl.V3 2-6-2T	36	27.3	22	41	63	3	66	244	79★
SR									
BR Cl.4 2-6-4T	23	44.4	12	41	53	9	62	247	80
LM Cl.4 2-6-4T	34	32.3	17	64	81	23	104	205	66
BR Cl.3 2-6-2T	14	37.1	15	23	38	5	43	266	86
BR Cl.2 2-6-2T	10	35.2	1	62	63	29	92	217	70
LM Cl.2 2-6-2T	24	27.2	12	36	48	13	61	248	80
WR									
BR Cl.3 2-6-2T	20	25.3	31	38	69	8	77	232	75
LM Cl.3 2-6-2T	13	15.7	10	33	43	41	84	225	73
45xx 2-6-2T	101	24.6	19	37	56	9	65	244	79

★ ScR adopted 310 days as total possible   ¶ includes number of days stored.

TABLE 5.27
Main Line Non-Steam Traction
Comparison of Annual Mileage and Availability for the Years 1956 and 1958

| Loco Class | Operating Stock @ year end | Average Annual Miles ('000s) | Weekdays Out Of Service (WOOS) | | | | | In Service | |
| | | | Repairs | | | Not Required | Total WOOS | No. of Days | % of Total Possible (309 days) |
			Classified Shop & Shed	Running & Exams	Total Repairs				
1956 **Diesel**									
1Co-Co1 2,000 hp (10203)	1	31.7	188	38	226	Nil	226	83	27
1Co-Co1 1,750 hp (10201/2)	2	10.1	247	17	264	5	269	60	13
Co-Co 1,600hp (10000-01)	2	22.2	209	25	234	7	241	68	22
Bo-Bo 827hp (10800)	1	5.3	213	27	240	4	244	65	21
Electric									
Co-Co 1,470hp (20001-03)	3	72.0	46	nil	46	2	48	261	84
1958 **Diesel**									
1Co-Co1 2,000hp (10203)	1	69.4	98	61	159	nil	159	150	49
1Co-Co1 1,750hp (10201-02)	2	83.0	80	45	125	nil	125	184	60
Co-Co 1,600hp (10000-01)	2	111.4	50	58	108	1	109	200	65
Bo-Bo 827hp (10800)	1	11.3	57	103	160	37	197	112	36
Electric									
Co-Co 1,470hp (20001-03)	3	72.4	23	9	32	nil	32	277	90
EM1 Bo-Bo 1,740hp (26000-57)	58	43.0	16	1	17	2	19	290	94
EM2 Co-Co 2,490hp (27000-06)	7	66.4	62	2	64	3	67	242	78
Gas Turbine									
A-1-A-A-1-A 2,500hp (18000)	1	45.6	64	114	178	5	183	126	41

On 5th July 1964 the Locomotive Club of Great Britain sponsored a rail tour of various Southern Region lines in south London and Surrey. Titled the "Surrey Wanderer" the route included lines to Epsom Downs, Caterham and Tattenham Corner. The obvious attraction to those on the tour was the unusual motive power, 78038 from Willesden depot, seen here at Banstead.

Roy Hobbs

75075 rounds the curve on the central section of the Southern Region's main line at Clapham Junction, on the 3.50pm Victoria-Brighton via Uckfield on 19th April 1962. 75070/4/5 were transferred from the western section to the central section of the Southern Region in early 1959 to work the tightly timed commuter services on the Oxted line. The locomotives were based at Stewarts Lane and Three Bridges. A typical day for 75075 was a start on the 7.07am Three Bridges-Forest Row, completing its duty on the 9.54pm vans from Horsham to Three Bridges.

R. C. Riley

On 4th March 1967 a rather dirty green-liveried 73035 heading a special from Chester to Birkenhead is seen passing Mollington which lost its passenger service on 7th March 1960 and goods facilities on 4th January 1965. The locomotive was allocated to Patricroft shed where many of the class ended their days. Note the photographers on the right of the picture, not a high visibility jacket in sight!   *Gavin Morrison*

70003 *John Bunyan* departs from Thetford towards Ely on the RCTS "Great Eastern Commemorative" rail tour of 31st March 1962. The train was composed of six Gresley coaches and departed from Liverpool St., returning there in the early evening. J17 0-6-0 65567 was attached for the run to Dereham via Wymondham, then on to County School and Foulsham returning to Thetford via Swaffham.   *Roy Hobbs*

41307 and 80042 depart Sidmouth Jct. on the 11.45am through train from Waterloo to Exmouth and Sidmouth on 10th August 1963. The summer service offered by the Southern Region was very popular with holiday makers in the 1950s and 1960s with trains from Waterloo direct to many Devon and Cornish seaside resorts.

Peter Gray

72009 *Clan Stewart* departs Carstairs on the 9.25am Crewe to Aberdeen on 1st August 1964. The locomotive nameplates are red backed indicating by the condition of the locomotive that it has recently had an overhaul at Cowlairs Works. The short-posted semaphore signal adjacent to the leading van allows the crew to see the signal indication below the overbridge.

Ken Falconer

76064 attacks the long climb of nearly five miles of 1 in 74 steepening to 1 in 50 from Weymouth to Bincombe tunnels and signal box. The train is a local service from Weymouth to Bournemouth passing the closed Upwey Wishing Well Halt on 9th May 1967. The location has always been very popular with photographers recording steam hard at work on the long climb. A new road now intervenes.   *Derek Cross*

On 5th September 1965 the Warwickshire Railway Society ran the "Hants and Dorset" rail tour from Birmingham (Moor Street) to Eastleigh Works and Weymouth and return utilising no fewer than five locomotives, D2985, 7029, 34019, 60145 and 73085. In this illustration the last numbered locomotive is featured taking the Bournemouth line at Worting Jct. on the Basingstoke-Eastleigh leg of the tour.   *Roy Hobbs*

82033 skirts the Dovey estuary between Aberdovey and Dovey Jct. on the up portion of the "Cambrian Coast Express" from Pwllheli to join the portion from Aberstwyth at Dovey Jct. on 9th August 1963. The locomotive was built at Swindon Works in the batch 82030-34 in 1954/5 under lot number 399 at a cost of £14,632. 82033 was first allocated to Newton Abbot, then to various Welsh sheds, Bristol and finally Nine Elms from where it was withdrawn in September 1965.

Trevor Owen

80064 north of Watford on a local train from Euston to Tring on 31st August 1957. The locomotive was delivered new to Watford in June 1953; it survived until August 1965 and was sold to Woodham Brothers in January 1966. It was purchased for preservation in 1972 for £4,000 and currently is on the Bluebell Railway.

Kenneth Wightman

In the days when much of the north Wales coast route was four track between Chester and Llandudno Jct., Britannia 70023 *Venus* of Aston shed, with a down Saturdays only extra on 22nd June 1963, passes the site of Mochdre station which closed on 5th January 1931. This part of the trackbed is now the A55/M55 dual carriageway. *Gavin Morrison*

76114 stands in the down loop at Beattock station awaiting a path northwards while, with a clear road, a green Brush type 4 diesel, now Cl.47, approaches the station with an up express from the north in November 1966. *Douglas Hume*

80023 runs bunker first on the 9.30am Kirkcudbright to Castle Douglas service, half a mile south of Castle Douglas on 18th July 1963. The locomotive spent all its working life in Scotland being allocated first to Polmadie in November 1951, then Stranraer, Hurlford and Dumfries before being withdrawn from Carstairs in October 1965.   *Michael Mensing*

76101 blasts past the Glasgow & South Western Railway signal box at Barassie on the Ayrshire coast on a coal train bound for Glasgow from the Ayr coalfield on 22nd June 1966. 115 locomotives of the class were built between December 1952 and November 1957. Construction was shared between the works at Horwich (45) and Doncaster (70). 76101 spent all its life in Scotland, being withdrawn in December 1966 and scrapped by Shipbreaking Industries, Faslane in May 1967.   *Derek Cross*

76063 heads south from Brockenhurst on a mixed freight for Southampton on 19th September 1959. The locomotive was delivered new to Eastleigh in July 1956 and remained there for eleven years before withdrawal in April 1967.

K. L. Cook

92004 leaving Market Harborough from the now closed Rugby line on 24th April 1965. The photograph is full of interest with fine signals, bullhead track and a water softening tower in the background. The locomotive appears in a very rundown condition but it did survive for another three years before being withdrawn in March 1968.

Martin Gill

70040 *Clive of India* departs from Ipswich on the 3.45pm Norwich-Liverpool St. on 22nd May 1957. The locomotive was delivered new to Norwich depot in March 1953 and remained on the ER until December 1963 when it was moved to Carlisle based at both Upperby and Kingmoor depots. It was withdrawn from Kingmoor in April and cut up by J. McWilliams, Shettlestone in November 1967.   *R. C. Riley*

72007 *Clan Mackintosh* heads the RCTS Ribble-Lune rail tour at Halton on Saturday afternoon of 23rd May 1964. The tour was organised by the Lancashire and North Western Branch of the society and toured around Lancashire with a brief foray into the West Riding of Yorkshire. 72007 was well turned out by Carlisle Kingmoor depot staff, the stock consisting of a five-coach train plus a buffet car. Ivatt 2-6-0 46441 also was used between Heysham harbour and Morecambe Promenade (see also p.37).

Noel Machell

84005 at Luffenham on 24th April 1965. The train had stopped short of the platform to take water, much to the annoyance of the passengers wishing to alight! The service from Seaton to Stamford was formed of an ex-LMS 1930s push and pull set. This photograph was taken six months prior to the withdrawal of the locomotive. *Martin Gill*

92220 *Evening Star* stands at Templecombe No.2 signal box awaiting its signal to proceed to Bournemouth West on the 9.30am from Bristol on 1st September 1962. The train had been hauled from Templecombe station by Western Region 0-6-0PT 3758 to regain the S&D line to the south. One week later *Evening Star* worked the very last up and down "Pines Express" before the train's diversion away from the S&D line. 92220 was the last steam locomotive to be constructed at Swindon Works and is now preserved as part of the National collection. *R. C. Riley*

70039 *Sir Christopher Wren* at Brocklesby on 12th September 1963. The white refrigerated van indicates that this is the Grimsby to London express fish train. 70039 was transferred from Norwich to Immingham in November 1960 and moved to Carlisle Upperby the month after this picture was taken.

www.rail-online.co.uk

76031 approaches Shalford with a Reading-Redhill train having crossed the River Wey at Shalford Jct., south of Guildford in October 1966. The locomotive was delivered new to Stratford in November 1953 and spent the first nine years of its life on the Great Eastern before moving to the Southern Region, where it remained for the next five years before being withdrawn in July 1967.

Roy Hobbs

76011 at Henstridge in the final week of service on the Somerset & Dorset line on a beautiful spring day, 5th March 1966. The train is the 12.30pm from Bath to Bournemouth West.

Gavin Morrison

82041 passing its home shed as it pulls out of Bath Green Park on 13th November 1965 with the 1.10pm local to Templecombe. Under all the grime the livery is lined green, but the engine would never meet the cleaners again as it was withdrawn seven weeks later. The picture was taken from Bath Station signal box and shows the track layout and the station situated immediately on the east side of the River Avon bridge. The elegant train shed was opened by the Midland Railway in August 1870 and today remains in non-railway use.

Hugh Ballantyne

In deplorable external condition completely hiding its lined green livery, plus with a painted smokebox door numberplate, Bath allocated 82041 is waiting time at Bailey Gate on 23rd October 1965. The train is 'wrong line', standing at the down platform, as it is the return working, as a milk train, of the 3.35pm all stations passenger train from Templecombe. This view, looking south towards Corfe Mullen Jct. shows the single story Dorset Central Railway design of the station building, and behind, the large United Dairies Creamery which provided substantial traffic for the railway.

Hugh Ballantyne

Plenty of power at the head of the "Pines Express" climbing the 1 in 50 out of Bath towards Devonshire tunnel with 73051 and rebuilt West Country 34046 *Braunton* bound for Bournemouth West on 24th April 1962. 73051 was one of the few members of the class to be allocated to only one shed during its working life, in this case Bath Green Park.

Gavin Morrison

Double chimney, green livery 75004 departs on a local train from Pwllheli on 5th September 1963. The mix of three suburban coaches and one corridor suggest a very slow all stations train. The station at Pwllheli is still open for traffic but has seen many changes. Only the platform on the left of the picture remains; the signals, water column and the track under the Class 4 have all disappeared.

Martin Gill

Tyne Dock shed received an allocation of 10 of the 9F 2-10-0s for working the iron ore trains from Tyne Dock to Consett, all fitted with Westinghouse air pumps. Apart from 92060 to 92066 being on loan to the LM Region for around three months, all these locomotives spent their 10-year careers almost entirely working the ore trains. 92099 is shown ready to leave Tyne Dock with an afternoon working to Consett on 18th March 1964.

Gavin Morrison

92061 at Bank on the Tyne Dock to Consett iron ore working in 1963. The locomotive entered traffic in November 1955 and was withdrawn in September 1966. The class of 251 examples was constructed by Crewe Works, 198 examples and Swindon Works 53 examples. *Bill Potter*

The last rope-worked inclines were eliminated on the Tyne Dock-Consett line and through locomotive workings commenced on completion of the Beamish deviation in 1893. The 6.5 mile line was constructed with a ruling gradient of 1 in 50 but there was a short section of 1 in 35 to the west of Shield Row (West Stanley) station. 92064 is seen on a 500 ton iron ore train banked by 92099 working hard having just left the steepest section and is at Stanley crossing the bridge over the road to Tanfield Lea on 5th October 1963. *Howard Forster*

On a day when the West Riding Branch of the society was enjoying a brakevan trip on the Grassington branch, Standard 75042 was providing the power and is seen at Swinden quarry on 6th October 1965. The trip also visited Grassington which closed to freight on 11th August 1969, passenger service having ceased in 1930. Several standard 4MTs ended their working life at Skipton, having originally replaced the Midland 4Fs.

Gavin Morrison

A very grimy 73077 climbs the long haul mostly of 1 in 100 for nearly 15 miles from Settle to Blea Moor on a heavy freight from Leeds to Carlisle, seen at Horton-in-Ribblesdale on a dull and wet 29th June 1963. The need for a new 4-6-0 mixed traffic locomotive became apparent at Nationalisation. The conceept had been very successful with 1,500 4-6-0s of the LMS Class 5, LNER Class B1, GWR Halls and the SR King Arthur classes and an update was required. A total of 172 locomotives was built at Derby and Doncaster.

Rodney Lissenden

6. BR STANDARD CLASSES
RECORD OF REPAIRS

Repair records for the BR Standard classes not covered in the first four volumes of this series are listed here in Section 6.

The information was obtained mainly from the Engine History Cards (EHCs) in the archives at the Public Record Office at Kew and the National Railway Museum at York. In the EHCs, the dates recorded for the beginning of the repair period relate to the date the engine was 'Stopped for Repair". There is however another source of data for the repair period, i.e. Engine Record Cards (ERCs). For the same engine, the data from the latter source indicates the actual date of reception into works and is normally a few days later than that recorded on the EHCs. The release date from works is almost invariably the same on both EHCs and ERCs.

The authors are grateful for to Mr. Ian Sixsmith, Mr. Richard Derry and Mr. Chris Hawkins of the Irwell Press for providing information on a number of the Scottish-based Standard Class 5 4-6-0s for inclusion into Table 6.1.

In the Tables:

Column 1 refers to the Repair Classification.

Column 2 records the location at which the repair was carried out.

Column 3 records the dates for the period when the engine was either 'Stopped for Works' or actually 'On Works'.

The key to the repair table columns is given in Table 6.9.

77005 heads eastwards through Holytown station in East Lanarkshire towards Holytown Junction with a pick up goods on the ex-Caledonian Railway between Glasgow Central and Edinburgh Princes Street. The station is located about a mile from Holytown village in New Stevenston and today is served by the ScotRail DMU service between Glasgow Central and Edinburgh Waverley via Shotts. *Alan Sainty collection*

TABLE 6.1
BR Standard Class 5 4-6-0s 73000-73171 – Record of Repairs

No.	1	2	3
73000	NC	De	13.04.51 – 27.04.51
	NC	De	26.06.51 – 02.07.51
	LC	De	04.10.51 – 19.10.51
	LC(EO)	De	22.04.52 – 20.05.52
	NC(EO)	De	15.12.52 – 17.12.52
	LI	De	12.08.53 – 10.09.53
	LC	De	25.05.54 – 17.06.54
	LC	De	21.09.54 – 21.10.54
	HG	De	17.10.56 – 16.11.56
	LC(EO)	De	02.12.57 – 03.01.58
	HG	Do	09.12.58 – 23.01.59
	HG	Do	11.09.61 – 29.12.61
	LI	Co	16.06.65 – 06.09.65
73001	Dg	De	18.07.51 – 21.07.51
	V	De	04.09.51 – 27.09.51
	PV	De	15.11.51 – 12.12.51
	PV	De	14.02.52 – 11.03.52
	M	De	19.12.52 – 12.01.53
	LI	De	07.09.53 – 01.10.53
	HG	De	20.10.55 – 25.11.55
	NC	De	30.08.56 – 06.09.56
	U	Ss	18.10.57 – 21.11.57
	U	Cn	22.01.58 – 04.02.58
	U	S	14.02.58 – 04.03.58
	HI	Ss	02.08.58 – 19.11.58
	U	Ss	30.10.59 – 08.03.60
	U	Do	17.10.60 – 01.01.60
	HG	Cy	18.01.61 – 18.03.61
	LC	De	13.12.61 – 03.01.62
	HI	E	07.05.63 – 12.07.63
	LC	E	08.06.64 – 29.07.64
73002	LC	De	04.06.51 – 05.06.51
	NC	De	20.06.51 – 26.07.51
	PV	De	25.09.51 – 06.10.51
	LI	De	06.01.53 – 29.01.53
	CD	De	09.02.53 – 17.02.53
	TB	De	20.02.53 – 24.02.53
	LI	De	01.02.55 – 01.03.55
	HG	De	15.05.56 – 15.06.56
	LC	De	01.03.57 – 11.04.57
	HI	De	28.01.58 – 20.02.58
	HG	Do	03.08.60 – 17.09.60
	LI	E	10.01.63 – 09.02.63
	NC	E	26.02.64 – 07.03.64
	LC	E	12.08.65 – 15.09.65
	LC	E	25.03.66 – 12.04.66
73003	LC	De	21.08.51 – 01.09.51
	LC(EO)	De	18.02.52 – 08.03.52
	LC	De	10.06.52 – 05.08.52
	HI	De	23.11.53 – 31.12.53
	LC	De	10.02.54 – 31.03.54
	HG	De	01.02.56 – 27.03.56
	LC(EO)	De	08.06.56 – 14.06.56
	HI	De	04.01.58 – 30.01.58
	U	Br	22.10.58 – 19.12.58
	HI	S	04.08.59 – 12.11.59
	U	Br	08.11.60 – 21.12.60
	U	Br	29.04.61 – 17.06.61
	HG	Do	28.11.61 – 11.01.62
	LC	Wo	24.02.64 – 08.05.64
73004	LC	De	02.08.51 – 12.09.51
	NC(EO)	De	05.12.52 – 13.12.52
	LI	De	22.10.53 – 26.11.53
	HG	De	18.02.56 – 12.04.56
	HI	Do	15.10.58 – 26.11.58
	LC(EO)	De	24.03.60 – 21.04.60
	HG	Co	05.09.61 – 27.10.61
	HC	Da	16.04.64 – 05.06.64
	LC	Da	27.07.64 – 12.09.64
73005	NC	De	02.07.51 – 06.07.51
	LI	R	04.05.53 – 29.05.53
	LC(EO)	R	15.02.54 – 27.02.54
	LC(EO)	R	27.07.54 – 07.08.54
	NC	R	08.11.54
	LI	R	04.01.55 – 29.01.55
	LC(EO)	Pe	24.03.55 – 07.04.55
	NC(EO)	R	04.07.55 – 12.07.55
	NC(EO)	R	15.05.55 – 28.05.55
	HC(EO)	R	29.08.55 – 23.09.55
	HC(EO)	R	23.12.55 – 30.12.55
	HG	R	25.01.56 – 18.02.56
	NC(EO)	R	19.03.56 – 24.03.56
	NC(EO)	R	23.04.56 – 03.05.56
	LC(EO)	R	11.03.57 – 16.03.57
	HI	R	17.05.57 – 27.06.57
	LC(EO)	R	28.10.57 – 31.10.57
	LC(TO)	Co	05.05.58 – 07.06.58
	LI	Co	24.01.59 – 14.02.59
	NC(EO)	Co	05.03.59 – 07.03.59
	LC	Co	22.02.60 – 12.03.60
	NC(EO)	Co	11.05.60 – 28.06.60
	NC	Co	09.08.60 – 02.09.60
	NC(EO)	Co	18.10.60 – 04.11.60
	LC(EO)	Co	27.01.61 – 25.02.61
	HG	Co	21.08.61 – 07.10.61
	HI	Co	24.04.63 – 25.05.63
	LC(TO)	Co	03.01.64 – 04.02.64
73006	NC	De	05.07.51 – 11.07.51
	LC	R	12.06.52 – 26.06.52
	LI	R	09.06.53 – 27.06.53
	LC(EO)	R	06.04.54 – 23.04.54
	LI	R	02.11.54 – 26.11.54
	NC(EO)	R	13.01.55 – 20.01.55
	LC(EO)	R	01.02.55 – 12.02.55
	LC	R	15.11.55 – 24.11.55
	NC(EO)	R	07.02.56 – 09.02.56
	HG	R	23.04.56 – 25.05.56
	HI	R	10.10.57 – 14.11.57
	LC(EO)	R	28.10.58 – 08.11.58
	HI	Co	21.04.59 – 09.05.59
	NR	Co	20.05.59 – 21.05.59
	LC(EO)	Co	14.10.60 – 18.10.60

ID	Type	Code	Date range
	HG	Co	14.02.61 – 18.03.61
	LC(EO)	Co	24.10.61 – 25.10.61
	LC	Co	05.12.62 – 15.12.62
	LC	Co	12.09.63 – 20.09.63
	NC(EO)	Co	31.01.64 – 06.02.64
	LI	E	08.09.64 – 29.10.64
73007	LC(EO)	R	25.09.51 – 04.10.51
	LC(EO)	R	07.04.52 – 29.04.52
	LI	R	10.08.53 – 05.09.53
	LC(EO)	R	27.01.54 – 13.02.54
	NC(EO)	R	15.02.54 – 17.02.54
	LC(EO)	R	20.03.54 – 16.04.54
	NC(EO)	R	09.11.54 – 10.11.54
	HG	R	11.05.55 – 04.06.55
	NC(EO)	R	16.06.55 – 25.06.55
	LC	C	09.04.56 – 14.05.56
	NC(EO)	R	04.09.56 – 13.09.56
	HI	R	17.12.56 – 26.01.57
	NC(EO)	R	30.05.57 – 06.06.57
	LC(EO)	R	30.10.57 – 02.11.57
	NC(EO)	R	05.12.57 – 13.12.57
	HI	Co	26.05.58 – 21.06.58
	LC(EO)	Co	02.07.58 – 17.07.58
	HG	Co	24.12.59 – 05.03.60
	LC(EO)	Co	15.08.60 – 17.09.60
	LC	Co	22.11.61 – 02.12.61
	HI	Co	25.04.62 – 09.06.62
	LC(EO)	Co	03.06.63 – 22.06.63
	LI	Co	16.04.64 – 30.05.64
	NC	Co	11.05.65 – 15.05.65
	NC(EO)	Co	20.10.65 – 23.10.65
	NC	Co	21.12.65 – 31.12.65
73008	NC	De	23.05.52 – 28.05.52
	LI	R	26.09.53 – 17.10.53
	LC(EO)	R	15.12.53 – 09.01.54
	NC(EO)	R	16.11.54
	HG	R	08.03.55 – 09.04.55
	NC(EO)	R	14.04.55 – 16.04.55
	NC	R	27.02.56 – 29.02.56
	HI	R	28.04.56 – 02.06.56
	HC(EO)	R	03.09.56 – 13.10.56
	HC(EO)	R	05.11.56 – 16.11.56
	LC(EO)	R	20.11.56 – 01.12.56
	LC(EO)	R	02.08.57 – 06.09.57
	LC(EO)	R	26.09.57 – 26.10.57
	HI	R	28.11.57 – 21.12.57
	HC	Co	11.10.58 – 25.10.58
	LC(EO)	Co	28.11.58 – 24.12.58
	HG	Co	20.05.59 – 13.06.59
	LI	Co	02.11.60 – 10.12.60
	LC(EO)	Co	27.03.61 – 20.04.61
	LC(EO)	Co	20.09.61 – 14.10.61
	HI	Co	03.08.62 – 08.09.62
	NC(EO)	Co	05.11.62 – 14.01.62
	LC(EO)	Co	20.05.63 – 13.06.63
	LC(EO)	Co	28.05.64 – 27.06.64
73009	NC	C	30.07.51 – 03.08.51
	LI	R	11.04.53 – 30.04.53
	LC(EO)	R	07.07.53 – 17.07.53
	LI	R	13.09.54 – 16.10.54

ID	Type	Code	Date range
	NC(EO)	R	18.11.54
	LC(EO)	R	02.02.55 – 04.03.55
	NC(EO)	R	28.03.55 – 07.04.55
	NC(EO)	R	28.04.55 – 30.04.55
	NC(EO)	R	31.12.55 – 12.01.56
	NC	R	29.02.56 – 01.03.56
	HG	R	05.03.56 – 20.04.56
	HC(EO)	R	09.06.56 – 30.08.56
	HI	R	21.12.57 – 20.02.58
	LI	Co	12.09.59 – 10.10.59
	LC(EO)	Co	19.09.60 – 08.10.60
	NC(EO)	Co	20.06.61 – 30.06.61
	HG	Co	28.12.61 – 10.02.62
	LI	Da	22.09.64 – 14.11.64
	NC	Da	16.11.64 – 25.11.64
	NC(EO)	Co	06.08.65 – 14.08.65
73010	NC(EO)	De	02.01.53 – 08.01.53
	LI	De	10.08.53 – 02.09.53
	HG	De	23.05.55 – 07.07.55
	HI	De	25.09.56 – 24.10.56
	NC	Do	06.01.58 – 10.01.58
	LC	Do	31.05.58 – 14.06.58
	HI	Do	07.07.59 – 13.08.59
	LC(EO)	De	14.04.60 – 08.06.60
	HG	De	26.07.61 – 19.10.61
	LI	Co	11.05.65 – 29.05.65
73011	NC	De	21.01.53 – 28.01.53
	LC	De	07.04.53 – 23.04.53
	LI	De	23.08.54 – 23.09.54
	LC(EO)	De	10.11.54 – 25.11.54
	HG	De	24.09.56 – 26.10.56
	HG	Do	01.10.58 – 14.11.58
	HI	De	25.04.61 – 30.05.61
	HG	De	05.11.62 – 07.12.62
	LC	E	15.09.64 – 16.10 64
73012	LC(EO)	De	01.09.51 – 05.09.51
	NC(EO)	De	02.02.53 – 11.02.53
	U	Sa	20.01.54 – 03.02.54
	U	Sa	11.03.54 – 21.06.54
	LI	De	18.08.54 – 16.09.54
	U	Sa	10.08.55 – 05.09.55
	HG	De	19.03.56 – 26.04.56
	U	Ss	23.01.57 – 06.02.57
	U	Ss	21.10.57 – 13.11.57
	U	Ss	11.03.58 – 31.03.58
	HI	S	26.08.58 – 02.12.58
	LC	S	02.10.59 – 24.12.59
	U	Ss	05.04.60 – 19.04.60
	HG	Do	10.04.61 – 27.05.61
	U	Ss	06.07.62 – 23 07.62
	HG	De	24.08.62 – 20.09.62
	U	Ss	26.11.62 – 08.03.63
	LC	De	11.02.63 – 07.03.63
	U	Ss	08.04.63 – 07.06.63
	U	Ly	28.02.64 – 22.04.64
73013	LC	De	04.05.53 – 27.05.53
	LI	H	08.10.54 – 13.11.54
	HG	E	30.05.56 – 19.06.56
	HI	N	28.04.58 – 05.06.58

	LC(EO)	De	25.02.59 – 09.04.59
	LC(EO)	De	25.11.59 – 21.12.59
	LI	De	19.07.60 – 18.10.60
73014	PV	De	27.02.52 – 20.03.52
	RG	De	09.03.53 – 07.04.53
	RS	De	04.08.53 – 31.08.53
	LI	De	25.10.54 – 25.11.54
	LC	De	26.04.56 – 14.08.56
	HG	De	28.05.57 – 05.07.57
	LC	De	05.08.59 – 31.08.59
	HI	De	20.06.60 – 08.07.60
	AWS	De	16.03.61 – 13.04.61
	NC	De	09.06.61 – 23.06.61
	LC	De	15.01.63 – 12.02.63
	HG	E	15.01.63 – 14.03.64
73015	LC	De	02.08.52 – 02.09.52
	LC(EO)	De	24.11.52 – 29.12.52
	LC	De	06.02.53 – 04.03.53
	LC	De	29.07.53 – 08.09.53
	LI	De	25.10.54 – 19.11.54
	LC(EO)	De	15.01.55 – 22.02.55
	HG	De	28.01.56 – 16.03.56
	LC(EO)	De	28.09.56 – 01.11.56
	HI	De	04.09.57 – 07.10.57
	U	Bb	17.12.58 – 16.01.59
	HG	S	20.07.59 – 01.01.60
	U	Bb	15.03.60 – 11.04.60
	U	Bb	29.06.60 – 29.07.60
	U	Bb	05.12.60 – 18.02.61
	U	Bb	04.08.61 – 06.10.61
	HG	Do	11.04.62 – 19.05.62
73016	CD	De	25.09.51 – 02.10.51
	Wh	De	12.11.51 – 19.12.51
	PV	De	12.02.53 – 04.03.53
	LC	De	27.08.53 – 01.10.53
	LI	De	27.04.54 – 27.05.54
	LC(EO)	De	24.01.55 – 10.02.55
	LC(EO)	De	28.02.56 – 10.03.56
	LI	De	14.05.56 – 07.06.56
	HG	De	17.12.56 – 30.01.57
	HG	Do	02.01.59 – 13.02.59
	HI	Do	16.05.61 – 17.06.61
	NC	Do	20.02.62 – 08.03.62
	LC	De	02.10.62 – 02.11.62
	LC	E	18.10.63 – 09.11.63
	HI	E	11.05.65 – 18.06.65
	NC	E	25.03.66 – 28.03.66
73017	LC	N	28.03.53 – 25.04.53
	LI	De	21.05.55 – 30.06.55
	NC(EO)	De	21.06.56
	HG	De	19.03.57 – 26.04.57
	Wh	Br	09.09.58 – 21.10.58
	LI	E	10.09.59 – 26.09.59
	HG	E	03.08.61 – 09.09.61
73018	LC	N	15.06.53 – 04.07.53
	HI	De	18.10.54 – 17.11.54
	HG	De	17.04.56 – 21.05.56
	HI	S	12.08.57 – 08.11.57

	LC	S	11.03.58 – 24.04.58
	U	S	27.08.58 – 11.11.58
	HI	E	09.06.59 – 27.06.59
	HG	E	10.11.61 – 30.12.61
	LC	E	10.12.62 – 15.12.62
	LC	E	20.01.66 – 03.03.66
73019	PV	De	30.09.52 – 22.10.52
	U	Sp	27.09.53 – 20.01.54
	U	Sp	09.04.54 – 25.06.54
	LI	De	06.12.54 – 04.01.55
	U	Sp	12.04.56 – 05.05.56
	LC	De	14.05.56 – 30.05.56
	HG	De	18.12.56 – 25.01.57
	U	Br	25.09.57 – 06.11.57
	U	Sp	08.02.58 – 03.03.58
	HI	E	21.01.59 – 28.02.59
	HG	E	02.02.61 – 11.03.61
	LI	E	25.11.63 – 04.01.64
	LC	E	17.11.64 – 20.11.64
73020	PV	De	30.09.52 – 22.10.52
	NC(EO)	C	12.01.53 – 24.01.53
	LC	De	22.04.53 – 11.05.53
	LI	De	10.10.55 – 03.11.55
	LC	De	14.05.56 – 20.05.56
	NC(EO)	De	30.07.56 – 06.08.56
	AWS	S	06.09.56
	HG	De	29.01.57 – 06.03.57
	LI	E	19.08.59 – 05.09.59
	HG	E	13.10.61 – 25.11.61
	LC	E	05.04.66 – 06.05.66
73021	NC	C	19.02.53 – 25.02.53
	LC	De	25.09.53 – 15.10.53
	U	Ty	19.05.54 – 25.05.54
	LI	De	09.02.55 – 04.03.55
	U	Ch	03.09.55 – 16.09.55
	U	Ej	11.11.55 – 01.12.55
	U	Ch	14.05.56 – 01.06.56
	HG	De	06.08.56 – 05.09.56
	U1	Ch	12.11.57 – 28.11.57
	U	Ej	21.04.59 – 29.05.59
	U	Hd	28.08.59 – 17.09.59
	HG	S	15.10.59 – 15.02.60
	LC	Cy	17.10.60 – 04.11.60
	U	Gb	11.08.61 – 28.08.61
	LC	Gb	30.08.61 – 30.10.61
	LI	De	09.04.63 – 06.06.63
	U	Ss	19.12.63 – 15.01.64
	LC	S	06.03.64 – 05.05.64
73022	LC	De	02.10.52 -04.11.52
	LI	De	09.11.54 – 07.12.54
	NC	De	29.05.56 – 11.06.56
	HG	De	08.01.57 – 08.02.57
	LC	S	26.04.58 – 23.05.58
	NC	Br	21.08.58 – 05.10.58
	LC	E	06.05.59 – 30.05.59
	LI	E	24.03.60 -24.04.60
	Rect	E	25.04.60 – 21.05.60
	HG	E	15.08.62 – 22.09.62
	LC	E	04.10.65 – 04.11.65

73023	LI	De	08.04.54 – 11.05.54
	U	Ty	01.03.55 – 30.03.55
	U	Ch	26.05.56 – 15.06.56
	HG	De	13.08.56 – 14.09.56
	U	Ch	28.11.56 – 19.12.56
	U	Ox	14.11.57 – 03.12.57
	U	Sa	25.02.59 – 14.03.59
	HI	De	22.09.58 – 27.10.58
	U	Sa	25.02.59 – 14.03.59
	U	Cf	16.04.59 – 16.05.59
	U	Oo	08.06.59 – 10.07.59
	U	Cf	15.10.59 – 25.11.59
	HG	Do	23.03.60 – 13.05.60
	U	Ly	19.11.60 – 05.12.60
	U	Ly	13.12.60 – 05.01.61
	U	Ly	07.04.61 – 26.04.61
	U	Ly	08.08.61 – 22.08.61
	HC	Cy	11.04.62 – 12.07.62
	U	Ly	20.12.63 – 20.01.64
	U	Ly	13.05.64 – 18.08.64
73024	NC(EO)	C	11.12.51 – 28.12.51
	NC(EO)	C	16.03.53 – 25.03.53
	LC	De	29.06.53 – 12.08.53
	LI	De	01.05.55 – 16.06.55
	LC	De	26.10.55 – 08.11.55
	NC(EO)	De	20.08.56 – 23.08.56
	HG	De	08.05.57 – 18.06.57

	HG	S	02.09.59 – 18.02.60
	HI	Do	09.11.61 – 16.12.61
73025	LC(EO)	De	27.03.52 – 12.05.52
	NC(EO)	H	18.11.52 – 19.11.52
	LC	De	11.08.53 – 23.09.53
	LI	De	15.07.55 – 23.08.55
	LC	De	24.11.55 – 20.12.55
	NC(EO)	De	12.06.56 – 27.06.56
	HG	De	19.11.56 – 03.01.57
	LC(EO)	Cy	06.05.58 – 05.06.58
	HI	W	05.08.59 – 16.10.59
	NC	W	02.12.59 – 10.12.59
	LC	C	01.08.63 – 29.09.63
	LI	Co	04.06.65 – 28.08.65
73026	NC(EO)	H	20.11.52 – 25.11.52
	LI	De	19.10.54 – 10.11.54
	NC(EO)	De	xx.xx.xx – 02.10.56
	HG	De	30.01.57 – 21.03.57
	LC	S	28.01.58 – 06.05.58
	HG	S	10.11.59 – 07.04.60
	HG	Do	04.07.62 – 24.08.62
	LC	Da	09.06.64 – 09.07.64
	LI	Co	21.05.65 – 21.06.65
73027	NC(EO)	H	25.11.52 – 26.11.52
	LI	De	03.10.53 – 26.11.53

70002 *Geoffrey Chaucer* runs through Stratford on an up express from Norwich to Liverpool Street. The Stratford and Norwich locomotives worked the expresses from Liverpool St. but before they could enter service on diagrams requiring a quick turn round in Liverpool St. the turntable there had to be lengthened. As from 2nd July 1951, 12 engines of the class operated 11 diagrams on a regular interval service from Liverpool St. to Norwich. 70002 spent 12 years on the Great Eastern before moving to Carlisle Kingmoor in 1963. *Kenneth Wightman*

No.			
	HG	De	16.11.56 – 21.12.56
	LC	S	05.11.57 – 13.12.57
	HG	S	30.10.59 – 02.06.60
			No further data
73028	NC(EO)	H	27.11.52 – 29.11.52
	LC	De	13.03.53 – 08.04.53
	LC	De	07.12.53 – 31.12.53
	LI	De	01.09.55 – 26.09.55
	NC(EO)	De	28.06.56 – 04.07.56
	HG	De	28.08.57 – 20.09.57
	HI	E	07.10.59 – 31.10.59
	HG	E	29.06.62 – 11.08.62
	LC	E	19.11.63 – 23.12.64
73029	NC(EO)	C	13.10.52 – 20.10.52
	LC(EO)	De	22.10.52 – 19.11.52
	LC	De	10.06.53 – 24.06.53
	HI	De	14.11.55 – 07.12.55
	ATC	De	05.11.56 – 12.11.56
	HG	De	24.03.58 – 02.05.58
	HI	E	06.10.60 – 29.10.60
	HG	E	27.05.63 – 27.07.63
	LC	E	23.12.64 – 26.01.65
	LC	E	17.08.66 – 13.09.66
73030	LI	De	01.01.55 – 15.01.55
	LI	De	04.11.55 – 24.11.55
	NC(R)	De	02.01.56 – 14.01.56
	NC(R)	De	03.02.56 – 16.02.56
	LC(EO)	De	18.05.57 – 12.06.57
	HG	De	13.12.57 – 22.01.58
	LC(EO)	De	28.04.59 – 13.05.59
	HI	De	22.08.59 – 26.10.59
	HG	De	25.11.62 – 17.01.63
73031	LC	De	17.02.55 – 10.03.55
	LI	De	11.02.56 – 12.03.56
	LI	De	14.02.57 – 12.03.57
	LC(EO)	De	28.04.57 – 16.05.57
	HG	De	09.11.57 – 23.12.57
	NC(R)	De	30.12.57 – 22.01.58
	HG	S	??.??.60 – 01.07.60
73032	LI	De	30.07.56 - 24.08.56
	NC(EO)	De	12.11.56 - 29.11.56
	LC	De	17.05.58 – 14.08.58
	HG	De	20.03.59 – 15.05.59
	LC(EO)	C	13.06.59 – 30.07.59
	LC(EO)	De	19.04.60 – 10.06.60
	HI	De	16.05.63 – 06.08.63
73033	LI	De	28.09.55 – 08.12.55
	NC(EO)	De	28.06.56 – 11.07.56
	LC	W	14.10.57 – 29.01.58
	HG	De	26.05.59 – 02.07.59
	HI	De	17.04.61 – 08.06.61
	HI	Da	30.09.64 – 19.11.64
	NC	E	12.02.65 – 16.02.65
73034	LI	De	12.08.55 – 08.09.55
	NC(EO)L	De	17.10.56 – 30.10.56
	LI	W	12.11.57 – 14.02.58

No.			
	LI	S	03.11.58 – 06.02.59
	HG	Do	07.03.60 – 26.04.60
	HG	Do	15.03.62 – 05.05.62
	HI	S	01.05.64 – 24.11.64
73035	LI	De	12.12.55 – 03.01.56
	PV	De	14.08.56 – 20.08.56
	LI	W	31.10.57 – 17.01.58
	HG	S	07.03.59 – 12.06.59
	HG	Do	23.11.61 – 04.01.62
	LI	Da	13.05.64 – 08.08.64
	HC(EO)	Co	16.07.65 – 11.09.65
73036	LI	De	13.12.55 – 09.01.56
	NC(EO)	De	23.08.56 – 29.08.56
	LI	S	28.04.58 – 20.06.58
	HG	S	14.01.59 – 14.04.59
	LI	W	16.02.60 – 07.04.60
	HG	Do	25.11.62 – 03.03.62
	LC	E	01.05.64 – 22.05.64
73037	LI	De	02.03.56 – 28.03.56
	HC	W	19.06.56 – 05.07.58
	HI	W	11.01.60 – 25.03.60
	HC	W	20.04.61 – 03.08.61
	LI	E	20.01.64 – 29.03.64
	LC	E	21.05.65 – 01.06.65
	NC	E	12.09.66 – 13.09.66
73038	LI	De	07.09.56 – 04.10.56
	HG	De	02.01.59 – 17.02.59
	NC(EO)	De	17.08.59 – 31.08.59
	HI	De	28.08.61 – 07.10.61
	HC	C	22.08.63 – 17.10.63
73039	NC(EO)	De	07.12.56 – 24.12.56
	HG	De	26.09.57 – 28.11.57
	LC(EO)	De	09.07.58 – 01.09.58
	LC	De	10.04.59 – 06.05.59
	LI	De	20.05.60 – 04.07.60
	HC	De	17.03.61 – 02.05.61
	LC	De	04.05.62 – 01.06.62
	HI	E	24.08.64 – 13.10.64
73040	LI	De	20.03.56 – 12.04.56
	HG	De	31.08.58 – 17.10.58
	NC(EO)	De	19.10.59 – 04.11.59
	HI	De	11.06.60 – 10.08.60
	HG	De	20.12.62 – 29.01.63
	LC	C	28.08.63 – 19.09.63
73041	LI	De	16.03.56 – 10.04.56
	HI	De	15.08.57 – 03.09.57
	NC	De	19.11.57
	NC	De	26.11.57 – 04.12.57
	HG	E	08.10.58 – 08.11.58
	NC	A	09.04.59 – 01.05.59
	LC	E	09.06.61 – 01.07.61
	HI	E	08.08.62 – 08.09.62
73042	LI	De	11.04.56 – 03.05.56
	HI	De	12.09.57 – 17.10.57
	LC	E	30.09.58 – 01.11.58

ID			
	HG	E	19.10.59 – 14.11.59
	LI	E	24.05.62 – 16.06.62
73043	LI	De	12.01.56 – 31.01.56
	LC(EO)	De	13.09.56 – 11.10.56
	HI	Do	20.05.58 – 05.07.58
	HG	Do	12.07.61 – 18.08.61
	LI	E	29.06.64 – 21.08.64
73044	LI	De	05.03.56 – 09.04.56
	HG	De	12.11.58 – 29.12.58
	NC(EO)	De	22.01.59 – 09.02.59
	LC	De	06.03.59 – 07.04.59
	HI	De	17.11.61 – 20.12.61
73045	LI	De	10.01.56 – 30.01.56
	NC(EO)	De	14.05.56 – 30.05.56
	LC	Do	25.05.57 – 16.06.57
	HI	Do	15.04.58 – 20.05.58
	HI	De	18.11.59 – 13.01.60
	LC(EO)	De	23.12.60 – 20.02.61
	HG	De	09.02.63 – 23.03.63
73046	LI	De	03.04.56 – 26.04.56
	LC	De	18.12.56 – 15.01.57
	HI	Do	19.08.58 – 06.10.58
	HG	Do	11.01.61 – 15.02.61
	HC	De	06.11.62 – 07.12.62
	NC	E	25.02.64 – 06.03.64
73047	LI	E	13.03.56 – 07.04.56
	NC	B	14.05.57 – 20.05.57
	HI	E	25.03.58 – 03.05.58
	HG	E	17.03.60 – 28.05.60
	LI	E	28.05.62 – 16.06.62
73048	HI	De	20.08.56 – 25.09.56
	LC	De	16.09.57 – 10.10.57
	HG	Do	14.08.58 – 03.10.58
	HI	De	02.08.60 – 07.10.60
	HG	Da	14.09.63 – 07.01.63
73049	LC	B	07.11.55 – 29.11.55
	HI	E	17.01.57 – 16.02.57
	NC	B	04.07.57 – 11.07.57
	HG	E	25.11.58 – 20.12.58
	NC	Bg	15.10.59 – 03.12.59
	HI	E	19.04.61 – 13.05.61
	HI	E	23.07.63 – 31.08.63
73050	LC	E	14.03.55 – 26.03.55
	LI	E	03.04.56 – 27.04.56
	LC	De	11.06.56 – 19.06.56
	LC	E	04.03.57 – 13.03.57
	NC	B	21.10.57 – 01.11.57
	HI	E	10.04.58 – 10.05.58
	NC	E	11.09.58 – 01.10.58
	NC	E	23.01.59 – 14.02.59
	HG	E	20.01.60 – 27.02.60
	NC	E	23.01.61 – 09.02.61
	NC	E	27.12.61 – 17.01.62
	LC	E	21.02.62 – 17.03.62
	LC	E	12.06.62 – 30.06.62
	NC	Ss	12.07.63
	NC	Bg	17.12.63
	LI	E	15.06.64 – 12.08.64
	HC	EE	28.07.65 – 03.09.65
73051	LC	E	15.03.55 – 26.03.55
	LC	E	07.02.56 – 18.02.56
	NC	De	16.04.56 – 02.05.56
	HI	E	02.05.57 – 25.05.57
	HG	E	10.04.59 – 09.05.59
	HI	E	15.09.61 – 14.10.61
	LC	E	16.01.63 – 26.01.63
	LI	E	13.08.63 – 21.09.63
73052	LC	E	28.02.55 – 05.03.55
	LI	E	21.02.56 – 10.03.56
	LC	De	01.05.56 – 21.05.56
	NC	B	25.11.57 – 06.12.57
	HI	E	16.05.58 – 14.06.58
	LC	Ne	23.06.58 – 06.08.58
	NC	Bg	10.11.59 – 30.11.59
	NC	Bg	21.01.60 – 09.02.60
	HG	E	31.05.60 – 25.06.60
	LC	E	19.05.61 – 12.06.61
	LI	E	19.06.62 – 28.07.62
	LC	E	07.05.64 – 03.06.64
73053	LC	De	01.12.54 – 08.12.54
	NC	De	28.12.54 – 07.01.55
	LC(EO)	De	14.03.55 – 14.04.55
	HI	Do	11.02.57 – 20.03.57
	HG	Do	05.06.59 – 17.07.59
	HI	De	25.03.61 – 24.05.61
	LC	De	01.05.62 – 25.05.62
	NC	De	17.10.62 – 11.02.63
	HG	S	21.11.63 – 29.05.64
	LC	Co	03.05.65 – 12.05.65
73054	LC	C	02.11.55 – 29.11.55
	LI	De	01.04.57 - 25.04.57
	HG	S	20.03.59 – 10.09.59
	LI	Cy	23.02.60 – 03.03.60
	HG	Do	01.11.61 – 08.12.61
	HG	E	20.09.63 – 02.11.63
73055	NC	R	24.11.55
	LI	R	07.01.57 – 02.02.57
	LC	Co	27.03.58 – 02.05.58
	HG	Co	17.11.58 – 06.12.58
	HI	Co	09.01.61 – 04.03.61
	HG	Co	29.05.63 – 06.07.63
	LC(EO)	Co	21.09.65 – 06.10.65
73056	LC(EO)	R	05.05.55 – 12.05.55
	NC	R	29.11.55 – 30.11.55
	NC(EO)	R	09.01.56 – 20.01.56
	NC(EO)	De	04.04.56 – 25.04.56
	LI	R	08.04.57 – 02.05.57
	HG	R	01.06.59 – 20.06.59
	NC(EO)	Co	12.05.60 – 13.06.60
	LC	Co	17.11.60 – 24.12.60
	HI	Co	09.10.61 – 24.11.61
	LC	Co	11.10.62 – 02.11.62
	LC	Co	14.05.63 – 01.06.63

73057	NC(EO)	R	26.10.54 – 28.10.54		HC	R	18.03.60 – 15.04.60
	NC(EO)	R	15.12.54 – 22.12.54		LI	Co	26.02.62 – 06.04.62
	NC	R	26.10.55 – 28.10.55		HC(EO)	Co	16.09.63 – 19.10.63
	LC(EO)	De	28.04.56 – 07.06.56		LC	Co	07.09.64 – 03.10.64
	LI	R	09.02.57 – 02.03.57		LI	Co	11.06.65 – 03.07.65
	HG	Co	17.04.59 – 15.05.59				
	NC(EO)	R	08.06.59 – 13.06.59	73060	NC	R	04.11.55 – 05.11.55
	HI	Co	23.08.61 – 21.10.61		LI	R	15.04.57 – 17.05.57
	LI	Co	03.08.64 – 10.10.64		LC(EO)	Co	10.02.58 – 01.03.58
	NC(EO)	Co	03.12.64 – 19.12.64		HG	Co	08.06.59 – 27.06.59
					HI	Co	24.04.61 – 03.06.61
73058	NC(EO)	R	13.12.54 – 18.12.54		HG	Co	21.08.63 – 21.09.63
	LC(EO)	C	18.08.55 – 09.09.55		NC	Co	11.03.65 – 17.04.65
	LC(EO)	De	06.10.55 – 21.10.55		NC	Co	03.06.65 – 15.06.65
	NC	R	11.01.56 – 12.01.56				
	LI	R	20.06.56 – 10.07.56	73061	NC	R	10.11.55 – 11.11.55
	LC	R	17.12.57 – 28.12.57		LI	R	29.07.57 – 15.05.57
	HG	Co	27.10.58 – 27.11.58		HG	Co	31.07.59 – 05.09.59
	LC	Co	20.01.60 – 09.02.60		LC	Co	11.09.59 – 22.09.59
	HC	Co	18.03.60 – 23.04.60		HI	Co	06.02.62 – 10.03.62
	NC(EO)	Co	10.05.60 – 20.05.60		LC(EO)	Co	25.06.63 – 10.07.63
	LC	Co	11.10.61 – 28.10.61		NC(EO)	Co	30.07.63 – 06.08.63
	HI	Co	03.09.62 – 13.10.62		NC(EO)	Co	21.05.64 – 05.06.64
73059	NC	R	20.10.55 – 22.10.55	73062	NC	R	08.11.55 – 09.11.55
	LI	R	16.03.57 – 10.04.57		LI	R	12.08.57 – 31.08.57
	LC(EO)	Co	23.09.58 – 11.10.58		HG	Co	17.08.59 – 12.09.59
	HG	Co	16.02.59 – 14.03.59		HI	Co	20.03.62 – 04.05.62

Super power combination for the Manchester to Bournemouth West "Pines Express" with 75071 piloting 92245 as they approach Bath Jct. to leave the Midland line and turn on to Somerset & Dorset metals and take the single line to Midford on 9th June 1962. Both engines were allocated at Bath, 92245 having just been drafted in from Cardiff Canton for the summer season. Note the Whitaker automatic tablet exchange catcher is positioned on the 9F's tender in readiness to pick up the single line tablet and the crew of the piloting 75071 are watching to ensure the tablet will be caught in the catcher. On the left is part of the substantial engineering works of Stothert & Pitt, well known worldwide for its dockside cranes. 92245 is preserved at the Barry Railway Centre.

Hugh Ballantyne

	LC	Co	09.08.62 – 18.08.62
	NC(EO)	Co	16.07.63 – 06.08.63
	NC(EO)	Co	24.02.64 – 07.03.64
73063	NC	R	07.12.55
	LI	R	25.06.57 – 07.08.57
	LC	R	04.12.59 – 27.12.59
	HG	Co	26.10.59 – 28.11.59
	NC(EO)	Co	09.12.59 – 18.12.59
	HI	Co	01.09.62 – 12.10.62
73064	NC	R	27.12.55 – 28.12.55
	HI	R	29.04.57 – 01.06.57
	HG	Co	10.06.59 – 04.07.59
	HC(EO)	Co	08.09.60 – 29.10.60
	HI	Co	10.05.62 – 23.06.62
	NC(EO)	Co	05.06.63 – 12.06.63
	NC	Co	13.11.64 – 14.11.64
	NC	Co	16.11.64 – 20.11.64
	LC(EO)	Co	01.06.65 – 26.06.65
	U(EO)	Co	17.02.66 – 19.03.66
73065	LI	De	05.11.56 – 23.11.56
	LC	De	26.10.57 – 07.11.57
	HG	Do	30.10.58 – 13.12.58
	NC	Do	07.12.59 – 11.12.59
	HG	Do	23.03.61 – 06.05.61
	LI	E	30.10.64 – 16.12.64
73066	LI	De	05.11.56 – 23.11.56
	HG	Do	04.02.57 – 13.03.57
	NC	De	29.10.57 – 07.11.57
	LI	De	04.01.58 – 25.01.58
	HG	Do	13.01.59 – 19.02.59
	NC(EO)	Do	19.05.59 – 29.05.59
	NC	Do	11.08.59 – 17.09.59
	LC(EO)	De	06.11.59 – 23.11.59
	LC(EO)	De	13.07.60 – 27.09.60
	NC(R)	De	03.10.60 – 07.10.60
	LC	De	22.12.60 – 21.02.61
	LC(EO)	De	10.04.61 – 17.05.61
	HI	De	25.06.62 – 07.08.62
	HG	S	08.04.64 – 17.06.64
73067	LI	De	09.07.57 – 21.08.57
	HG	Do	24.06.59 – 01.08.59
	HI	De	19.06.61 – 13.07.61
	HI	E	16.10.64 – 01.12.64
73068	LI	De	10.09.56 – 11.10.56
	HG	Do	28.03.60 – 07.05.60
	HG	De	??.??.?? – 28.01.63
			No further data
73069	NC	De	16.12.54 – 31.12.54
	LC(EO)	De	13.01.55 – 09.02.55
	HG	Do	21.01.57 – 02.03.57
	HG	Do	03.04.59 – 07.05.59
	HC	De	12.09.60 – 03.11.60
	NC(R)	De	10.11.60 – 16.11.60
	HI	De	10.01.63 – 08.02.63
	HC	C	01.08.66 – 30.09.66

73070	NC	De	25.02.56 – 01.03.56
	LI	De	12.03.57 – 01.04.57
	LC	De	11.05.57 – 17.05.57
	NC(R)	De	10.06.57 – 13.06.57
	LC	De	01.11.58 – 02.12.58
	HG	De	02.01.60 – 26.02.60
	HI	De	10.06.62 – 13.07.62
	NC	H	19.10.63 – 05.11.63
73071	NC	Do	23.03.56 – 17.04.56
	LI	De	31.05.57 – 20.06.57
	NC(R)	De	01.07.57 – 05.07.57
	LC	De	20.09.57 – 26.09.57
	LC	De	18.10.57 – 31.10.57
	LI	De	15.06.59 – 07.07.59
	LC	C	01.10.59 – 28.11.59
	LC(EO)	De	22.11.60 – 10.02.60
	HG	De	31.07.61 – 06.10.61
	HI	Da	05.02.64 – 20.05.64
73072	LI	De	02.01.57 – 21.01.57
	LC	De	02.07.57 – 15.07.57
	NC	De	10.04.58 – 07.05.58
	HG	Co	29.04.59 – 22.05.59
	HI	Co	14.02.62 – 24.03.62
	NC(EO)	Co	29.01.65 – 30.01.65
	HI	Co	18.03.65 – 22.05.65
	LC(EO)	Co	02.02.66 – 05.03.66
	NC(EO)	Co	26.04.66 – 07.05.66
73073	LI	De	05.12.56 – 27.12.56
	HG	Do	18.02.59 – 03.04.59
	HI	De	25.09.61 – 16.11.61
	HI	E	28.09.64 – 06.11.64
73074	LI	De	03.12.57 – 23.12.57
	NC	Do	31.07.58 – 09.08.58
	LC	Do	23.04.59 – 16.05.59
	HG	Do	14.12.60 – 17.01.61
	LC	De	20.12.62 – 22.01.63
73075	NC	R	02.11.55 – 03.11.55
	LI	R	07.03.57 – 30.03.57
	HG	Co	24.06.59 – 16.07.59
	LC	Co	04.07.60 – 06.08.60
	HI	Co	04.06.62 – 11.07.62
73076	LC(TO)	R	10.10.55 – 15.10.55
	LC	R	16.12.55 – 22.12.55
	LC(TO)	R	18.01.56 – 21.01.56
	NC(EO)	R	25.06.56 – 28.06.56
	LI	R	21.11.57 – 13.12.57
	HG	Co	25.11.59 – 19.12.59
	LC(EO)	Co	20.10.60 – 03.11.60
	HI	Co	31.10.62 – 24.11.62
	NC(EO)	Co	15.10.63 – 16.10.63
	NC(EO)	Co	30.10.63
73077	NC	R	27.06.56
	NC	R	05.11.56
	LI	R	11.03.57 – 05.04.57
	LI	R	07.08.58 – 06.09.58
	NC(EO)	R	23.02.59 – 04.03.59

	NC(EO)	Co	30.05.59 – 10.06.59	73083	NC	De	13.09.56 – 27.09.56
	HG	Co	07.03.60 – 30.04.60		HI	E	30.07.57 – 17.08.57
	NC(EO)	Co	11.04.61 – 15.04.61		HC	E	15.11.57 – 14.12.57
	LC	Co	17.05.61 – 10.06.61		HG	E	14.09.59 – 10.10.59
	NC(EO)	Co	30.08.61 – 02.09.61		LI	E	06.03.62 – 31.03.62
	LI	Co	31.01.63 – 09.03.63		LC	E	16.10.62 – 03.11.62
	NC(EO)	Co	04.04.63 – 19.04.63		HC	E	09.06.64 – 02.07.64
	NC(EO)	Co	11.06.63 – 22.06.63		LC	E	02.03.66 – 07.03.66
	LC(EO)	Co	13.11.63 – 16.11.63				
	LC(EO)	Co	26.06.64 – 14.08.64	73084	NC	De	08.10.56 – 24.10.56
	NC	Co	10.11.64 – 14.11.64		LC	E	28.05.57 – 08.06.57
					LI	E	23.09.57 – 12.10.57
73078	LC	R	20.12.55 – 28.12.55		NC	E	06.01.58 – 11.01.58
	NC	R	15.02.56 – 16.02.56		HG	E	30.09.59 – 31.10.59
	NC	R	04.07.56		LI	E	15.02.62 – 17.03.62
	NC	R	23.10.56		LC	E	28.09.64 – 30.10.64
	LI	R	09.05.57 – 25.05.57		LC	E	05.08.65 – 09.08.65
	LC(EO)	Co	24.03.58 – 27.03.58				
	NC(EO)	Co	05.07.58 – 07.07.58	73085	NC	De	15.11.56 – 16.12.56
	HI	Co	14.10.58 – 05.11.58		HI	E	31.12.57 – 18.01.58
	NC(EO)	R	23.02.59 – 04.03.59		NC	A	27.04.59 – 15.05.59
	LC	Co	25.08.59 – 17.09.59		LC	E	02.07.59 – 08.08.59
	HG	Co	17.12.59 – 30.01.60		HG	E	23.08.60 – 17.09.60
	LC(EO)	Co	30.11.60 – 03.12.60		LC	E	04.05.62 – 12.05.62
	LC	Co	04.07.61 – 13.07.61		LC	E	27.09.62 – 03.11.62
	LC(EO)	Co	27.11.61 – 01.12.61		LC	E	18.12.63 – 04.01.64
	LI	Co	17.09.62 – 20.10.62		LC	E	27.05.64 – 25.06.64
	NC(EO)	Co	28.03.63 – 30.03.63		LI	E	20.05.65 – 25.06.65
					LC	E	07.12.65 – 16.12.65
73079	LC	R	30.11.56 – 21.12.56		LC	E	16.05.66 – 19.05.66
	LI	R	10.09.57 – 12.10.57		NC	E	19.12.66 – 20.12.66
	LC(EO)	Co	12.05.58 – 31.05.58				
	HC(EO)	Co	10.08.59 – 03.09.59	73086	LC	De	01.02.57 – 13.02.57
	HC	Co	09.04.60 – 30.04.60		HI	E	04.09.57 – 21.09.57
	HG	Co	21.02.61 – 22.04.61		HC	E	18.12.57 – 11.01.58
	LC	Co	07.06.62 – 29.06.62		HG	E	11.11.59 – 12.12.59
	HI	Co	01.08.63 – 31.08.63		LC	E	08.07.60 – 09.07.60
	NC(EO)	Co	19.07.64 – 07.08.64		LC	E	16.05.61 – 07.06.61
	LC(EO)	Co	30.11.64 – 26.12.64				No further data
	LC	Co	24.05.66 – 10.06.66				
				73087	LC	E	18.01.57 – 02.02.57
73080	HI	E	10.03.58 – 12.04.58		NC	De	06.06.57 – 17.06.57
	NC	A	28.05.59 – 12.06.59		LI	E	09.10.57 – 26.10.57
	LC	E	21.09.60 – 01.10.60		HI	E	20.01.59 – 07.02.59
	HG	E	30.12.60 – 06.02.61		NC	E	26.02.59 – 28.02.59
	HI	E	24.02.64 – 11.04.64		HG	E	21.04.61 – 27.05.61
	NC	E	11.07.66 – 12.07.66		HI	E	06.03.64 – 18.04.64
73081	LC	C	05.12.55 – 19.01.56	73088	LI	De	26.02.57 – 19.03.57
	LC	E	14.09.56 – 20.10.56		NC	E	24.09.57 – 04.10.57
	LI	E	23.10.57 – 09.11.57		HC	E	20.11.57 – 07.12.57
	HI	E	13.03.59 – 11.04.59		LC	E	11.02.58 – 03.01.59
	HG	E	09.01.61 – 11.02.61		NC	E	25.02.59 – 07.03.59
	LC	E	05.12.62 – 18.12.62		LC	E	26.05.60 – 18.06.60
	LI	E	07.11.63 – 14.12.63		HG	E	28.03.61 – 06.05.61
					NC	E	20.07.62 – 23.07.62
73082	LC	C	28.12.55 – 17.02.56		HI	E	09.04.64 – 14.05.64
	HI	E	28.10.57 – 30.11.57		LC	E	18.08.65 – 17.09.65
	LI	E	28.07.59 – 15.08.59				
	LC	E	04.03.60 – 19.03.60	73089	LC	De	05.04.57 – 02.05.57
	LC	E	05.12.60 – 24.02.60		LI	E	17.10.57 – 09.11.57
	HG	E	01.08.61 – 02.09.61		LC	E	26.11.57 – 06.12.58
	LI	E	15.11.63 – 21.12.63		LC	E	15.04.59 – 02.05.59

75072 is seen leaving Radstock with the 9.05am local train from Templecombe to Bath Green Park on 9th June 1962. This locomotive was one of three double-chimney members of this class allocated to Bath at the time. The picture was taken from Radstock North A signal box, one of the tallest on the S&D, necessary for sighting purposes over the top of Tyning's Arch, a restricted bridge carrying a colliery tubway up to a spoil tip. On the left is the two-road loco shed, a sub-depot to Bath, with two class 3F 0-6-0Ts outside, of which the one on the left is standing on the line leading to the coal hoist. On the extreme left is the siding which led to Ludlow's colliery and, indirectly, made a physical connection to the Great Western Bristol to Frome branch.

Hugh Ballantyne

	HG	E	13.04.60 – 04.06.60			LC	S	03.07.62 – 17.09.62
	LI	E	11.09.62 – 29.09.62			LC	E	27.04.65 – 30.04.65
	HC	E	13.05.64 – 10.06.64					
					73094	LC	De	21.05.57 – 06.06.57
73090	LI	De	11.11.57 – 11.12.57			HI	De	25.02.58 – 25.03.58
	NC(EO)	De	10.06.58 – 26.06.58			LC	W	08.01.60 – 05.02.60
	HG	Do	29.06.60 – 12.08.60			LI	Cy	22.03.60 – 07.04.60
	NC	Do	07.10.60 – 14.10.60			HI	Do	22.09.60 - 03.11.60
	LC	De	28.06.63 – 07.07.63			LI	E	06.08.64 – 23.09.64
	HC	C	22.08.63 – 04.10.63					
					73095	LI	De	08.07.57 – 15.08.57
73091	NC(R)	De	08.11.55 – 11.11.55			HG	Do	21.05.60 – 14.07.60
	NC(T)	De	26.08.56 – 01.09.56			HG	Do	17.05.62 – 18.07.62
	LC(T)	De	09.04.57 – 11.04.57				No further data	
	LC	De	19.09.57 – 03.10.57					
	LI	De	13.02.58 – 06.03.58		73096	NC(T)	De	13.03.56 – 15.03.56
	LC	W	02.02.59 – 24.02.59			LC(T)	De	05.06.57 – 07.06.57
	HG	Do	19.04.60 – 27.05.60			LI	De	19.03.58 – 14.04.58
		No further data				LC	Sa	14.08.59 – 07.09.59
						LI	W	19.11.59 – 31.12.59
73092	LI	De	05.02.58 – 24.02.58			HG	Do	09.02.61 – 24.03.61
	HG	Do	05.04.60 – 27.05.60			LI	C	26.08.63 – 02.10.63
	HI	Da	18.10.63 – 14.02.64					
	LC	E	20.04.65 – 20.05.65		73097	NC(EO)	De	26.11.56 – 04.12.56
						LC	De	13.02.57 – 27.03.57
						LI	De	06.12.57 – 07.01.58
73093	LI	De	25.11.57 – 19.12.57			LI	W	02.09.59 – 16.10.59
	LC	De	02.09.58 – 25.09.58			HG	Do	02.12.60 – 11.01.61
	HI	W	22.02.60 – 19.05.60			HC	Da	05.02.64 – 20.04.64

73098	LC(TO)	De	29.01.57 – 04.02.57		LC(EO)	Co	11.08.59 – 28.08.59
	LC	De	09.10.57 – 23.10.57		HG	Co	17.12.59 – 06.02.60
	LI	De	23.11.57 – 24.12.57		NC(EO)	Co	12.04.61 – 20.04.61
	LC	Co	30.06.59 – 14.07.59		LC(EO)	Co	12.04.62 – 04.05.62
	NC(EO)	Co	28.03.60 – 30.04.60		HI	Co	30.07.62 – 01.09.62
	HG	Co	27.03.61 – 29.04.61		LC(EO)	Co	29.06.64 – 28.08.64
	LC	Co	01.02.62 – 17.03.62		NC	Co	18.11.64 – 20.11.64
	LC(TO)	Co	20.09.62 – 12.10.62		LI	Co	25.02.65 – 01.05.65
	NC(EO)	Co	13.12.62 – 21.12.62		NC	Co	16.08.65 – 28.08.65
	HI	Co	22.08.63 – 19.10.63		NC	Co	25.01.66 – 02.02.66
	NC(EO)	Co	08.11.63		LC(EO)	Co	14.06.66 – 25.06.66
	LC(EO)	Co	17.02.64 – 28.02.64				
	NC	Co	29.09.65	73101	LC(EO)	R	11.10.56 – 07.11.56
					LI	R	07.10.57 – 09.11.57
73099	LI	De	12.01.58 – 03.02.58		LC(EO)	Co	27.01.59 – 02.03.59
	NC(EO)	Co	03.04.59 – 28.04.59		HG	Co	05.07.60 – 20.08.60
	LC(TO)	R	15.12.59 – 31.12.59		HI	Co	19.01.63 – 23.02.63
	HG	Co	03.07.61 – 16.09.61		LC(EO)	Co	17.08.64 – 29.09.64
	HI	Co	20.06.63 – 03.08.63		NC(EO)	Co	16.02.65 – 20.02.65
	NC(EO)	Co	09.12.64 – 11.12.64		NC(EO)	Co	03.08.65 – 04.08.65
	LC	In	21.04.65 – 01.05.65		LC(EO)	Co	05.01.66 – 29.01.66
	LC	Co	26.05.66 – 10.06.66		NC(EO)	Co	18.03.66 – 30.03.66
	LC(EO)	Co	13.07.66 – 16.07.66		NC(EO)	Co	24.04.66 – 07.05.66
73100	LC	R	26.06.56 – 04.07.56	73102	LC(EO)	R	18.12.56 – 26.12.56
	LI	R	04.09.57 – 03.10.57		LC	R	11.03.57 – 23.03.57
	NC	R	29.10.57 – 06.11.57		LC	R	11.10.57 – 12.10.57
	NC(EO)	Co	23.05.58 – 03.06.58		HI	R	24.10.57 – 15.11.57
	NC(EO)	Co	30.06.59 – 04.07.59		LC(EO)	Co	14.10.58 – 30.10.58

Gourock on the south bank of the River Clyde was the Caledonian Railway's answer to the Glasgow & South Western Railways bid for a share of the lucrative Clydeside steamer and ocean liner traffic, hence the extensive siding accommodation with the River Clyde, a paddle steamer and the station in the background. Although normally the preserve of Class 4 2-6-4 tanks, here 73072 is waiting to back down to the station to work a return service to Glasgow Central in March 1966. Withdrawal came seven months later.

Douglas Hume

	LC	Co	03.08.59 – 17.08.59
	HG	Co	25.04.60 – 18.06.60
	LC(TO)	Co	18.02.61 – 11.03.61
	HI	Co	26.05.62 – 23.06.62
	LI	Co	31.12.64 – 27.02.65
	NC	Co	30.12.65 – 15.01.66
73103	LC	R	16.10.57
	LI	Co	27.01.58 – 01.03.58
	HG	Co	15.09.59 – 30.10.59
	HI	Co	27.03.62 – 18.05.62
	HI	Co	21.05.64 – 27.06.64
	NC(EO)	Co	19.02.65 – 20.02.65
	NC(EO)	Co	30.08.65 – 09.09.65
73104	LC(EO)	R	15.02.56 – 17.02.56
	NC	R	15.08.56 – 18.08.56
	LI	R	12.12.57 – 26.12.57
	LC(EO)	Co	29.05.58 – 20.06.58
	HG	Co	30.05.60 – 02.07.60
	HI	Co	17.06.63 – 10.07.63
	NC(EO)	Co	10.01.64 – 11.01.64
	LC(EO)	Co	13.11.64 – 12.12.64
	LC	In	21.01.65 – 22.01.65
73105	LI	Co	24.02.58 – 29.03.58
	NC(EO)	R	05.03.59 – 12.03.59
	LC(EO)	Co	14.09.59 – 08.10.59
	HG	Co	16.03.60 – 07.05.60
	HI	Co	11.06.62 – 11.08.62
	LC(EO)	Co	21.08.64 – 12.09.64
	NC(EO)	Co	19.02.65 – 27.02.65
	NC	Co	20.09.65 – 25.09.65
	LC	Co	26.10.65 – 20.11.65
	LC(EO)	Co	30.05.66 – 18.06.66
73106	NC	Do	03.01.56 – 05.01.56
	NC	R	30.01.56 – 03.02.56
	LC(TO)	R	31.01.57 – 09.02.57
	LI	Co	17.02.58 – 22.03.58
	NC(EO)	Co	06.06.58 – 07.06.58
	NC(EO)	Co	20.06.58 – 21.06.58
	NC(EO)	Co	21.11.58 – 01.12.58
	LC(EO)	Co	06.04.59 – 28.04.59
	HG	Co	22.03.60 – 21.05.60
	NC(EO)	Co	19.04.61 – 27.04.61
	HI	Co	12.03.62 – 21.04.62
	LC(EO)	Co	08.01.63 – 09.02.63
	NC(EO)	Co	29.05.63 – 07.06.63
	NC(EO)	Co	14.06.63 – 06.07.63
	LC(EO)	Co	20.02.64 – 20.03.64
	LC(EO)	Co	05.08.64 – 04.09.64
	NC(EO	Co	29.01.65 – 30.01.65
73107	LI	Co	23.12.57 – 08.02.58
	NC(EO)	Co	27.09.58 – 04.10.58
	NC(EO)	Co	08.12.58 – 13.12.58
	LC(EO)	Co	10.08.59 – 20.08.59
	HG	Co	28.09.59 – 07.11.59
	LC(EO)	Co	23.01.61 – 04.02.61
	LC(EO)	Co	30.06.61 – 19.08.61
	LC(EO)	Co	04.01.62 – 03.02.62
	HI	Co	10.04.62 – 01.06.62
	HI	Co	30.09.64 – 31.10.64
	NC(EO)	Co	19.08.65 – 21.08.65
	NC(EO)	Co	29.11.65 – 04.12.65
73108	NC(EO)	R	28.06.56
	LC(EO)	R	16.11.56 – 20.11.56
	LI	Co	22.04.58 – 17.05.58
	NC(EO)	R	09.03.59 – 14.03.59
	NC(EO)	Co	02.07.59 – 04.07.59
	NC(EO)	Co	15.09.59 – 16.09.59
	NC(EO)	Co	21.09.59 – 23.09.59
	NC(EO)	Co	13.04.60 – 14.04.60
	NC(EO)	Co	05.05.60 – 07.05.60
	HG	Co	22.06.60 – 06.08.60
	NC(EO)	Co	21.06.61 – 23.06.61
	NC(EO)	Co	08.08.61
	LC(EO)	Co	28.09.61 – 07.10.61
	HI	Co	03.04.63 – 02.05.63
	NC	Co	25.12.65 – 18.01.66
	LC(EO)	Co	13.07.66 – 16.07.66
73109	LC(EO)	R	30.01.57 – 06.02.57
	LI	Co	09.01.58 – 01.02.58
	NC(EO)	R	18.03.59 – 24.03.59
	HG	Co	16.02.60 – 26.03.60
	LI	Co	10.05.62 – 02.06.62
	NC(EO)	Co	30.01.63 – 31.03.63
73110	HI	E	30.09.57 – 19.10.59
	HG	E	21.12.59 – 23.01.60
	NC	E	02.11.60 – 19.11.60
	NC	E	05.10.61 – 25.10.61
	LI	E	26.10.62 – 01.12.62
	LC	E	22.05.63 – 29.05.63
	NC	E	10.09.63 – 14.09.63
	LC	E	21.02.64 – 14.03.64
	LC	E	14.10.64 – 15.10.64
	NC	E	28.03.66 – 31.03.66
73111	LC	B	22.05.55 – 21.06.55
	HI	E	24.01.56 – 15.02.56
	LC	E	15.05.58 – 19.06.58
	LC	A	04.08.59 – 05.09.59
	HG	E	20.10.60 – 26.11.60
	LC	E	03.05.61 – 19.05.61
	LI	E	06.02.63 – 09.03.63
	NC	E	06.06.63 – 22.06.63
	LC	E	20.10.63 – 16.11.63
	LC	E	12.02.64 – 29.02.64
	LC	E	05.05.65 – 15.05.65
	LC	E	22.06.65 – 25.06.65
73112	PV	B	03.09.56 – 28.09.56
	LI	E	09.12.57 – 04.01.58
	NC	E	30.04.59 – 03.05.59
	HG	E	04.03.60 – 02.04.60
	LC	E	16.05.61 – 18.05.61
	LI	E	27.12.62 – 26.01.63
73113	LC	B	23.04.56 – 24.05.56
	LC	E	11.11.57 – 30.11.57
	LI	E	24.11.59 – 12.12.59
	LC	E	22.12.60 – 07.01.61

ID	Code	Type	Dates
	HG	E	21.11.61 – 20.01.62
	LC	E	26.02.65 – 25.03.65
	NC	E	18.04.66 – 26.04.66
73114	NC	B	10.12.56 – 22.12.56
	HI	E	20.02.58 – 15.03.58
	NC	A	03.07.59 – 25.07.59
	HG	E	16.02.60 – 19.03.60
	LC	E	02.01.61 – 28.01.61
	LC	E	26.11.62 – 06.12.62
	HI	E	27.04.64 – 30.05.64
	LC	E	27.01.65 – 01.02.65
73115	PV	B	06.07.56 – 09.08.56
	HI	E	13.12.57 – 11.01.58
	NC	A	23.10.59 – 13.11.59
	HG	E	05.01.60 – 30.01.60
	LI	E	22.11.62 – 22.12.62
	HI	E	22.03.65 – 30.04.65
73116	USX	E	09.07.56
	NC	B	21.02.57 – 14.03.57
	LI	E	26.02.58 – 28.03.58
	LC	E	16.12.58 – 23.12.58
	NC	E	06.04.59 – 11.04.59
	LC	E	02.09.59 – 19.09.59
	HG	E	06.09.60 – 01.10.60
	LI	E	02.08.62 – 15.09.62
	NC	E	24.04.63 – 25.04.63
73117	LC	B	14.01.57 – 01.02.57
	HI	E	19.08.58 – 13.09.58
	NC(R)	E	15.10.58 – 21.10.58
	NC	E	27.01.59 – 11.02.59
	HG	E	06.03.61 – 15.04.61
	LC	Se	05.02.63 – 15.02.63
	LC	E	05.06.63 – 14.06.63
	HI	E	17.02.64 – 28.03.64
	LC	E	22.12.64 – 15.01.65
	LC	E	07.03.66 – 16.03.66
	NC	E	20.04.66 – 22.04.66
73118	NC	B	01.04.57 – 18.04.57
	HI	E	14.01.58 – 08.02.58
	NC	E	12.11.59 – 20.11.59
	HI	E	26.01.60 – 20.02.60
	HG	E	12.12.63 – 02.02.63
	LC	E	21.11.65 – 23.12.65
	NC	E	09.05.66 – 17.05.66
73119	NC	B	31.10.56 – 17.11.56
	LI	E	06.02.58 – 22.02.58
	NC	E	26.05.59 – 11.06.59
	LI	E	11.03.60 – 02.04.60
	LC	E	02.09.60 – 17.09.60
	HG	E	01.02.62 – 10.03.62
	LC	E	15.11.62 – 22.11.62
	LC	E	31.03.64 – 24.04.64
	LC	E	26.04.66 – 06.05.66
73120	HI	R	04.10.57 – 02.11.57
	LC(EO)	Co	16.02.59 – 17.03.59
	LI	Co	06.08.59 – 29.08.59

ID	Code	Type	Dates
	LC(EO)	Co	13.10.59 – 31.10.59
	NC(EO)	Co	09.04.60 – 21.04.60
	NC(EO)	Co	26.04.60 – 14.05.60
	NC(EO)	Co	04.01.61 – 10.01.61
	HG	Co	29.05.61 – 14.07.61
	NC(EO)	Co	29.03.62 – 24.05.62
	HI	Co	24.01.63 – 01.03.63
	LC(EO)	Co	01.04.63 – 20.04.63
	LC	Co	14.05.65 – 05.06.65
	NC	Co	18.10.65 – 06.11.65
	LC(EO)	Co	16.04.66 – 12.05.66
73121	LI	Co	03.02.58 – 01.03.58
	NC	Co	31.08.59 – 10.09.59
	HG	Co	14.03.60 – 30.04.60
	HI	Co	25.08.62 – 29.09.62
	NC(EO)	Co	03.01.63 – 12.01.63
	LI	Co	02.07.64 – 19.09.64
	LC	Co	22.04.65 – 29.05.65
	LC	Co	26.08.65 – 04.09.65
	NC	Co	24.11.65 – 27.11.65
73122	LI	Co	09.06.58 – 28.06.58
	LI	Co	27.01.60 – 19.03.60
	HC(EO)	Co	30.08.60 – 17.10.60
	NC(EO)	Co	13.09.61 – 19.09.61
	NC(EO)	Co	25.04.62 – 01.05.62
	LI	Co	12.09.62 – 26.10.62
	NC(EO)	Co	06.11.62 – 14.11.62
	NC(EO)	Co	27.09.63 – 11.10.63
	NC(EO)	Co	10.09.64 – 03.10.64
	LC	Co	19.10.64 – 28.11.64
73123	LI	Co	12.05.58 – 06.06.58
	HI	Co	08.02.60 – 02.04.60
	HG	Co	14.11.61 – 06.01.62
	LC(EO)	Co	31.10.62 – 15.11.62
	NC(EO)	Co	23.07.64 – 07.08.64
	NC(EO)	Co	07.09.64 – 12.09.64
	LC	Co	08.02.65 – 27.02.65
73124	LI	Co	22.03.58 – 19.04.58
	HI	Co	05.03.60 – 09.04.60
	NC(EO)	Co	19.05.60 – 10.06.60
	NC(EO)	Co	29.11.60 – 14.12.60
	NC(EO)	Co	09.01.62 – 16.01.62
	HG	Co	06.03.62 – 19.04.62
	LC	Co	24.10.63 – 10.11.63
	NC(EO)	Co	28.12.62 – 05.01.63
	LC(EO)	Co	27.04.63 – 17.05.63
	LC(EO)	Co	27.04.64 – 16.05.64
	LC	Co	20.08.64 – 24.10.64
	NC	Co	21.11.64 – 27.11.64
	NC(EO)	Co	06.04.65 – 10.04.65
73125	LC	De	09.02.59 – 27.02.59
	HI	De	12.08.61 – 27.09.61
	HC	C	15.08.63 – 16.10.63
	HI	Co	08.06.65 – 14.08.65
73126	LC	De	29.01.59 – 19.02.59
	HG	De	29.03.61 – 05.05.61
	LI	E	30.11.64 – 08.02.65

73127	U	W	30.01.57 – 01.02.57
	LC(EO)	Ru	24.04.59 – 07.05.59
	NC(EO)	De	01.12.59 – 24.12.59
	LI	De	27.02.61 – 25.04.61
	LC(EO)	De	10.05.61 – 08.06.61
	LC(EO)	De	03.07.61 – 21.08.61
	HG	C	05.09.63 – 25.01.64
73128	LC	De	29.01.59 – 18.02.59
	LC	De	01.06.59 – 25.06.59
	LI	De	28.06.60 – 09.09.60
	LC(EO)	De	26.05.61 – 15.06.61
	HG	C	11.09.63 – 17.12.63
73129	LC(EO)	Ru	27.02.59 – 17.03.59
	NC(EO)	De	14.12.59 – 06.01.60
	HG	Co	14.09.61 – 14.10.61
	NC(EO)	Co	18.10.61 – 21.10.61
	LI	Co	01.05.65 – 18.05.65
73130	LC(EO)	De	09.02.59 – 16.03.59
	NC(EO)	H	01.02.60 – 18.02.60
	LI	De	24.07.61 – 21.09.61
	NC	De	18.02.62 – 08.03.63
	NG	Da	21.09.63 – 17.01.64
73131	LC(EO)	Ru	10.03.59 – 14.04.59
	LI	De	06.10.59 – 17.11.59
	HG	De	18.06.62 – 13.08.62
73132	LC	De	21.04.59 – 14.05.59
	NC(EO)	De	14.12.59 – 05.01.60
	HG	De	07.04.61 – 09.06.61
	HI	De	26.08.64 – 09.10.64
73133	NC	W	17.01.58 – 02.02.58
	LC	De	25.06.59 – 03.08.59
	NC(EO)	De	13.01.60 – 01.02.60
	HG	De	16.11.61 – 18.01.62
	CD	Da	30.06.64 – 12.08.64
	HI	E	15.09.65 – 27.10.65
73134	LC	De	06.07.59 – 10.08.59
	NC(EO)	De	18.01.60 – 01.02.60
	HG	Co	26.10.61 – 18.11.61
	LI	Co	28.05.65 – 08.07.65
73135	NC(EO)	De	31.01.57 – 20.02.57
	LC(EO)	Ru	03.01.59 – 03.02.59
	LI	De	01.07.60 – 26.08.60
	HG	C	05.09.63 – 21.11.63
	NCR	C	04.12.63 – 07.12.63
	LC	Da	25.06.64 – 22.08.64
73136	NC(EO)	De	02.05.57 – 02.05.57
	LI	De	25.04.59 – 27.05.59
	LC(EO)	De	02.12.60 – 04.01.61
	LC	De	06.11.61 – 07.12.61
	HG	De	13.11.62 – 14.12.62
73137	LC(EO)	Ru	22.12.58 – 30.01.59
	LI	De	24.10.59 – 26.11.59
	LC	De	11.09.61 – 24.10.61
	HG	De	01.07.62 – 12.09.62
	LC	Da	03.02.64 – 15.05.64
73138	LC(EO)	De	05.05.57 – 31.05.57
	LC(EO)	Ru	06.02.59 – 12.03.59
	LC	De	29.05.59 – 25.06.59
	LI	De	07.11.60 – 08.12.60
	HC	De	17.06.62 – 03.08.62
	HG	Da	08.11.63 – 05.03.64
73139	LC(EO)	De	14.01.59 – 11.02.59
	HI	De	21.05.60 – 23.06.60
	HG	De	22.10.62 – 16.11.62
73140	LI	De	26.03.59 – 05.05.59
	LC	De	03.11.60 – 02.12.60
	HG	De	27.03.62 – 02.05.62
73141	LC	De	20.02.59 – 19.03.59
	HI	De	30.05.60 – 14.06.60
	HG	De	04.11.62 – 21.12.62
	LC	Co	12.07.65 – 09.10.65
73142	LI	De	06.02.59 – 16.03.59
	HI	De	16.11.61 – 20.12.61
	HG	Da	23.12.63 – 29.02.64
	NC(EO)	De?	12.03.64 – 06.05.64
73143	LC	De	05.06.59 – 22.06.59
	HI	De	24.06.60 – 15.08.60
	HG	C	20.08.63 – 25.10.63
	NC(EO)	Co	18.02.65 – 20.02.65
73144	LC	De	12.05.59 – 21.05.59
	HI	De	22.06.60 – 08.09.60
73145	LI	Co	05.11.58 – 22.11.58
	LC(EO)	R	22.06.59 – 01.07.59
	LC(EO)	Co	13.09.60 – 23.09.60
	HG	Co	22.02.61 – 29.04.61
	LC	Co	18.03.63 – 20.04.63
	HI	Co	29.01.64 – 07.03.64
	NC(EO)	Co	15.12.65 – 18.12.65
	LC	Co	30.05.66 – 17.06.66
73146	LI	Co	12.11.58 – 06.12.58
	LC(EO)	Co	08.06.59 – 05.08.59
	LI	Co	29.11.60 – 07.01.61
	NC(EO)	Co	02.11.61 – 11.11.61
	HG	Co	17.12.62 – 02.02.63
	LC(EO)	Co	20.01.64 – 06.02.64
	HI	Co	31.12.64 – 30.01.65
	LC	Co	02.06.65 – 10.07.65
	NC	Co	10.08.65 – 04.09.65
	NC(EO)	Co	29.11.65 – 11.12.65
	LC	Co	19.01.66 – 12.02.66
73147	LI	Co	06.12.58 – 27.12.58
	NC(EO)	R	30.06.59 – 09.07.59
	NC(EO)	Co	24.11.59 – 01.12.59
	LC(EO)	Co	06.10.60 – 19.10.60
	HG	Co	25.10.61 – 16.12.61

	LC(EO)	Co	06.01.63 – 13.01.63		LC(EO)	Co	26.12.63 – 18.01.64
	LC(EO)	Co	17.07.62 – 18.08.62		LC(EO)	Co	19.06.64
	LC	Co	04.11.64 – 05.12.64		LI	Co	03.05.65 – 12.05.65
73148	LI	Co	10.12.58 – 31.12.58	73155	AD	Do	31.01.57 – 06.02.57
	NC(EO)	R	10.06.59 – 18.06.59		HI	Do	13.12.58 – 30.01.59
	LC(EO)	Co	27.06.60 – 08.07.60		HG	Do	22.12.60 – 25.01.61
	HG	Co	21.04.61 – 20.05.61		LC	E	07.01.64 – 25.01.64
	LC(EO)	Co	23.11.62 – 05.12.62		HI	E	20.06.65 – 27.08.65
	HI	Co	11.12.63 – 25.11.64		NC	E	01.04.66 – 06.04.66
	NC(EO)	Co	11.05.64 – 20.05.64				
	LC(EO)	Co	29.03.65 – 03.04.65	73156	HI	Do	03.02.59 – 19.03.59
					LI	Do	26.11.59 – 01.12.59
73149	LC	R	16.09.57 – 26.09.57		HG	De	31.10.61 – 15.12.61
	LI	Co	18.12.58 – 10.01.59		HC	De	31.01.63 – 02.02.63
	NC(EO)	R	08.06.59 – 11.06.59				
	LC(EO)	Co	01.08.60 – 26.08.60	73157	LI	De	16.02.59 – 23.03.59
	HG	Co	26.12.61 – 27.01.62		LC(EO)	De	18.09.60 – 24.11.60
	LI	Co	24.03.65 – 10.04.65		LI	De	24.03.61 – 11.05.61
					HI	E	18.11.64 – 08.01.65
73150	LI	Co	22.12.58 – 16.01.59				
	LC(EO)	Co	24.10.59 – 11.12.59	73158	HC	Do	28.10.58 – 17.11.58
	HG	Co	08.05.61 – 17.06.61		Ty	Do	18.05.59 – 04.06.59
	NC(EO)	Co	11.02.63 – 21.02.63		LI	De	02.05.60 – 17.06.60
	HI	Co	19.03.64 – 25.04.64		LC(EO)	De	20.09.61 – 21.11.61
					HG	De	30.04.62 – 01.06.62
73151	LI	Co	20.01.59 – 13.02.59		LC	Co	19.03.65 – 27.03.65
	LC	Co	01.09.60 – 16.09.60				
	HG	Co	02.06.61 – 12.08.61	73159	LI	De	06.02.59 – 27.02.59
	LC(EO)	Co	05.02.62 – 22.02.62		LC(EO)	De	07.10.59 – 05.11.59
	HI	Co	11.11.64 – 26.12.64		LC(EO)	N	05.12.60 – 31.12.60
	NC	Co	04.02.65 – 06.02.65		LI	De	29.08.61 – 30.10.61
	LC	Co	07.05.65 – 17.05.65		HC	De	09.08.62 – 31.08.62
					HC	De	08.03.63 – 24.04.63
73152	LI	Co	19.02.59 – 28.02.59		NC	De	01.05.63 – 10.05.63
	NC(EO)	Co	13.04.59 – 20.04.59		LC	Bn	30.09.63 – 12.10.63
	HG	Co	06.02.61 – 07.04.61		LC	Da	15.04.64
	LC(EO)	Co	27.11.61 – 15.12.61		LI	E	14.09.64 – 20.10.64
	LC	Co	10.12.62 – 21.12.62				
	LI	Co	30.10.63 – 07.12.63	73160	HI	Do	04.09.59 – 14.10.59
	NC(EO)	Co	13.12.63 – 17.12.63		LI	E	03.07.64 – 28.08.64
	NC(EO)	Co	28.04.64 – 15.05.64		LC	E	19.01.65 – 09.02.65
	NC(EO)	Co	22.05.64 – 12.06.64				
	LC	Co	16.10.64	73161	H	Do	28.05.59 – 02.07.59
	LC	Co	12.05.65 – 22.05.65		LI	C	30.07.62 – 24.08.62
					LC	H	03.07.63 – 02.08.63
73153	LI	Co	04.02.59 – 27.02.59		LC	E	17.01.64 – 15.02.64
	LC(EO)	Co	04.07.60 – 15.07.60				
	HG	Co	11.01.61 – 18.02.61	73162	H	Do	23.04.59 – 23.05.59
	LC(EO)	Co	27.11.61 – 20.12.61				No further data
	LI	Co	08.11.62 – 01.12.62				
	LC(EO)	Co	04.06.63 – 15.06.63	73163	H	Do	25.07.59 – 27.08.59
	LC(EO)	Co	25.03.64 – 01.05.64				No further data
	NC(EO)	Co	13.05.64 – 20.05.64				
	LC(EO)	Co	25.06.64 – 15.07.64	73164	AD	Do	29.05.57 – 03.06.57
	LC(EO)	Co	14.12.64 – 26.12.64		H	Do	17.06.59 – 25.09.59
	NC(EO	Co	11.01.65 – 16.02.65		HC	De	22.11.62 – 28.12.62
	LC(EO)	Co	03.02.66 – 05.03.66				
				73165	LC	Do	17.04.59 – 23.04.59
73154	LI	Co	06.03.59 – 28.03.59		HG	Do	17.07.59 – 15.08.59
	LC(EO)	Co	04.11.60 – 25.11.60		NC	Do	09.11.61 – 23.11.61
	HG	Co	23.01.62 – 24.02.62		Ty	Do	14.05.62 – 30.05.62
	LC(EO)	Co	13.02.63 – 06.04.63		LI	E	12.01.65 – 26.02.65

73166	H	Do	06.08.59 – 05.09.59		NC	Do	09.05.61 – 19.05.61
	LI?	C	23.07.63 – ??.??.??		CD	Do	22.08.61 – 30.09.61
					LI	E	04.12.63 – 11.01.64
73167	NC	Do	20.09.57 – 30.09.57		LC	E	07.04.64 – 25.04.64
	HI	Do	13.04.59 – 15.05.59				
	HI	De	15.08.62 – 05.09.62	73170	HI	Do	27.08.59 – 06.10.59
	LC	E	07.01.64 – 25.01.64		HG	Do	27.09.61 – 27.10.61
	LC	E	17.09.64 – 14.10.64		HI	E	05.12.63 – 18.01.64
					LC	E	31.12.64 – 25.01.65
73168	NC	Do	20.09.57 – 30.09.57				
	HI	Do	20.08.59 – 24.09.59	73171	AD	Do	06.06.57 – 15.06.57
	HG	Do	16.05.62 – 06.07.62		HI	Do	23.04.59 – 03.06.59
					HG	Do	09.08.61 – 22.09.61
73169	HI	Do	16.12.59 – 28.01.60		HI	E	18.12.63 – 25.01.64
	LC	Do	23.02.60 – 12.03.60		N	E	22.06.65 – 01.07.65

84029 stands at Ramsgate station awaiting departure on the service to Ashford via Canterbury West on 14th May 1960. Delivered new to Ramsgate depot as one of the batch, 84020-29, allocated to the Eastern Section of the Southern Region in 1957 to replace the SECR H Class 0-4-4T. However, they were not able to work push and pull trains because their equipment was on the vacuum system whereas the Southern locomotives used the compressed air system. 84029 was the last BR tank engine to be built and was the very last locomotive to be constructed at Darlington North Road Works.

R. C. Riley

TABLE 6.2
BR Standard Class 4 4-6-0s 75000-75079 – Record of Repairs

No.	1	2	3
75000	LC	S	19.01.55 – 16.02.55
	HC	S	30.11.55 – 09.02.56
	HC cont.	S	20.02.56 – 01.03.56
	HI	S	27.06.57 – 05.09.57
	LC	S	08.11.58 – 16.01.59
	LI	Ty	01.09.59 – 28.10.59
	LI	Ty	26.02.60 – 12.03.60
	HG	W	14.06.60 – 07.09.60
	HC	C	08.08.63 – 09.11.63
75001	HI	S	24.04.54 – 06.08.54
	HI	S	13.07.55 – 11.10.55
	LC	Bb	25.10.56 – 01.11.56
	LC	S	09.05.57 – 09.09.57
	HG	S	24.07.58 – 03.10.58
	HI	Cy	20.04.61 – 08.09.61
75002	LC	S	15.01.54 – 22.02.54
	HI	S	07.02.55 – 06.04.55
	HI	S	18.01.56 – 24.01.56
	HG	S	15.08.57 – 11.11.57
	HG	S	18.09.59 – 07.10.59
	HG	Gb	01.02.60 – 24.02.60
	HI	Cy	02.08.60 – 16.09.60
	HG	E	17.03.64 – 02.05.64
75003	RVC	S	22.12.53 – 01.01.54
	U	S	23.01.56 – 25.01.56
	HI	S	07.12.56 – 21.02.57
	LC	S	23.12.59 – 22.05.60
	LC	S	15.10.59 – 11.01.60
75004	HI	S	01.02.54 – 31.03.54
	LC	S	10.01.56 – 17.02.56
	HG	S	04.09.56 – 12.12.56
	HG	S	22.06.59 – 21.09.59
75005	HG	S	14.06.56 – 18.10.56
	HI	De	19.04.59 – 27.05.59
	LC	E	15.04.64 – 20.05.64
75006	HI	S	26.07.54 – 14.10.54
	HI	S	30.10.56 – 28.01.57
	HI	De	31.10.58 – 08.12.58
75007	NC	De	29.11.56 – 04.12.56
	LC	De	06.03.57 – 27.03.57
	LI	De	11.12.57 – 07.01.58
	LC	W	07.09.59 – 16.10.59
	NC	W	06.11.59 – 09.11.59
	HI	Do	02.12.60 – 11.01.61
	HC	W	10.05.62 – 19.07.62
75008	HI	S	17.11.53 – 19.01.54
	U	S	19.03.56 – 27.03.56
	HG	S	22.05.56 – 03.08.56
	HI	S	30.07.58 – 22.10.58
	HG	Cy	08.09.60 – 19.11.60
	HG	S	20.06.62 – 24.09.62
75009	HI	S	16.12.53 – 19.02.54
	U	S	13.02.56 – 17.02.56
	HG	S	31.08.56 – 05.11.56
	HI	W	29.04.59 – 25.06.59
	G	De	20.09.62 – 20.11.62
	I	Da	26.11.64 – 02.02.65
	BLR	C	10.03.66 – 07.04.66
75010	NC(EO)	C	15.05.53 – 30.05.53
	LC(EO)	H	01.09.53 – 01.10.53
	LI	De	08.05.54 – 17.06.54
	HG	De	15.10.56 – 30.11.56
	LC(EO)	De	08.03.57 – 28.03.57
	HI	De	05.11.58 – 11.12.58
	NC	De	12.05.59 – 29.05.59
75011	NC(EO)	C	09.06.53 – 20.06.53
	LI	De	03.07.54 – 23.08.54
	HG	De	01.12.56 – 16.01.57
	LC(EO)	De	19.02.57 – 13.03.57
	LC(EO)	De	06.09.57 – 26.09.57
	HI	De	16.05.60 – 11.06.60
	HC(EO)	De	17.04.61 – 07.06.61
75012	NC	C	23.02.53 – 27.02.53
	LI	De	21.05.54 – 17.06.54
	HG	De	05.11.56 – 12.12.56
	LC(EO)	De	27.08.57 – 12.09.57
	LC(EO)	De	16.09.58 – 14.11.58
	HI	De	21.03.60 – 05.05.60
	LC	E	16.02.65 – 10.03.65
75013	LC(EO)	C	20.04.53 – 02.05.53
	LI	De	28.06.54 – 12.08.54
	HG	De	23.11.56 – 04.01.57
	LC(EO)	De	06.05.57 – 01.07.57
	LC(EO)	De	10.08.58 – 16.09.58
	HI	De	19.10.59 – 12.11.59
	LC	E	09.03.64 – 04.04.64
75014	NM	C	21.07.53 – 01.08.53
	LI	De	26.07.54 – 02.09.54
	HG	De	28.08.56 – 13.10.56
	LC(EO)	De	30.01.57 – 27.02.57
	LC(EO)	De	10.04.57 – 27.06.57
	HI	De	31.01.60 – 24.03.60
75015	NC(EO)	H	06.11.52 – 07.11.52
	NC	H	24.01.53 – 07.05.53
	LI	De	21.09.54 – 21.10.54
	HG	De	19.09.56 – 09.11.56
	LC(EO)	De	05.11.57 – 03.12.57
	LI	De	16.02.59 – 24.03.59
	LI	De	18.09.61 – 26.10.61
75016	NC(EO)	H	11.11.52 – 12.11.52
	NC(EO)	H	08.05.53 – 29.05.53
	NC(T)	H	04.05.54 – 17.05.54
	LI	De	15.11.54 – 14.12.54
	HI	De	09.05.56 – 11.06.56
	LC(EO)	De	02.11.56 – 01.01.57
	HG	De	06.05.58 – 05.06.58
	LC(EO)	Bo	05.03.59 – 15.04.59

ID			
	LI	De	30.01.61 – 09.03.61
	LI	E	04.06.64 – 31.07.64
75017	NC(EO)	H	28.10.52 – 31.10.52
	NC(EO)	H	04.06.53 – 22.06.53
	LI	De	08.02.55 – 10.03.55
	LC(EO)	De	31.05.55 – 11.07.55
	HG	De	23.02.57 – 05.04.57
	LC(EO)	De	14.07.58 – 08.09.58
	HI	De	01.01.59 – 02.02.59
	HI	De	04.09.61 – 17.10.61
75018	NC(EO)	H	04.11.52 – 05.11.52
	LC(EO)	H	01.07.53 – 11.07.53
	LI	De	28.12.54 – 27.01.55
	LC(EO)	De	26.05.55 – 07.07.55
	LI	De	12.04.56 – 17.05.56
	LC(EO)	De	05.10.56 – 06.11.56
	HG	De	20.04.57 – 31.05.57
	LC	De	10.09.57 – 26.09.57
	LI	De	16.03.59 – 17.04.59
	LI	De	29.08.61 – 09.10.61
	HI	E	23.09.64 – 04.11.64
75019	NC(EO)	H	13.11.52 – 15.11.52
	LC(EO)	H	10.09.53 – 05.10.53
	LI	De	14.02.55 – 17.03.55
	HG	De	03.12.56 – 24.01.57
	HI	De	01.04.58 – 13.05.58
	LI	De	07.03.60 – 26.04.60
	HI	E	30.07.65 – 17.09.65
75020	HI	S	26.12.55 – 07.03.56
	HG	De	27.10.58 – 28.11.58
75021	HI	S	11.06.56 – 31.08.56
	HI	S	25.02.59 – 29.04.59
	I	Da	21.12.64 – 06.02.65
75022	HI	S	21.04.56 – 06.07.56
	U	S	29.08.56 – 13.09.56
	HG	S	17.12.58 – 20.02.59
	U	Br	28.11.59 – 23.12.59
	HG	S	18.04.62 – 25.06.62
75023	HI	S	01.06.56 – 09.08.56
	LC	Bb	13.12.56 – 18.12.56
	HG	S	28.05.59 – 01.09.59
75024	HI	S	09.04.56 – 13.06.56
	U	Sa	13.06.58
	HG	S	10.12.58 – 13.02.59
	HI	Co	13.07.65 – 04.09.65
75025	HI	S	29.12.56 – 12.03.57
	HG	S	26.05.59 – 13.08.59
75026	HI	S	26.10.56 – 02.01.57
	HG	De	03.11.58 – 08.01.59
75027	LI	E	02.06.65 – 09.07.65
75028	LC	Na	23.07.55 – 29.07.55
	HI	S	05.12.56 – 11.03.57
	HG	De	23.02.59 – 02.04.59
	LC	De	29.02.60 – 29.03.60
75029	HI	E	20.03.64 – 25.04.64
75030	LI	De	29.05.56 – 21.06.56
	HG	De	26.07.58 – 12.09.58
	LC(EO)	De	24.11.59 – 09.12.59
	HI	De	25.09.61 – 10.11.61
	LI	E	05.07.65 – 07.09.65
75031	LI	De	08.08.56 – 30.08.56
	HG	De	24.02.59 – 08.04.59
	LC	De	24.08.60 – 02.11.60
75032	LI	De	15.08.55 – 08.09.55
	HG	De	26.07.58 – 14.10.58
	HI	De	14.08.61 – 05.10.61
75033	LI	De	25.11.55 – 21.12.55
	HG	De	30.06.58 – 26.09.58
	LI	De	07.02.61 – 29.03.61
	HI	E	02.04.65 – 15.05.65
75034	LI	De	11.11.55 – 08.12.55
	HG	De	30.05.58 – 19.08.58
	HI	De	01.09.61 – 13.10.61
	HI	E	06.11.64 – 24.12.64
75035	LC	De	07.04.54 – 13.05.54
	LI	De	23.01.56 – 16.02.56
	HG	De	06.01.59 – 06.02.59
	LI	De	02.10.61 – 01.11.61
	LI	E	10.06.65 – 05.08.65
75036	LI	De	22.12.55 – 17.01.56
	HG	De	12.02.58 – 14.03.58
	HC	De	10.11.59 – 30.11.59
	LC(T)	De	02.04.60 – 21.04.60
	LC	E	29.04.64 – 23.05.64
75037	LC	De	31.05.54 – 24.06.54
	LI	De	05.04.56 – 10.05.56
	HG	De	02.06.58 – 01.08.58
	NR	De	05.08.58 – 14.08.58
	NR	De	26.11.59 – 14.12.59
	HI	De	29.05.61 – 23.06.61
75038	LI	De	07.11.55 – 06.12.55
	LC(EO)	De	12.12.56 – 21.01.57
	HG	De	14.12.57 – 30.01.58
	HI	De	23.01.60 – 24.02.60
75039	LI	De	30.09.55 – 26.10.55
	HG	De	04.06.58 – 02.09.58
	HI	De	07.02.61 – 23.03.61
75040	LI	De	21.07.55 – 18.08.55
	LC(EO)	De	26.07.56 – 16.08.56
	LC(EO)	De	29.09.56 – 23.10.56
	HG	De	23.09.58 – 31.10.58
	HI	De	30.05.61 – 21.06.61
75041	LI	De	27.07.55 – 24.08.55
	LC(EO)L	De	24.10.55 – 10.11.55

75003 passes a Great Western lower quadrant signal and a busy yard on a southbound freight at Beaconsfield on 25th March 1962. At the time of the photograph the locomotive was based at Tyseley and was used on secondary passenger duties to Shrewsbury and Oxford and fitted freights to London.

K. L. Cook

	C(EO)LC	De	06.12.55 – 26.01.56		HG	De	05.05.58 – 12.06.58
	(EO	De	17.09.56 – 16.10.56		HI	De	24.08.59 – 12.10.59
	LC(EO)H	De	07.12.56 – 01.01.57				
	G	De	21.02.59 – 26.03.59	75047	LI	De	29.08.55 – 21.09.55
	HI	De	31.07.61 – 13.09.61		P	H	04.09.56 – 19.09.56
	HI	E	16.06.65 – 20.08.65		LC(EO)	De	25.10.56 – 15.11.56
	NR	E	31.08.65 – 07.09.65		HG	De	28.05.58 – 11.07.58
					LI	De	20.06.60 – 12.08.60
75042	LI	De	14.05.55 – 15.06.55		HI	E	09.10.64 – 18.11.64
	HG	De	24.08.57 – 04.10.57				
	HI	De	12.10.60 – 30.11.60	75048	LI	De	16.01.56 – 02.02.56
					LC(EO)	De	02.11.56 – 07.12.56
75043	LC(EO)	De	10.12.53 – 06.01.54		HG	De	30.12.57 – 12.02.58
	HI	De	09.08.55 – 06.09.55		HI	De	02.05.60 – 30.06.60
	LC(EO)	De	09.08.56 – 11.09.56		NR	De	25.07.60 – 09.08.60
	HG	De	31.07.58 – 23.10.58				
	HI	De	04.04.61 – 11.05.61	75049	LI	De	10.04.56 – 26.04.56
					HG	De	23.12.57 – 29.01.58
75044	LI	De	23.05.55 – 22.06.55		LI	De	05.07.60 – 29.09.60
	HG	De	09.01.57 – 15.02.57				
	NR	De	25.02.57 – 27.02.57	75050	LI	De	02.11.59 – 08.12.59
	HI	De	11.09.59 – 05.11.59		LC(EO)	De	07.01.61 – 16.03.61
					NC(EO)	De	24.06.61 – 24.08.61
75045	LI	De	27.07.55 – 26.08.55				
	HI	De	23.04.57 – 23.05.57	75051	LI	De	29.12.59 – 29.01.60
	HG	De	24.03.59 – 12.05.59				
	LI	De	11.04.61 – 17.05.61	75052	LC(EO)	Ru	17.12.58 – 07.01.59
					LI	De	01.07.59 – 06.08.59
					NC(EO)	De	02.12.59 – 24.12.59
75046	LI	De	21.02.56 – 19.03.56		LC	De	28.09.61 – 16.11.61
	LC(EO)	De	27.11.56 – 17.12.56		NC(EO)	De	22.11.61 – 04.12.61

75053	LI	De	05.03.60 – 14.04.60		NC	E	20.10.60 – 05.11.60
					HG	E	23.01.60 – 25.02.61
75054	LI	De	05.12.59 – 14.01.60		LC	E	26.07.63 – 27.07.63
	NR	De	04.03.60 – 27.04.60		LC	E	25.03.65 – 15.04.65
75055	LC	De	18.06.59 – 06.07.59	75071	NC	E	12.03.57 – 14.03.57
	LI	De	16.07.60 – 23.09.60		LC	E	28.10.57 – 02.11.57
					LI	E	16.04.58 – 03.05.58
75056	LI	De	01.01.59 – 24.02.59		HG	E	03.02.61 – 18.03.61
75057	LI	De	21.07.59 – 20.08.59	75072	NC	E	29.03.57 – 04.04.57
					LI	E	03.07.58 – 09.08.58
75058	LI	De	17.11.59 – 23.12.59		HG	E	12.10.60 – 12.11.60
	L	De	30.05.61 – 11.07.61		HI	E	03.03.64 – 11.04.64
					LC	E	17.08.64 – 17.09.64
75059	LI	De	08.12.58 – 13.01.59				
	LI	De	16.01.61 – 29.03.61	75073	NC	E	26.10.56 – 10.11.56
					LI	E	03.10.58 – 25.10.58
75060	LI	De	02.05.60 – 10.06.60		HG	E	23.06.61 – 19.08.61
					LC	E	17.10.63 – 09.11.63
75061	LI	De	18.12.59 – 28.01.60				
				75074	NC	E	26.04.57 – 04.05.57
75062	LI	De	06.08.60 – 21.10.60		HI	E	07.07.58 – 16.08.58
					HG	E	09.06.61 – 29.07.61
75063	LI	De	17.10.59 – 19.11.59		LI	E	23.01.64 – 29.02.64
75064	LI	De	15.12.59 – 18.01.60	75075	NC	E	13.05.57 – 17.05.57
					LI	E	05.06.58 – 04.07.58
75065	NC	A	01.02.57 – 14.02.57		NC	E	21.10.58 – 25.10.58
	LI	E	13.02.58 – 08.03.58		HG	E	25.08.61 – 30.09.61
	HG	E	24.03.61 – 22.04.61		LC	E	10.03.64 – 20.03.64
	HI	E	30.10.63 – 07.12.63		LC	E	28.06.66 – 18.07.66
75066	NC	A	26.02.57 – 01.03.57	75076	LC	E	14.03.57 – 23.03.57
	NC	A	20.01.58 – 08.02.58		LI	E	18.09.58 – 11.10.58
	LI	E	01.10.58 – 18.10.58		LC	E	11.05.60 – 21.05.60
	HG	E	23.02.61 – 01.04.61		HG	E	24.05.61 – 24.06.61
	NC	E	27.03.63 – 05.04.63		LI	E	08.07.65 – 10.09.65
	LC	E	02.01.64 – 23.01.64				
				75077	NC	E	29.05.57 – 06.06.57
75067	NC	A	12.03.57 – 14.03.57		LI	E	19.06.58 – 30.07.58
	LI	E	27.02.58 – 22.03.58		HG	E	09.05.61 – 10.06.61
	HG	E	25.10.60 – 03.12.60		LC	E	28.01.64 – 08.02.64
	LC	E	30.08.62 – 15.09.62		LC	E	27.05.65 – 23.06.65
75068	NC	A	25.03.57 – 04.04.57	75078	NC	E	19.06.57 – 22.06.57
	LI	E	05.03.58 – 29.03.58		LI	E	12.08.58 – 30.08.58
	LC	A	26.03.59 – 25.04.59		HG	E	12.09.61 – 14.10.61
	HG	E	15.12.60 – 21.01.61		NC	E	08.01.63 – 11.01.63
	LC	Se	04.06.63 – 06.06.63		LI	E	26.01.65 – 05.03.65
	HI	E	25.03.64 – 07.05.64				
				75079	NC	E	03.07.57 – 09.07.57
75069	NC	A	16.04.57 – 23.04.57		NC	E	12.09.57 – 21.09.57
	LI	E	14.03.58 – 05.04.58		LI	E	05.11.58 – 22.11.58
	HG	E	23.09.60 – 22.10.60		NC	E	19.06.59 – 27.06.59
	HI	E	31.07.63 – 14.09.63		HG	E	20.10.61 – 25.11.61
					NC	E	12.02.63 – 13.02.63
75070	NC	E	14.02.57 – 22.02.57		LI	E	09.09.64 – 25.09.64
	LI	E	13.11.57 – 23.11.57				

TABLE 6.3
BR Standard Class 4 2-6-0s 76000-76114 – Record of Repairs

No.	1	2	3
76000	LC	R	08.12.52 – 12.12.52
	NC	Do	21.07.55 – 17.08.55
	HI	Do	07.07.56 – 17.08.56
	NC(EO)	Co	22.10.57 – 26.10.57
	LI	Co	24.06.58 – 19.07.58
	NC(EO)	R	01.02.60 – 27.02.60
	HG	Co	24.01.62 – 03.03.62
	LC(EO)	Co	14.09.64 – 31.10.64
76001	HI	Do	27.06.55 – 09.08.55
	NC	Co	02.12.57 – 04.12.57
	LI	Co	20.06.58 – 19.07.58
	HG	Co	29.06.62 – 17.08.62
	NC(EO)	Co	16.02.66 – 19.03.66
76002	CD	Do	12.02.53 – 06.03.53
	HI	Do	17.05.55 – 28.06.55
	NC	Co	10.12.57 – 13.12.57
	LI	Co	12.06.58 – 12.07.58
	HG	Co	15.02.62 – 26.03.62
76003	HI	Do	12.04.55 – 27.05.55
	NC	Co	02.11.57 – 16.11.57
	LI	Co	13.05.58 – 06.06.58
	LC(EO)	Co	30.06.59 – 06.08.59
	NC(EO)	Co	03.11.60 – 19.11.60
	HG	Co	11.12.61 – 12.01.62
	LC	Co	17.02.65 – 27.03.65
76004	NC(EO)	R	27.10.53 – 07.11.53
	HI	Do	30.04.55 – 04.06.55
	NC(EO)	Co	23.10.57 – 02.11.57
	LI	Co	06.08.58 – 06.09.58
	LC(EO)	Co	06.04.60 – 14.06.60
	HG	Co	15.03.61 – 11.04.61
	LC(EO)	Co	02.06.63 – 08.06.63
	LC(EO)	Co	20.06.66 – 16.07.66
76005	LI	E	08.03.55 – 02.04.55
	HG	E	22.05.57 – 22.06.57
	NC	E	19.02.58 – 20.02.58
	LI	E	31.12.59 – 16.01.60
	LC	E	16.02.62 – 24.02.62
	HG	E	14.01.63 – 23.02.63
	LC	E	15.07.66 – 26.08.66
76006	NC	E	25.02.53 – 07.03.53
	HI	E	30.06.55 – 30.07.55
	LC	B	22.03.57 – 05.04.57
	HG	E	08.10.57 – 02.11.57
	LI	E	23.06.59 – 11.07.59
	NC	E	01.12.60 – 24.12.60
	HG	E	01.11.62 – 08.12.62
	LC	E	30.06.66 – 27.07.66
76007	LI	E	27.07.55 – 13.08.55
	LC	E	11.06.56 – 23.06.56
	LC	E	30.08.57 – 18.09.57
	HG	E	17.02.58 – 19.03.58
	LI	E	14.02.61 – 11.03.61
	NC	E	28.08.61 – 09.09.61
	HG	E	26.06.63 – 24.08.63
	LC	E	31.05.66 – 17.06.66
76008	LC	Fr	27.03.54 – 07.05.54
	HI	E	31.08.55 – 17.09.55
	HG	E	31.01.58 – 01.03.58
	HI	E	26.08.60 – 17.09.60
	HG	E	04.04.63 – 11.05.63
	LI	E	24.05.66 – 10.06.66
76009	LI	E	06.01.55 – 22.01.55
	LC	E	24.11.55 – 03.12.55
	LC	E	17.05.56 – 08.06.56
	HG	E	17.04.57 – 25.05.57
	NC	E	17.03.58 – 23.03.58
	LI	E	18.09.59 – 03.10.59
	LC	E	03.08.60 – 13.08.60
	LC	E	22.09.61 – 07.10.61
	HG	E	06.04.62 – 12.05.62
	LC	E	31.08.64 – 01.10.64
76010	HI	E	03.08.55 – 20.08.55
	LC	E	24.04.56 – 25.05.56
	NC	E	06.09.57 – 14.09.57
	HG	E	22.04.58 – 23.05.58
	LC	E	06.11.59 – 28.11.59
	LI	E	30.05.60 – 18.06.60
	LC	E	15.03.62 – 31.03.62
	HG	E	13.12.62 – 05.01.63
	LC	E	23.08.63 – 05.10.63
76011	HI	E	20.10.55 – 11.11.55
	HG	E	11.06.58 – 11.07.58
	LC	E	27.01.60 – 06.02.60
	LC	E	08.06.60 – 25.06.60
	LI	E	13.09.60 – 01.10.60
	LC	E	26.06.61 – 06.07.61
	LC	E	10.09.62 – 22.09.62
	HG	E	23.11.63 – 04.01.64
76012	LI	E	12.05.55 – 28.05.55
	LC	E	20.09.56 – 05.10.56
	HG	E	31.03.58 – 02.06.58
	NC	E	05.05.60 – 14.05.60
	LI	E	24.11.60 – 10.12.60
	NC	E	20.11.61 – 02.12.61
	HG	E	01.10.63 – 16.11.63
	NC	E	12.04.65 – 14.04.65
	NC	E	15.11.65 – 26.11.65
76013	LC	E	20.01.55 – 29.01.55
	LI	E	29.12.55 – 14.01.56
	LC	E	10.04.57 – 13.04.57
	HG	E	03.12.57 – 04.01.58
	LC	E	05.01.59 – 17.01.59
	LI	E	10.08.60 – 27.08.60
	LC	E	18.01.61 – 01.02.61

	HG	E	06.06.63 – 17.08.63
76014	HI	E	14.11.55 – 01.12.55
	NC	E	16.12.55
	NC	E	23.02.56 – 07.03.56
	NC	E	14.06.56 – 21.06.56
	LC	B	08.10.56 – 03.11.56
	NC	E	04.11.57 – 15.11.57
	HG	E	09.06.58 – 14.06.58
	LC	E	06.11.59 – 21.11.59
	LI	E	10.01.61 – 04.02.61
	NC	E	21.08.61 – 02.09.61
	NC	E	06.12.62 – 19.12.62
	HG	E	11.05.63 – 25.06.63
76015	LC	E	07.09.54 – 18.09.54
	LC	E	16.03.55 – 26.03.55
	LI	E	11.01.56 – 04.02.56
	LC	E	27.06.57 – 13.07.57
	NC	E	02.04.58 – 09.04.58
	HG	E	23.10.58 – 15.11.58
	LC	E	14.09.59 – 25.09.59
	LI	E	14.10.60 – 05.11.60
	NC	E	01.12.61 – 13.12.61
	HI	E	12.02.63 – 16.03.63
	LC	E	01.01.64 – 19.01.64
76016	HC	B	16.03.55 – 29.04.55
	LC	B	22.07.55 – 06.08.55
	LI	B	22.02.56 – 16.04.56
	NC	B	27.08.56 – 20.09.56
	HG	E	16.01.58 – 01.02.58
	LI	E	17.08.60 – 03.09.60
	LC	E	26.02.62 – 03.03.62
	HG	E	01.01.63 – 09.02.63
	NC	E	24.06.65 – 01.07.65
76017	LI	E	22.10.54 – 13.11.54
	LC	E	26.09.55 – 01.10.55
	LC	E	29.12.55 – 07.01.56
	LI	E	04.10.56 – 27.10.56
	LC	E	12.12.57 – 21.12.57
	HG	E	03.04.59 – 02.05.59
	LC	E	14.10.59 – 16.10.59
	LI	E	14.12.61 – 20.01.62
	NC	E	14.01.64 – 25.01.64
76018	LI	E	06.05.55 – 21.05.55
	LC	E	03.04.56 – 14.04.56
	HG	E	18.11.57 – 14.12.57
	LC	E	01.04.59 – 11.04.59
	LI	E	02.06.60 – 25.06.60
	HG	E	10.05.63 – 15.06.63
76019	HI	E	12.05.55 – 28.05.55
	LI	E	06.03.57 – 23.03.57
	LC	E	02.04.58 – 19.04.58
	HG	E	04.06.59 – 27.06.59
	LI	E	19.01.62 – 10.02.62
	HI	E	15.01.64 – 15.02.64
76020	LC	Da	01.12.53 – 12.12.53
	HI	Do	09.02.56 – 14.03.56

	AD	Do	08.05.56 – 29.05.56
	LI	H	23.12.58 – 27.02.59
	LC	H	15.03.60 – 05.04.60
	LC	H	23.08.60 – 03.09.60
	AWS	H	30.10.61 – 10.11.61
	HG	H	28.02.62 – 05.04.62
	HC	H	30.07.62 – 28.08.62
	LC	Da	25.08.64 – 05.10.64
76021	NC	Do	20.01.55 – 02.02.55
	HI	Do	29.09.55 – 01.11.55
	HG	St	27.10.58 – 17.12.58
	NC	Do	02.01.61 – 07.01.61
	HG	Do	15.01.62 – 16.02.62
	LC	In	03.03.65 – 10.04.65
76022	HI	Do	21.11.55 – 29.12.55
	LI	H	13.08.58 – 03.10.58
	LC	H	21.05.59 – 10.06.59
	HG	H	05.05.61 – 09.06.61
	LC	H	10.11.61 – 23.11.61
	LI	E	14.08.64 – 29.09.64
76023	HI	Do	06.10.55 – 09.11.55
	LI	H	02.07.58 – 12.09.58
	LC	H	22.09.59 – 10.10.59
	HG	H	17.06.60 – 07.10.60
	AWS	H	06.10.61 – 24.10.61
	LC	H	18.01.62 – 02.02.62
	HC	H	24.01.63 – 14.02.63
	LC	H	02.10.63 – 25.10.63
76024	NC	Do	02.12.54 – 24.12.54
	HI	Do	02.01.56 – 03.02.56
	HG	St	10.09.58 – 31.10.58
	LC	Do	30.04.60 – 21.05.60
	NC	Do	07.11.60 – 24.11.60
	LC	Co	05.05.65 – 15.05.65
76025	LC	E	18.08.54 – 28.08.54
	LI	E	03.02.56 – 10.03.56
	LC	E	10.10.57 – 26.10.57
	LC	E	06.06.58 – 14.06.58
	HG	E	20.11.58 – 03.01.59
	NC	E	18.12.59 – 31.12.59
	LI	E	29.11.60 – 17.12.60
	NC	E	04.09.61 – 09.09.61
	HI	E	19.06.63 – 10.08.63
76026	LI	E	13.01.56 – 10.02.56
	NC	E	03.05.57 – 11.05.57
	HG	E	19.02.58 – 28.03.58
	HI	E	29.02.60 – 19.03.60
	NC	E	01.09.61 – 09.09.61
	HG	E	16.11.62 – 29.12.62
	LC	E	01.07.66 – 16.08.66
76027	LI	E	02.03.56 – 17.03.56
	NC	E	23.01.58 – 25.01.58
	HG	E	04.11.58 – 06.12.58
	NC	E	14.04.60 – 30.04.60
	HI	E	22.03.61 – 15.04.61
	LI	E	20.11.63 – 28.12.63

No.			
76028	LC	B	15.03.55 – 03.04.55
	LI	E	22.03.56 – 14.04.56
	NC	E	28.04.58 – 10.05.58
	HG	E	20.10.58 – 15.11.58
	LI	E	03.01.61 – 28.01.61
	LC	E	26.06.61 – 29.07.61
	LC	E	01.06.62 – 09.06.62
	LC	E	20.08.63 – 07.09.63
76029	LI	E	17.05.56 – 09.06.56
	LC	E	01.05.58 – 17.05.58
	HG	E	08.12.58 – 17.01.59
	LI	E	14.08.61 – 09.09.61
	LC	E	12.03.62 – 17.03.62
	LC	E	05.07.63 – 15.08.63
76030	LC	St	xx.xx.xx – 18.06.55
	SI	Do	04.05.56 – 09.05.56
	LC	St	xx.xx.xx – 23.02.57
	HG	St	15.08.57 – 30.11.57
	LC	St	12.03.58 – 26.03.58
	UC	St	22.02.60 – 11.03.60
	LC	Do	14.07.60 – 19.08.60
	UC	Do	10.01.61 – 24.01.61
	LI	H	02.11.62 – 13.12.62
	HC	H	03.05.63 – 20.03.63
	LC	E	30.01.64 – 15.02.64
76031	NC	St	26.09.55 – 06.10.55
	NC	Do	28.05.56 – 30.05.56
	HI	St	22.03.57 – 10.05.57
	NC	Do	04.02.61 – 17.02.61
	HG	Do	25.04.61 – 02.06.61
	NC	Do	22.11.61 – 30.11.61
	LC	E	08.10.63 – 10.10.63
	HI	E	12.04.65 – 28.05.65
76032	SI	Do	25.05.56 – 30.05.56
	LI	St	26.11.57 – 18.01.58
	HC	St	17.02.61 – 15.04.61
	LC	Se	01.07.63 – 03.07.63
	LI	E	22.11.63 – 14.12.63
76033	NC	Do	06.06.56 – 08.06.56
	LI	St	08.04.57 – 23.05.57
	NC	St	02.12.57 – 22.02.58
	HG	Do	04.01.61 – 04.02.61
	LC	Do	12.06.62 – 07.07.62
	LC	Bs	01.03.63 – 28.03.63
	LC	E	08.04.64 – 13.04.64
	LI	E	27.08.64 – 15.10.64
	NC	E	14.02.66 – 02.03.66
	NC	E	23.05.66 – 27.05.66
76034	LC	St	P.E. 03.12.65
	LI	St	04.11.57 – 28.12.57
	LC	St	P.E. 26.01.59
	LC	St	22.07.60 – 25.11.60
	NC	Do	23.02.61 – 07.03.61
	LI	Do	22.07.61 – 23.08.61
	LC	E	18.06.63 – 04.07.63
76035	NC	Do	27.06.55 – 05.07.55
	NC	Do	04.06.56 – 06.06.56
	HI	Do	21.11.56 – 02.01.57
	HG	H	17.02.59 – 03.04.59
	NC	H	30.06.59 – 06.07.59
	LI/AWS	H	16.10.62 – 23.11.62
76036	NC	Do	18.07.55 – 22.07.55
	UC	St	07.09.56 – 20.09.56
	HI	Do	27.09.56 – 02.11.56
	LI	H	12.12.58 – 13.02.59
	NC	H	22.05.59 – 08.06.59
	LC	H	22.01.60 – 15.02.60
	LC	N	03.01.61 – 18.01.61
	HG	H	12.03.63 – 03.05.63
76037	NC	Do	28.07.55 – 05.08.55
	HI	St	18.02.57 – 09.04.57
	LC	Bo	29.04.59 – 12.06.59
	HG	H	18.02.60 – 22.04.60
	LC	H	02.08.61 – 17.08.61
	I	S	20.12.63 – 26.06.64
76038	NC	Do	01.09.55 – 15.09.55
	HI	Do	23.10.56 – 27.11.56
	LC	H	30.01.59 – 27.02.59
	LI	H	01.06.60 – 13.07.60
	HG/AWS	H	30.01.62 – 03.03.62
76039	NC	Do	23.09.55 – 03.10.55
	HI	St	15.01.57 – 08.03.57
	LC	H	01.08.59 – 18.08.59
	HG	H	09.02.60 – 11.03.60
	HI	E	27.07.64 – 10.09.64
76040	NC	Do	10.11.55 – 17.11.55
	HI	St	01.01.57 – 23.02.57
	HG	H	10.11.59 – 12.12.59
	HI	H	23.05.63 – 03.07.63
	NR	H	08.07.63 – 05.07.63
	NR	H	30.07.63 – 10.08.63
	Su	Da	10.01.66 – 03.02.66
	Su	C	17.03.66 – 13.04.66
76041	LC	Do	25.11.55 – 03.12.55
	HI	St	06.12.56 – 14.02.57
	HG	H	11.06.60 – 01.08.60
	NR	H	11.10.60 – 03.11.60
	NR	S	06.12.63 – 14.04.64
76042	NC	Do	12.10.55 – 28.10.55
	LC	Kx	20.04.57
	LI	St	03.02.58 – 11.04.58
	LC	H	06.12.60 – 26.02.60
	LC	H	18.10.60 – 24.11.60
	HG	H	18.08.61 – 27.09.61
	HC	H	18.06.62 – 05.07.62
	HC/AWS	H	25.09.62 – 05.10.62
76043	LC	Do	22.12.55 – 07.01.56
	HI	St	04.03.57 – 11.04.57
	LC	Bo	21.04.59 – 28.05.59
	HG	H	26.07.60 – 28.10.60
	HC	H	14.06.62 – 29.06.62

ID			
76044	HI	St	28.01.57 – 21.03.57
	LC	Bo	30.10.58 – 31.12.58
	HG	H	13.06.60 – 18.11.60
	LC	E	11.04.64 – 01.05.64
76045	LI	St	17.04.58 – 06.06.58
	HI	Do	28.03.60 – 21.05.60
	NC/AWS	Do	10.11.60 – 26.11.60
	LC	Do	01.11.61 – 18.11.61
	HI	H	29.05.63 – 08.07.63
76046	LI	St	12.01.58 – 15.03.58
	NC	Do	25.08.60 – 12.10.60
	NC	Do	28.11.60 – 16.12.60
	NC	Do	24.03.61 – 29.03.61
	HG	Do	01.01.62 – 01.02.62
	HC	Co	03.12.63 – 11.01.64
	LC(EO)	Co	13.01.64 – 24.01.64
	NC(EO)	Co	21.10.64 – 28.10.64
	LC	Co	04.11.64 – 15.12.64
	LC(EO)	Co	03.06.66 – 16.07.66
76047	HC	Do	06.04.55 – 21.04.55
	LI	St	12.09.57 – 16.11.57
	LC	H	05.04.59 – 03.05.59
	HG	H	02.05.63 – 05.08.60
	HC	H	18.12.61 – 28.01.62
	LI	E	02.09.64 – 20.10.64
76048	LI	St	11.10.57 – 14.12.57
	LC	H	11.11.58 – 28.11.58
	HG	H	12.04.60 – 27.05.60
	LC	H	22.04.61 – 08.05.61
	HG	H	05.10.62 – 22.11.62
76049	LI	St	05.02.58 – 18.04.58
	NC	Do	07.12.59 – 12.12.59
	NC	Do	12.01.61 – 20.01.61
	NC	Do	20.03.61 – 24.03.61
	HG	Do	09.06.61 – 27.06.61
	NC	Do	24.11.61 – 04.01.62
	NC	Do	20.03.62 – 07.04.62
76050	HI	St	20.01.59 – 27.02.59
	NC	Do	05.12.60 – 17.12.60
	NC	Do	26.06.61 – 21.07.61
	LC(EO)	Co	18.06.64 – 03.07.64
	LC	Co	07.04.65 – 15.05.65
76051	LI	H	16.04.58 – 21.05.58
	LC	H	16.02.60 – 14.04.60
	HC	H	21.04.60 – 09.05.60
	HG	H	29.11.61 – 26.01.62
	NC/AWS	H	14.02.63 – 22.02.63
	HC	Da	11.05.64 – 13.06.64
76052	LI	H	25.11.58 – 24.12.58
	LC	H	03.10.59 – 04.11.59
	LC	H	21.04.60 – 06.05.60
	HG	H	25.05.62 – 26.06.62
	SU	Co	31.01.66 – 05.02.66
76053	HC	B	30.08.55 – 26.09.55
	LC	E	25.09.56 – 06.10.56
	HI	E	05.09.57 – 21.09.57
	NC	E	06.03.58 – 08.03.58
	LC	E	23.01.59 – 31.01.59
	NC	E	04.05.59 – 23.05.59
	NC	E	29.07.59 – 01.08.59
	HG	E	16.12.59 – 16.01.60
	LI	E	24.08.62 – 22.09.62
	LC	E	01.07.64 – 19.08.64
76054	NC	B	14.09.55 – 01.10.55
	LC	E	24.08.56 – 08.09.56
	TC	Re	04.11.56
	LI	E	15.11.57 – 07.12.57
	HG	E	10.06.59 – 11.07.59
	LI	E	08.01.62 – 27.01.62
	LC	E	10.08.64 – 21.08.64
76055	HC	B	16.09.55 – 28.10.55
	LC	B	27.07.56 – 15.09.56
	LI	E	16.10.57 – 02.11.57
	LC	A	17.06.58 – 12.07.58
	HG	E	12.08.59 – 12.09.59
	LC	E	08.03.60 – 19.03.60
	HI	E	07.11.62 – 08.12.62
	LC	E	24.07.63 – 10.08.63
76056	HC	B	04.10.55 – 20.10.55
	NC	B	01.02.56 – 18.02.56
	LC	E	29.06.56 – 17.07.56
	HI	E	21.11.57 – 07.12.57
	LC	E	07.11.58 – 22.11.58
	HG	E	02.12.59 – 09.01.60
	LI	E	18.09.62 – 20.10.62
76057	HC	B	28.10.55 – 18.11.55
	LC	B	31.12.56 – 26.01.57
	LC	B	11.03.57 – 05.04.57
	LI	E	27.05.58 – 21.06.58
	LC	E	12.01.59 – 31.01.59
	LC	E	14.05.59 – 30.05.59
	LC	E	19.05.60 – 04.06.60
	HG	E	16.03.61 – 22.04.61
	HI	E	03.12.63 – 11.01.64
76058	HC	B	03.11.55 – 24.11.55
	LC	B	11.02.57 – 09.03.57
	LI	E	02.12.57 – 21.12.57
	NC	E	25.05.59 – 12.06.59
	HG	E	16.09.60 – 15.10.60
	NC	E	16.10.61 – 28.10.61
	LC	E	03.04.62 – 14.04.62
	LI	E	08.11.63 – 20.12.63
76059	HC	B	23.11.55 – 16.12.55
	LC	B	23.07.56 – 02.08.56
	LC	E	22.03.57 – 06.04.57
	LI	E	17.12.57 – 11.01.58
	NC	E	13.05.59 – 28.05.59
	HG	E	27.07.60 – 27.08.60
	LC	E	31.10.61 – 18.11.61
	LI	E	11.06.63 – 03.08.63
76060	HC	B	14.12.55 – 12.01.56
	LC	E	04.05.56 – 12.05.56

76038 with red background to the numberplate piloting an unidentified 4MT 4-6-0 approaching Talerddig summit on the up "Cambrian Coast Express" on 20th August 1966. The climb from Llanbrynmair to the summit is almost three miles at 1 in 52. The photograph demonstrates a period when lineside photographers cleaned locomotives on the side to be photographed and also used white paint on the front end. It looks as if the crew expected to be photographed!

Trevor Owen

	LC	A	14.03.57 – 13.04.57		LC	E	14.10.60 – 20.10.60
	LC	E	31.07.57 – 03.08.57		LC	E	01.06.61 – 02.06.61
	LI	E	01.05.58 – 24.05.58		HG	E	15.02.62 – 17.03.62
	LC	E	05.06.59 – 20.06.59		LC	E	26.07.63 – 16.08.63
	HG	E	06.10.60 – 12.11.60		LC	E	16.06.64 – 02.07.64
	NC	E	30.10.61 – 09.11.61				
	LC	E	25.02.63 – 11.03.63	76064	LI	E	19.12.58 – 17.01.59
	LI	E	11.10.63 – 23.11.63		LC	E	12.04.60 – 30.04.60
					HG	E	15.08.61 – 16.09.61
76061	HC	B	16.11.55 – 10.12.55		LC	E	27.09.63 – 12.10.63
	LC	E	30.10.56 – 10.11.56		LC	E	12.10.64 – 06.11.64
	HI	E	11.02.58 – 07.03.58				
	HC	E	28.01.59 – 14.02.59	76065	LI	E	29.10.58 – 15.11.58
	LC	E	08.12.59 – 12.12.59		LC	E	20.01.60 – 30.01.60
	HG	E	04.05.61 – 10.06.61		LC	E	26.07.60 – 06.08.60
	LI	E	20.12.63 – 08.02.64		LI	E	09.02.61 – 11.03.61
					LC	E	02.08.61 – 11.08.61
76062	HC	B	02.01.56 – 21.01.56		LC	E	02.08.62 – 11.08.62
	LC	B	12.11.56 – 24.11.56		HG	H	12.03.63 – 16.04.63
	HI	E	09.08.57 – 31.08.57				
	NC	E	14.02.58 – 19.02.58	76066	LC	E	19.10.56 – 26.10.56
	NC	E	24.04.58 – 07.05.58		LC	E	03.07.57 – 13.07.57
	HG	E	26.08.59 – 26.09.59		LI	E	20.02.59 – 07.03.59
	LC	E	12.09.61 – 30.09.61		HG	E	13.01.61 – 18.02.61
	LC	E	12.04.62 – 21.04.62		HI	E	13.09.63 – 26.10.63
	NC	E	17.09.62 – 26.09.62		NC	E	06.06.66 – 16.06.66
	HI	E	31.12.62 – 02.02.63				
				76067	LC	E	27.01.58 – 22.02.58
76063	LC	E	02.10.57 – 12.10.57		LI	E	18.03.59 – 04.04.59
	LI	E	29.01.59 – 23.02.59		HG	E	15.06.61 – 12.08.61
	LC	E	08.04.60 – 29.04.60				

LC	E	03.07.62 – 04.08.62
HI	E	13.05.64 – 17.06.64

76068	HI	E	12.09.58 – 04.10.58
	HG	E	11.11.60 – 17.12.60
	NC	E	03.11.61 – 18.11.61
	LI	E	05.09.63 – 19.10.63
76069	LC	E	26.09.57 – 05.10.57
	LI	E	09.01.59 – 31.01.59
	LC	E	15.10.59 – 23.10.59
	HG	E	17.05.61 – 23.06.61
	LI	E	13.12.63 – 18.01.64
76070	LI	Co	11.05.60 – 25.06.60
	HG	Co	20.05.63 – 22.06.63
76071	LI	Co	16.01.60 – 27.02.60
	HG	Co	28.03.62 – 03.05.62
76072	LI	Co	15.04.59 – 02.05.59
	HG	Co	31.01.61 – 24.02.62
	NC(EO)	Co	08.03.62
	LC(EO)	Co	13.04.62 – 14.04.62
76073	LI	Co	01.05.59 – 23.05.59
	LC(EO)	Co	28.09.59 – 20.10.59
	HG	Co	01.09.61 – 04.11.61
	NC(EO)	Co	31.05.62 – 13.06.62
	NC(EO)	Co	01.11.62 – 10.11.62
	HI	Da	06.10.64 – 05.12.64
	LC	Da	30.12.64 – 14.01.65
76074	NC(EO)	Co	03.08.59 – 08.08.59
	LI	In	21.03.60 – 13.05.60
	LC(EO)	Co	14.10.60 – 11.11.60
	NC(EO)	Co	20.03.61 – 25.03.61
	HG	Co	18.04.63 – 08.06.63
	NC(EO)	Co	09.04.64
76075	NC	H	15.05.57 – 06.06.57
	LC	H	08.10.59 – 18.11.59
	LI	H	21.08.61 – 05.10.61
	HC	S	20.01.64 – 27.08.64
76076	LC	H	21.12.57 – 04.01.58
	LI	H	18.08.61 – 28.09.61
	HC	H	29.12.61 – 19.01.62
	LC	H	03.12.62 – 12.12.62
	NC	H	21.02.63 – 14.03.63
	HC	S	17.01.64 – 28.08.64
76077	NC	H	05.06.57 – 28.06.57
	LC	H	18.08.59 – 02.09.59
	LI	H	19.10.60 – 28.11.60
	LC	H	07.03.61 – 22.03.61
	AWS	H	14.11.61 – 28.11.61
	HC	H	04.07.62 – 10.08.62
	HG	E	09.01.64 – 22.02.64
76078	BLR	H	27.02.57 – 12.03.57
	LC	H	29.02.58 – 20.03.58
	NC	H	27.03.58

	LI	H	16.11.60 – 16.12.60
	AWS	H	23.11.61 – 05.12.61
	HC	H	30.01.63 – 19.12.63
76079	NC	H	07.08.57 – 23.08.57
	LC	H	15.01.58 – 04.02.58
	LC	H	25.11.58 – 05.12.58
	LI	H	24.11.61 – 05.01.62
	HG	E	27.02.64 – 11.04.64
76080	LI	H	26.09.59 – 05.11.59
	HG	H	22.10.63 – 26.11.63
	LC	Da	04.02.65 – 23.03.65
76081	LI	H	06.04.61 – 05.06.61
	NC/AWS	H	02.11.62 – 13.11.62
	HG	S	24.12.63 – 24.06.64
	LC	Da	13.11.64 – 31.12.64
76082	HI	H	15.05.61 – 16.06.61
	LC	E	19.05.64 – 24.06.64
76083	LI	H	21.02.61 – 17.03.61
	NC/AWS	H	24.08.62 – 12.09.63
	LC	Co	27.05.64 – 30.05.64
	LC	Co	27.04.65 – 01.05.65
	LC	Co	25.08.65 – 04.09.65
76084	LI	H	20.01.61 – 17.02.61
	NC	H	27.09.62 – 12.10.62
	HC	Co	18.06.64 – 09.07.64
	LC	Co	24.05.65 – 29.05.65
76085	LI	H	06.12.60 – 05.01.61
	HC	H	11.02.61 – 03.03.61
	LC	Co	12.06.64 – 27.06.64
	NC	Co	02.07.64 – 03.07.64
76086	LI	H	31.10.59 – 03.12.59
	HG	H	07.09.62 – 18.10.62
76087	LI	H	29.10.60 – 05.12.60
	LC/AWS	H	08.08.62 – 17.08.62
	HC	H	23.04.63 – 12.06.63
76088	HI	H	14.11.59 – 23.12.59
	LC	E	28.01.64 – 15.02.64
76089	LI	H	13.01.60 – 12.02.60
	HI	H	16.01.62 – 19.02.62
	LC	E	12.08.64 – 11.09.64
	LC	E	14.09.64 – 22.09.64
	LC	E	07.12.65 – 08.12.65
76090	NC(EO)	Co	08.09.59 – 16.09.59
	LI	Co	05.03.60 – 16.04.60
	NC(TO)	Co	27.02.61 – 02.03.61
	LI	Co	18.04.64 – 13.06.64
76091	LI	Co	04.01.60 – 20.02.60
	NC(TO)	Co	02.05.62
	HG	Co	26.12.62 – 02.02.63
	NC	Co	25.10.63 – 16.11.63
	NC(EO)	Co	01.06.66 – 03.06.66

ID			
76092	NC(EO)	Co	22.09.59 – 02.10.59
	LC(EO)	Co	04.12.59 – 15.01.60
	LI	Co	29.08.60 – 01.10.60
	HG	Co	17.07.63 – 30.08.63
76093	LC(EO)	Co	26.08.57 – 12.09.57
	LI	Co	30.05.60 – 15.07.60
	HG	Co	01.06.63 – 29.06.63
76094	LI	Co	28.10.60 – 26.11.60
	HG	Co	03.04.63 – 04.05.63
76095	–	–	Data not traced
76096	LC(EO)	R	28.01.59 – 28.02.59
	LI	Co	22.11.60 – 24.12.60
	LI	In	10.05.64 – 21.06.64
76097	LI	Co	26.06.61 – 05.08.61
76098	LC(EO)	Co	04.12.57 – 20.12.57
	LC(EO)	Co	22.09.58 – 11.10.58
	LI	Co	28.11.60 – 31.12.60
	HG	Co	21.01.64 – 29.02.64
76099	LI	Co	12.11.60 – 10.12.60
	LC(EO)	Co	26.03.63 – 04.06.63
	LC	Co	26.02.64 – 13.03.64
	LC	Da	11.09.64 – 14.11.64
	NR	Da	16.11.64 – 20.11.64
76100	NC(EO)	Co	18.05.59 – 26.05.59
	LI	Co	25.01.60 – 19.03.60
	NC(EO)	Co	17.05.60 – 03.06.60
	NC(EO)	Co	24.10.60 – 01.11.60
	LC(EO)	Co	10.11.60 – 26.11.60
	HG	Co	17.04.63 – 01.06.63
76101	LI	In	15.08.60 – 23.09.60
	LI	Co	19.03.64 – 02.05.64
	LC	Co	02.11.64 – 11.11.64
76102	NC(EO)	Co	27.05.59 – 04.06.59
	LI	Co	15.12.60 – 21.01.61
	HG	Co	15.04.64 – 30.05.64
	NC	Co	26.11.64
	NC	Co	26.12.64 – 06.02.65
76103	NC(EO)	Co	27.05.59 – 10.06.59
	LI	Co	05.01.61 – 11.02.61
	HI	Co	03.06.64 – 04.07.64
76104	LI	In	04.01.60 – 06.02.60
	HG	Co	19.09.62 – 26.10.62
	NC	Co	12.03.65 – 20.03.65
76105	LI	Co	26.12.58 – 24.01.59
	NC	Co	27.01.59 – 29.01.59
	LC(EO)	Co	27.05.60 – 30.06.60
	LI	Co	11.06.62 – 13.07.62
	NC(EO)	Co	16.10.62 – 27.10.62
	LC	Co	11.09.64 – 14.11.64
76106	LI	Co	09.09.59 – 03.10.59
	LC(EO)	Co	08.03.61 – 28.03.61
	LC(EO)	Co	11.01.62 – 19.01.62
	LI	Co	02.07.62 – 11.08.62
76107	LI	In	08.01.60 – 12.02.60
	LC(EO)	Co	03.08.60 – 27.08.60
	LC(EO)	Co	12.10.60 – 18.11.60
	LC	Co	03.12.64 – 28.01.65
76108	LI	In	22.02.60 – 08.04.60
	LC(EO)	Co	11.08.60 – 16.09.60
	LC(EO)	Co	31.01.63 – 09.03.63
	LI	Co	19.02.64 – 29.03.64
	NC(EO)	Co	03.04.64 – 15.04.64
	LC(EO)	Co	04.06.64 – 27.06.64
76109	NC(EO)	Co	24.10.59 – 05.11.59
	LI	Co	12.12.60 – 19.01.61
	HG	Co	25.03.64 – 16.05.64
76110	LC(EO)	Co	11.08.59 – 31.08.59
	HG	Co	23.05.61 – 24.06.61
	LI	Da	23.10.64 – 03.01.65
	NC	Da	11.01.65 – 13.01.65
76111	NC(EO)	Co	09.11.59 – 21.11.59
	LI	In	28.03.61 – 02.06.61
	HC(EO)	Co	07.01.63 – 07.02.63
	LC	In	27.05.64 – 19.06.64
	NC	In	13.10.64 – 19.10.64
	LC(EO)	Co	11.12.64 – 23.01.65
76112	LI	Co	19.10.59 – 12.11.59
	LC(EO)	Co	09.09.60 – 01.10.60
	LC	Co	10.08.61 – 15.08.61
	HG	Co	21.03.62 – 13.04.62
	LC(EO)	Co	28.08.64 – 05.09.64
76113	LC(EO)	Co	02.03.59 – 23.03.59
	NC(EO)	Co	03.08.59 – 11.08.59
	LI	Co	20.08.59 – 19.09.59
	HG	Co	25.09.62 – 27.10.62
	NC(EO)	Co	16.12.64 – 09.01.65
76114	NC(EO)	Co	02.06.59 – 11.06.59
	LI	Co	29.11.60 – 14.01.61
	LI	In	14.05.64 – 19.06.64

73112 hurries through Esher on a Waterloo to Basingstoke train on a frosty morning of 18th January 1964. Named *Morgan le Fay* in April 1960, being one of 20 Southern Region locomotives in groups 73080-89 and 73110-9 given the names of recently withdrawn Urie King Arthur class N15 4-6-0s.

Rodney Lissenden

The penultimate Horwich-built locomotive in October 1957, 76098 has an easy task ascending the north side of Beattock incline with a featherweight goods train from Carstairs to Beattock on 30th May 1966. The train is passing the elegant Caledonian signal box situated on the down platform of Elvanfoot, located in the sparsely inhabited and windswept upland country near the Lowther Hills. This station once had been the junction for the Wanlockhead & Leadhills Light Railway but by the time of this picture most traces of that railway had disappeared. 76098 was withdrawn in May 1967 after a service life of just under ten years.

Hugh Ballantyne

TABLE 6.4
BR Standard Class 3 2-6-0s 77000-77019 – Record of Repairs

No.	1	2	3
77000	LI	Da	06.10.56 – 03.11.56
	LC	Da	30.01.59 – 23.03.59
	HC	Da	19.07.60 – 18.11.60
	NC	Da	20.01.62 – 02.02.62
	HI	C	18.01.63 – 16.02.63
	HG	C	22.06.65 – 14.08.65
77001	HG	Da	25.02.57 – 05.04.57
	HG	Da	31.08.61 – 20.09.61
	LC	C	02.08.62 – 01.09.62
77002	NC	Da	24.05.54 – 27.05.54
	NC	Da	08.12.54 – 16.12.54
	NC	Da	07.07.56 – 25.07.56
	HI	Da	07.09.56 – 11.10.56
	LC	Da	07.09.57 – 17.10.57
	HG	Da	09.05.60 – 23.06.60
	NC	Da	30.11.61 – 12.12.61
	HI	C	31.10.63 – 17.12.63
	NC	C	30.12.63 – 06.01.64
	NR	C	08.01.64 – 25.01.64
77003	NC	Da	29.05.54 – 05.06.54
	NC	Da	12.12.54 – 24.12.54
	HG	Da	28.08.56 – 19.10.56
	HG	Da	16.06.60 – 12.09.60
	NC	Da	18.12.61 – 22.12.61
	I	Co	15.07.64 – 22.08.64
	NC	Co	31.08.64 – 03.09.64
77004	HG	Da	23.04.57 – 25.05.57
	HG	C	21.08.62 – 12.10.62
77005	NC	S	19.05.54 – 26.06.54
	NC(EO)	R	22.11.54
	LI	Co	14.02.57 – 16.03.57
	NC	Co	13.12.57 – 26.12.57
	LC(T)	Co	13.01.58 – 08.03.58
	HC	Co	06.05.59 – 28.05.59
	HG	Co	28.11.60 – 21.01.61
	LI	Co	26.02.65 – 20.03.65
77006	NC	S	08.06.54 – 11.06.54
	NC(EO)	R	16.11.54 – 18.11.54
	LC	R	26.04.56 – 19.05.56
	LI	Co	20.11.57 – 14.12.57
	HG	Co	28.02.61 – 20.06.61
	LC(EO)	Co	21.12.61 – 11.01.62
77007	NC	S	11.06.54 – 23.06.54
	LC(EO)	R	04.10.54 – 08.10.54
	NC(EO)	R	29.11.54
	LC	R	16.08.56 – 30.08.56
	LI	Co	05.11.57 – 07.12.57
	HG	Co	30.12.59 – 17.03.60
	LI	Co	08.07.63 – 17.08.63
	LC(T)	Co	09.06.64 – 20.06.64
	NC(EO)	Co	21.06.66 – 25.06.66
77008	LC(EO)	R	26.11.54
	LC	R	20.09.56 – 06.10.56
	LI	Co	03.02.57 – 06.04.57
	LC	Co	02.12.57 – 27.12.57
	LC(EO)	Co	24.06.59 – 15.07.59
	HG	Co	02.08.60 – 07.10.60
	LC(T)	Co	29.11.60 – 10.12.60
77009	NC(EO)	R	15.08.54 – 17.08.54
	LC(EO)	R	10.12.54
	LC(EO)	Co	26.01.57 – 02.02.57
	LI	Co	07.09.57 – 05.10.57
	HG	Co	15.10.59 – 12.12.59
	HI	Co	05.10.62 – 10.11.62
77010	LI	G	23.11.56 – 28.12.56
	NC	Da	20.01.59 – 22.03.59
	HG	Da	05.09.60 – 22.10.60
	NC	Da	15.10.62 – 27.12.62
77011	–	–	Data not traced
77012	LI	Da	18.03.58 – 26.04.58
	HG	Da	19.06.61 – 06.08.61
	LC	Da	16.11.61 – 20.12.61
	LC	C	09.06.65 – 11.06.65
77013	LI	Da	27.08.57 – 25 09.57
	NC	Da	10.12.59 – 05.01.60
	LC	Da	07.12.60 – 14.02.61
	LC	Da	20.07.61 – 09.09.61
	HC	C	31.01.63 – 02.03 63
77014	LC	Da	27.05.57 – 20.06.57
	HG	Da	23.08.58 – 02.10.58
	HC	Da	17.01.61 – 01.03.61
77015	NC(EO)	R	18.11.54
	LC(EO)	R	17.12.54 – 21.12.54
	LI	R	14.06.57 – 05.07.57
	HG	Co	03.03.60 – 25.05.60
	HI	Co	02.10.62 – 03.11.62
	LC	Co	04.02.65 – 15.03.65
77016	LC(EO)	R	24.11.54
	LC(EO)	R	24.03.55 – 02.04.55
	LI	R	17.06.57 – 09.08.57
	LC(EO)	Co	30.06.58 – 10.07.58
	HG	Co	26.11.59 – 16.01.60
	HI	Co	05.04.62 – 19.05.62
77017	LC(EO)	R	08.12.54 – 11.12.54
	LI	In	17.06.57 – 02.08.57
	HG	Co	15.02.60 – 09.04.60
	HI	Co	10.08.62 – 01.09.62
77018	LC(EO)	R	15.12.54
	LI	Co	17.06.57 – 11.07.57
	NC	Co	25.12.57 – 28.12.57
	HG	Co	17.12.59 – 20.02.60
	HI	Co	04.12.61 – 12.01.62
	LC(EO)	Co	10.01.64 – 01.02.64
77019	LC(EO)	R	13.12.54 – 18.12.54
	LI	R	17.06.57 – 06.07.57
	NC	R	31.07.57 – 01.08.57
	HG	Co	07.03.60 – 14.05.60
	HI	Co	28.05.62 – 30.06.62
	LC(EO)	Co	13.12.63 – 29.02.64
	LC	Co	31.05.65 – 15.06.65

76063 runs into Basingstoke on the Great Western line from Reading on the through service to Portsmouth. 76063 was delivered new to Eastleigh depot in July 1956 and withdrawn after nearly 11 years at that depot. One of a class of 115 built between December 1952 and November 1957 it was withdrawn in April 1967 and scrapped eight months later by J. Buttigieg, Newport. *Kenneth Wightman*

On 1st September 1962 76015 and 92220 *Evening Star* approach Midford on the single line section from Bath on the 09.30am Bristol-Bournemouth West, a train which did not need a pilot engine with a class 9F, but the Bournemouth-based 2-6-0 was attached to Evercreech Jct. to avoid a light engine working. The train was later photographed minus 76015 leaving Templecombe; Dick Riley was obviously in the company of photograper Ivo Peters making good use of his Bentley. *R. C. Riley*

75004 leaves Towyn (now spelt Tywyn) station on 26th September 1964 with a short freight containing a gunpowder van. For greater protection and as stated in the BR Rule Book the gunpowder van is marshalled in the middle of the train and forms part of the vacuum head allowing the locomotive to show a class 6 headcode.

Roy Hobbs

75048 passes through Silverdale station in the direction of Barrow-in-Furness with a pick up goods. Probably the mineral wagons are destined for the small yard at Grange-over-Sands. This section of the railway saw a rather bizarre incident in September 1966 when LMS Class 5 4-6-0 45095 ran away driverless out of Carnforth MPD yard for a distance of nearly nine miles ending up near Grange-over-Sands, passing three signal boxes, various level crossings and over the Kent viaduct in the process.

Roy Hobbs

92249 passing Carstairs no.2 signal box with an up empty coaching stock working from Glasgow on 1st August 1964, returning the coaching stock south, after it was used on a return Glasgow Fair holiday extra.   *Ken Falconer*

75012 pilots an unidentified member of the same class about to pass milepost 62 nearly at the summit at Talerddig of the 1 in 52 and 1 in 56 climb from Llanbrynmair. The train was a working from Pwhelli to Birmingham on 20th August 1966, just over six months before the last BR steam working over Talerddig.   *Trevor Owen*

78028, one of two of the class shedded at Leicester Midland, which received modifications at Crewe in December 1963 and January 1964 to cut down their cab height and profile to enable them to negotiate Glenfield tunnel on the Leicester West Bridge to Desford Junction line. 78028 is seen arriving at Ratby in March 1966 with a pick up freight. *Keith Mapley*

Summer Saturdays always were very busy on the Midland main line in the West Riding of Yorkshire. In a scene that no longer exists 73043 brings M17 the 2.20pm SO Blackpool North-Sheffield off the freight only branch from Thornhill Jct. on the Calder Valley L&Y main line past Royston Junction signal box to join the Midland main line heading towards Royston and Notton station in August 1958. *David Kelso*

Skipton shed had two Standard 2MTs allocated to it for nearly two years between 1962 and 1964 and these locomotives often were used on the Barnoldswick branch. Here we see 78036 leaving Hellifield with a train for Morecambe, a duty which by this date, 26th January 1963, would normally be in the hands of a Standard Class 4. The shed, which can be seen to the left of the signal box, closed in 1963. *Gavin Morrison*

77000, ready to depart on a local pickup freight, stands by the fine signal box at Calverley & Rodley in Leeds on 19th August 1966. The photograph was taken only four months before withdrawal. *Gavin Morrison*

73101 stands at the south end of Dumfries station with a local service to Carlisle in April 1965, two months before the closure of the Port Road from Dumfries to Stranraer. In the background stands the massive Caledonian Railway goods warehouse in the Lockerbie branch station yard. Formally a bonded warehouse to serve the local whisky distilleries and latterly used for commercial purposes. The branch closed completely in April 1966. *Douglas Hume*

Diverted due to a derailment near Beamish on 10th December 1964, 92099 runs on to the viaduct at Durham on a set of empty wagons, passing a southbound coal 'trip working' hauled by an EE Type 3 diesel. The coal train consists exclusively of the 20 ton coal hoppers used widely in the north east, most of which were not fitted with vacuum brakes. The brake tender attached to the diesel was a regular feature in the area to aid the braking capabilities of the locomotive when used on unfitted or partially braked trains. *Mike Robinson*

84008 at Northampton Bridge Street on the 12.10pm to Wellingborough on 28th September 1963. This was a Wellingborough engine on a local job, and it would be a surprise if any passengers boarded or alighted such was the paucity of passenger traffic at that period. The flower garden belies the service was running down to its final day (Saturday 2nd May 1964). The coaling plant at Northampton shed, in the left background, would be required only for a further short period, closure coming on 25th September 1965. *Alan Sainty collection*

72001 *Clan Cameron* leaves Crianlarich Upper station in very poor June weather for the Scottish Highlands with the 1956 Clan Cameron Gathering special from Glasgow Queen St. to Spean Bridge and return. 72001 had spent the previous week working between Glasgow and Fort William before the special ran on 16th June. This is thought to be the only time that a Clan worked over the West Highland line.

David Kelso

92120 departs southwards from York under the Holgate road bridge with a train of empty 16 ton mineral wagons on 10th October 1963. It was allocated to Leicester Midland at the time, and stayed there until transferred to Birkenhead in April 1965.   *www.rail-online.co.uk*

73049 on an up inter-regional train from Bournemouth West passes ex-Somerset and Dorset 2-8-0 53807 at Wellow on 6th July 1959. The 2-8-0 was working a freight for Bath and had been shunted into the sidings to allow this train and the "Pines Express" to pass. The village of Wellow was situated about seven miles from Bath; it was poorly served by buses due to the many steep hills in the area. Consequently the station was well patronised by local people.

R. C. Riley

70052 having lost its *Firth of Tay* nameplates crosses over the Crook road bridge at Ings between Staveley and Windermere with a lightweight train of four vehicles (probably through coaches from London Euston off a train to Barrow-in-Furness). The opening of this branch in 1847 by the Kendal and Windermere Railway gave rise to the composition by the famous Lakeland poet, William Wordsworth, of a sonnet as a protest against the construction of the line proving that "nimbyism" is not a recent phenomenon!
Roy Hobbs

80055 on ECS duties leaves Craigentinny carriage sidings bound for Edinburgh Waverley on 17th September 1962. These sidings remain to this day as the main rolling stock maintenance facility for the East Coast main line north of the border.
Ken Falconer

A well turned out 76096 stands at platform 3 at Ayr station with a northbound train possibly the Heads of Ayr to Edinburgh return holiday camp train in July 1965. The station building and hotel dominate the background and a DMU set introduced on the Ayr-Glasgow services in 1959 stands at bay platform 1.

Douglas Hume

92224 stands at Bath Green Park on 14th September 1963 waiting to depart with the 1.10pm all stations to Templecombe. The locomotive spent only a short time on the S&D during the summer of 1963 as the 9Fs were not fitted with steam heating facilities and therefore did not work passenger trains during the winter period.

Hugh Ballantyne

75002 climbs towards the summit at Talerddig from Carno near Clatter. The climb to the summit of 1 in 132 was less severe than the 1 in 52 for eastbound trains. The working was a Paddington to Pwllheli holiday train on 22nd August 1964. 75002 was the third locomotive of the class of 80, built at Swindon works in 1951. It survived 16 years before being withdrawn in August 1967. *Trevor Owen*

During the floods in mid-Wales during December 1964, when the railway was breached near Dovey Junction, services were terminated at Aberdovey. Standard 3MT 82003 is seen at Aberdovey after working a train from Portmadoc on 19th December 1964. *Gavin Morrison*

A photograph full of interest taken on 27th June 1962. 70038 *Robin Hood* on a northbound express from Kings Cross to Cleethorpes passes the yard at Hornsey. A BR Sulzer Type 2 is crossing the flyover and a further member of the class is in the goods yard on the right of the photograph.

www.rail-online.co.uk

92062, one of Tyne Dock's fleet of ten 9Fs allocated for the onerous Consett steel works iron ore and coal train workings, is seen at South Pelaw Jct. on 21st September 1965 drawing forward to split its coal train before continuing up to Consett. From here the engine faced a formidable unbroken nine miles slog of 1 in 50, and steeper gradients, up beyond Annfield and 600 feet above South Pelaw, followed by another five miles of undulating railway to the steel works at Consett.

Hugh Ballantyne

75058 storms up grade through Halton station in the Lune valley with the 12.40pm Heysham (Moss sidings) to Tees yard tank train in August 1965.

Noel Machell

92117 carrying reporting number WT35A approaches Llandudno Junction in May 1959 with a a mixed bag of coaching stock forming a relief to a regular service indicated by the suffix A in the reporting number. The track curving away to the right of the picture is the Conway Valley branch to Blaenau Festiniog.

Kenneth Field (Rail Stephenson Archive)

92162 heads towards Mirfield along the Calder Valley main line past Heaton Lodge Jct. with its fine array of signals with a summer Saturdays holiday extra in July 1958 watched by locospotter cyclists. The Leeds New Line to Huddersfield is in the background and will pass under the main line between the two sets of signals in the distance.
David Kelso

73082 heads past Durnsford Road, Wimbledon with an evening Waterloo to Southampton service in August 1966. Maintenance problems are evident as 73082's offside injector is blowing through, discharging steam and feedwater to the track. The train is about to run over a track 'wet spot' where defective foundation ballast is allowing the train's weight to pump water upwards, contaminating the top ballast and interfering with drainage and causing the rails to dip.
Roy Hobbs

82020 takes water at Portmadoc on 24th June 1964. The locomotive was delivered new in September 1954 to Hull Botanic Gardens before being moved to the Midlands to work the Nuneaton-Coventry-Leamington Spa stopping trains. Finally it was transferred to the Western Region. Note the WR yellow route availability disc on the bunker side. In its short life of eleven years it received three liveries, lined black, lined green and finally unlined green.

Ken Falconer

Former Crosti-boilered 92021 has just passed under the former Cheshire Lines Committee flyover at Mickle Trafford and is approaching Chester on 26th August 1966 with a mixed goods train. At the time it was allocated to Birkenhead shed, where its more usual duties would have been working Stanlow oil or Shotwick ore trains. 92021 was built at Crewe with a Crosti boiler in May 1955, converted to conventional boiler in June 1960 and withdrawn when Birkenhead closed in November 1967.

Hugh Ballantyne

Murrayfield on the Caledonian branch from Edinburgh Princes Street was the nearest station to the home of Scottish Rugby Union football. Winter Saturdays could see an almost continuous procession of excursions from all over Scotland, which were able to arrive directly at Murrayfield by using the spur between Gorgie East and Dalry North Jct. which line now forms part of the electrified link to Haymarket East Jct. Here 73075 and 73076 arrive with a special in February 1963 after the passenger service to Leith (North) had been withdrawn in April 1962.

Douglas Hume

Apart from the last two and half years of its life 92108 spent all its time allocated to the sheds at the southern end of the Midland main line. This photograph was taken on 20th April 1961 at Shipley whilst the engine was working a freight from Carlisle; 92108 was allocated to Leicester Midland at this time. Note the track workers without an obvious look out or high visibility vests!

Gavin Morrison

TABLE 6.5
BR Standard Class 2 2-6-0s 78000-78064 – Record of Repairs

No.	1	2	3
78000	HI	S	09.10.56 – 11.02.57
	HG	S	10.08.60 – 19.04.61
	NC	C	11.12.63 – 02.01.64
78001	HI	S	15.11.56 – 23.01.56
	HI Cont.	S	23.02.56 – 08.03.56
	HC	W	11.07.58 – 12.09.58
78002	–	–	Data not traced
78003	LC	W	11.11.54 – 29.11.54
	HI	S	24.10.56 – 30.01.57
	XS	S	01.02.57 – 02.03.57
	HI	W	06.04.60 – 27.05.60
	HG	C	15.08.63 – 02.10.63
78004	HI	S	25.10.56 – 21.12.56
	HC	S	22.01.59 – 14.09.59
	U	Hd	13.02.60 – 14.03.60
78005	HI	S	27.03.56 – 01.06.56
	LC	Os	10.08.57 – 27.08.57
	HI	Cy	08.08.60 – 14.04.60
78006	HI	S	23.01.57 – 28.03.57
78007	HI	S	12.06.56 – 11.09.56
	HG	S	14.05.60 – 18.08.60
	LI	C	24.04.64 – 18.06.64
78008	LC	W	08.11.56 – 16.12.56
	HI	S	26.02.58 – 18.06.58
	U	Wo	16.12.59 – 02.01.60
	LC	C	22.01.64 – 29.02.64
78009	LC	S	31.08.55 – 09.11.55
	HI	S	17.01.58 – 28.03.58
	HC	W	18.08.60 – 28.10.60
78010	HG	Da	26.06.59 – 14.08.59
	NC	Da	13.06.61 – 24.06.61
	I	C	15.05.64 – 19.06.60
78011	–	–	Data not traced
78012	LC	Da	01.04.54 – 08.04.54
	G	Da	24.04.59 – 27.05.59
	NC	Da	15.06.61 – 04.07.61
	G	C	03.10.62 – 17.11.62
	NC	Da	25.10 63 – 07.11.63
78013	G	Da	24.09.56 – 30.10.56
	G	C	28.10.59 – 11.12.59
	LC	C	26.05.60 – 14.06.60
78014	–	–	Data not traced
78015	HG	Da	13.11.56 – 19.12.56
	LC	Da	12.02.59 – 05.03.59
	LC	Da	20.05.60 – 30.05.60
	LC	Da	06.10.60 – 17.10.60
	LC	Da	05.01.61 – 27.02.61
	NC	Da	20.07.61 – 29.07.61
78016	LC	Co	03.09.64 – 17.10.64
78017	CD	Da	13.10.55 – 02.12.55
	LC	Da	02.08.56 – 01.09.56
	HG	Da	30.01.58 – 01.03.58
	HG	C	05.02.60 – 12.03.60
	AWS	C	20.09.61 – 12.10.61
	LI	C	24.04.64 – 06.06.64
78018	HG	Da	04.01.57 – 13.02.57
	HG	C	13.01.60 – 13.02.60
	LI	C	27.05.63 – 21.06.63
	LC	C	18.09.63 – 18.10.63
78019	CD	Da	08.10.55 – 25.11.55
	HG	Da	01.02.57 – 06.03.57
	HG	C	14.05.59 – 17.06.59
	AWS	C	16.08.61 – 29.08.61
	HI	C	27.02.63 – 23.03.63
78020	LI	C	27.06.57 – 03.08.57
	HG	C	25.04.60 – 24.05.60
	HG	C	08.01.64 – 13.02.64
	NR	C	19.02.64 – 21.02.64
78021	LC	C	25.07.55 – 06.08.55
	LI	C	04.10.57 – 30.11.57
	HG	C	03.05.61 – 07.06.61
	NC	C	18.12.63 – 10.01.64
	I	C	11.05.65 – 08.06.65
78022	LI	C	24.02.58 – 15.03.58
	NC	C	24.03.58 – 08.04.58
	G	Da	22.06.61 – 05.08.61
78023	CD	De	09.05.56 – 15.05.56
	HG	Da	28.11.58 – 02.01.59
	NC	C	13.12.63 – 01.01.64
	LI	C	01.07.64 – 17.10.64
78024	HG	Da	14.01.59 – 12.02.59
78025	NC	Da	18.06.54 – 25.06.54
	HG	Da	31.07.58 – 05.09.58
78026	LI	C	13.02.58 – 14.03.58
	HG	Da	03.12.59 – 23.02.60
	I	Da	04.07.61 – 19.01.62
78027	LC	Da	15.08.58 – 26.09.58
	HI	Da	10.02.60 – 11.03.60
	HC	C	27.09.63 – 29.10.63
	NR	C	22.11.63 – 28.11.63
78028	CD	C	18.12.56 – 17.01.57
	HG	C	30.07.59 – 05.09.59
	LI	C	11.11.63 – 21.12.63
	HC	C	24.02.65 – 24.03.65

During 1963 Willesden received an allocation, initially of seven, Standard Class 2 2-6-0s in exchange for a similar number of Ivatt Class 2s, as the former were fitted with AWS equipment. These locomotives were mainly employed by Willesden for ballast trains, pilot duties and, as seen here, empty coaching stock workings to and from Euston. On 14th May 1964 78039 is passing Kensal Rise station taking the empty stock of the up "Caledonian" from Euston station out to Wembley carriage sidings.

Hugh Ballantyne

78029	LI	C	22.01.59 – 18.02.59		HG	C	24.11.61 – 02.01.62
	LC	C	31.12.59 – 29.01.60				
	HG	C	26.07.61 – 02.09.61	78036	LC	H	08.12.54 – 18.12.54
	NC	C	10.01.63 – 02.02.63		LI	C	27.03.58 – 26.04.58
					HG	C	12.12.61 – 20.01.62
78030	LI	C	11.05.58 – 06.06.58		NC	C	03.01.63 – 18.01.63
	NC	C	16.08.59 – 03.09.59				
	HG	C	28.01.61 – 06.03.61	78037	LI	C	14.03.58 – 13.04.58
	NR	C	11.03.61 – 24.03.61		LC	C	29.06.60 – 16.09.60
	NC	C	28.08.61 – 23.09.61				
				78038	LI	C	27.01.58 – 21.02.58
78031	LI	C	18.04.58 – 10.05.58		HG	C	28.08.61 – 23.11.61
	LC	C	17.12.58 – 09.01.59				
	HG	C	01.05.61 – 01.06.61	78039	LI	C	28.03.58 – 24.04.58
	NC	C	18.12.62 – 07.01.63		LC/AWS	C	30.08.61 – 06.10.61
					HG	C	15.01.62 – 24.02.62
78032	LI	C	21.01.58 – 12.02.58				
	HG	C	22.03.61 – 04.05.61	78040	HG	C	28.04.61 – 08.06.61
					HG	C	18.04.63 – 28.06.63
78033	LI	C	19.12.57 – 18.01.58				
	HG	C	28.08.61 – 05.10.61	78041	LI	C	12.06.58 – 11.07.58
	NC	C	10.12.62 – 04.01.63		HG	C	23.06.60 – 05.08.60
	HC	C	01.11.63 – 08.01.64		LC	C	23.10.62 – 16.11.62
					I	C	31.12.63 – 28.01.64
78034	HI	C	23.01.58 – 21.02.58		NR	C	31.03.64 – 01.04.64
	HG	C	01.03.61 – 11.04.61				
	AWS	C	23.08.61 – 23.09.61	78042	LI	C	21.08.58 – 17.09.58
					HG	C	02.11.61 – 02.12.61
78035	I	C	16.12.57 – 11.01.58		LC	C	28.06.62 – 26.07.62
	AWS	C	24.07.61 – 14.08.61		NC	C	08.01.63 – 26.01.63

78043	LI	C	04.02.59 – 06.03.59	78054	LI	In	18.07.58 – 29.08.58
	HG	C	07.09.61 – 20.10.61		LC	In	03.02.59 – 24.02.59
	NC	C	07.02.63 – 27.02.63		LC(EO)	In	12.08.59 – 11.09.59
78044	LI	C	06.01.58 – 07.02.58		NC(EO)	In	16.09.59 – 23.09.59
	HG	C	15.04.60 – 23.06.60		HG	Co	07.02.61 – 25.03.61
					HI	In	27.07.64 – 11.09.64
78045	LI	Co	20.06.58 – 19.07.58		NC	In	29.09.64 – 07.10.64
	LC(EO)	Co	27.11.59 – 08.01.60		LC	In	15.02.65 – 03.04.65
	HG	Co	26.01.62 – 03.03.62				
				78055	LI	C	25.06.59 – 30.07.59
78046	LI	Co	15.08.58 – 13.09.58		HG	C	23.09.63 – 02.12.63
	LC	Co	17.03.60 – 14.04.60				
	HG	Co	21.09.60 – 12.11.60	78056	HI	C	23.03.59 – 17.04.59
	NC(EO)	Co	28.03.62 – 04.04.62		HG	C	22.08.61 – 22.09.61
	HG	Co	12.02.64 – 04.04.64		NC	C	18.01.63 – 05.02.63
	NC(EO)	Co	29.12.64		LC	C	28.08.63 – 02.10.63
78047	LI	Co	12.04.58 – 23.08.58	78057	LI	C	30.01.61 – 02.03.61
	LC(EO)	Co	13.06.60 – 11.07.60		HC	C	28.08.63 – 04.10.63
	HG	Co	27.12.60 – 04.02.61				
				78058	LI	C	20.04.60 – 14.05.60
78048	LC(EO)	Co	12.02.60 – 26.02.60		HG	C	10.09.63 – 26.10.63
	HG	Co	03.05.61 – 27.05.61				
				78059	LI	C	13.10.60 – 16.11.60
78049	LC(EO)	Co	27.01.60 – 03.03.60		HC	C	18.09.63 – 05.11.63
	HG	Co	06.03.61 – 06.05.61				
	LI	Co	26.05.64 – 27.06.64	78060	HG	C	06.02.62 – 08.03.62
	U	In	29.07.65 – 20.08.65		NC	C	29.03.62 – 05.04.62
					NC	C	17.01.63 – 16.02.63
78050	LI	Co	28.01.59 – 20.02.59				
	LC(EO)	R	01.02.60 – 04.03.60	78061	LI	C	18.05.61 – 16.06.61
	HG	Co	19.12.61 – 20.01.62		HC	C	27.05.63 – 15.06.63
	NC(EO)	Co	26.01.62 – 30.01.62		NC	C	04.09.63 – 06.09.63
	LC	Co	01.05.63 – 17.05.63				
				78062	LI	C	01.05.61 – 26.06.61
78051	LI	Co	10.02.59 – 06.03.59		LC	C	02.11.62 – 21.11.62
	LC(EO)	Co	03.05.61 – 20.05.61		HC	C	23.10.63 – 10.12.63
	HG	Co	22.10.62 – 17.11.62				
				78063	LC	C	28.01.60 – 27.02.60
78052	HG	Co	13.12.61 – 13.01.62		HG	C	22.01.63 – 19.02.63
	NC(EO)	Co	23.02.65 – 27.02.65				
				78064	LI	C	03.03.61 – 06.04.61
78053	LI	In	30.09.58 – 24.10.58		HC	C	02.12.63 – 25.01.64
	LC(EO)	In	27.03.59 – 17.04.59				
	LC(EO)	In	05.09.60 – 14.10.60				

An unidentified Standard Class 5 4-6-0, with rear end assistance, climbs the 1 in 74 out of Weymouth on a northbound freight at Upwey in the summer of 1958.

Kenneth Wightman

TABLE 6.6
BR Standard Class 4 2-6-4 Tank Engines 80000-80154 – Record of Repairs

No.	1	2	3
80000	LI	R	24.11.54 – 14.12.54
	G	R	24.08.57 – 19.09.57
	LC	Co	19.09.58 – 23.10.58
	LI	Co	30.07.60 – 09.09.60
	G	Co	10.09.63 – 12.10.63
80001	LI	R	23.05.55 – 18.06.55
	LC	R	05.04.56 – 21.04.56
	G	R	23.08.57 – 10.10.57
	LC	Co	06.11.58 – 15.11.58
	G	Co	31.08.61 – 25.11.61
	LI	Co	11.12.64 – 16.01.65
80002	LI	R	21.06.55 – 15.07.55
	LC	R	19.12.56 – 29.12.56
	G	R	19.08.57 – 14.09.57
	LC	R	09.11.57 – 30.11.57
	HI	Co	15.08.60 – 24.09.60
	G	Co	20.10.62 – 17.11.62
	NC	Co	23.11.62 – 24.11.62
	NC	Co	30.09.65 – 02.10.65
80003	LC	R	24.07.54 – 12.08.54
	LI	R	15.04.55 – 14.05.55
	G	Co	03.03.58 – 05.04.58
	NC	Co	11.04.58 – 17.04.58
	LC	Co	13.07.59 – 17.07.59
	HI	Co	04.05.61 – 10.06.61
	LC	Co	06.09.62 – 15.09.62
80004	LC	R	24.05.54 – 05.06.54
	LI	R	13.01.55 – 04.02.55
	LC	In	22.06.55 – 15.07.55
	NC	In	17.04.56 – 18.04.56
	G	R	10.12.56 – 12.01.57
	HI	Co	13.03.59 – 18.04.59
	NC	In	24.10.59 – 06.11.59
	LC	In	01.12.59 – 29.12.59
	G	Co	05.02.64 – 29.02.64
	LC	Co	11.05.64 – 16.05.64
80005	LC	In	01.03.54 – 26.03.54
	LI	R	20.10.54 – 13.11.54
	NC	In	27.03.56 – 28.03.56
	G	R	03.12.57 – 27.12.57
	NC(EO)	In	09.07.59 – 10.07.59
	LI	Co	14.01.60 – 27.02.60
	G	Co	10.08.63 – 14.09.63
80006	LI	R	17.06.55 – 09.07.55
	G	R	24.09.57 – 26.10.57
	HI	Co	23.09.59 – 24.10.59
	LC	Co	20.04.62 – 11.05.62
	LC	Co	17.02.65 – 17.04.65
80007	LI	R	03.05.55 – 28.05.55
	G	R	02.11.57 – 30.11.57
	LC	Co	11.02.60 – 24.03.60
	HI	Co	05.12.60 – 14.01.61
	LC(EO)	Co	27.01.61 – 15.02.61
	LI	Co	24.03.64 – 13.06.64
80008	LI	R	22.10.54 – 06.11.54
	LC	R	01.03.55 – 05.03.55
	G	R	26.04.57 – 16.05.57
	NC	R	23.05.57 – 25.05.57
	LI	Co	17.03.59 – 04.04.59
	LC	Co	26.11.59 – 17.12.59
	LC	Co	16.03.60 – 29.04.60
	NC	Co	15.09.61
	LC	Co	07.12.61 – 14.12.61
	G	Co	04.06.62 – 30.06.62
	LC	Co	01.07.63 – 06.07.63
80009	LI	R	19.04.55 – 07.05.55
	G	R	20.11.57 – 07.12.57
	HI	R	25.04.60 – 30.04.60
	G	Co	13.06.63 – 12.07.63
	NC	Co	27.08.63 – 28.08.63
	LC	Co	02.04.64 – 17.04.64
80010	LC	B	23.06.53 – 01.08.53
	LC	A	01.04.54 – 15.04.54
	LI	B	08.06.55 – 20.07.55
	LC	B	28.12.56 – 11.01.57
	G	E	05.08.57 – 31.08.57
	LI	E	30.06.59 – 01.08.59
	LI	E	30.01.62 – 17.02.62
80011	LC	B	02.12.52 – 17.01.53
	LI	E	27.09.54 – 16.10.54
	LC	B	21.04.55 – 03.06.55
	G	E	13.12.56 – 12.01.57
	LC	B	06.06.57 – 12.06.57
	LC	B	29.11.57 – 05.12.57
	LC	B	03.02.58 – 07.02.58
	LC	A	07.08.58 – 29.08.58
	LI	E	30.09.60 – 22.10.60
	LC	E	18.08.61 – 02.09.61
	LC	E	07.05.62 – 19.05.62
	G	E	10.02.64 – 04.04.64
	RET	E	21.07.64 – 22.07.64
80012	LC	B	30.01.53 – 14.02.53
	LC	E	25.08.53 – 05.09.53
	LI	E	28.06.55 – 09.07.55
	RET	E	09.09.55 – 15.09.55
	G	E	25.01.57 – 16.02.57
	LC	B	18.09.57 – 24.09.57
	HC	E	23.06.58 – 11.07.58
	LI	E	09.06.60 – 25.06.60
	LC	Ba	26.07.61 – 17.09.61
	LC	Ba	05.02.61 – 16.03.61
	G	E	11.03.64 – 25.04.64
80013	RET	A	22.09.52 – 09.10.52
	LC	E	12.03.53 – 21.03.53
	LI	E	26.11.54 – 18.12.54

ID				ID			
	LC	B	16.07.56 – 01.09.56		LI	E	24.02.61 – 18.03.61
	LC	B	11.03.57 – 14.03.57		G	E	28.02.63 – 30.03.63
	G	E	28.08.57 – 21.09.57	80019	C	B	16.09.53 – 15.11.53
	NC	E	21.10.58 – 25.10.58		C	B	09.03.54 – 26.03.54
	LI	E	01.01.60 – 23.01.60		C	B	29.06.54 – 07.07.54
	LI	E	26.06.61 – 29.07.61		LI	De	19.01.55 – 10.02.55
	G	E	01.04.63 – 04.05.63		C	B	03.10.55 – 14.10.55
	LC	E	12.12.63 – 21.12.63		C	B	26.04.56 – 11.05.56
80014	RET	A	19.05.52 – 30.05.52		G	E	05.07.56 – 18.08.56
	LC	B	29.06.53 – 06.08.53		LI	E	28.08.58 – 20.09.58
	LI	E	09.12.54 – 24.12.54		C	A	27.11.59 – 12.12.59
	LC	B	30.01.56 – 11.02.56		LI	E	04.12.61 – 06.01.62
	G	B	04.04.57 – 29.05.57		G	E	23.01.64 – 07.03.64
	LI	A	12.01.59 – 17.02.59	80020	NC	R	27.11.51
	LC	E	30.10.59 – 14.11.59		NC	In	13.08.52
	NC	E	10.10.61 – 21.01.61		LI	R	27.04.54 – 13.05.54
	G	E	29.05.62 – 23.06.62		NC(EO)	In	08.05.56 – 09.05.56
80015	RET	A	01.08.52 – 12.09.52		G	R	06.12.56 – 22.12.56
	LC	B	21.05.53 – 20.06.53		HI	Co	12.05.59 – 30.05.59
	LI	E	23.08.54 – 11.09.54		LC	Co	25.01.60 – 12.02.60
	G	E	26.07.56 – 08.09.56		NC	In	21.07.60 – 22.07.60
	LC	B	13.08.57 – 28.08.57		G	Co	21.12.62 – 19.01.63
	LI	E	17.10.58 – 01.11.58	80021	LI	R	08.04.54 – 29.04.54
	HC	E	02.10.59 – 17.10.59		G	R	29.08.56 – 29.09.56
	G	E	02.05.61 – 03.06.61		LI	R	23.09.58 – 18.10.58
	LI	E	26.07.63 – 07.09.63		NC?	R	25.06.59 – 30.06.59
	LC	E	04.10.63 – 15.10.63		LC	R	10.12.59 – 18.12.59
	LC	E	25.09.64 – 08.10.64		LC	Co	05.07.60 – 15.01.60
80016	RET	A	08.06.53 – 04.07.53		LC	Co	27.10.60 – 10.11.60
	LC	B	09.09.53 – 26.09.53		G	Co	11.06.62 – 07.07.62
	LC	B	12.10.54 – 22.10.54	80022	LI	R	13.05.54 – 09.06.54
	LI	E	04.01.55 – 22.01.55		G	R	14.03.57 – 19.04.57
	NC	E	16.08.55 – 19.08.55		NC	Co	24.10.58 – 31.10.58
	NC	E	11.11.55 – 19.11.55		LI	R	08.02.60 – 11.03.60
	LC	B	26.03.56 – 10.04.56		LC	Co	15.12.61 – 28.12.61
	G	E	31.10.56 – 03.12.56		G	Co	13.04.63 – 25.05.63
	LI	A	21.11.58 – 13.12.58		LC	Co	28.10.63 – 14.12.63
	G	E	26.07.61 – 26.08.61	80023	LI	R	20.08.54 – 04.09.54
	NC	Ba	07.01.63 – 11.01.63		LC	R	15.03.55 – 24.03.55
	HI	E	08.05.64 – 13.06.64		LC(EO)	R	29.03.55 – 30.03.55
80017	LC	E	12.03.53 – 21.03.53		G	R	17.04.57 – 09.05.57
	I	B	02.04.53 – 07.05.53		LC	R	09.10.57 – 12.10.57
	LC	B	20.07.55 – 06.08.55		NC	R	23.09.58 – 10.10.58
	LC	B	02.07.56 – 11.07.56		HI	Co	13.11.59 – 12.12.59
	G	E	18.09.56 – 13.10.56		G	Co	16.08.62 – 08.09.62
	LC	B	09.10.57 – 16.10.57		NC	Co	04.10.63 – 05.10.63
	LC	B	26.02.58 – 20.03.58		NC	Co	12.06.64 – 20.06.64
	LI	E	16.04.59 – 02.05.59		NC	Co	17.06.65 – 19.06.65
	G	E	05.12.60 – 14.01.61	80024	LI	R	12.04.54 – 08.05.54
	HC	E	08.08.62 – 08.09.62		NC	R	19.03.55 – 24.03.55
80018	C	E	16.01.53 – 24.01.53		G	R	17.11.56 – 08.12.56
	RET	A	12.03.53 – 27.03.53		HI	Co	22.03.58 – 26.04.58
	LI	E	26.08.54 – 18.09.54		LC	Co	14.11.58 – 22.11.58
	NC	B	15.11.55 – 18.11.55		NC	Co	20.06.59 – 30.06.59
	LC	E	14.05.56 – 26.05.56		G	Co	19.11.61 – 23.12.61
	G	E	16.01.57 – 09.02.57		LI	Co	09.02.65 – 13.03.65
	LC	B	22.01.58 – 24.01.58				
	LI	E	16.09.58 – 11.10.58				

80025	LI	R	13.02.54 – 13.03.54
	G	R	24.01.57 – 20.02.57
	LC	Co	24.02.58 – 05.04.58
	NC	Co	10.02.59 – 25.02.59
	LI	Co	06.06.59 – 27.06.59
	G	Co	28.08.62 – 05.10.62
	LC	Co	23.07.63 – 10.08.63
	NC	Co	26.11.63 – 20.12.63
80026	LI	R	29.07.54 – 20.08.54
	G	R	05.09.56 – 13.10.56
	NC	R	16.10.56 – 18.10.56
	HI	Co	08.02.60 – 26.03.60
	G	Co	29.09.62 – 03.11.62
	LC	Co	08.11.62 – 20.11.62
80027	LI	R	24.02.54 – 26.03.54
	LC	R	05.12.55 – 17.12.55
	G	R	23.10.56 – 30.11.56
	NC	R	21.02.57 – 02.03.57
	LI	Co	27.05.59 – 19.06.59
	G	Co	17.01.63 – 23.02.63
80028	LI	R	26.04.54 – 22.05.54
	NC	In	20.09.56 – 21.09.56
	G	R	05.02.57 – 08.03.57
	LI	Co	06.09.58 – 16.10.58
	NC	In	19.05.59 – 20.05.59
	NC	In	22.07.59 – 23.07.59
	NC	In	19.08.59
	NC	In	15.01.60 – 18.01.60
	LI	Co	02.07.60 – 27.08.60
	NC	In	17.02.61 – 24.02.61
	LC	Co	18.09.61 – 06.10.61
	G	Co	24.08.62 – 22.09.62
80029	LI	R	04.05.54 – 29.05.54
	G	R	19.02.57 – 23.07.57
	NC	In	21.05.59 – 27.05.59
	NC	In	13.10.59 – 22.10.59
	LI	Co	21.12.59 – 30.01.60
	NC	In	06.04.60 – 15.04.60
	LC	Co	02.07.62 – 12.07.62
	NC	Co	23.07.62 – 02.08.62
	G	Co	10.04.63 – 18.05.63
	NC	Co	19.11.64 – 12.12.64
80030	LI	R	15.09.53 – 09.10.53
	LI	R	07.12.55 – 24.12.55
	LC	R	30.11.56 – 07.12.56
	G	Co	21.04.58 – 10.05.58
	LI	Co	04.10.60 – 29.10.60
	LC	Co	21.03.61 – 31.03.61
	LC	Co	22.08.61 – 09.09.61
80031	LC	E	01.09.53 – 12.09.53
	LC	B	16.06.54 – 26.06.54
	LI	E	09.03.55 – 26.03.55
	LC	B	05.12.55 – 13.12.55
	G	E	31.08.56 – 29.09.56
	HC	E	07.03.58 – 29.03.58
	NC	A	08.09.58 – 03.10.58

92227 from Banbury with a Class 6 freight at Gloucester Central on 4th July 1964, passing GWR 4300 class 7318 in the platform road. The 9F still is quite clean following a casual overhaul at Crewe, completed on 25th June 1964.

www.rail-online.co.uk

No.				No.			
	LI	E	03.07.59 – 08.08.59	80040	LI	De	29.04.55 – 26.05.55
	G	E	29.03.61 – 06.05.61		NC(R)	De	22.06.55 – 25.06.55
	LC	A	05.09.61 – 23.09.61		G	De	04.02.57 – 13.03.57
	LC	E	28.08.63 – 07.09.63		LI	De	09.09.59 – 13.10.59
					LC	A	14.02.61 – 23.03.61
80032	LC	E	24.04.53 – 07.05.53		G	E	19.09.61 – 21.10.61
	LI	E	21.03.55 – 09.04.55				
	LC	B	19.09.55 – 23.09.55	80041	PV	De	28.07.53 – 20.08.53
	LC	B	16.04.56 – 25.04.56		I	De	18.04.55 – 13.05.55
	LC	E	24.09.56 – 05.10.56		U	De	20.05.55 – 23.05.55
	G	E	07.02.58 – 08.03.58		HG	De	14.08.57 – 25.09.57
	LI	E	19.01.61 – 11.02.61		HI	E	29.04.60 – 21.05.60
	G	E	14.05.63 – 22.06.63		NC	A	11.07.60 – 23.07.60
					NC	A	20.03.61 – 21.03.61
80033	NC	A	20.10.52 – 29.10.52		LC	A	14.06.61 – 08.07.61
	LC	E	31.03.53 – 11.04.53		G	E	08.08.63 – 14.09.63
	LC	B	05.02.54 – 11.02.54				
	LI	De	29.11.54 – 20.12.54	80042	I	De	17.08.55 – 08.09.55
	G	E	23.10.56 – 17.11.56		HB	De	19.09.55 – 29.09.55
	LC	B	09.09.57 – 13.09.57		HG	De	22.10.57 – 04.12.57
	LI	E	09.02.59 – 28.02.59		HI	E	25.02.60 – 19.03.60
	G	E	15.09.60 – 15.10 60		LC	A	02.05.61 – 27.05.61
	LI	E	22.06.62 – 04.08.62		NC	E	09.10.61 – 21.10.61
	LC	E	03.10.63 – 31.10.63		LC	Ex	03.01.63 – 05.02.63
80034	I	De	06.12.54 – 04.01.55	80043	I	De	21.08.55 – 21.09.55
	HG	De	28.05.57 – 05.07.57		HC	De	10.09.58 – 20.10.58
	LC	Ru	13.01.59 – 22.01.59		LC	A	20.07.60 – 06.08.60
	LI	E	01.09.60 – 24.09.60		LI	E	14.02.61 – 11.03.61
	G	E	17.01.63 – 23.02.63		NC	E	13.04.61 – 21.04.61
					LC	E	04.01.63 – 23.01.63
80035	I	De	10.05.55 – 02.06.55				
	G	De	17.02.58 – 02.04.58	80044	I	De	08.09.55 – 29.09.55
	LI	E	31.08.60 – 24.09.60		G	De	07.07.58 – 27.08.58
	HC	E	10.01.62 – 03.02.62		W	H	11.11.59 – 23.11.59
	LC	E	23.01.63 – 16.02.63		LC	Co	30.06.60 – 12.07.60
					HI	Co	04.10.61 – 28.10.61
80036	I	De	26.07.55 – 22.08.55		LC	Co	18.02.63 – 23.02.63
	G	De	15.05.58 – 13.06.58				
	HI	E	28.10.60 – 19.11.60	80045	LI	De	20.12.54 – 18.01.55
	LC	A	20.12.61 – 13.01.62		HG	De	19.06.57 – 01.08.57
					G	Co	26.08.61 – 30.09.61
80037	I	De	16.02.55 – 10.03.55		LI	Co	28.02.64 – 18.04.64
	HG	De	08.08.57 – 05.09.57				
	LI	E	23.06.60 – 30.07.60	80046	LI	De	17.08.54 – 20.09.54
	LC	A	06.09.61 – 30.09.61		G	De	27.06.57 – 16.08.57
					HI	Co	25.04.60 – 11.06.60
80038	I	De	20.06.55 – 27.07.55		G	Co	29.10.63 – 28.12.63
	TB	De	03.08.55 – 05.08.55		LC(EO)	Co	01.02.66 – 05.02.66
	G	De	04.10.57 – 07.11.57				
	C	De	03.06.58 – 26.06.58	80047	LI	De	17.03.55 – 14.04.55
	LC	Ru	23.01.59 – 05.02.59		LC	De	21.10.56 – 22.11.56
	HI	E	29.04.60 – 14.05.60		G	De	02.04.58 – 09.05.58
	LC	A	12.07.61 – 05.08.61		NC	Co	21.04.60 – 22.04.60
					LI	Co	27.04.61 – 27.05.61
80039	NC	De	02.02.53		LC	Co	20.04.62 – 12.05.62
	LI	De	22.04.55 – 16.05.55		NC	Co	27.08.63 – 07.09.63
	LC	De	14.09.55 – 29.09.55		G	Co	27.01.64 – 14.03.64
	G	De	08.10.57 – 08.11.57				
	HI	E	26.02.60 – 12.03.60	80048	HC(BLR)	De	08.05.53 – 03.06.53
	LC	A	19.04.61 – 07.10.61		LC(TK)	De	11.11.54 – 26.11.54
	NC	E	12.09.61 – 07.10.61		LI	De	04.08.55 – 30.08.55
	G	E	02.07.62 – 11.08.62		LC	De	16.02.56 – 03.03.56

ID	Col2	Col3	Dates
	LC	De	26.09.56 – 26.10.56
	HG	De	27.05.58 – 01.07.58
	HI	Co	10.11.61 – 08.12.61
80049	I	De	08.09.55 – 29.09.55
	G	De	09.12.57 – 24.01.58
	LI	Co	07.09.60 – 08.10.60
	HC	Co	14.12.62 – 29.12.62
80050	I	De	18.10.55 – 02.11.55
	G	De	26.03.58 – 07.05.58
	LI	Co	13.12.61 – 13.01.62
80051	LI	De	28.09.55 – 19.10.55
	G	De	13.01.58 – 14.02.58
	HI	De	15.02.60 – 24.03.60
	NC	De	09.05.60 – 26.05.60
	LC	Co	21.11.61 – 08.12.61
	G	Co	15.06.63 – 10.08.63
	NC	Co	02.12.64 – 19.12.64
80052	CD	De	18.02.54 – 11.03.54
	I	De	21.09.55 – 13.10.55
	G	De	31.03.58 – 29.05.58
	NC	Co	17.05.60 – 09.06.60
	HI	Co	04.09.61 – 07.10.61
80053	I	De	01.11.55 – 22.11.55
	C	De	14.03.56 – 29.03.56
	G	De	29.01.58 – 28.02.58
	HI	Co	17.03.61 – 15.04.61
80054	LI	Co	23.12.57 – 25.01.58
	LC	Co	10.12.58 – 27.12.58
	G	Co	27.11.61 – 06.01.62
80055	NC	R	07.06.56
	LC	R	07.09.56 – 28.09.56
	LI	R	01.06.57 – 21.06.57
	LC	Co	28.04.58 – 16.05.58
	G	Co	26.04.60 – 18.06.60
	HI	Co	23.07.63 – 24.08.63
80056	–	–	Data not traced
80057	LI	R	11.11.57 – 06.12.57
	LC	Co	22.08.58 – 20.09.58
	LC	Co	17.11.57 – 09.12.57
	G	Co	01.05.61 – 10.06.61
80058	LI	R	19.10.57 – 16.11.57
	G	Co	16.11.60 – 17.12.60
	HI	Co	12.02.64 – 25.02.64
80059	LI	De	25.05.56 – 14.06.56
	HB	De	20.06.56 – 27.06.56
	G	De	04.11.57 – 17.12.57
	HI	E	12.04.60 – 30.04.60
	LC	A	26.05.61 – 24.06.61
	G	E	03.08.62 – 08.09.62
80060	LC	De	24.08.54 – 08.09.54
	LI	De	02.05.56 – 24.05.56
	HG	De	14.10.58 – 03.12.58
	LC	Co	08.08.60 – 03.09.60
	G	Co	09.06.62 – 07.07.62
80061	T	De	29.07.54 – 18.08.54
	LI	De	14.08.55 – 29.08.55
	HG	De	15.08.58 – 18.09.58
	HI	Co	29.11.61 – 30.12.61
	G	Co	22.01.64 – 14.03.64
	U	Co	05.08.65 – 28.08.65
80062	I	De	26.01.56 – 16.02.56
	G	De	10.02.58 – 17.04.58
	LI	De	25.05.59 – 18.06.59
	HI	Co	12.01.62 – 03.02.62
	LC	Co	13.08.63 – 17.08.63
80063	Ty	De	16.09.54 – 06.10.54
	LI	De	16.09.55 – 06.10.55
	CD	De	18.01.56 – 01.02.56
	G	De	05.12.57 – 13.01.58
	HI	Co	01.04.61 – 06.05.61
	NC	Co	05.05.62 – 16.05.62
	G	Co	11.02.64 – 11.04.64
80064	LI	De	05.04.56 – 26.04.56
	HG	De	22.10.58 – 28.11.58
	LI	E	25.04.61 – 20.05.61
	NC	E	28.02.62 – 14.03.62
	HI	E	14.06.62 – 07.07.62
80065	LI	De	27.06.56 – 31.07.56
	LC	Ru	16.01.59 – 06.02.59
	G	De	11.11.59 – 09.12.59
	LC	E	25.09.61 – 14.10.61
	LC	E	26.01.62 – 10.02.62
	HI	E	09.10.63 – 23.11.63
	NC	E	17.05.65 – 20.05.65
80066	LI	De	13.11.56 – 30.11.56
	G	De	02.01.59 – 17.02.59
	LC	Ba	06.07.61 – 24.08.61
	LI	E	23.01.62 – 17.02.62
	LC	A	16.04.62 – 05.05.62
80067	I	De	29.11.56 – 19.12.56
	LC	De	21.02.58 – 13.03.58
	TB	De	21.03.58 – 24.03.58
	HG	De	05.03.59 – 09.04.59
	HI	E	24.04.62 – 19.05.62
80068	C	De	25.08.54 – 22.09.54
	LI	De	07.11.56 – 29.11.56
	LC	Ru	01.05.59 – 12.05.59
	G	E	24.05.60 – 18.06.60
	HI	E	11.09.63 – 19.10.63
80069	NC	Bo	28.10.53 – 03.11.53
	NC	Bo	06.11.53 – 11.11.53
	NC	St	13.05.54 – 14.05.54
	HI	St	06.04.56 – 23.06.56
	LC	St	01.07.58 – 06.08.58
	G	Da	07.08.59 – 11.09.59

LC	Da	17.08.60 – 20.10.60
H	Da	04.09.61 – 07.12.61

80070	NC	St	03.05.54 – 04.05.54
	H	St	16.08.54 – 01.10.54
	I	St	27.04.56 – 01.08.56
	H	Da	27.04.59 – 03.06.59
	NC	Bo	11.06.59 – 12.06.59

80071	-	-	Data not traced

80072	NC	Bo	01.12.53 – 04.12.53
	NC	St	29.04.54 – 30.04.54
	NC	St	10.09.54 – 23.09.54
	HI	St	12.04.56 – 25.06.56
	G	Da	28.01.59 – 11.03.59
	Cas	C	07.10.64 – 22.01.65

80073	-	-	Data not traced

80074	NC	Bo	18.12.53 – 23.12.53
	NC	St	05.05.54 – 06.05.54
	NC	Pl	19.06.54
	CD	St	25.10.54 – 04.12.54
	NC	Pl	23.04.55
	H	St	08.03.56 – 29.03.56
	LC	St	05.10.56 – 08.12.56
	NC	St	07.09.59 – 11.09.59
	H	Da	06.04.60 – 17.06.60

80075	NC	Bo	28.12.55 – 29.12.55
	NC	St	27.04.54 – 28.04.54
	NC	Pl	17.07.54
	NC	Bo	30.04.55 – 06.05.55
	H	St	10.12.56 – 01.02.57
	H	Da	23.11.59 – 01.01.60
	LC	Da	11.05.61 – 15.08.61

80076	NC	Bo	04.01.54 – 06.01.54
	NC	St	11.05.54 – 12.05.54
	I	St	29.12.55 – 14.04.56
	LC	St	25.04.58 – 27.06.58
	G	Da	12.06.59 – 21.08.59
	NC	Bo	10.09.59 – 14.09.59

80077	NC	Bo	22.01.54 – 26.01.54
	NC	St	15.05.54 – 17.05.54
	I	St	20.06.56 – 01.08.56
	NC	Da	14.06.60 – 12.08.60

80078	NC	Bo	19.02.54 – 22.02.54
	NC	St	24.04.54 – 26.04.54
	HI	St	04.09.56 – 12.10.56
	NC	Bo	22.10.56 – 23.10.56
	LC	Da	15.12.58 – 23.01.59
	NC	Bo	09.02.59
	G	Da	28.10.60 – 10.12.60

80079	NC	Bo	16.03.54 – 22.03.54
	HI	St	12.11.56 – 11.01.57

80019 runs bunker first past the rock cutting at East Hill at Corfe Castle on the branch service from Wareham to Swanage on 29th March 1966. This was the final year of steam operation on the branch. Hampshire DEMUs took over the service until the branch closed in January 1972. Subsequently the line was taken over by the Swanage Railway Society. 80019 entered service in 1951 being delivered to Tunbridge Wells West to replace the LMR Fairburn tanks on local services, finally being withdrawn from Bournemouth in March 1967. *Rodney Lissenden*

	LC	St	12.02.58 – 02.05.58
	LC	St	05.12.58 – 05.01.59
	H	Da	12.09.60 – 03.12.60
	I	C	11.09.63 – 02.11.63
80080	NC	Bo	01.04.54 – 02.04.54
	NC	St	18.05.54 – 19.05.54
	U	St	28.12.55 – 25.02.56
	HC	St	05.04.57 – 25.05.57
	NC	Bo	04.06.57 – 05.06.57
	LC	St	16.02.59 – 11.03.59
	LC	Da	11.04.60 – 13.06.60
	HI	C	10.02.64 – 18.03.64
80081	LI	De	30.07.56 – 15.08.56
	HG	De	02.12.58 – 07.01.59
	HI	E	13.02.61 – 11.03.61
	LC	E	24.06.63 – 05.07.63
80082	LI	De	07.01.57 – 24.01.57
	LC	De	23.12.57 – 16.01.58
	LC	Ru	02.02.59 – 12.02.59
	G	De	11.11.59 – 18.12.59
	LI	E	13.12.62 – 19.01.63
	LC	E	02.09.63 – 21.09.63
	CAS	E	13.04.65 – 28.04.65
80083	I	De	09.10.56 – 29.10.56
	LC	De	03.06.58 – 26.06.58
	LC	Bo	12.05.59 – 19.06.59
	G	E	12.02.60 – 12.03.60
	HI	E	31.01.63 – 23.02.63
	LC	E	12.05.65 – 27.05.65
80084	I	De	16.06.56 – 09.07.56
	HG	De	05.11.58 – 18.12.58
	HI	E	09.03.62 – 31.03.62
	LC	E	31.08.64 – 06.10.64
80085	LC	De	21.03.56 – 09.04.56
	G	De	06.12.56 – 16.01.57
	LC	De	18.01.57 – 22.01.57
	HI	E	01.02.60 – 20.02.60
	LC	Ba	13.05.60 – 15.06.60
	G	E	29.10.63 – 14.12.63
80086	LI	De	07.01.57 – 24.01.57
	C	De	11.02.57 – 20.02.57
	G	De	24.11.59 – 24.12.59
	G	Co	06.05.63 – 08.06.63
80087	LI	De	07.05.57 – 23.05.57
	G	E	02.08.60 – 27.08.60
80088	C	De	06.04.55 – 25.04.55
	C	De	12.10.55 – 20.10.55
	I	De	18.02.57 – 13.03.57
	HG	De	04.02.59 – 27.02.59
	HI	E	11.05.61 – 03.06.61
	LI	E	23.05.63 – 22.06.63
	LC	E	03.09.64 – 24.09.64
80089	LI	De	03.07.57 – 07.08.57
	G	E	07.01.60 – 30.01.60
	NC	E	12.09.60 – 17.09.60
	HI	E	07.06.62 – 30.06.62
	LC	E	11.11.64 – 09.12.64
80090	LI	De	21.07.57 – 21.08.57
	HG	Co	13.04.60 – 28.05.60
	LI	Co	03.08.62 – 08.09.62
	LI	Co	12.06.63 – 09.08.63
80091	LI	De	27.08.57 – 03.10.57
	G	De	11.08.59 – 14.10.59
	LC	Co	21.01.61 – 18.02.61
	NC(EO)	Co	22.02.61 – 04.03.61
	LC	Co	16.10.61 – 30.11.61
	HI	Co	02.05.63 – 01.06.63
	LC	Co	13.03.64 – 10.04.64
80092	LI	De	18.09.57 – 10.10.57
	G	De	03.02.60 – 09.03.60
	HI	Co	30.11.62 – 22.12.62
80093	LI	De	02.04.57 – 02.05.57
	HG	De	02.09.59 – 02.10.59
80094	LI	De	30.10.57 – 20.11.57
	G	E	23.03.60 – 23.04.60
	LC	E	28.11.62 – 12.12.62
	HI	E	22.10.63 – 23.11.63
80095	LI	De	27.11.57 – 19.12.57
	G	E	02.02.60 – 27.02.60
	LC	A	23.05.61 – 10.06.61
	LI	E	20.03.63 – 20.04.63
80096	NC	Bo	16.12.54 – 20.12.54
	LI	St	21.05.57 – 19.07.57
	C	Da	09.07.58 – 27.08.58
	NC	Bo	02.09.58
80097	NC	Bo	30.12.54 – 03.01.55
	LI	St	16.10.57 – 22.11.57
	LC	Da	27.02.58 – 21.04.58
	NC	Bo	24.04.58 – 25.04.58
80098	NC	Bo	13.01.55 – 17.01.55
	LC	St	10.11.55 – 09.12.55
	HC	St	31.01.57 – 11.02.57
	I	St	16.09.57 – 07.11.57
	NC	Bo	12.11.57 – 13.11.57
	G	Da	01.03.60 – 13.04.60
80099	NC	Bo	25.02.55 – 02.03.55
	LC	St	28.05.56 – 16.06.56
	G	Da	07.02.58 – 20.03.58
	NC	Bo	08.04.58
	HI	Da	01.06.61 – 01.07.61
80100	NC	Bo	17.02.55 – 22.02.55
	LC	St	06.10.55 – 05.11.55
	U	St	06.03.56 – 16.03.56
	G	Da	10.03.58 – 17.04.58

ID			
	NC	Bo	12.05.58
	G	Da	19.05.61 – 24.06.61
80101	NC	Bo	10.03.55 – 14.03.55
	H	St	12.08.57 – 21.09.57
	NC	Bo	26.09.57 – 27.09.57
	LC	St	26.11.57 – 08.12.57
	NC	St	10.01.58 – 02.04.58
	NC	St	29.09.58 – 21.10.58
	G	Da	18.02.61 – 15.04.61
80102	NC	Bo	20.03.55 – 24.03.55
	LC	St	05.03.57 – 25.03.57
	NC	Bo	08.04.57
	G	Da	27.06.58 – 14.08.58
	NC	Bo	05.09.58
	G	C	08.11.62 – 22.02.63
80103	–	–	Data not traced
80104	NC	Bo	25.04.55 – 27.04.55
	G	Da	23.04.58 – 30.05.58
	NC	Bo	12.06.58 – 15.06.58
	LC	Da	22.04.60 – 31.05.60
80105	NC	Bo	06.05.55 – 11.05.55
	NC	Bo	23.12.56 – 28.12.56
	HI	St	18.08.57 – 13.10.57
	NC	Bo	18.10.57
	LC	Da	04.03.59 – 27.04.59
	NC	Bo	02.05.59 – 04.05.59
	G	Da	12.09.60 – 11.11.60
	I	C	27.09.63 – 17.12.63
80106	NC	R	15.12.54 – 16.12.54
	LI	R	10.06.57 – 03.05.57
	LC	Co	06.05.58 – 17.05.58
	LC	Co	13.02.59 – 25.02.59
	G	Co	05.05.61 – 03.06.61
80107	LI	R	29.07.57 – 10.08.57
	LC	Co	03.04.58 – 12.04.58
	LC	Co	09.09.58 – 25.09.58
	NC	Co	01.05.59 – 06.05.59
	G	Co	16.11.61 – 09.12.61
80108	NC	In	13.07.55
	NC	In	08.11.55 – 10.11.55
	NC	In	25.01.56 – 26.01.56
	NC	In	01.05.56 – 02.05.56
	LI	Co	10.04.57 – 18.05.57
	LC	Co	19.03.58 – 29.03.58
	G	Co	24.02.60 – 09.04.60
	HI	Co	30.04.62 – 26.05.62
	LC	Co	06.06.62 – 16.06.62
80109	LI	R	19.06.57 – 05.07.57
	LC	Co	10.04.58 – 19.04.58
	G	Co	30.09.60 – 22.10.60
	LC(EO)	Co	16.11.60 – 18.11.60
	LC	Co	13.12.60 – 15.12.60
	LI	Co	06.03.64 – 11.04.64
80110	LI	R	11.07.56 – 17.08.56
	LC	R	12.10.56 – 27.10.56
	G	Co	13.04.59 – 08.05.59
	HI	Co	06.09.62 – 06.10.62
	NC	Co	12.12.63 – 24.12.63
	NC	Co	19.02.64 – 26.02.64
80111	LI	R	07.11.57 – 04.12.57
	G	Co	01.08.60 – 17.09.60
	HI	Co	08.03.63 – 06.04.63
	LC	Co	20.01.65 – 10.02.65
80112	LI	Co	06.05.57 – 11.05.57
	NC	In	09.09.57 – 10.09.57
	NC	In	07.10.59 – 22.10.59
	G	Co	11.01.60 – 27.02.60
	NC	In	19.07.60 – 20.07.60
	HI	Co	03.06.63 – 06.07.63
	HC	Co	07.10.64 – 28.11.64
80113	LI	R	25.09.57 – 24.10.57
	NC	In	26.05.59 – 02.06.59
	G	Co	31.10.59 – 19.12.59
	NC	In	22.07.60
	LC	Co	06.09.61 – 20.10.61
	HI	Co	11.01.62 – 12.02.62
	LC	Co	08.03.63 – 24.05.63
	LC	Co	30.08.63 – 20.09.63
	LC	Co	09.07.65 – 21.08.65
80114	–	–	Data not traced
80115	LI	Co	18.04.58 – 10.05.58
	NC	In	15.04.59 – 17.04.59
	NC	In	31.08.59 – 04.09.59
	NC	In	03.05.60 – 06.05.60
	NC	In	19.05.60 – 09.06.60
	G	Co	26.12.61 – 20.01.62
80116	LI	Co	03.05.65 – 05.06.65
80117	–	–	Data not traced
80118	LC	Co	25.06.65 – 17.07.65
80119	LI	Da	07.01.58 – 15.02.58
	G	Da	18.01.62 – 09.03.62
80120	G	Co	28.12.63 – 01.02.64
80121	LI	R	19.08.57 – 13.09.57
	LC	In	21.11.58 – 02.12.58
	LC	Co	01.05.59 – 27.05.59
	G	Co	10.10.60 – 19.11.60
	HI	Co	28.08.63 – 05.10.63
80122	LI	Co	17.05.58 – 13.06.58
	LC	Co	19.06.59 – 13.07.59
	G	Co	13.03.61 – 13.05.61
	HI	Co	15.04.65 – 08.05.65
80123	LI	Co	11.01.58 – 15.02.58
	LC	Co	07.01.59 – 04.02.59

ID			
	G	Co	22.09.61 – 11.11.61
	LI	Co	04.10.63 – 30.11.63
80124	LC	R	xx.xx.xx – 06.04.56
	LI	Co	30.04.58 – 26.05.58
	LC	Co	27.05.59 – 10.06.59
	G	Co	07.06.61 – 05.08.61
	LI	Co	19.08.63 – 14.09.63
80125	-	-	Data not traced
80126	NC	R	21.11.55 – 22.11.55
	LI	Co	26.03.58 – 26.04.58
	LC	Co	11.08.58 – 23.08.58
	G	Co	29.08.60 – 15.10.60
	LI	In	20.08.63 – 04.10.63
80127	LI	Co	30.04.58 – 24.05.58
	LC	Co	11.12.58 - 25.12.58!
	G	Co	16.10.61 – 11.11.61
80128	LC	R	17.08.56 – 25.08.56
	LC	R	11.11.57 – 23.11.57
	LI	Co	25.11.58 – 13.12.58
	G	Co	18.08.60 – 22.10.60
	LI	In	25.06.64 – 14.08.60
80129	-	-	Data not traced
80130	LI	Co	08.09.58 – 04.10.58
	G	Co	21.12.60 – 11.02.61
	LI	Co	24.02.64 – 09.04.64
80131	NC	Bo	19.03.56 – 24.03.56
	G	Da	09.09.58 – 10.10.58
	NC	Bo	03.11.58
80132	CD	St	02.07.56 – 01.09.56
	G	Da	25.09.58 – 03.11.58
	NC	Bo	04.12.58
80133	LC	B	22.05.56 – 01.06.56
	LI	Da	28.05.59 – 08.07.59
	NC	Bo	27.07.59 – 28.07.59
	HG	C	29.11.62 – 14.02.63
80134	NC	Bo	15.05.56 – 17.05.56
	LI	Da	26.05.59 – 25.06.59
	NC	Bo	15.07.59 – 16.07.59
80135	LI	Da	24.03.59 – 04.05.59
	HG	C	18.10.62 – 17.11.62
80136	LI	Da	31.07.59 – 10.09.59
	HG	C	11.10.62 – 12.01.63
	LC	C	08.03.63 – 20.04.63
80137	I	De	06.08.58 – 04.09.58
	LC	Ne	14.03.59 – 08.04.59
	HI	E	18.02.60 – 05.03.60
	G	E	06.06.62 – 07.07.62
80138	LI	De	18.08.58 – 09.09.58
	G	E	25.11.60 – 31.12.60
	LI	E	17.04.63 – 11.05.63
	LC	E	29.01.65 – 26.02.65
80139	LI	De	08.09.58 – 29.09.58
	LC	Bo	01.07.59 – 25.09.59
	LC	E	09.02.60 – 20.02.60
	LC	E	07.06.60 – 25.06.60
	G	E	16.01.62 – 10.02.62
	LI	E	04.12.64 – 15.01.65
80140	LI	De	03.11.58 – 25.11.58
	LC	E	18.02.60 – 05.03.60
	LC	E	14.09.60 – 24.09.60
	G	E	24.01.61 – 25.02.61
	LC	E	21.06.61 – 06.07.61
	HI	E	26.09.63 – 02.11.63
80141	LI	De	01.12.58 – 18.12.58
	LC	De	24.11.59 – 24.12.59
	LC	E	09.12.60 – 24.12.60
	G	E	19.02.62 – 24.03.62
	LC	E	17.06.64 – 11.08.64
	RET	E	25.11.64 – 08.12.64
80142	RET	B	26.09.56 – 06.10.56
	LI	De	22.10.58 – 20.11.58
	LC	De	25.11.59 – 18.12.59
	LC	A	11.04.60 – 30.04.60
	NC	E	01.11.60 – 19.11.60
	G	E	26.04.62 – 26.05.62
	LI	E	26.10.64 – 02.12.64
80143	LI	De	14.10.58 – 04.11.58
	LC	E	05.02.60 – 13.02.60
	LI	E	04.11.60 – 26.11.60
	G	E	06.05.63 – 01.06.63
80144	LI	De	14.10.58 – 30.10.58
	LC	De	28.07.59 – 20.08.59
	G	E	23.11.60 – 31.12.60
	LI	E	05.03.63 – 06.04.63
80145	LI	A	12.03.59 – 11.04.59
	G	E	04.10.61 – 04.11.61
	HI	E	14.05.64 – 19.06.64
80146	LC	B	08.05.57 – 14.05.57
	LI	E	12.01.59 – 31.01.59
	LI	E	06.12.60 – 31.12.60
	G	E	30.05.63 – 03.08.63
80147	LC	B	22.03.57 – 27.03.57
	LC	B	09.07.57 – 26.08.57
	LI	E	25.05.59 – 06.06.59
	LI	E	09.08.60 – 27.08.60
	G	E	19.03.62 – 14.04.62
	LC	E	27.06.63 – 05.07.63
80148	LI	A	18.11.58 – 13.12.58
	G	E	02.06.61 – 06.07.61

80149	LC	B	11.12.57 – 18.12.57			LC	E	17.01.63 – 02.02.63
	LI	E	23.03.59 – 11.04.59			HI	E	18.02.64 – 28.03.64
	G	E	08.12.61 – 20.01.62		80153	LC	B	31.12.57 – 03.01.58
80150	LC	B	19.11.57 – 13.12.57			LI	E	25.03.59 – 18.04.59
	LI	E	27.04.60 – 14.05.60			LC	A	05.04.60
	LC	E	12.09.62 – 27.10.62			G	E	18.04.62 – 19.05.62
	G	E	24.07.63 – 03.08.63			LC	E	28.07.64 – 19.08.64
	LC	E	23.09.63 – 04.10.63		80154	LI	E	16.06.59 – 04.07.59
80151	LC	B	26.05.57 – 28.06.57			NC	E	12.08.60 – 20.08.60
	LC	A	23.10.58 – 08.11.58			LI	E	16.11.61 – 16.12.61
	G	E	09.02.62 – 05.03.62			NC	E	10.04.63 – 19.04.63
	LC	E	01.10.64 – 02.11.64			NC	E	10.06.63 – 14.06.63
80152	LI	A	28.01.59 – 21.02.59			HI	E	20.04.64 – 13.06.64
	G	E	14.06.61 – 05.08.61					

An overcast day saw 84015 about to leave Barnoldswick with the very last passenger train on the branch for the short journey back to Earby on 25th September 1965. The train had previously arrived as the 11.45am, Saturdays only from Earby and normally would have returned ECS, but as a last day concession, it made the return journey as a service train. Following this 84015, together with sister engine 84028, were placed in store at Skipton shed and in November 1965 were earmarked, with others, for potential use on the Isle of Wight. In the event this never happened and 84015 and others of the class were withdrawn in December 1965.

Hugh Ballantyne

No.	1	2	3		No.	1	2	3
						LC	Os	01.01.60 – 08.01.60
						G	C	28.02.64 – 21.04.64
82000	HI	S	26.07.54 – 20.09.54					
	HG	S	06.08.56 – 25.10.56		82010	HC	S	21.11.53 – 23.12.53
	LC	Os	05.05.58 – 06.06.58			HI	S	02.12.54 – 07.02.55
	HI	W	08.12.59 – 10.02.60			LI	E	13.11.56 – 01.12.56
	G	C	03.10.63 – 03.12.63			G	E	02.07.58 – 16.08.58
						G	E	28.09.60 – 29.10.60
82001	LC	S	22.03.54 – 21.05.54					
	U	Ba	27.08.54		82011	NC	S	16.03.54 – 09.04.54
	HI	S	23.04.55 – 21.06.55			HI	S	18.01.55 – 15.03.55
	HG	S	21.10.57 – 30.12.57			G	E	22.08.57 – 14.09.57
	U	Ba	11.03.58 – 11.03.58			HI	E	27.02.59 – 21.03.59
	HI	W	15.06.60 – 19.08.60			LI	E	08.03.61 – 08.04.61
	HG	C	03.06.63 – 19.07.63			LI	E	25.09.62 – 10.11.62
82002	HG	S	06.02.58 – 21.04.58		82012	U	E	10.11.53 – 14.11.53
	NC	W	02.04.60 – 19.08.60			HI	S	12.03.55 – 11.05.55
	LC	W	15.09.60 – 10.10.60			G	E	17.10.57 – 16.11.57
	NR	W	04.11.60 – 02.12.60			NC	E	27.11.59 – 28.11.59
						HI	E	09.12.60 – 07.01.61
82003	HI	S	17.05.54 – 06.08.54			LC	E	17.08.61 – 26.08.61
	HG	S	25.02.57 – 07.05.57					
	C	W	25.11.58 – 23.12.58		82013	HI	S	03.02.55 – 16.05.55
	HI	W	23.12.59 – 18.02.60			LI	E	09.01.57 – 01.02.57
	HI	W	22.03.60 – 30.03.60			G	E	08.08.58 – 06.09.58
	LC	W	01.07.60 – 12.08.60			LI	E	30.11.60 – 17.12.60
	G	C	12.02.64 – 07.04.64			NC	E	25.10.61 – 08.11.61
82004	HI	S	28.09.54 – 26.11.54		82014	NC	E	17.11.53 – 21.11.53
	HG	S	30.01.57 – 05.04.57			LC	Fr	04.11.54 – 27.11.54
	LI	Ba	30.04.57 – 06.06.57			LC	Bk	11.08.55 – 08.09.55
	LC	W	22.12.58 – 05.03.59			LI	E	18.01.57 – 09.02.57
	HC	W	19.08.59 – 25.09.59			G	E	21.08.58 – 20.09.58
						LI	E	17.01.61 – 04.02.61
82005	LC	S	21.04.54 – 09.06.54			LC	E	08.09.61 – 23.09.61
	HI	S	31.03.55 – 27.06.55			LC	E	14.01.63 – 24.01.63
	LC	Ba	13.06.57 – 12.07.57					
	HG	S	15.03.58 – 05.06.58		82015	NC	E	27.11.53 – 03.12.53
	LC	W	25.09.59 – 26.11.59			LC	Fr	27.09.54 – 15.10.54
	HC	W	20.04.60 – xx.xx.xx			LC	S	23.09.55 – 21.11.55
	I	C	18.04.63 – 16.05.63			HI	E	11.11.56 – 08.12.56
						G	E	06.10.58 – 11.11.58
82006	–	–	Data not traced			NC	E	01.09.60 – 03.09.60
						LC	E	20.02.61 – 04.03.61
82007	HI	S	05.08.54 – 04.10.54			LI	E	01.08.61 – 01.09.61
	HG	S	26.11.56 – 06.02.57					
	LC	W	01.05.58 – 03.06.58		82016	NC	E	07.12.53 – 11.12.53
	U	Bb	22.10.59 – 05.04.59			LC	S	03.08.54 – 14.10.54
						LC	Na	18.04.55 – 27.05.55
82008	LC	Cf	11.06.54 – 19.08.54			HI	S	11.03.56 – 16.05.56
	HI	S	08.09.55 – 04.11.55			G	E	02.09.58 – 27.09.58
	HC	W	09.09.57 – 08.10.57			LI	E	03.07.61 – 12.08.61
	U	Wo	27.08.58 – 18.09.58			LC	E	01.02.63 – 21.02.63
	HI	W	27.09.59 – 06.08.59					
					82017	HI	S	10.11.54 – 21.01.55
82009	HI	S	26.01.55 – 24.03.55			LI	E	05.10.56 – 27.10.56
	HG	S	15.03.57 – 24.05.57			G	E	24.03.58 – 25.04.58
	U	We	09.04.58 – 03.05.58			LI	E	25.07.60 – 13.08.60
	HI	W	20.08.59 – 09.10.59			LI	E	05.07.62 – 18.08.62
						LC	E	25.11.63 – 06.12.63

82018	HI	S	10.01.55 – 03.03.55
	G	E	05.03.57 – 30.03.57
	HI	E	19.03.59 – 11.04.59
	G	E	14.04.61 – 13.05.61
	LI	E	14.12.64 – 05.02.65
82019	HI	S	21.02.55 – 11.05.55
	LC	S	14.02.56 – 23.05.56
	G	E	06.02.57 – 02.03.57
	HI	E	16.04.59 – 02.05.59
	NC	E	03.12.59 – 12.12.59
	LI	E	04.05.61 – 27.05.61
	LC	E	02.10.62 – 20.10.62
	G	E	02.04.64 – 16.05.64
82020	NC	Da	26.06.57 – 29.06.57
	HI	S	14.05.58 – 31.07.58
82021	HI	S	09.04.58 – 19.06.58
	U	Os	16.03.60 – 30.03.60
82022	LI	E	21.03.57 – 12.04.57
	LI	E	29.04.59 – 16.05.59
	G	E	16.11.60 – 17.12.60
	LC	E	31.08.61 – 16.09.61
	LC	E	23.01.63 – 02.02.63
	LI	E	19.11.63 – 21.12.63
82023	LI	E	21.02.57 – 16.03.57
	G	E	26.03.59 – 18.04.59
	LI	E	12.06.61 – 07.07.61
	G	E	11.03.63 – 06.04.63
82024	LI	E	12.12.56 – 11.01.57
	LI	E	12.09.58 – 04.10.58
	G	E	14.10.60 – 19.11.60
	G	E	03.12.62 – 19.01.63
82025	LI	E	25.04.57 – 16.05.57
	G	E	26.05.59 – 20.06.59
	NC	E	18.01.60 – 28.01.60
	G	E	31.05.61 – 24.06.61
82026	LI	Da	26.11.57 – 28.12.57
	G	Da	12.12.61 – 10.02.62
82027	HI	Da	24.06.57 – 15.08.57
	HC	Da	04.03.60 – 20.05.60
	LI	Da	12.09.60 – 28.10.60
	NC	Da	26.01.62 – 12.02.62
	LC	E	05.11.63 – 27.11.63
	LC	E	06.04.64 – 29.04.64
82028	LI	Da	22.11.56 – 28.12.56
	G	Da	13.08.59 – 02.10.59
	HI	E	05.11.63 – 30.11.63
82029	LI	Da	24.09.56 – 30.10.56
	G	Da	30.05.60 – 19.08.60
	LC	E	13.11.63 – 07.12.63
	LC	E	03.12.64 – 01.01.65
82030	LC	S	08.12.55 – 21.02.56
	HI	S	27.04.57 – 14.08.57
	HG	S	11.08.59 – 21 10.59
	LC	Cy	07.09.60 – 05.10.60
	LC	C	20.08.63 – 27.09.63
82031	LC	W	04.09.56 – 21.09.56
	HI	S	25.09.58 – 11.12.58
	LI	E	04.08.64 – 11.09.64
82032	LI	Ba	06.02.57 – 08.03.57
	HI	S	13.01.58 – 03.03.58
	U	Ba	28.04.58
	HG	S	15.12.60 – 28.02.61
82033	LC	Ba	03.12.56 – 11.01.57
	U	Ba	25.04.58
	HI	S	20.05.58 – 01.09.58
	HI cont.	S	15.10.58 – 18.11.58
82034	LC	Ba	10.09.57 – 01.10.57
	U	Ba	25.04.58
	HC	S	19.06.58 – 16.09.58
	HC	S	18.10.60 – 09.12.60
	I	C	02.12.64 – 16.01.65
82035	LI	Ba	16.05.57 – 20.06.57
	U	Ba	19.03.58
	HG	S	30.04.58 – 30.06.58
82036	LI	Ba	08.02.57 – 18.05.57
	HI	S	01.09.58 – 31.10.58
	HC	W	22.11.60 – 03.02.61
82037	LI	Ba	19.02.57 – 05.04.57
	HI	S	20.09.58 – 15.12.58
	U	Bb	31.12.59 – 15.01.60
82038	HI	S	16.04.57 – 09.08.57
	U	Sa	20.10.59 – 03.11.59
	HG	Bb	01.12.59 – 15.01.60
82039	-	-	Data not traced
82040	LI	Ba	28.05.57 – 05.07.57
	HI	S	03.11.58 – 06.01.59
82041	HI	S	05.10.57 – 10.12.57
	U	Bg	13.11.59 – 05.12.59
	U	Br	11.02.60 – 26.02.60
82042	LI	Ba	07.08.57 – 05.09.57
	HI	S	20.04.59 – 01.07.59
82043	LI	Ba	09.04.57 – 15.05.57
	U	Ba	02.04.58
	HG	S	27.11.58 – 26.01.59
	LC	Na	26.02.59 – 06.03.59
82044	LI	Ba	21.06.57 – 19.07.57
	HI	W	25.08.59 – 30.10.59

No.	1	2	3
84000	LI	C	10.12.56 – 05.01.57
	LC	C	11.08.58 – 28.08.58
	HG	C	28.07.60 – 01.09.60
84001	–	–	Data not traced
84002	LC	C	28.12.53 – 20.01.54
	LI	C	05.06.56 – 28.06.56
	HG	C	06.08.58 – 29.08.58
	LC	C	13.04.60 – 10.05.60
84003	C	C	20.08.53
	LI	C	18.12.56 – 18.01.57
	HC	C	18.03.57 – 18.05.57
	LC	C	27.10.58 – 13.11.58
	HG	C	29.11.60 – 04.01.61
	NC(AWS)	C	24.12.62 – 17.01.63
84004	LI	C	22.02.57 – 15.03.57
	HG	C	25.03.59 – 17.04.59
	LC	C	19.10.59 – 18.11.59
84005	HI	C	24.04.56 – 16.05.56
	HG	C	14.08.58 – 12.09.58
	LC	C	01.09.61 – 04.10.61
84006	HG	C	10.03.58 – 03.04.58
84007	HG	C	25.08.58 – 26.09.58
84008	HI	C	27.01.58 – 21.02.58
	HG	C	11.01.60 – 13.02.60
	LI	C	07.01.64 – 07.02.64
84009	I	C	19.07.56 – 08.08.56
	LC	Da	28.07.58 – 30.09.58
	LC	Da	25.08.59 – 14.10.59
	G	Da	27.10.60 – 03.12.60
84010	LC	C	29.03.54 – 27.04.54
	LI	C	20.11.57 – 14.12.57
	HG	C	14.09.60 – 13.10.60
84011	LI	C	13.11.59 – 07.12.59
	HG	C	19.09.60 – 08.12.60
84012	LI	C	11.11.57 – 07.12.57
	HG	C	16.09.60 – 21.10.60
	LC	C	11.02.61 – 06.03.61
84013	HI	C	15.01.58 – 18.02.58
	HG	C	14.09.60 – 25.10.60
84014	LI	C	16.06.56 – 18.07.56
	HG	C	23.01.60 – 03.03.60
84015	LI	C	11.12.57 – 11.01.58
	HG	C	03.10.60 – 10.01.61
84016	LI	C	15.03.57 – 18.04.57
	LC	C	13.11.58 – 19.12.58
	HG	C	07.10.60 – 28.11.60
84017	LI	C	19.03.57 – 18.04.57
	LC	C	27.05.57 – 20.06.57
	LC	C	07.06.58 – 08.07.58
	HG	C	27.02.60 – 30.08.60
84018	HI	C	20.08.56 – 24.09.56
	LC	C	12.09.57 – 12.10.57
	HG	C	24.10.60 – 22.12.60
84019	–	–	Data not traced
84020	LI	E	18.01.60 – 13.02.60
	HC	E	15.04.60 – 30.04.60
	HG	E	13.04.61 – 13.05.61
84021	NC	Da	29.04.57 – 01.05.57
	LI	E	02.10.59 – 24.10.59
	NC	E	14.12.59 – 24.12.59
84022	LC	A	23.01.59 – 21.02.59
	LI	E	16.06.60 – 30.07.60
84023	AD	Da	30.04.57 – 07.05.57
	LI	E	12.10.59 – 07.11.59
84024	LI	E	20.04.59 – 30.05.59
84025	AD	Da	01.05.57 – 10.05.57
	LI	E	08.09.59 – 03.10.59
	NC	E	21.01.60 – 28.01.60
	NC	E	18.04.60 – 04.05.60
	LC	A	07.06.60 – 02.07.60
84026	AD	Da	01.05.57 – 10.05.57
	LC	A	16.10.58 – 31.10.58
	LI	A	10.11.59 – 19.12.59
84027	LI	E	13.11.59 – 28.11.59
	C	A	23.02.61 – 25.03.61
84028	LI	E	14.09.59 – 03.10.59
	LI	E	21.06.61 – 12.08.61
84029	LI	E	10.12.59 – 02.01.60
	LC	E	24.03.61 – 15.04.61

TABLE 6.9
Repair Tables Column Key

Column 1 – Repair Classification		Column 2 – Repair Location		Column 3 – Date Repair Period. Dates either 'On Works' or 'Stopped'
AD	Adjustment (= Rectification)	A	Ashford Works	
ATC	Automatic Train Control	B	Brighton Works	
AWS	Automatic Warning System	Ba	Bricklayers Arms	
		Bb	Bristol Bath Road	
BLR	Boiler repair	Bg	Bath Green Park	
		Bn	Bolton	
C or Cas	Casual	Bo	Bow Works	
CB	Boiler change	Br	Bristol Barrow Road	
CD	Collision Damage	Bs	Brighton MPD	
		By	Barry	
Dg	Drawbar gear	C	Crewe Works	
		Cf	Cardiff	
EO	Executive Order	Ch	Chester	
		Cn	Croes Newydd	
G	General	Co	Cowlairs Works	
		Cy	Caerphilly Works	
H	Heavy	Da	Darlington Works	
HB	Hand Brake	De	Derby Works	
HC	Heavy Casual	Do	Doncaster Works	
HG	Heavy General			
HI	Heavy Intermediate	E	Eastleigh Works	
		Ej	Ebbw Junction	
I	Intermediate	Ex	Exeter	
		Fr	Fratton	
L	Light			
LC	Light Casual	G	Gateshead	
LI	Light Intermediate	Gb	Gloucester Barnwood	
M	Modification	H	Horwich Works	
NC	Non Classified	Hd	Hereford	
NC(R)	Non Classified Rectification			
NM	Non Classified Modification	In	Inverurie Works	
NR	Non Classified Rectification			
		Kx	Kings Cross	
P	Pistons			
PV	Pistons and Valves	Ly	Llanelly	
Rect.	Rectification	N	Nottingham	
RET	Return (= Rectification)	Na	Newton Abbot	
RG	Reversing gear	Ne	Neasden	
RS	Reversing shaft			
RVC	Regulator valve change	Oo	Old Oak Common	
		Os	Oswestry	
SI	Speed indicator	Ox	Oxford	
SU	Superheater header			
		Pe	Perth	
T	Tender	Pl	Plaistow	
TB	Tender Brake			
TK	Tank	R	St. Rollox Works	
TO	Tender Only	Re	Redhill	
Ty	Tyres	Ru	Rugby Works	
U	Unclassified	S	Swindon Works	
UC	Unclassified	Sa	Shrewsbury	
USX	Ultrasonic Axle Test	Se	Stewarts Lane	
		Sp	Bristol St. Philips Marsh	
V	Valves	Ss	Swindon MPD	
		St	Stratford Works	
W	Weighing	Ty	Tyseley	
Wh	Wheels			
		W	Wolverhampton Stafford Road Works	
XS	Special attention ?	We	Wellington	
		Wo	Worcester	

Engine No	Boiler No.	Fitting Date
73005	841N	20.06.51
73006	842N	28.06.51
73007	843N	09.07.51
73008	844N	13.07.51
73009	845N	19.07.51
	841	Date not traced
73021	837	15.02.60
73023	847	12.07.62
73030	1910	01.07.60
73050	966N	14.04.54
73059	1619	27.12.60
73068	1171N	13.08.54
73081	1496N	17.06.55
	1909	25.01.63
73082	1620	07.11.61
73085	1497N	24.06.55
73112	1500N	07.08.55
73115	1621N	22.10.55
73127	1002	22.12.62
73128	1768	25.01.64
73135	1784	17.12.63
73143	865	21.11.63
73144	1764	25.10.63
73145	1750	01.04.64
73146	1770N	24.01.57
73147	1771N	12.01.57
73148	1772N	13.02.57
73149	1773N	07.03.57
73150	1774N	20.03.57
73151	1775N	04.04.57
73152	1776N	18.04.57
73153	1777N	09.05.57
73154	1778N	24.05.57
73156	1779N	14.06.57
73158	1498	15.12.61
	1781	01.06.62

N: fitted from new

7. AMENDMENTS TO PREVIOUS VOLUMES

7.1 VOLUME ONE
BACKGROUND TO STANDARDISATION AND THE PACIFIC CLASSES

Page iii. The poster illustrated is believed to date from between mid-1954 and early 1956 due to the combination of locomotives illustrated and the liveries carried.

Page 2. Contents section 9.2 commences at p.135 (not p.134).

Page 4. RH column, first line: amend 'Page 7' to read 'Page 6'.

Page 6. Add to list of abbreviations: 'ihp- indicated horse power'.

Page 10. Fig 3: The total number of Stanier class 5s was 842 (not 841).

Page 11. RH col, para 3, line 2: amend '1923-48' to '1923-47'.

Page 12. RH col vi: A second possible reason for the choice of the Laird crosshead was to ease the dropping of the small end during maintenance (no lower slide bar to obstruct this).

Page 14. In the table the cylinder stroke for the WD 2-10-0 should read 28. In the bottom line of the table, weights should be in tons/cwt and read '72t 2cwt, 72t 0cwt, 78t 6cwt' respectively..

Page 14. LH column, line 1: The twelve locomotives for the Kowloon-Canton Railway were 2-8-0s (not 2-10-0s).

Page 14. LH column, end of para 1: Four examples of the 2-10-0 type have been preserved.

Page 14. RH column, line 15 from the end, amend 'Linberg' to read 'Limberg'.

Page 17. Table 2. 94xx, the period of building commenced in 1949 (not 1948) whilst the number built should read '200'. Add to the table in the GWR section '0-6-0T 74xx, 1948-50, 20'. These amendments do not affect the total of locomotives built in the GWR section.

Page 18. LH column, para 1, last line: amend '1948-52' to 1948-53'.

Page 19. LH column: under the 'entirely new design' heading the Class 5 should be a 4-6-2, not a 4-6-0; similarly in the RH col, 3rd line from the end.

Page 19. RH column, line 3: 'bought' should be 'brought'.

Page 22. Those shown in the picture, left to right are: C. S. Cocks (LMR), J. W. Caldwell (LMR), G. E. Scholes (WR), F. C. Mattingley (WR), E. S. Cox (Executive Officer (Design)), E. Windle (ER/NER), R. G. Jarvis (SR) and W Durban (SR).

Page 23. Table: amend 'sanding brake gear' to 'sanding and brake gear', and 'two axle trucks' to 'two wheel trucks'.

Page 23. RH column, last line: amend 'Table 5' to 'Table 7'.

Page 23. Additional to final paragraph. An additional feature was the provision of several extra inches of unused travel on the slide bars. This was done to aid piston examination, which would otherwise have required the slide bars to be dismantled.

Page 26. The firebox maximum width for the 73xxx class should read 3' 11$^7/_8$". The barrel outside diameter for the

77xxx/82xxx classes should read 5' 0$^1/_2$". In both halves of the table in column 1, line 8 'Total area sq in' refers to the superheater.

Page 27. Section 3.5, 3rd line from bottom, 'fire' should read 'fine'. RH col, 9 lines from the end of the large paragraph: add to end of sentence '(except 71000)'.

Page 28. Both halves of table 6, column 1, line 4: the area should be in 'sq ft', not 'sq in'. Column 3, line 3 should read 1' 02 x 2, (not 1' 0" x 2").

Page 29. Table 7: data for Class 3 locomotives and subsequent entries - move all one column to the left. In 'Key' at base of table 'exhause' should be 'exhaust'.

Page 31. Fig 12, the locomotive is fitted with a 'tritone' whistle.

Page 32. Section 3.12. Amend text to read 'Table 10 gives a summary of the Standard locomotive classes.......the former railway companies are given in Table 9'.

Page 33. Table 10: Length over buffers for the Class 4 2-6-4 tanks should read 44' 9$^7/_8$".

Page 34. LH column, para 2, 3rd line from end: delete '15 Class 2 2-6-2T' and replace with '18 Class 3 2-6-2T'.

Page 34. 4.1.2) insert after 4-6-0s 'to be built, 73125-54'.

4.1.4) para 3, additional. Subsequently the 9F 2-10-0s appeared in unlined black. Applications of power classifications to locomotive cabsides appeared to vary with nothing on ex-works Doncaster examples through to e.g. 4P4F on a class 4 locomotive. It appears that an edict was issued sometime in 1957 or 1958 to require just the single number to be applied.

Page 34, Table 11:

　　1953, delete entry 71000 '1', add 1954 71000 '1'
　　1956, delete entry 84000 '10', add 1957 84000 '10'
　　1960, delete entries for 71000 '1' and 84000 '30'
　　Totals, add entry for 71000 '1' and 84000 '30'.

Page 35. RH column. In researching the information for Volume 2 it has been established that Ivatt Class 2 46413 was evaluated as apart of the 78xxx development programme. (See p.232, Volume 2).

Page 38. Lower photograph. Amend caption to read… 'last day of British Rail *scheduled* steam operations'.

Page 39. Upper photograph, location is Manchester Victoria, not Exchange. Lower photograph location is Salterwath.

Page 40. Lower photograph. The train is not the 5.45pm from Norwich. It is believed to be the 9.45am service.

Page 42. Upper photograph: the location should read 'Whitehall', not 'Whitehill'.

Page 50. Section 7.4, line 1: amend 'Hueson' to 'Hulson'. Section 7.5, paragraph 8, 2nd line: 'screw in the cab' should read 'wheel in the cab'. Para 9, end: amend 'section 8.7' to read 'sections '8.2 and 8.7'.

Page 51. RH column, Line 10: add 'and 10.3'.

73006 at Carstairs awaiting departure on the 9.25am Crewe-Aberdeen on 18th August 1962. The locomotive was delivered new to Perth in July 1951 and remained on the Scottish Region for thirteen years before being reallocated to Patricroft in July 1964. It was withdrawn from service in March 1967.   *Ken Falconer*

Page 52. RH column, Section 7.7: re names of 72015-24; it is now understood that F. A. Pope (a member of the British Transport Commission) did object in writing to the use of Clan names on the basis that these locomotives might eventually be allocated to any part of the system.
Section 8.2: the 'steam lap' figure should be '1 11/16'.

Page 54. Table of weights: amend as follows:

Line 2 Col 4: 21.80 to 21.08
Line 4 Col 2: 16.30 to 16.03
Line 4 Col 3: 14.30 to 14.03
Line 4 Col 4: 15.30 50 15.03   All weights in tons/cwts.

Additional - The Western Region gave the class a 'Red' route classification, this being the same as the Castles and Halls.

Page 57. LH column, para 1, 5th line from the end: add after 1959 'facing left'. There were two sizes of crest used and whilst the larger size was employed on the Britannias, at least 70003 was noted in October 1965 with the smaller size. Add to end of paragraph. 'Most Britannias carried the power classification '7' but some were noted with '7P' e.g. 70046 in 2/61, 70017 6/62 and 70052 3/67.

LH column, para 2. The change to yellow axlebox covers started about 1961. This change, which was not applied to all locomotives/tenders, is now thought to indicate that the axle boxes were filled with grease rather than oil. Only some locomotives had the subsequent red stripe applied, the significance of which has not been established. This applies to all the Pacific classes.

LH column, 3rd para from bottom: amend height of name-plate letters to 4".

LH column final para: the naming date for 70000 should read 30th January 1951.

RH column, para 3. The reference to Sir Alfred Tennyson should not refer to 'Lord' Tennyson. Sir Alfred was the grandson of Lord Tennyson.

RH column. Amended naming dates: 70001 6th March 1951 (also on Page 63 LH col), 70043 May 1957, 70044 to 16th March 1959, 70046 September 1959, 70048 23rd July 1958 (also p.63 LH col).

Page 60. Table showing Britannia Livery Modifications. Following reference to recently published photographs, information in the table has been updated as follows:

New Emblem Dates

70009 by 3/61; 70010 by 3/59, 70013 by 8/58;
70015 by 7/60†; 70022 by 4/59†; 70023 1/57-5/60;
70029 by 8/59†; 70030 by 10/58; 70036 by 4/61
70039 by 4/58; 70044 6/59-2/61; 70051 8/57-5/58
note †: probable date locomotive in works.

Route Discs

70018 5/60; 70023 12/51, 5/60, no 8/62.

Notes on interpretation:

Lined green cylinders. Dates shown are those noted on photographs. There were probably several other examples but this feature is particularly difficult to confirm on less than clean engines.

Plain Green. Only observations from mid-1964 are recorded which appears to be the earliest that unlined green was applied. Due to the generally unkempt state of locomotives after that date it is very difficult to be sure which livery was carried. Only dates from clear photographs are quoted.

Nameplates removed. It would appear from dates quoted that in fact most plates were removed at the end of 1964/early 1965.

Route discs. The application of these to WR locomotives seems (surprisingly) to have been quite random. In most cases they were not carried when new.

New emblem. This was generally applied from around 3/57 on repaint. Given the normal shopping frequency of the Britannias it is likely that all carried the new emblem from the end of 1960 at the latest.

Background colour to nameplates. It is suggested that all of 70050-4 were new with BLUE backed nameplates, the original entry for 70052 with a red backed plate then being incorrect. This had been deduced from the light background colour of the plate in a black and white photograph. In this context, see Fig.31 which appears to indicate that 70021 sported a red backed plate when new. An undated photo of 70011 also suggests a red-backed nameplate.

Page 63. LH column. List of locomotive names. Amend dates in 70048 name to 1908-1958 and for 70050 amend 'Forth' to 'Firth'.

RH column, para 1' line 4' amend '46' to '41'.

Para 3. The fourth locomotive referred to in line 5 was 70005 which went to the test plant at Rugby twice in 1951 (see 8.6).

Para 4. Last line: 'LMR' should read 'ER'.

Page 65, LH column, para 1. Additional - The journal of the Stephenson Locomotive Society at the time suggested that the loan of the three West Country Pacifics was to cover 70004/9/14 being used on the Southern Region.

RH column, Stratford diagram 4; the start time should read 10.30am and the finish time 3.56am.

Page 66. Norwich diagram 5, departure time for second working not traced.

Page 66. LH column, Stratford diagram 9, line 1. Insert 'to' after Liverpool St. Diagram 2, final line, amend to 4.45pm.

Page 66. RH column, diagram 2. Delete line 3. Diagram 3: add at start '10am Liverpool St.-Norwich'

Page 68. LH column, line 6. Substitute 'Type' for 'Class'.

Page 68. Diagram at bottom of LH column and top of RH column should go at the end of Stewarts Lane duty 4, 8 lines from the bottom of the RH column.

Page 72. Fig.41. The train shown is entering the docks and therefore the caption should refer to the Waterloo-Southampton service. Contemporary reports suggest that the engine subsequently fouled the docks platform precluding further use of the class on services to and from the docks.

Page 74. LH column, final para, line 3. Amend 70030-5 to 70030-3.

RH column, para 2, line 9. Amend to Mowbray (not Mobray).

RH column, 28 lines from end: 'down' should be 'up'.

Page 76. Fig 48. The single lamp on the locomotive suggests that rather than arriving at Paddington, it was on the rear of the empty coaching stock being towed to Old Oak Common.

Page 77. LH column, final paragraph. Delete the reference to Newton Heath locomotives working St. Pancras duties, these were always Trafford Park turns. Newton Heath duties took the class north to Glasgow replacing Jubilees and westwards to Southport and north Wales. The demise of the Longsight allocation was due to the electrification of Manchester-Euston services which started on 12th September 1960.

RH column, December 1962 allocations. 70021 add to 1A and delete from 5A.

Line 21. Amend 'engine' to 'engines'.

Para 5. The Polmadie Britannias worked primarily south from Glasgow on Manchester/Liverpool duties with less frequent visits north to Perth.

Reference the transient Neasden and Annesley allocations, these locomotives initially replaced five ex-LNER B1s on Great Central duties.

Page 78. RH column, para 4, line 1. Amend 41 to read 42.

Line 10. Add at end of sentence '(but see 70045 opposite)'.

Page 79. LH column, para 2, line 2. Amend Stetchford to Stechford.

Page 83. LH column, additional at end of first line. 70000/26/43/4 were the only class members that were not allocated to a Carlisle depot at some point in their service.

Page 83. RH column, additional exhibition appearances were, 70009, Marylebone 23/5/51; 70009 Eastbourne at the summer meeting of the Institute of Locomotive Engineers on 2/6/51; 70037 at Willesden May-June 1954 for the International Railway Congress.

8.4.1 Allocations. Additional. The LMR and possibly initially the Scottish depots under its control used 'four-week' accounting periods rather than calendar months for their locomotive allocation information denoted e.g. p1/53. The 'P' should be inserted in any LMR allocation where it has been omitted. Various contemporary publications list alternative versions of allocations. The authors have taken the view that to avoid confusion only dates gleaned from official records and those published in the *Railway Observer* will be quoted.

Add to 'N.B.' Where an allocation is shown as e.g. 04/51 – Stratford-Norwich the locomotive concerned moved twice in that period with actual dates not being recorded.

70025 6/57 - Cardiff Canton should read 12/52.

70043 P10/63 – Toton (on loan) should read P10/53.

Page 85. LH column, para 3' line 2: 'Coeur de lion' should read 'Coeur de Lion'.

Page 86. Fig.57. Add to caption 'and that grease is used for lubrication'.

Page 88. Table 1. Locomotive number should read 70035. At 8.4 miles, Needham: move both value entries in table one column to the right.

Page 89. Table 6:

    Hemel Hempstead, move both entries 1 col to right
    Bletchley, move Spd '77.5' 1 col to right
    Blisworth, move Spd '77' 1 col to right
    Colwich, move Spd '61' 1 col to right
    Blisworth, Distance, amend to '62.85'.

Page 90. Both tables, Garstang: amend distance to 9.5 miles. Table 8, run 1: Time at Oxenholme should read '41.55'

Page 93. Another reason suggested for the unpopularity of the Britannias on the WR was the left hand driving position which made the sighting of signals difficult. In order to avoid having to stop on banks when slowing following an adverse distant, Britannias were driven slowly uphill, hence losing more time which meant more paperwork, a further cause of their unpopularity.

Page 97. LH column, 8.6. 70005, additional trial date at Rugby was 7/51.

RH column, penultimate para, line 1. '3 miles' should read '3³/₄ miles'.

Pages 98/99. Figs 67-69. The carriage immediately behind the locomotives is not a dynamometer car although it may have contained some test equipment.

Page 100. LH column, para 1, line 5. '22 per cent' should read '22¹/₂ per cent'.
Para 3, line 25. '54 miles' should read '54¹/₂ miles'.
9 lines from end of para: amend '77' to '77¹/₄' and '75' to '75¹/₄'.

Page 100. RH column, para 2, 3rd line from the end: add a full stop after 'ihp'. Penultimate para, line 2: 'Liverpool' should read 'Liverpool Street'.

Page 101, table 15, column headings: amend 'Randane' to 'Rankine'.

Page 103 LH column. Additional. Close study of photographs shows that early engines have a larger diameter hole in the centre of the bogie wheels than later engines. It is not clear where the change occurs (probably from 70030 onwards) neither has it been established why it was done but it may be related to the wheel shifting problem where similar action was taken on the driving axles.

Page 103, RH column, 2nd line: insert 'centre' before 'driving wheel'.

Page 105, LH column, 2nd line from the end: 'new quite' should read 'quite new'.

Page 106, Fig 74: add to action 'In addition some Western Region engines also had the ejector moved to a lower position as seen here. Compare this with Fig 75, below'.

Page 107, LH column, para 6, line 10: amend 'two short stantions' to read 'a second short stantion'.

4 lines from bottom: add table number '16'

Additional/amended information. A recent article in *Steam World* magazine by John Pearse goes into considerable detail concerning the handrail modifications. Quoting from a list published over 20 years ago he asserts that five of the class that received the MR type modification did not have cups behind the handholds, these being 70017/20/4/8/9. Photographic evidence of this has been seen for 70020/4.

There is some doubt around the claimed modification of 70031 and further confirmation of fitting (or not) would be welcome. It would appear that only engines based at some point on the ER, NER or WR were modified. 70031 was always an LMR engine.

Page 107, RH column, para 3, line 3: amend 91,493' to 96,332'.

Line 5: amend '88,000' to '89,717'.

Para 4: In addition to Fig 52, see also Fig 51. Both show the AWS protective plate but in Fig 51 the signal detection shoe is also visible. For AWS-fitted engines, a vacuum cylinder had to be fitted, this normally being beneath the cab floor, but in some instances it was located on the right-hand running plate ahead of the AWS battery box. At least 70014/25/9/48 were so fitted.

Page 107, para 6, additional: At the same time the centre lamp bracket at buffer beam level was also moved to the right (as viewed from the front of the locomotive) to remain in line with the smokebox door bracket, see Fig 52.

Para 7, RH column, line 2: add after 1959 '(other than 70044 - see earlier)'.

Para 8: Delete reference to 'Scottish Region'. 70053 was allocated to Leeds, Holbeck at the time. 70001 (Norwich) was apparently sent north to compensate, being noted working the "Thames Clyde Express" at Skipton on 14th November 1959.

Page 108, Fig 76: In this view it would seem that the lining out of both engine and tender was still to be carried out.

Page 109, LH column, para 3, line 4: add after batches '(except 70025-9)'.

At entry for 70040-9, add to the end of this paragraph, 'see column, axlebox mod' in Table 16'.

70043, Add. This statement has been disputed, it being argued that the Westinghouse brake equipment was mistaken for a water heater by a caption writer for C. J. Allen's book *British Pacific Locomotives*.

P109 RH column final paragraph. re Sanders. A study of column photographs seems to indicate that where the sanders were modified on 70000-29 only the rear two sand box fillers received the extension pipe and thus the cover that stands proud of the running plate. 70030 onwards have three covers per side.

During the course of the research for subsequent volumes details of a number of the modifications carried out by the Southern Region have been established. Some modifications are common to all classes. The following is a listing of all the SR modification numbers encountered with details where known.

2081 Regulator valves and various boiler valves modified with 'special material' (stainless steel).

    2216 Grease lubrication modification (oil to grease)
    2237 Clack valve modification
    2243 Unknown
    2244 Unknown

2249 Unknown
2253 Unknown
2254 Split feed to side bars
2263 Piston rod, modified packing, same as Mod Ref 8895
2270 Not known
2272 Piston head modifications (3 rings)
2273 Pony truck axle guides
2276 Injector steam valves
2278 Provision of modified steam brake pipes
2283 Connecting and coupling rod bushes
2286 Wheel flange lubrication
2289 Manganese guide liners
2291 Modification of tender coal hole door plates for improved access
2298 Modification of BR standard firebars to permit improved steaming by reduction of clinker build-up
2303 Improved axlebox grease lubrication
2317 Coupling rod joint pin arrangement
2335 Unknown
2337 Unknown: applied to two Cl. 9F 2-10-0s, 92205/6
2338 Modification of boiler fusible plug system. Front plug: SR type, back plug; BR type.

Page 110, Additional: modifications recorded on 70014 were Mod 2263, M/C/L 1595 and 1825

Mod 3208: Amend cost to £33 14s 3d

Mod 3242: Amend 70000-34 to 70000-29 see Table 16

Mod 3329: Delete entry for 70052

Mod R4194 Delete reference to 'Table'

Mod R4341: add at end 'despite the fact that the latter four were never so fitted'

Mod E5173: Amend to 70045-54.

Page 111, RH column, 10 lines from bottom. Amend 'everlasting' to 'Everlasting' (name of company).

Line 4 from bottom: add to end of line 'least in part at'.

Page 112, LH column, line 3: '40ft/min' should read '40 cu ft/min'.

Para 2, line 2: 'UIG' should be 'UIC'.

Penultimate para: add after 70000 '(see Fig. 57)'.

Additional to final item 'reversing springs': see p.56, Fig 26, where the spring is clearly visible. Fig 36 on p.67 appears to show the spring covered. Presumably this modification was to stop the ingress of any item which might jam in the spring and render the reversing gear inoperable. This may be mod 3622, see p.110.

Additional modifications noted:

Problems were found with excessive flexing of the regulator control rodding. This was overcome by the fitting of two small brackets (see Fig 76 p.108), the first halfway along the side of the firebox and the second about one foot behind the second handrail mounting from the front of the boiler cladding. These were fitted from new on 70045-54. 70025-44 carried only the front bracket from new. 70000-24 were retro fitted with the front bracket and engines of both groups were subsequently modified to have the rear bracket added although it is possible that not all were so fitted.

At least one engine had a 'bracket' fitted to the cabside to carry the name of the crew - see fig 83. This was 70045 and the 'bracket' is visible above the seven and the first zero. Others that may have had this fitting were 70031/2/43/4/6-9.

70004/14 were fitted with bolts on the smoke deflectors to allow the emblem for the "Golden Arrow" to be carried (see Fig 88). Following accident damage 70004 lost these on the right-hand smoke deflector only after visiting Darlington Works in 1966.

70004 also appears to have two bolt heads on the smokebox door below the bottom door hinge bracket. Their purpose has not been established.

Some members of the class appear to have acquired an additional 'pipe' running under the edge of the left hand running plate. 70005 was so fitted but see also Figs 56 & 57.

Pages 114-115: Following a study of recently published photographs, Table 16 should be amended as shown.

70002 Handrail M by 6/59
70003 Front step mod 8/51-5/57; Handrail Mod M 5/57-8/62
70004 Front pipe 2/55-9/55
70006 Front step 6/54-2/56; Front pipe by 6/54; Lub. by 6/54
70009 Handrail M by 3/59; Front pipe 9/51-3/61
70010 Handrail M by 3/59
70011 Front pipe 4/52-8/53; Lub. 7/51-4/52
70012 Handrail M 2/57-8/59
70013 LMS ret. by 8/58; Front step 6/54-8/58; Handrail M 8/58-5/59
70014 Lamp bracket removed 6/64-8/66
70015 Front step by 5/60; Handrail W by 5/60; Front pipe by 5/60; Lub. by 5/60; Sander by 5/60
70017 LMS crank by 3/58
70018 Front pipe 9/52-4/55; Sander ??/52-4/55; LMS crank by 5/60
70019 LMS crank 8/60-8/64
70022 Front step 8/54- 7/57; Handrail W by 4/59
70024 Front step 8/54-7/57
70029 Handrail M 8/58-6/61
70030 Handrail M 8/57-10/58
70035 LMS crank by 7/63
70039 Front step by 4/58; Handrail M by 4/58
70040 Handrail M by 4/58
70042 Lub. pipe still fitted 9/55
70044 LMS crank 10/57-6/59
70050 Top lamp by 10/63
70052 AWS by 7/62
70053 Top lamp by 11/64.

There were a number of anomalies noted during the research, detailed as follows:

70023 noted with LMS lamp bracket bottom right with GWR at top by 7/61.

70031 still did not have handrail mod 8/62.

70023/34 still carried additional SR lamp brackets in 60/64 respectively.

70036 the front step mod top plate overhangs the vertical plate.

70042 originally had a vertical spike support for the front step (9/55) but by 7/62 this had been modified to the standard pattern.

70042 originally fitted with plain trailing truck bearings had roller bearings by 4/62. Apparently no locomotive subsequently appeared with plain bearings, so it was not a swap. Presumably a spare set was used.

Most WR locomotives had two bolt heads on either side of the smokebox door approximately at the level where a lamp bracket was fitted when lowered. The reason for this has not been traced. 70023 had them only on the right-hand side of the smokebox door in 7/61.

Notes on modifications.

ATC and GWR lamp bracket removal. It is believed that neither were removed prior to transfer away from the WR.

LMS return crank. Locomotives where there is no entry, appear to have carried the original pattern throughout.

Handrail mods, as per LMS return crank. No locomotives would have been modified prior to the date of the Didcot derailment.

Lubricator mods, it seems likely that this modification took place on all relevant locomotives within a few months of entering service.

Top lamp bracket. In general this modification appears actually to have taken place during 1964 or early 1965.

Page 116 Fig 81: Add 'The additional foot platforms are clearly visible on the rear of the tender (see 8.8.1) and compare this with Fig 80 above'.

Page 117, Section 8.8, final paragraph, additional: If the tenders mentioned as being paired with 70004/21 were from 9F 2-10-0s then modifications would have been necessary to match the height of the fall-plate between engine and tender.

Pages 117–118

Additional/amended data have come to light concerning tender pairings as follows:

Tender No.

726	70027	23/4/60
769	70016	13/4/66
770	70035	23/8/61
778	70020	31/10/59
779	70019 amended to 31/10/59 then to 70023 26/5/65	
781	70025	8/59
782	70025	10/12/56, amend 70022 to 8/59. Exchange with 70040 may have been in 4/65, not 4/64
844	amend to 70023 18/1/57 then to 70029 26/5/65	
845	amend to 70029	13/9/60
846	amend to 70029 6/10/56 then 70018 19/5/61, 70010 13/4/66	
847	amend to 70026 11/10/60, 70011 u/d	
848	add 70027 6/10/56, 70016 23/4/60 then 70024 28/4/61	
853	add 70039	23/3/65
854	70011	23/8/61, 70026 u/d
982	add 70050	12/10/66
983	amend: delete 70046 entry, replace with 70048 30/6/64	
984	add 70047	12/10/66
985	amend date of 70054 to 29/4/64	
988	amend date of 70051 to 29/4/64.	

The unique 71000 *Duke of Gloucester* at Ashby Jct., one mile north of Nuneaton Trent Valley station on the northbound "Midday Scot" on 20th June 1959. This title was officially conferred in September 1927 and over the years included portions in its formation for Blackpool, Edinburgh and Aberdeen. The title was lost upon the outbreak of war but it was formally given back in September 1949. The title was removed from the timetable in June 1965.

Peter Glenn

The swap of tenders between 70011 and 70035 took place at Norwich depot. Other tender swaps are suggested and indeed known to have taken place but the tenders concerned cannot positively be identified.

Page 119. Table re repair mileages: boiler lift mileage ER should read 184,817.

Pages 122, 124, 125. The following amendments should be made as follows:

   70008 column 4: mileage is 274,235
   70022 column 4: mileage is 302,271
   70023 column 5, line 4: amend 'S' to 'D'
   70026, delete reference to 70025 at top of RH column listing.
   70027 column 3: mileage is 136,188
   Col 4: amend 348,652 to 349,652
                435,851 to 436,851
   Col 5, line 4: amend 'S' to 'D'
   70028 column 5, line 3: add 'S'
   70046, delete lines 2-4 and replace with 'LI 8/57 C, HI 4/49 C, HG 2/61 C,
   LI 5/63 C, mileages not recorded.
   70052 column 4 amend 199.55 to 199,557.

Additional overhaul information has been supplied but mileages are not recorded. Some variance with the dates already published have been noted but in most cases this is thought to be due to one source quoting an arrival date whilst another is quoting a 'return to traffic' date.

70002 HI 12/56 D, HG 6/58 D, HG 3/60 D, HG 7/62 D, L1 11/64 C.
70003 HI 8/56 D, HG 3/58 D, HI 12/59 D, HG 2/62 D, HI 3/65 C.
70004 Also LI 5/59.
70005 HG 8/57 D, HG 5/59 D, HG 6/61 D, L1 2/66 C.
70006 HG 7/57 D, HG 12/59 D, HG 1/62 D, L1 8/65 C.
70008 HI 10/56 D, HG 4/58 D, HG 10/59 D, HG 12/61 D, L1 2/65 C.
70009 HI 10/56 D, HG 4/58 D, HG 8/60 D, HI 9/62 C
70010 HG 3/58 D, HG 9/59 D, HG 5/61 D, HI 4/64 C.
70011 HI 9/56 D, HG 5/58 D, HG 4/60 D, HG 6/62 D.
70012 HG 10/57 D, HG 11/59 D, HG 9/61 D, L1 5/65 C.
70013 HG 9/57 D, HG 5/59 D, HG 11/61 D, L1 11/65 C.
70014 L1 4/62 C, HI 9/65 C.
70015 HI 2/65 C.
70016 HI 11/65 C.
70018 HG 1/63 C.
70020 HG 8/63 C.
70021 HG 6/63 C.
70023 ? I 2/65 C.
70025 HG 12/62 C, ? I 12/65 C.
70026 HI 7/63 C.
70027 L1 10/65 C.
70029 HI 2/62 C, H1 12/65 C.
70030 Also HI 11/56DD, and HG 5/60 D, LI 10/63 C.
70031 HG 1/62 C, HI 6/65 C.
70032 HI 5/65 C.
70033 HI 11/64 C.
70034 HG 3/57 D, HI 4/59 D, HG 8/61 D, LI 11/64 C.
70038 HG 12/57 D, ? G 10/61 D, HI 12/64 C, HI 4/66 C.
70039 HG 10/56 D, HG 2/58 D, HG 6/59 D, HG 8/61 D, H1 12/64 C.

70040 HG 11/56 D, HG 7/58 D, HG 2/60 D, HG 6/62 D, HI 1/66 C.
70041 HG 1/57 D, HG 7/59 D, HG 12/61 D, H1 4/65 C.
70042 ? I 12/65 C.
70043 L1 12/61 C.
70044 HG 7/60 D, H1 12/62 C.
70045 L1 11/63 C, H1 12/66 C.
70047 ? I 6/64 C.
70048 LI 11/59 C, HG 12/61 C, L1 6/64 C.
70049 HI 5/63 C.
70051 HI 1/66 C.
70052 LI 3/65 C.
70053 HI 10/59 D, HG 5/62 D, LI 10/64 C.
70054 HI 7/59 D, H1 2/61 D, HI 10/62 D, L1 7/65 C.

'?' indicates severity of overhaul not specified. Casual repairs are not included in the list.

70036 was noted in 'ex-works' condition on 5/12/65. As this was at Eastfield and the locomotive carried 'Carlisle Kingmoor' painted on the buffer beam, this suggests a visit to Cowlairs Works.

Page 124, RH column, top line: delete reference to 70025. Move '70026' up one line.

Page 125, LH column: The HI overhaul given to 70026 in 5/56 was probably a full overhaul following the Didcot derailment but would have been booked to 'accident reapairs'.

Pages 125 and 126: headings for columns on boiler changes should read:

Engine Number
Boiler No. when new
Subsequent changes/fitting dates.

Add to 70013, boiler 809 7/57, 819 5/59.

Page 127, RH column, para 2: The maintenance of WR Britannias transferred to Crewe in 9/61 as stated, but this was because the locomotives were reallocated to the LMR.

Para 3: an additional works which dealt with a Britannia was Brighton, 70014 being recorded there on 16th July 1951. See also reference to 70036 at Cowlairs above.

Para 4, line 3: amend 1965 to 1966.

Para 7, line 2: substitute 'connecting rod' for 'coupling rod'.

Page 129, Fig 92: amend 8 am to 8.30 am.

Page 130, LH column, para 2, line 1: amend Ten to Eleven.

Para 3: rumours also circulated in South Wales as to who was driving at this time, it being not unknown for drivers to take a turn on the shovel.

RH column, line 17: amend 'from' to 'to'.

Pages 130 and 131, Disposals: 70025 to G. H. Campbell.

70018/27/36/54 'Inslow Works' should read 'Inshaw Works'.

70044 withdrawal date is w/e 29/10/66.

70045 date to traffic, speculation exists around the exact date to traffic for this engine. Official documents quote w/e 19/6/54. It was complete at Crewe on 13th June and noted at Birmingham on 18th June.

*Note (additional) The movements listed are for transfers with known dates. 70000 moved to and from Preston Park, Brighton, exact dates unknown.

Page 131, Section 8.13, line 3: amend 'June' to 'May'.

DUKE OF GLOUCESTER

Page 135, LH column, penultimate para, lines 6-8: Subsequent information suggests that E. S. Cox was involved in the Riddles design, to the extent that he proposed the use of the British Caprotti valve gear.

Last line: barrel should read 'ring'.

Page 137, LH column, para 1, line 1: frame plate thickness is $1\frac{1}{4}$" and spacing is 3' $2\frac{1}{4}$".

Para 4, line 1: amend 'everlasting' to 'Everlasting'.

Page 138, LH column additional. Presumably because it was not intended that 71000 work on the Western Region, except on a trial basis, it was not painted with a route colour code disc. However a WR working timetable shows that it was restricted to the same routes and tracks as a King and so presumably would have carried a Double Red disc if this had been applied.

Page 138, 9.3 Livery, para 1, line 4: amend 'BR1' to 'BR1J'.

Additional: The original power classification was applied as '8' but amended to '8P' before the locomotive's appearance at the International Railway Conference exhibition at Willesden.

RH column, par 3, line 1: amend 'Stetchford' to 'Stechford'.

Line 3: amend 'Cammel' to 'Cammell'

Page 139, Fig 104: photo is by G. Wheeler.

Page 141, run 3: On analysis of this log it would appear that the speeds quoted are, at best, maxima. Average speeds calculated show:

Cheddington-Leighton Buzzard 76.8mph
Bletchley-Wolverton 81.1mph
Wolverton-Castlethorpe 77.1mph etc.

Page 142: Due to the use of incorrect data for calculations by O. S. Nock the original table should be disregarded and the following substituted:

		King		Duchess		71000	
Spd	Steam Rate	ihp lb/hr	dbhp	ihp	dbhp	ihp	dbhp
30	20,000	1,220	1,025	1260	1,120	1,330	1,140
50		1,380	950	1320	1,010	1,470	1,080
70		1,430	650	1265	750	1,580	860
30	22,000	1,350	1,290	1400	1,265	1,450	1,280
50		1,530	1,160	1475	1,170	1,625	1,245
70		1,590	800	1465	930	1,750	1,040
30	30,000	1,870	1,640	1895	1,735	1,970	1,800
50		2,000	1,540	2070	1,765	2,220	1,850
70		2,020	1,190	2100	1,570	2,350	1,630

Page 143, Table, Run 1: Amend load to read '250/285'.

Page 145, LH column, line 6: Amend 'Kirby' to read 'Kirkby'.

RH column, line 5: amend 'Rated' to 'Rate'.
Line 8: amend 'valve' to 'value'.
Section 9.7, line 2: amend 'ATC' to 'AWS' and delete reference to LMS return crank fitting in para 2.

Page 146, LH column: The extended 'heavy general' time was probably due to the fact that there was no spare boiler for this engine and thus boiler 1603 was carried throughout.

Page 147, RH column para 3: In recent years the assertion has been made that the ashpan design fault was the prime reason for the poor steaming performance of 71000 in BR service. This theory has been rejected by the restoring group. The main reason for the improved performance is attributed to the Kylchap blast pipe.

Page 148, Paragraph 1: The Goodfellow tips fitted reduced the blastpipe area to 34.5 sq in.

Page 148, Preservation update. Various runs have shown that 71000 has performance levels at least comparable to Duchess Pacific 46229 *Duchess of Hamilton* and A2 60532 *Blue Peter*. Following expiry of its boiler certificate 71000 has spent a long time under going overhaul and further modifications at the East Lancashire Railway, re-entering service in 2004.

CLANS

Page 149, RH column: Adhesive weight should read 56t 18cwt, not 56t 8cwt.

Page 151, Liveries - additional: The class as built carried the first BR totem.

Sightings with the second totem were:

72000 not before 5/59
72001 by time of withdrawal
72002 9/57 and 9/58
72003 unique in class as retaining first totem to withdrawal
72004 1/57 and 6/58
72005 4/59 and 11/63
72006 7/57 and 8/61
72007 9/57 and 8/58
72008 9/57 and 4/60
72009 undated.

All were of the 'large' size. The class originally carried power classification '6' on the cabside. On some locomotives this was changed to '6MT' for a period.

Background colour to nameplates: in most cases the use of blue or red backing for nameplates has been determined by studying photographs. However, with black & white photos it is not easy to distinguish between blue and red backing colours (see Fig.119). It is believed that at least 72000-3/5/7-9 had blue backed plates soon after entering service. 72007 was reported with a red backed plate in 1962 whilst photographs on p.44 show 72008 (5/61) and 72005 (5/63) so adorned.

Photographic evidence shows 72009 sporting green cylinder covers with red lining in September 1962.

It has been suggested that 72008 had at least an unlined green cabside when seen in 1965.

Names: the naming ceremony for 72000 is given variously as 15th and 16th January with the majority of reports favouring 15th.

Amend the name for 72019 to read *Clan Douglas*.

Page 153, Section 10.4, para 2, line 3: amend 'eight' to 'six'.

RH column, end, Kingmoor diagram: It has been suggested that the parcels elements of this diagram are incorrect and that the duty involved working the "Northern Irishman" from Carlisle returning the next day's London bound train of the same name. It is possible that as the locomotives were new in 1952 the parcels trains formed part of the diagram but once confidence in the class was established this was amended to include the "Northern Irishman". The class certainly did work the train on occasions, a photograph of 72006 with headboard being taken on 20/7/59.

Page 153, LH column, running-in turns: the reports for 72005 (23/1/52) and 72008 (22/1/52) predate the release of these locomotives to traffic, therefore they should be deleted. Additional sightings may be added as follows: 72003 (17/2/52) Manchester Victoria-Blackpool, 72002 (2/3/52) 9.40 am Manchester-Southport.

RH column, penultimate line: for 'Filey' read 'Otley'.

Page 155, Figs 121/2: Close study of these photographs seems to suggest that these locomotives (72008/9) have had 'standard' whistles substituted for chime units.

Page 158, LH column: the reference to 72005 working to Bristol should state that the outward working was a through service to Paignton, the Clan coming off at Bristol. It set out on 8th July returning on 9th July.

72005 also featured in other unusual wanderings e.g. 1.40pm Llandudno-Derby (8/9/56) via Stoke-on-Trent and it also covered several duties at the southern end of the GC lines in December 1964.

RH column, final paragraph: amend Solway Ranger to read 'Ribble-Lune'.

Page 159, additional: Transfers to Edinburgh depots always were to provide motive power for the seasonal potato trains.

Page 159, Table; Eglington should be 'Eglinton'.

Page 160, Run 1: Beattock, amend actual time to '3.28' from '3.38'.

Run 3, Carstairs: amend actual time to '7.04' from '7.0'.
Run 4: Coal consumption per mile should read 28.2.
Upper table footnote: Abingdon should be Abington.
Lower table, LH column: move 'Beattock' and 'Carstairs' one line higher.
Eglington should be Eglinton.

Page 161, LH column: amend Abingdon to Abington.

RH column, Log: amend Greskin to Greskine.

Page 162, Log: In 'West Coast 4-6-0s at Work' by P. Atkins (p.33) it states that in reality the tare weight of the train hauled by 903 was 237 tons.

Page 163, table, Long Marton/72007 entry: remove '60' from 'scheduled' line.

RH column, section 10.7, line 3: amend 'everlasting' to 'Everlasting'.

Page 164, Modification R3208, 1st line: delete 'in'.

Page 165, Mod R4542: 72004 amend to 10/57.

LH column, fitting of LM return crank: additional/amended dates as follows:

72002 by 9/60, 72003 by 4/56, 72004 by 5/61, 72006 amend to 'by 4/56', 72009 amend to 'by 6/58'.

AWS: 72001 amend to 'by 9/60', 72006 amend to 'by 8/60'. Speedometers: 72000 fitted 'by 10/61', 72005 amend to 'not by 7/59', 72006, the works card shows the fitting date as 8/61; however a dated photograph appears to show a speedometer fitted in 8/60.
72008 amend from, not by 5/61 to '5/61-7/65'.

Additional information: regulator control rodding - see additional comments for the Britannias (amendments to p.112) 72000-9 as 70000-24.

Moving of the centre lower lamp brackets, additional comments as per p.107 (see also Fig.132 which illustrates this modification). RH col, 1st para: Add, undated, 72005-9 fitted with cabside bracket for Bryson tablet catcher. This was for working the Stranraer-Dumfries line, see Fig.134, protrusion just above cabside number.

Section 10.8. Tenders: additional - Tender numbers 1186-1200 were allocated for the subsequently cancelled 72010-24, five being of the BR1B type for 72010-4 with the remainder being of the BR1C design.

Section 10.9. 72000: 1958 HI, amend works to Cowlairs.

72001: amend last entry in column 4 - mileage to 177,099.

Page 166, section 10.9: 72004 HG date 2/61 should be 12/61.

72005: HI 9/58 was at Cowlairs (not Crewe).

72006: add HI 9/63 Cowlairs. column 4, line 4: mileage amend 264,482 to 264,532.

72007; from the time remaining in service it is likely that this locomotive received a HI at the end of 1963 or early 1964, but no record of this has been found.

72008: as per 72007, but probably at the end of 1962 or early 1963.

Page 167, Fig 133, 2nd line of caption: 'pistons' should read 'piston valves'.

Page 168, boiler records: 826 add '72006 5/61'.

832: amend to '72002 5/61'.
833: remove reference to 72002 U/D.
If the speculation on the shopping of 72007/8 (above) is correct, then further boiler changes may have taken place.

Section 10.10: 72006 amend withdrawal date to 5/66. Additional: 72000-4 were stored at Polmadie from 12/62 to 5/63 and at Parkhead 5-9/63.

Page 168 Additional. A scheme is underway to construct a new Clan Pacific in the guise of the cancelled order for 72010. A considerable number of parts have been acquired or manufactured although entry into service appears to be many years away.

Page 169, Line 3: amend initials to 'D.L.

Bibliography, Line 1: add 'The' in front of the book title.
Line 5: amend 'with' to 'in'.
Line 7, add: 'A Pictorial Record of' in front of the book title.
Line 8, add: 'the' in front of the book title.
Line 9, add after title: 'Volumes 1 & 2'.

Page 170: The last entry should read '4.15 pm Paddington-Penzance via Bristol TM as far as Plymouth North Road'.

Page 171, RH Col, section '20-24,000 mile examinations', line 7: amend 'Cottar' to 'Cotter'.

84001 stands in Amlwch station after working the 12.32pm service from Bangor on 12th August 1963. The branch to Amlwch which left the main Holyhead line at Gaerwen Jct. was opened in 1866 and closed to passenger traffic on 5th December 1964, although freight services used the line until 1993 together with the occasional rail tour. The line has been the subject of much interest as a re-opening candidate with a feasibility study into restoring passenger services to an intermediate station, Llangefni, having been carried out in early 2011. The section from Llangefni to Amlwch possibly could be operated as a preserved railway.

Noel Machell

7.2 VOLUME TWO
THE 4-6-0 AND 2-6-0 CLASSES

Page 16. Table 3, column 1: Programmme should read programme.

Page 20. Column. 1, paragraph 1: Chime whistles. In view of the unsatisfactory performance of the design, class members were fitted with the ordinary monotone whistle from 73090 onwards not 73100.

Page 25. Table 5. For 73165, delete 1453, 26.02.65 which refers to a tender number,

Page 26. Fig.9; the train is an Inverness-Perth local running via Grantown-on-Spey. It would probably be combined at Aviemore with a train from Inverness via Carr Bridge.

Page 30. Table 8, column 4, 73098. Although reported as carrying lined green livery from November 1960, this engine was transferred from Chester West to Polmadie in November 1958, only one month after the first BR Standard 5 4-6-0 to be painted in green livery. 73068 had had this applied at Swindon Works. 73098 does not appear to have visited a WR works during its lifetime; hence it seems unlikely that the engine ever carried a lined green livery.

Page 33. Column. 2, paragraph 1: The 5FA portion of the 5P5FA designation did not refer to the former LSWR power classification. The author is indebted to Mr. E. S. Youlden and Mr. Peter Groom for the following information. In the BR locomotive classification scheme the SR alone considered that the freight categories for Classes 2 and 5 were too wide-ranging and so split these into 2FA and 2FB, 5FA and 5FB, the A group having the higher number of wagons permitted for any given route; sometimes the last two letters were reversed and rendered as eg. 5AF. The criterion for assignment of classes to either A or B has not been traced but it may have been associated with braking power rather than tractive effort, or perhaps a combination of the two.

Mr. Groom confirmed that the LSWR power classification scheme was introduced in 1916 when Robert Urie was the CME. Engine classes were given a designation between A and K, with A representing the highest power. The letters were painted on the platform valance close to the front buffer beam and in Southern Railway days, most engines passing through Eastleigh works carried the code, including classes such as the Schools 4-4-0s which were of post-LSWR design. After nationalisation, this letter could still be seen on some ex-LSWR locomotives but by the early 1950s, if it was carried at all, it was likely to be on the cabside beneath the engine number. These topics are covered in an article by Mr. Groom in *British Railways Illustrated*, Vol.11, January 2002, Irwell Press.

Page 34. Column 1, paragraph 3. The Leicester Standard Class 5s had a freight diagram which took them to Carlisle throughout the mid-1960s. The engines were serviced at either Durran Hill or Kingmoor. At least twice, Kingmoor borrowed them for their Stranraer/Glasgow diagram noted in the section on the Clan Pacifics; 73003 and 73046 were the engines involved and were observed at Ayr.

Page 34. Column 2, last paragraph The engine 73008 probably did not reach Scotland at this time.

Page 36. Fig. 22. The train is an up postal, possibly the 15.30 ex-Aberdeen. This train was booked for a Polmadie Duchess Pacific as far as Carstairs.

Page 37. Column 2, paragraph 3. Although it stayed for a brief time only, Polmadie-allocated 73037 did cross the border and was used on similar workings to those featuring 73033-6.

Pages 39/40. The 8.46am Bradford Forster Square-Scarborough was EWD (each weekday).

Page 49. Column 1, final paragraph. On the Highland main line, the diesel classes operating were Cl.24s and 26s. The Cl.27s were at Eastfield and worked on the West Highland line to Fort William and Mallaig; the Cl.27s did not work to Inverness at this time.

Page 64. 73031. Although the Rugby testing station was closed in 1959, the engine does not appear to have been officially reallocated until much later but certainly by February 1961.

Page 71. Fig.62. 73170 is arriving at Scarborough, not departing.

Page 76. Table 11, column 2, WR. Some repairs to BR Standard Cl. 5 4-6-0s were carried out on an ad hoc basis until the end of 1965.

Page 87. Table 13, column 4, 73116. Although the engine was reported as named on 15th October 1960, at least one name-plate does not appear to have been affixed until 15th September 1962.

Page 82. Column 1, paragraph 3. The Corkerhill Standard Cl. 5s, 73079, 73100-4/21-4, were fitted at one time with the bracket on the cabside for the Bryson tablet catcher as used on the Dumfries-Stranraer line.

Page 91. Tables 14 and 15: Caxton Road should read Cuxton Road.

Page 104. 73119 was reported as being cut up at the yards of J. Cashmore, Newport.

Page 108. Table 23, column 9. The tractive effort for the BR Standard 4 4-6-0 should read 25,515lb and in column 10, the weight in working order should read 67 tons 18 cwt.

Page 119. Fig. 110; the train is leaving Oxford, not arriving.

Page 128. May 1961 allocation. Mold Junction allocation should read 75013/4/28.

Page 148. Table 34, column 2. WR. Some repairs to BR Standard Cl. 4 4-6-0s were carried out on an ad hoc basis until the end of 1965.

Pages 164/5. 75036/56 were both reported as cut up in the yards of J. Cashmore, Great Bridge.

Page 182. Column 2, paragraph 2. The author is indebted to Mr. Bill Hamilton for the following information. The Corkerhill group, 76090-9 were not used on passenger trains to Stranraer as this was a demanding route and Corkerhill by then had received its full allocation of Standard Class 5s, while retaining the Jubilee and Stanier Class 5 4-6-0s. The 4MTs were used instead of Standard Class tank engines on the locals to Girvan on occasion.

Trains to and from Stranraer were exclusively the preserve of Kingmoor and Corkerhill Class 5s and Class 6s. Similarly 76112 did not work passenger trains to Glasgow St. Enoch from Stranraer; Stranraer locomotives did not work north on any regular basis. The boat trains to Stranraer at this time were not regularly double-headed and that would be only between Ayr and Stranraer, probably only during Glasgow Fair. A relief would be far more likely to have been run at this time as a long, double-headed train would have required double draw-ups at intermediate stations, clearly an operational nightmare.

Page 193. 76010 first allocation 3.52 should read 3.53.

Page 212. Table 50, column 9. BR Standard 3 weight in working order should read 57 tons 10 cwt.

Page 219. Fig. 225. Caledonian Railway semaphores were carried by at least one of the BR Standard Class 5 4-6-0s,

73033, allocated new to Polmadie in 1953. A photograph of this engine so fitted and heading a Glasgow Central-Lanark local was published in *The Railway Magazine* Vol.99, No.622, February 1953, p.88.

Page 232. Table 56, column 9. BR Standard 2 tractive effort should read 18,513 lb.

Page 236. Some interchangeability did occur, see Volume 3, p.134; there may have been others.

Page 244 column 2, paragraph 4. Ex-HBR should read ex-NBR.

Page 251 col. 1, paragraph 3. Cl.26 diesels worked on the Waverley route, not Cl.27s which at this time were all at Eastfield.

Page 266. Fig. 279. 78022 worked for a period on the K&WVR whilst fitted with the Giesel ejector.

The RCTS ran the "Stainmore Limited" rail tour on the last day that the line was open, 20th January 1962. The special started from Darlington Bank Top at 10.46am calling at most stations west of Barnard Castle to Tebay, where locomotives 77003 and 76049 were turned and serviced. The train returned to Kirkby Stephen East and then headed for Penrith and Carlisle. The special did not leave Carlisle until 8.13pm to ensure that it was the last train to travel over the Stainmore summit and Belah viaduct. The train is seen at Kirkby Stephen East on the outward journey.

Gavin Morrison

7.3 VOLUME 3
THE TANK ENGINE CLASSES

Page 8, RH column paragraph 2, line 3: after '…high running plates' insert (except 78xxx).

Page 9, Section 1.2, paragraph 2, line 2, add at end of sentence 'but the thickness varied per class'.

Add after penultimate paragraph: Attachment of drawhook - this varied per class with both dragboxes and stiffened channelling behind the buffer beam being used. The Class 4 tank employed both stiffening at the front and dragbox at the rear. The Class 3 design used stiffening front and rear whilst the Class 2s employed dragboxes at both ends.

Page 9, RH column, paragraph 9, last line: amend to 'die blocks for the back surface'.

Page 11, Fig 5: The I3 classification was first given to the class by the London, Brighton & South Coast Railway, not the Southern Railway.

Page 13, RH column 1st line: The 'cutaway' was applied to all locomotives from 80059 (see following additional information on p.14).

Page 14, RH column, line 6: insert after a 953, '(and the later built 80054-8)'.

Additional: Lubricators - 80000-53 were fitted with Silvertown mechanical lubricators but 80054-154 received Wakefield lubricators. These were mounted on the running plate immediately in front of the side tanks. No doubt due to the need to have improved access for the Wakefield design, a small section of running plate edge was omitted from these engines (except 80054-8 built at Derby).

Derby had also been responsible for another variant when building 80000-9 where the casing covering the outer edge of the piston valve spindle was round, whereas on 80010-154 it had a flat section.

Page 16, Fig.11: Add 'rod' after 'piston'.

Page 17, main table: 80116-20 additional fittings - add 'Speedometer'.

80079-95, 80145-54: delete 'Cab lifting hooks'.

Page 18, LH column, 2.4 Boilers, paragraph 2: Amend total number built to 163, with the Crewe build being 20.

Add to list at bottom of page: boiler 1598, order 1357/1516, Crewe.

Amend Brighton build to show 1599, not 1598.

Page 19. Livery - additional. Although the new totem was first shown in 1956 it was not generally applied until 1957. 80154 was the only member of the class to carry the second totem from new.

Illustrations in Volume 3 showed various minor livery variations viz:
Page 10: 80140, Page 55: 80146, Yellow dot on bunker side.
Page 15: 80030, Page 26: 80070, Page 32: 80027, power classification omitted.
Page 63: 80154, Page 72: 80089, Page 75: 80143, Page 84: 80153, all show a yellow triangle on the bunkerside.

Page 84, 80101: Large numerals.

The photograph of 80089 on p.72 also shows 'electrification' flashes added.

Power classification, when shown, could be anything from '4' to '4P'4F' as close inspection of the various illustrations shows.

The yellow dot was applied to Southern region engines to denote that they were fitted with water treatment equipment. The symbol was later changed to a triangle to avoid confusion with the Western region route disc. This also applied to the 82xxx and 84xxx.

80000-9 had slightly different shaped numerals on their front number plates when new.

Locomotives repainted at Cowlairs received large bunkerside numerals and had the depot allocation painted on the buffer-beam.

Page 22, Fig 16: the perforations mentioned are air vents, not spray holes.

Page 23, RH column, amend allocations: Brighton, delete 80138.

Tilbury, 2nd line: should read 80100-5/31/2/4-6.

Page 24, LH column, storage dates: 1/8/62, delete 80079.

RH column, amend allocation, Shrewsbury: should read 80048/70, 80100/2/35/6.

RH column lower, line 4: WR to SR – amend date to '8/64'.

Page 25, RH column, paragraph 2, line 6: amend to read '…as in July 1962 80072 and 80131 were transferred…'.

Page 26, Fig.20: note that the speedometer is disconnected.

Page 27, Duties, additional: 80083/5 to Rugby 1/55 - these were for trials on Rugby-Peterborough services to see if they were faster then the Fairburn tanks normally employed; apparently they were not!

Page 41, LH column, paragraph 1, line 3: amend 80106-9 to 80106-9/15.

Page 43, LH column, 3rd line from bottom: for 1955 read 1965.

Page 45, Figs.49 and 50: Note modification to positions of front hose mountings to accommodate the fitting of snow ploughs.

Page 56, Fig.64: The location is Hammersmith and Chiswick, not Hammersmith, Grove Road.

Page 58, Paragraph 2, line 2: Delete 'being monopolised by' and substitute 'mainly in the hands of'.

Page 68, General, additional: Water tank filler caps. Both the Standard Class 3 and 4 tanks had a change to the method of securing the filler caps. During the production run. 80000-58 (probably) and 82000-19 (probably) had a screwdown type securing clip and an inverted 'u' shaped rest behind the filler cover to prevent it dropping on to the tank top.

Later engines had a toggle similar to those fitted to the GW 51xx tanks (Fig.93), the cover only falling back to an angle of about 45 degrees.

See Figs.35 and 140 and compare with Figs.18 and 88.

Locomotives to 80058 had wooden handles on the injector steam valves, later engines having four-spoked brass wheels.

It has been suggested that the bunker steps were wider on later locomotives but conclusive evidence is not to hand.

Page 68, bottom of LH column, AWS, additional: there were problems finding space for AWS equipment on this class. The SR put the battery box in the base of the bunker on the drivers side.

AWS fitting dates - amendments /additions

3/60 add 80138	4/60 add 80094
5/60 80038/41 80150	6/60 80068
8/60 80087 80147/54	9/60 80034/5/89 80140
10/60 80011/33	11/60 80036 80242/3
12/60 add 80138/41/4/6	
1/61 80017, alternative date	
to 2/62 as originally given	
3/61 80018/43/81	5/61 80031/64
6/61 80015/88	7/61 80013 80148
8/61 80016 80152	10/61 80014/39/40/2/65
11/61 80145	1/62 80019 80149
2/62 80010, alternative date	
to 8/57 originally given; 80066	
3/62 80084 80151	5/62 80067 80153
7/62 80137	1/63 80082
2/63 80083	4/63 80095

Speedometer Fitted

1/62 80019	2/62 80010 (not 8/57)
5/62 80011	8/62 80033/9
1/63 80037 (not 7/60)	2/63 80034
3/63 80018	5/63 80013
6/63 80032	9/63 80015/41
6/64 80016	U/D additional 80055.

Page 69, LH column - top: add heading 'Provision of New Type Pony Truck Lifeguards'.

Anti Glare screen: query on date for 80010, given as both 1/57 and 8/57.

Fitting of cab lifting brackets: amended data

6/60 80012/68	1/61 80017
7/60 80037	3/61 80043/80
8/60 80087, 80147	11/61 80145
9/60 80034/5	1/62 80149
10/60 80011/33	3/62 80151
11/60 80036 80143	5/62 80142/53
12/60 80144/6	
U/D 80015/32/42, 80138/40/54	

Briquette Tube Feeders - additional

4/54 80071	5/54 80076
5/60 80041	11/60 80036
3/61 80043/80	6/61 80088
9/61 80040	2/62 80139
3/62 80084	5/62 80067
1/63 80082	11/63 80065
80087/96-9 80100-5/31-4/6/43/7/8 remain U/D	

RH column, Removal of Water Pickup Apparatus: amended/additional data

2/60 add 80095	3/60 add 80089

4/60 80059	6/60 add 80012/68
8/60 80087	3/61 80043
5/61 80064	6/61 add 80088
2/62 80066	1/63 80082
11/63 add 80065	80103 claimed as ON 6/56, OFF 8/58

Manual Blowdown Valve and silencer

3/61 80043	6/61 80084/8
1/63 80082	11/63 80065.

Page 70 LH column

Snow Plough fitments 80004/5 80121
Tank Steadying Brackets 3/61 80043 (was U/D)
Two SR fusible plugs 1/63 80082 (was U/D)
Cab Gangway Doors 3/62 add 80119
Cab weatherboard mod 80094 4/60 (was undated).

Additional items:

DC 'U' bracket fitted 9/60 80034

Handrails by front steps removed
By 4/55 80032 see Fig 17   by 8/63 80141
By 9/64 80134   by 3/67 80143.

Additional bunker and front lamp brackets 4/60 80059. (this occurred soon after the locomotive was transferred to the Southern where extra brackets would be required for the route discs. Presumably the same modification was carried out on all locomotives transferred in but no other records have been noted.

Injectors: Add '★' at end of numbers for locomotives fitted with two 8mm injectors (80080, 80116/33/6★)

Section 2.8.1

Experiment 1323 (RH column) should be prefixed M/D/L and refers to 'Piston valve liners –shape of ports'.
Mod 2081 - it appears that this is the SR code for modifications STL 20 and 1384 carried out on other regions. Amended additional data:

M/D/L 1384 U/D 80037/8/9/41/6. 6/60 80068, was U/D (said to be ex-80038).

2081 8/59 – 2/62 80010   1/61 80017
additional 2/60 80085   off by 1/62 80149 (No record of fitting)
6/59-4/62 80147, mod 1384 also done with a valve said to be ex-80038.

2216 8/59 80010   10/59 80015
11/59 80014   1/60 80013

2263 see also HO8895 Page 69.
11/59 80014   6/60 80012 off at this date

2270 U/D 80015

2273 5/60 80012

2276 removed 8/59 80010

2286 10/59 80015   11/59 80014

2289 7/59 80154   U/d 80150/3

2338 8/61 80016 (not 12/51)   9/63 80031

Modification numbers 2081-2338 are in the Southern Region series. The same modifications could have been carried out on other regions under different reference numbers. Crossed out modification numbers on engine record/history cards appear to have three meanings

1) transferred to another locomotive,
2) cancellation (SR term or
3) conclusion (LMR/ER use).

Page 71 RH column, para 1: add to list of engines receiving a second overhaul – 80043.

Page 71 RH column, 80019 general repairs, sixth entry: dates to works and traffic should be reversed.

Page 74 Table 3, 80xxx Scottish: amend mileage to General Repair to '189,854'.

Page 77 Additional - 80132 was cut up w/e 2/4/66 at Eastleigh shed.

Page 78 Additional. Documents have come to hand which giving the selling price at the time of disposal for scrap. Prices paid include free delivery to the final destination.

80039 £2,678
80065 £1,895
80069 £2,746 (actual disposal point- Feltham, not Nine Elms as originally given)
80070 £1,970
80082 £1,895
80094 £1,755 (actual disposal point – Eastleigh, not Feltham as originally given)
80150 £2,215 (actual removal date 10.1.66).

Page 78 Liveries in preservation.

80002. When out shopped after its first overhaul it carried large numbers and large second totem. After its second overhaul it appeared with small numbers and small first totem.
80079 has also run in unlined black.
80135 has run only in lined green, although this has been in two distinct shades.

Page 81, Fig 76. This locomotive displays an 'additional' plate on the bunker above the bottom right hand step. It is believed it is simply a repair rather than a modification.

Page 84, Fig 82. The 'missing' bits are con rod, coupling rod, eccentric rod and return crank.

Page 89, LH column, line 12: No.4 should be No.2.

Page 93, LH column: Superheater Surface Area: amend to 82000-29/31-5 190 sq ft.; 82030/6-44 184.5 sq ft.
Section 3.3.1, Para 2, lines 4/5: amend to 'probably the first engine so fitted was 82000 in October 1956, see Fig 150.
Para 3: all engines had the LNER pattern return crank when new.
Additional: 82000-19 were fitted with Silvertown lubricators. Subsequent engines received Wakefield lubricators.

Page 93 RH column, line 10: delete 'bogie'.
Additional. The WR locomotives were classified as Yellow route engines. Despite the marginal extra weight of 82030/6-44, the WR working timetable carried a stipulation that these engines were not to be coupled to another member of the class when working on Yellow routes.

Page 95. Column 1, para 7: Transfer of boilers, 1105 1345/79 were transferred from Swindon to Eastleigh, the latter on 28/11/56.

82007 received boiler 1348 10/60.
82016 received boiler 1345 (probably 8/58).
82019 boiler 956: delete 'spare'.
Section 3.4 para 2: amend 1577-62 to 1577-94.

It has been suggested, but not verified during research for Volume 2 that boiler 1376 (Darlington) found use on 77001/3/4. It should be noted that the spare boilers for this class also formed the spare pool for the 77xxx.

Page 96. Variations in thickness of bunkerside numbers: see photographs of 82001 in 1952 and 1958.
Para 2: The second BR totem, introduced in 1956, was not generally applied until Q2 1957.
Para 3: Delete comments re totems carried by 82003/4 (see above).
The WR route disc was not carried from new, a later addition – see Fig.102 and others.

Page 98, Fig 107: 82029 carries 'large' numerals (see also Fig.118). Despite being a WR engine, 82008 is not carrying its route disc in 1958 (see p.85), likewise 82007 (p.89) and 82021 noted 8/60.
Fig.109: 82014 appears to have additional lettering in front of its power classification on the bunker.
Fig.110: 82024 carries a yellow triangle – see additional notes 80xxx.
Figs.108 and 140: 82006/9 are carrying electrification flashes.

Page 99, LH column, 1st para, additional: A route disc was not carried.

Livery data - delete all the information and replace as follows:

Engine	Probable Green Paint Date	Comments
82000	10/63	Lined/standard sized second crest
82001	11/57	Lined by 11/57/ standard sized second crest
82002	4/58	Lined by 29/9/63, standard sized second crest
82003	5/57 & 6/64?	Lined by 6/58. Believed to have carried small crest to withdrawal
82004	4/57	Lined by 8/58, standard sized second crest, Unlined, large crest by 8/62 (Also reported as first crest at 8/58!)
82005	6/58	Lined by 9/62, standard sized second crest
82006	8/57	Lined by 9/62, unlined 'economy green' by 5/65, standard second crest.
82007	1/57	Unlined, large first crest, later to second crest
82008		Lined, first crest by 30/3/59
82009	5/57 & 6/64	Lined, both first and second crests (standard size)
82020	9/58 & 7/61	Lined green/standard sized second crest, then unlined green, large second crest
82021	5/58 and 1961	Unlined green, large second crest by 9/62 Lined at 5/58 repaint

195

82030	8/57 & 10/59	Lined, standard sized second crest	
82031	12/58	Unlined, large second crests as at 1/62	
82032	3/58 and 1961	Lined, standard sized second crest and then unlined large second crest by 8/9/62	
82033	9/58	Lined, standard sized second crest then unlined green	
82034	9/58	Lined, second crest suggested unlined by 7/4/67	
82035	5/58	Unlined green, standard sized second crest by 29/10/62 Possibly large crest by 4/5/63	
82036	10/58	Lined, standard sized second crest	
82037	12/58	Lined standard sized second crest	
82038	8/57	Lined standard sized second crest	
82039	10/57 & 1961	Lined standard sized second crest; unlined, possibly large second crest by 27/4/63, crest by 4/5/63	
82040	1/59	lined, standard sized second crest then unlined/large second crest by 6/62	
82041	12/57	Lined, standard sized second crest	
82042	7/59	Lined, standard sized second crest	
82043	1/59	Lined, standard sized second crest.	

All the above liveries are taken from photographs. Unfortunately not all photographers were accurate with their dating. Any further accurately dated reports would be appreciated.

82044 received a hybrid black repaint on 20/4/63 when the running number was painted under on the cabside rather than the bunker (see Fig.106).

Page 99, LH column, section 3.6.1: amend Newton Abbot to Plymouth.

Page 101, Fig.111: It is believed that the unidentified 82xxx are 82028 (right) and 82001 (behind).

Page 105, Section 3.6.4: Duties from Exmouth Junction were Exeter Central-Exmouth, Exmouth-Tipton St Johns, Sidmouth-Sidmouth Junction, Exeter Central-Axminster locals and Halwill-Bude.

Page 106. The move of 82xxx to Exmouth Junction (first main paragraph) did lead directly to the transfer of 42072/2/93/4. It allowed locomotives to be transferred to other depots which in turn released the 2-6-4 tanks.

RH column, paragraph 2: 31613 is a U class locomotive, not a U1.

Page 109, LH column, line 14: amend Fig. 72 to Figs. 72 and 125.

Page 109, RH column, top:

Although 82020/1 were allocated to 70A it is queried if they ever worked from there as they were not sighted during the course of several visits at that time. One was sighted in store at Willesden on 9/5/65 but had gone by 22/5/65.

Page 116, RH column, line 12: Amend to read '....in June that year. Several of the …'

Page 118, Fig 139: The locomotive shown is 82032.

Page 126, RH column, additional information

Fitting of AWS

11/59	82012	1/60	82025
8/60	82017	10/60	82010
11/60	82024	2/61	82014
4/61	82011	5/61	82018
7/61	82023 (or 4/63?)	8/61	82016
9/61	82022	11/61	82013

Briquette Tube Feeders

1/60	82025	8/60	82017
10/60	82010	11/60	82024
2/61	82014	4/61	82011
5/61	82018	9/62	82015
8/61	82016	11/63	82028
4/63	82023		

Extra Washout Plugs

10/60	82010	11/60	82022/4
12/60	82013/20/2	1/61	82012
2/61	82014	5/61	82018

Continuous Blowdown Apparatus

12/60	82013/22

UK Piston Road Packing

2/57	82013	5/57	82023
9/57	82011 (or 3/59?)	11/57	82012
5/59	additional 82020		

Injector Overflow Pipe Mods

11/60	82024/5	12/60	82013/22
1/61	82012	11/63	82026/7

Speedometer Fitted

Additional U/D 82020	10/54-10/56	82021

Other Modifications

S/C BHP (abbreviation not known) 12/56 82015, 3/57 82018 W/SW/L/95, W/SW/L/96, 82030-concluded 15/6/61
Running plate cut away below mechanical lubricator: U/D 82004/6/10/1/4/9/20/1/3/9/31/2/5/9/40/3
Additional footsteps below smokebox located between main frames: U/D 82005/10-4/6/8/9/22-9/42/4
Transverse handrail on top of side tank at front, immediately in front of tank filler: 82000/1/3/4/5/7/8/32/5-44 (possibly fitted from new on 82035-44)
Longitudinal handrail on top of boiler: U/D 82000-7/9/20/1/30-5/7/9-43
LMS pattern return crank U/D 82000/5
Enlarged cab roof ventilator: U/D 82006. (See Fig 140 and Fig 118 for comparison). This was shown on drawing dated SL/SW/149 dated 21/6/65
Mod 2081 3/59 82011
Mod 2289 U/D 82023
Mod 2338 U/D 82011 4/63 82023.

Page 127, section 3.9: The SR 82xxx were the responsibility of Swindon Works until 1956.

Page 129. Disposal of 82001 was ex-Bath Green Park.

82029 departs from Waterloo on an empty stock working to Clapham yard in September 1964. The locomotive was delivered new to the North Eastern Region, being moved to the Southern Region in September 1963 to join other engines of the class working on duties previously undertaken by M7 0-4-4Ts and E4 0-6-2Ts which had been withdrawn. The workings were mainly empty stock movements and local freight and vans on the Western section. The background now is dominated by the train shed erected for the Eurostar service, now unused.   *R. C. Riley*

Disposal of 82021 may not have been from Nine Elms. It was at Feltham on 27/12/65.
Table: entries for 82000/3 in the 'contract no.' column should appear under 'sold'.

Page 130. Additional. Documentation has become available which gives information of the selling prices of some of the class when sent for scrapping at private yards. These prices include free delivery to the relevant yard.

82011 £1,430
82012 £1,431
82013 £1,432
82014 £1,429
82021 £1,720. Date of removal 12/1/66, actually from Feltham, not Nine Elms as originally given.
82022 £1,720 Date of removal 13.1.66
82025 £1,428
82028 £1,738 ex-Feltham, not Nine Elms as previously given.

There has been much discussion in the enthusiast press about the need to build new locomotives for various heritage railways. The 82xxx design is considered to be one of the most suitable for this work and the same group who are constructing the new Clan Pacific intend to move on to the construction of a new 82xxx as 82045.

Page 131, Section 4.2: add to end of 1st paragraph 'but some received it later, see Page 153'.

Page 133, LH column, additional: 84000-19 were built with

LNER pattern return cranks but 84020-9 were new with the LMS type.

Page 134, LH column, line 21: delete 'bogie'.

Section 4.4, paragraph 2: Amend 1107-27 to read 1108-27. The spare boilers for this class were also considered to be spares for the 78xxx.
It has been suggested that boiler 1275 from 78022 was fitted to 84009 in 1962.

Page 134, Section 4.5: The Darlington-built locomotives had the larger size of cabside numerals when new. 84025/7-9 at least later carried the standard size numerals. In addition to 84015, 84022-5 and possibly 84028 appeared in unlined black (84023/4 were recorded as such as early as August 1962 and 84025 was noted on 27/7/65). It is suggested that Crewe handpainted the locomotive numbers at times and that this is evident from the figure '8' on 84000.

The following variations can be seen in the various illustrations:

A difference in lining can be seen in Figs.157/8. At the point where the bottom of the side tank steps up, 84021 displays a more curved line than 84000.

Fig.158, 84021: probably the first use of the new totem at Darlington Works was on this locomotive, see the A8 tank in the background, also ex-works. This locomotive also shows the large numbers and carries no power classification (see also Figs.177 and 180).

Figs.171 and 172: no power classification carried.

Figs.183 and 185: Yellow dot under number – see 80xxx additional information.

Figs.182 and 184, 84015/25 both carry 'electrification' flashes.

Page 139, additional: The Neasden allocation of 84xxx worked the Chesham branch. 84005/8 were the first to arrive ousting 41270/2/84. 84005 was at Bedford by 12/61 and was replaced by 84006 which in turn was replaced by 84029.

Page 145, section 4.6.3, second paragraph, additional: 84020 was used at Bedford for two weeks from 14/4/57 whilst 'on delivery'.

Page 148, LH column, paragraph 4: 84020-3 moved to London from Ashford but after four months passed to Exmouth Junction. Their stay was equally short (according to official data) although some in fact stayed for an extra two months. Whilst at Exmouth Junction they worked turn and turn about with the Ivatt Class 2s on duties such as the Lyme Regis branch.

Para 5, Line 4: Amend 'May' to 'June'.

Page 149 Fig.181. The locomotive in the background may be 92024 rather than 92224.

Page 153, Additional/amended information:

Removal of LMS motor apparatus:
1/60   84029   8/61   84028
by 1963 84009

Front footsteps. Delete the listing and substitute:

Footsteps were provided from new on 84020-9. It is probable, but not confirmed, that all of 84000-19 were subsequently fitted. Two positions of footstep were noted (see Figs.157 and 166).

Confirmed fittings were:

Low:	84000 by 29/8/60	84004 by 9/5/59
	84018 by 8/9/62	
High:	84003 by 7/62	84005 by 4/61
	84006 by 1960	84007 by 13/6/59
	84008 by 14/7/63	84013 U/D
	84015 by 25/9/65	

In addition 84004 had steps on the sloping sides of the bunker (fig 172) and may have been unique.
Vacuum operated regulator removed: U/D 84020/8/9.
Grease lubrication applied to pony trucks: 84028.
Briqutte Tube Feeder fitted U/D 84028.
LMS pattern return cranks fitted U/D 84003/9.

84020-9 were fitted with additional lamp brackets on the sides of the smokebox from new for use on the SR (LH column, bottom). On some locomotives these were removed subsequently (see Figs.184 and 185).

Page 153, LH column, 9 lines from bottom: Heating surface. It is suggested that the amendment from 1,025 sq ft to 1,149 sq ft is in fact the inclusion of the superheater area (124 sq ft).

Page 153, RH column, Works visits: 84026, at least, received attention at Horwich. 84026/8 received attention at Crewe as late as 1964.

The record card for 84002 has been traced recently. This shows that the locomotive made four visits to Crewe for attention up to the end of 1960; these being 23/12/53-20/1/54 (LC), 5/6/56-28/6/56 (LI), 6/8/58-29/8/58 (HG), and 13/4/60-10/5/60 (LC). The date for the heavy general repair would suggest a minor amendment to the boiler change date given on Page 134.

Page 154, Update: Work continues on the project to construct 84030 from 78059. However an entry into service still appears some way off.

7.4 VOLUME FOUR
THE 9F 2-10-0 CLASS

Page 51, column 2, paragraph 4 under Brakes; the WR 9F 2-10-0s were fitted with the WR vacuum ejector.

Page 73. Fig. 64 and page 270, column 2, paragraph 4; the photographer Mr. Hugh Ballantyne, has confirmed that the lining for 92203 *Black Prince* was orange, not red.

Page 78, Fig. 70: The last sentence of the caption is misleading. The busiest period for the southbound workings from the Peterborough yards, including those to Ferme Park, was not in the 1950s but during the years of the First World War. It seems that the GN main line south of Peterborough was legendary for its congestion at the time with block to block working during parts of the day and night for many months. Timed departures from New England together with substantial direct traffic, mainly from Colwick in the East Midlands but also some from south Yorkshire, meant that movements of up to three trains per hour were occasionally reported.

Details of the Working Timetable for southbound Class E freights from New England i.e. those for which the 9F 2-10-0s were rostered, have been kindly supplied by Mr. Ray Townsin for the period 15th September 1958 to 14th June 1959. There were 13 weekday departures:

Reporting No.	Departure from New England	Arrival at Ferme Park
1017	04.43	07.20
1027	07.12	09.43
1129	07.40	10.30
1135	08.10	11.08
1139	09.15	12.2.
1149	10.30	xx.xx
1187	02.13	04.10
1215	02/40	05.50
1239	03.58	07.04
1265	05.28SO	08.30
	05.43SX	08.30
1287	08.29	11.18
1371	09.30SX	00.35
	09.51SO	00.35
1379	11.08	01.52

Other southbound traffic from the Peterborough yards during the same period gave a combined weekday total of 31 trains to 13 different destinations.

Page 90, column 1, paragraph 1; South Pelaw Jct. is situated not on the ECML but approximately half a mile further towards Consett. The Tyne Dock-Consett route crosses the ECML at Ouston Jct.

Page 149. A further example of a 9F 2-10-0 noted on passenger work has been supplied by Mr. David Percival. 92043 (Annesley) was observed on the 2.38pm from Marylebone to Nottingham at an unspecified date in 1964.

Pages 194, and 253. A letter to the editor from Mr. Tom Greaves, an officer on the Eastern Region during the 9F era, adds commentary on the firehole door modification (p.194), provides further details of the exploits of Driver Bauer and 92184 on the Grantham-Kings Cross log (p.253) and describes another exhilarating 9F run on the Midland Main Line.

Page 194. The Firehole Door Saga: Mr. Greaves writes: "When the Class 9Fs came to New England, there was adverse reaction, to quote "this ...awful Derby firebox door which jams". As a young technical assistant at GN HQ, I was directed to look into the issue, have a ride and put in a report. The old District Motive Power Superintendent was a character and said "Greaves, let's try a GN trapdoor!", so we relieved an O2 2-8-0 bound for shops, the blacksmith welded new brackets and we tried the locomotive in service. It was well accepted on the Ferme Park 'heavies' (Class E freights ex-New England) and a submission went from the Eastern to the Board Mechanical and Electrical Engineer and was accepted, although, of interest, the North Eastern would not support us".

Page 253. Log of 92184 on the Grantham-Kings Cross run. Mr. Greaves comments: "In my role as Depot Master Finsbury Park, Peter Townsend, Shed Master Kings Cross and I used to cover each other on alternate weekends to ensure we both had a break from the job at least once a fortnight. On the cover days, one task was the booking out of the Pacific power at Kings Cross, particularly in the mornings as the pressure point was up to around 11.30 to midday when up road power could be turned round to alleviate any specific power shortage.

On Saturday 16th August 1958, I saw Driver Bauer as we were low in power and for the down semi-fast I had either a run-down York class V2 or a Cl.9 (92184) which had been well run-in during the week on the Kings Cross-Cambridge service. We had 34 (A4 Pacific 60034, *Lord Faringdon*) unbalanced at Grantham and as I explained to Driver Bauer, I would wire Grantham to make it ready for the return leg as the General Manager's saloon, with party, was to be attached following his opening of Colwick MPD's staff association sports stadium. However, Grantham hijacked the A4 for a Newcastle working and with the 9F watered, it re-engined the Edinburgh-Kings Cross, resulting in the incredible run on the up road.

I went home in the evening when Bert Dixon, the Chief Locomotive Inspector, who was one of the railways' gentlemen, called with a question out of the blue. "Mr. Greaves, how fast can a 9F go"? It had been timed at 92mph by Robin Johnson, the Eastern Region's development officer, a very enthusiastic railwayman, travelling as a member of the GM's party. At Kings Cross, they intended congratulating Driver Bauer on the excellent run, only to be dumbfounded by seeing the 9F simmering on the blocks. Bert had been contacted, hence the call to me. My reply was that I thought they were fit for 80-85mph. On the following Monday morning, depots were advised that 9Fs must not exceed 80mph and this I believe was later reduced to 70mph.

Page 249. Class 9Fs on the Midland Main Line. Mr. Greaves describes a run on the MML from Wellingborough to St. Pancras: "While the Grantham-Kings Cross was an event, it pales into insignificance compared with a run I experienced in the following year. As Traction Engineer, Sheffield, I was travelling to London for a high level meeting at Great Northern House on the morning business Leeds-St. Pancras which was relieved by Sheffield men. On the platform, there was the normal comment of "Are you riding with us, boss?", my reply being "No, I have work to do for my meeting". The train came in with one of Holbeck's Type 4 Cl.46s and off we went.

All well and on time to Wellingborough where we came to a stand, the driver coasting to a position outside the loco depot. Dropping the window with the Sulzer engine quiet, I dropped on to the ballast and went forward. The fault was easy to detect with the engine room full of water from a blown hose, a common fault at that time. I instructed the driver to uncouple, we restarted the engine and within three minutes we were in the depot limits on a dead road. The shed master had appeared and the only locomotive available was a typically filthy Wellingborough single-chimney 9F. I have a recollection that it was 92082, as I took a photo later believing it was the locomotive involved.

It was here that the fun started. I asked the fireman (second man) to get an extra shovel and as we moved off shed, we brewed up from 130 to 150psi, spreading the fire with the jet hard on. By the time we were on the train and had a vacuum, we had about 175psi and after whistling up had to wait for the Midland Pullman to pass. I can recall the driver saying "Eh, I haven't had one of these before; what's the best way, Class Five 'em"? My reply was "No, when we get to 200psi, put the regulator in the roof and wind her down until she slips and we'll get to see that Pullman's tail light!"

The crew entered into the spirit and with the Wellingborough muck in the tender, I fired left and the second man right with the driver helping on the door. Light spread of shovelfuls on alternate sides with a high proportion going up the chimney, she still would not get higher than about 205 psi until the fireman found a plastic bag with sand under the shovel plate. With her going full bore, a rule was broken with a shovel full scattered over the 40 square feet and part of the Bedford

approach was momentarily blacked out.

Almost immediately, the safety valves started to hum. A bit more down the scale rectified the lift and it was as continuous light but constant firing from the two on the shovel putting them down only as we passed Cricklewood. The first time the regulator was completely closed was as we emerged from Dock Junction tunnel (approx. $3/4$ mile from St. Pancras). The smooth running and exhaust roar from the single chimney gave way to the most horrendous banging from the right-hand big end. Stopping at the blocks, an oil smoke trace lifted from the big ends into the marvellous roof, from the big end now almost devoid of fusible metal. I parted from the crew with the comment "If they can't maintain them on the Midland, they deserve to repair them"!

A sequel to the event was that I joined the meeting in the GN Line Motive Power Superintendent Fred Clements' office where the immediate reaction from Fred, a gentleman who rarely resorted to bad language, was "Tom, look at my '...so-and-so...' carpet!". I had not appreciated the laughter until I was persuaded to visit the bathroom and divest myself of my Al. Jolson image.

To sum up, the boiler of the 9F is excellent and the locomotive shares the Peterborough V2 stand-by qualities in the ability to raise steam fast and accept a thrashing. Without doubt, it was the most exhilarating run of my career, including those with Bill Hoole."

Page 272. The tender on 92212 is plated 1181 of 1956 and not 1161 of 1954.

92122 takes the goods only line between Stenson Jct. and Sheets Stores Jct., Trent with iron ore empties from South Wales in October 1965.

Roy Hobbs

8.1. Origins of Basis for Classification

The original conception of a method of power classification for steam locomotives derives from the Midland Railway which commenced to place small brass numerals "1" to "4" on the upper cabsides from 1906. This was associated with the intoduction between 1907 and 1909 of Sir Cecil Paget's Midland Railway control system.

Following the amalgamation in 1923, the LMS developed this method, employing results represented by a curve on a graph deduced by the Lancashire and Yorkshire Railway (L&Y) giving the 'Mean Effective Pressure' (MEP), expressed as a percentage of the boiler pressure, for various piston speeds.

Attached as Appendix A on p.203 is a copy of the LMS memorandum of 23rd February 1923 that recommends the basic considertions required.

The original classification of LMS locomotives was therefore based on the following:

A. The cylinder tractive effort based on MEPs as given in Aspinall's L&Y curve taken at 50mph for passenger locomotives and 25mph for freight locomotives.

B. The boiler power based on a maximum combustion rate of 130lb. of coal per sq. ft. of grate area per hour, 6.15lb. of steam per lb. of coal and a steam rate of 25lb. and 20lb. of steam per indicated horse power (IHP) for saturated and super-heated locomotives respectively.

The lesser of the two values of A or B was then used for classification purposes. The original LMS classification was:

Class	Passenger tractive effort in tons at 50mph	Freight tractive effort in tons at 25mph
1	1.5 - 2.0	2.85 - 3.60
2	2.0 - 2.5	3.60 - 4.35
3	2.5 - 3.0	4.35 - 5.10
4	3.0 - 3.5	5.10 - 5.85
5	3.5 - 4.0	5.85 - 6.60
6	not specified	6.60 - 7.35.

Examples of the the classification of some of the LMS locomotives built subsequently to 1923 are as follows:

LMS Classification	L&Y MEP basis	Boiler Power Basis
4-6-2 Class 7 Duchess	Cl.7	Cl.8
4-6-2 Class 7 Princess	Cl.7	Cl.8
4-6-0 Class 6 Royal Scot	Cl.7	Cl.6
4-6-0 Class 5XP Jubilee	Cl.8	Cl.6
4-6-0 Class 5 Black Five	Cl.6	Cl.5

Due to the generally improved performance of the modern locomotive, it therefore became apparent to the LMS that the L&Y classification basis could give misleading results when applied to such locomotives and a revised MEP curve was evolved from indicator cards and extensive dynamometer car trials. It was assumed by the LMS that their locomotives could work to the normal plus 20% increase curve without difficulty but it was proposed to work on an MEP curve lying half way between the normal and the normal plus 20% line i.e. normal plus 10% increase to be on the safe side for normal running conditions. Although consideration was given by the LMS to the adoption of this revised curve to establish the power classification of the modern locomotives it was never actually used and the LMS fleet at the time of nationalisation was therefore classified on the L&Y basis formula but with considerable latitude having been used in relation to the modern locomotive where the classification was, in effect, representative of its known performance in service.

8.2. British Railways Classification

In 1948, Nationalisation resulted in the creation of a BR fleet officially reported as amounting to 20,023 steam locomotives of some 400 different types. It was clearly essential to have a common system of power classification and, as a temporary step, a temporary classification using tractive effort only as a basis was adopted by the motive power department.

This was clearly not sound engineering practice particularly for passenger and mixed traffic locomotives where boiler power rather than calculated cylinder tractive effort is the determing factor in power output. The first steps therefore were to develop the basic principles of the LMS system as none of the other railway companies had evolved such a widely applied classification. The basis was brought up to date in the form of Chart RD.2 attached as Appendix B on p.206.

The application of this method still resulted in a number of anomalies when applied to all locomotive classes and in 1949 it was agreed to undertake a general re-classification in which a considerable number of locomotives would be re-classified into a wider range. The effect was to divide the class 7 locomotives between classes 7 and 8, to leave class 5 and 6 locomotives broadly as they were and to spread the class 4, 3 and 2 locomotives over classes 4, 3, 2 and 1. In addition, it was necessary to re-classify a relatively small number of locomotives because the tractive effort formula did not indicate correctly their capabilities. Finally, recognition was given to the importance of the mixed traffic locomotives and certain anomalies of their classification removed.

8.3. The new BR Classification

The basis for this classification was as follows:

8.3.1. Passenger Classification

Locomotives classed as 'Passenger' and 'Mixed Traffic' were assesses according to the value of a factor aobtained by the following formula.

$$\frac{FGA \times GRA \times TE}{10,000}$$

where FGA = Free Gas Area in sq. ft.
GRA = Grate Area in sq. ft.
TE = Tractive Effort

This factor is reduced by 25% for locomotives with 'old' front ends and short lap valves.

It will be seen that this formula was based on the ability of the boiler to burn fuel in such a way that any unbalance in the boiler proportions would penalise the locomotives' power classification, just as it would penalise its maximum performance.

The classes are broadly as follows:

Class	Factor
1	up to 65
2	66–100
3	101–180
4	181–300
5	301–420
6	421–600
7	601–900
8	901 and over

Individual adjustments were made where the known locomotive characteristics were well outside any of the above divisions.

8.3.2. Freight Classification

Locomotives classed as freight were assessed to the lower of the following values:

A) Nominal Tractive Effort (at 85% of boiler pressure).

B) Adhesion weight divided by 4.5 as representing the maximum drawbar pull which they can sustain at low speeds.

Class	Value
1	up to 15,500
2	15,500–19,000
3	19,000–23,000
4	22,500–26,000
5	25,500–28,000
6	27,500–30,000
7	29,500–32,000
8	31,500–35,000
9	34,500 upwards

In some cases, brake power caused a downward revision of the classification. This was based on experience as any calculation of brake power is influenced by numerous extraneous factors.

This basic method was used for the power classification of the BR Standard steam locomotives, the freight classes being extended to make provision for the 2-10-0 locomotives.

In conclusion it must be reiterated that, as with the LMS classification, the strict application of the BR formula could give rise to anomalies. Considerable latitude was therefore used, where necessary, to ensure that the classification reflected as accurately as possible the known performance of the individual types of locomotives on the services to which they were allocated.

A very work-stained 92131 approaches Royston Jct. with the 2.25pm Water Orton to Normanton yard Class D freight in July 1958. In the background towards Royston and Notton station the scene is dominated by the Monckton Coke & Chemical Company plant and the Monckton Main colliery. All that remains of this section of the four-track Midland main line is the up slow which forms a single line branch to the Redfearn Glass plant at Monk Bretton.

David Kelso

APPENDIX A
LMS memorandum
Locomotive Power Classification
23rd February 1923

The value of an engine as a means of hauling a train depends upon the drawbar pull it is capable of producing at the speeds at which the class of traffic for which it was designed normally runs. Strictly speaking, the drawbar pull depends not only on engine dimensions, such as cylinder, grate area, etc. but also on the resistance of the engine and tender as a vehicle, this dependent on the weight and number of coupled wheels.

It is suggested, however, that for the present purposes consideration of factors, such as engine resistance, are an unnecessary refinement and that for practical classification the value of an engine may be based on the simple tractive effort, neglecting friction and resistance as a vehicle.

It may be pointed out that the nominal resistance tractive effort is not a satisfactory measure of the power of an engine at normal running speeds. For instance, a high nominal tractive effort may be due to a small wheel diameter but since the mean effective pressure in a cylinder falls off as the piston speed increasees, it follows that the tractive effort of an engine having a small driving wheel will fall off more quickly as the speed of the train increases than does the tractive effort of an engine with a larger wheel.

The method suggested is to use a curve deduced from experiments on the L&Y which gives a mean pressure (expressed as a percentage of boiler pressure) for various piston speeds.

The mean effective pressure for any piston speed depends, of course, not only on the size of the ports, steam pipes etc. but also on the ability of the boiler to supply the necessary quantity of steam. It is therefore necessary after working out the tractive effort at the selected speeds in accordance with the above curve to make sure that the boiler is adequate to supply the necessary steam.

The speeds at which it is suggested that the tractive effort should be worked out are 25mph for freight engines and 50mph for passenger engines, the engines being rated according to the maximum tractive effort they may be expected to develop at these speeds.

As regards boiler power, any given tractive effort at any given speed represents a definite horse power. The method of ascertaining the maximum tractive effort for which the boiler can provide steam may be as follows:

"Taking a maximum combustion rate of 130lb. of coal per sq. ft. of grate per hour and an actual evaporation of 6.15 lb. of steam per lb. of coal this is equivalent to 800lb. of steam per sq. ft. of grate per hour. Taking the the steam consumption per horsepower hour as 35lb. and 20lb. for saturated and super-heated engines respectively, this is equivalent to 32 and 40 horsepower per sq. ft. of grate. If it is thought necessary to introduce a further refinement, these figures can be multiplied by a coefficient depending on the ratio of heating surface to grate area. However, from a practical point of view, having regard for a number of other factors which it is difficult to take into consideration, this appears to be a questionable utility.

Two variants of the ultimate in Standard power with rebuilt Crosti 92021 alongside original 92123, standing at Holbeck on 19th June 1967.
Gavin Morrison

73023 of Llanelly shed carrying the rather unusual reporting number (1O05 is more likely) runs into Swansea High Street on a summer Saturday service while a pair of early diesel multiple units await departure on an adjoining platform on 26th August 1961. It is interesting to note the two boys with notebooks in hand ready to record the locomotive number, and also the fine array of Great Western signals. *Peter Glenn*

73143 fitted with British Caprotti valve gear and a BR1C tender stands at Bakewell on the former Midland main line from Derby to Manchester with a class H mixed unfitted freight in August 1960. *David Kelso*

TABLE 9
BR STANDARD CLASSES
PRESERVATION STATUS AT JUNE 2011

Loco	Owner/Operator	Location	Status	Notes
70000★	Jeremy Hosking	Southall Railway Centre	Op	ML
70013★	National Museum of Science and Industry	Great Central Railway	Op	ML
71000★	71000 (Duke of Gloucester) Steam Locomotive Trust Ltd.	East Lancashire Railway	Op	ML
73050★	Peterborough City Council	Nene Valley Railway	Rep	–
73082★	73082 Camelot Locomotive Society	Sheffield Park, Bluebell Railway	OH	–
73096	John Bunch (on hire to Mid Hants Railway until 2014)	Mid-Hants Railway	Op	–
73129	Derby City Council	Butterley, Midland Railway	Op	–
73156	Bolton Steam Locomotive Company Ltd.	Loughborough, Great Central Railway	Rest	–
75014★	Dartmouth Steam Railway and Riverboat Co.	Churston, Dart Valley Railway	OH	–
75027	Bluebell Railway plc	Sheffield Park, Bluebell Railway	SD/AO	–
75029	North Yorks. Moors Historical Railway Trust	North York Moors Railway	Op	Bat–Whit
75069	The 75069 Fund	Bridgnorth, Severn Valley Railway	Rest	–
75078	Standard 4 Preservation Society	Haworth, Keighley & Worth Valley Railway	OH	–
75079	Mid-Hants Railway Ltd.	Ropley, Mid-Hants Railway	AR	–
76017	Standard 4 Locomotive Group	Ropley, Mid-Hants Railway	AO	–
76077	Unknown	Toddington, Gloucestershire Warwickshire Railway	AR	–
76079	North Yorks. Moors Historical Railway Trust	North York Moors Railway	Op	ML
76084	76084 Locomotive Company Ltd.	Morpeth, Ian Storey Engineering Ltd.	Rest	–
78018	Darlington Railway Preservation Society	Darlington Railway Preservation Society	Rest	–
78019	Loughborough Standard Locomotive Group	Great Central Railway	Op	–
78022	Standard 4 Preservation Society	Oxenhope, Keighley & Worth Valley Railway	SD	–
78059	Bluebell Railway plc	Sheffield Park, Bluebell Railway	C	–
80002	Unknown	Keighley & Worth Valley Railway	Op	–
80064	80064 Locomotive Fund	Sheffield Park, Bluebell Railway	AO	SD
80072	80072 Steam Locomotive Co. Ltd.	Llangollen Railway	Op	–
80078	Southern Locomotives Ltd.	Swanage Railway	Op	–
80079	Severn Valley Railway (Passenger Tank Fund)	Highley, Severn Valley Railway	SD	–
80080	Princess Royal Class Locomotive Trust	Butterley, Midland Railway	Rest	–
80097	Bury Standard 4 Group	Bury, East Lancashire Railway	Rest	–
80098	Princess Royal Class Locomotive Trust	Churnet Valley Railway	Op	–
80100	Bluebell Railway plc	Sheffield Park, Bluebell Railway	AR/SD	–
80104	Southern Locomotives Ltd.	Swanage Railway	Op	–
80105	Locomotive Owners' Group (Scotland)	Bo'ness and Kinneil Railway	OH	–
80135	North Yorks. Moors Historical Railway Trust	North York Moors Railway	Op	–
80136	Unknown	Crewe, LNWR Heritage Co. Ltd.	OH	–
80150	Mid Hants Railway Ltd.	Ropley, Mid-Hants Railway	AR	–
80151	80151 Locomotive Company Ltd.	Sheffield Park, Bluebell Railway	Op	Ticket expires 2011
92134	Howard and Heather Self	Crewe, LNWR Heritage Co. Ltd.	Rest	–
92203★	David Shepherd CBE	North Norfolk Railway	Op	–
92207★	The 92207 Railway Company Ltd.	Shillingstone station, North Dorset	Rest	No tender
92212	Locomotive Services Ltd. (Jeremy Hosking)	Severn Valley Railway	Rep	–
92214★	PV Premier Ltd. (Stuart Whitter)	North York Moors Railway	Op	–
92219	The 9F Locomotive Charitable Trust Company	Butterley, Midland Railway	S	For spares
92220★	National Museum of Science and Industry	Great Hall, National Railway Museum, York	SD	–
92240	Bluebell Railway plc	Sheffield Park, Bluebell Railway	AO/SD	–
92245	Cambrian Transport Ltd.	Barry Rail Centre	AR	No tender or pony truck

Key: ★ **Names** 70000 *Britannia* (in BR black livery, temporarily unnamed), 70013 *Oliver Cromwell*, 71000 *Duke of Gloucester*, 73050 *City of Peterborough*, 73082 *Camelot*, 75014 *Braveheart*, 92203 *Black Prince*, 92207 *Morning Star*, 92214 *Cock o' the North* (named at Grosmont, 22.04.2011), 92220 *Evening Star*.

AO – Awaiting overhaul, **AR** – awaiting restoration, **Bat–Whit** – cleared for main line working between Battersby and Whitby only, **C** – under conversion to Cl. 2 2-6-2T 84030, **ML** – cleared for working on specified sections of Network Rail, **OH** – undergoing overhaul, **Op** – operational, **Rest** – under restoration, **Rep** – under repair, **S** – retained for spares, **SD** – on static display.

Note Information on the above locomotives has been drawn from various issues of the following publications, *Railways Restored 2011, The Railway Magazine, Railway Observer, Steam Railway*; various other publications and websites were also consulted.

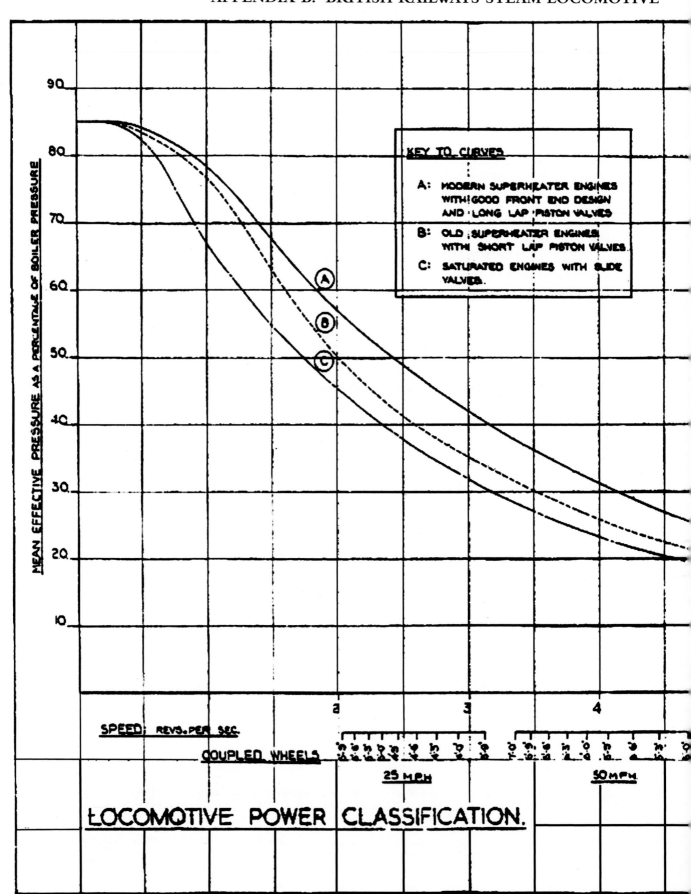

APPENDIX B

CYLINDER TRACTIVE EFFORT

CYLINDER TRACTIVE EFFORT = $\dfrac{N d^2 S P}{4480\, D}$ TONS.

WHERE

- N = NUMBER OF CYLINDERS
- d = CYLINDER DIAMETER — INS.
- S = CYLINDER STROKE — INS.
- P = MEAN EFFECTIVE PRESSURE LBS./SQ. IN.
  (AS GIVEN BY APPROPRIATE CURVE)
- D = COUPLED WHEEL DIAMETER — INS.

2. BOILER TRACTIVE EFFORT

ASSUME

(a) FIRING RATE OF 130 LBS. PER SQ. FT. OF GRATE PER HOUR IN NARROW FIREBOXES, AND 100 LBS. PER SQ. FT. OF GRATE PER HOUR IN WIDE FIREBOXES.

(b) UPPER LIMIT OF CAPACITY OF FIREMAN IS 4480 LBS. PER HR.

(c) EVAPORATION UNDER THESE CONDITIONS IS 6·5 LBS. OF WATER PER LB. OF COAL.

(d) STEAM CONSUMPTION PER D.B.HP. HOUR IS 20 LBS. FOR SUPERHEATER ENGINES AND 25 LBS. FOR SATURATED ENGINES.

THEN THE D.B.HP. DEVELOPED IS GIVEN BY:

	NARROW FIREBOX.	WIDE FIREBOX.
SUPERHEATER ENGINES	40 × GRATE AREA	30·7 × GRATE AREA
SATURATED ENGINES	32 × GRATE AREA	24·6 × GRATE AREA

SUBJECT TO LIMITS IMPOSED BY ASSUMPTION (b)

THE DRAWBAR PULL IN TONS IS GIVEN BY:

PASSENGER & MIXED TRAFFIC ENGINES   0·00535 × D.B.HP.
FREIGHT ENGINES   0·0067 × D.B.HP.

3. POWER CLASSIFICATION

TAKING THE LOWER OF THE TWO DRAWBAR PULL FIGURES, OBTAINED AS ABOVE, THE POWER CLASSIFICATION CAN NOW BE READ OFF THE APPROPRIATE DRAWBAR PULL CHART.

5·5

THE RAILWAY EXECUTIVE
222 MARYLEBONE ROAD
LONDON N.W.1.

DRAWING Nº   RD.2

ACKNOWLEDGEMENTS

The Society is very grateful to those photographers who have been kind enough to research and provide the colour slides for the enhancement of this volume.

Thanks are due to Hugh Ballantyne, John Edgington, Ken Falconer, Howard Forster, Martin Gill, Peter Glenn, Peter Gray, Roy Hobbs, Douglas Hume, John Jennison, David Kelso, Rodney Lissenden, Noel Machell, Keith Mapley, Michael Mensing, Gavin Morrison, Bill Potter and Mike Robinson for providing images used in this volume.

Thanks also to David Clark (for providing images from the Ken Wightman collection), David Cross (from the collection of his father, Derek Cross), Rodney Lissenden (for providing images from the Dick Riley collection), Trevor Owen (whose collection now is part of the Colour Rail catalogue), the Alan Sainty collection, Brian Stephenson (for providing images from the Kenneth Cook collection) and Kenneth Field collection (part of Rail Archive Stephenson).

Thanks are also due to the following who have freely given advice and help in the preparation of this book: Mr. J. B. Arnold, Mr. C. P. Atkins, Mr. P. Doggett and Mr. D. Percival. We have also made use of information from *The Book of the 9F 2-10-0s* by Richard Derry, Irwell Press, 2006 and extend our thanks for permission to use said extracts.